8/00

Domestic government

Society and culture in the modern Middle East
Series editor: Michael Gilsenan

Domestic government: kinship, community and polity in North Yemen

MARTHA MUNDY

I.B.Tauris Publishers
LONDON · NEW YORK

Published in 1995 by
I.B.Tauris & Co Ltd
45 Bloomsbury Square
London WC1A 2HY

175 Fifth Avenue
New York NY 10010

In the United States of America
and in Canada distributed by
St Martin's Press
175 Fifth Avenue
New York NY 10010

A full CIP record for this book is available from the British Library

A full CIP record for this book is available from the Library of Congress

ISBN 1 85043 918 4

Library of Congress catalog card number 94-61502

Set in Monotype Ehrhardt by
Ewan Smith, London E8

Printed and bound in Great Britain by
WBC Ltd, Bridgend, Mid Glamorgan

Contents

Maps

Figures

Tables

Tables

Note on anthropological terms and Arabic transliteration

The following abbreviations are used in the text: FBD (father's brother's daughter), FBS (father's brother's son), MBS (mother's brother's son), FZS (father's sister's son), and MZS (mother's sister's son). A parallel cousin refers to the child of a parent's sibling of the same sex as that parent; a cross-cousin refers to the child of a parent's sibling of the opposite sex as the parent, i.e. an FBS is a parallel cousin, an MBS is a cross-cousin.

The system of Arabic transliteration adopted here is that found in the *International Journal of Middle Eastern Studies*. In the case of vernacular poetry, I have adopted transliteration similar to that current for classical Arabic, without attempting a phonetic transcription. Likewise, when citing from unpublished manuscripts, local documents or vernacular poetry, I have not corrected the occasional departure from standard grammar but have transcribed the text verbatim.

Arabic words found in the *Oxford English Dictionary* have been spelt according to the form given there. An exception is the word sheikh, which has been spelt as shaikh throughout.

Preface and acknowledgements

The research for this study extended over a period of three and a half years between October 1973 and April 1977 in Wadi Ḍahr, Hamdān in what was then the Yemen Arab Republic. The historical present used for stylistic reasons in this study is thus that of the mid-1970s. All place names in this study are genuine but pseudonyms have been adopted for all persons, in both the text and the documents transcribed in Appendix 3. The time elapsed since the events described in these pages means, I trust, that a change of personal names should prove sufficient protection for those who so graciously admitted me into their confidence. The world described in these pages has changed with such rapidity that even to the actors the present text should appear a study in history. Such in a sense is its aim.

My first debt is to those about whom I write. Because of the use of pseudonyms in the text, I cannot, however, thank by full name those who have helped me the most. This study is beholden to the two men who served as shaikh during my stay, to the *amīn* (scribe), and to the friend who acted as irrigation supervisor in the early 1970s; I am myself beholden to the luminous companionship of Taqiyah, the late Ummi Taqwa, Sayyidah, Ummi Khairiyah, Rahah, the late Ummi Habibah, and al-Sharifah Fatimah.

Qāḍī Isma'il 'Ali al-Akwa', Director of the Department of Antiquities and Libraries, Ṣan'ā', and Ahmad al-Marwani, Director of the Yemeni Studies Centre, Ṣan'ā', secured official permission for my research and helped me in ways far beyond the responsibility of their posts. I was particularly honoured to carry out this work under the aegis of Yemeni institutions of research.

The Foreign Area Program of the Social Science Research Council, New York City (1972–73), U.S.P.H.S. Grant 1R01 DA-00974 (1974–75), and the Yemeni Studies Centre, Ṣan'ā', in conjunction with the Ford Foundation, Amman (1975–76), provided financial support for research in Yemen. Clare Hall College, Trinity College and Girton College, Cambridge supported writing of the Ph.D. dissertation (1977–81) on which this study draws. Fellowships from the S.S.R.C., New York City (1991), the Ministère de Recherche et Technologie (1992) and the Ecole des Hautes Etudes en Sciences Sociales, Paris (1993) allowed the preparation of this book. I am most grateful for the support of all these institutions.

At the different stages of this work I have been honoured by the friendship, aid, and insight of the late Mahmud al-Ghul, Ian Manners, the late Robert Serjeant, Jerry Erbach, Huriyah al-Mu'ayyid, Fernando Varanda, the late Amat al-Rahman and 'Abd al-Rahman al-Wazir, John Kennedy, 'Abdo 'Ali 'Uthman, the late Qāḍī Ahmad Zahir, Muhammad al-Shami, Sylvia Kennedy, Husein and Amat al-Hasib al-'Amri, Hamidah al-Qa'i, 'Abd al-Salam Nur al-Din, 'Ali Abu Rijal, Nikki Keddie, Lucette Valensi and Aziz al-Azmeh. Jack Goody supervised the doctoral work from which this study has grown and, for the last twelve years, has continued to give generous attention to its themes and its fate. Richard Saumarez Smith, Ashraf Ghani, Marlène Shamay, Basim Musallam and Michael Howley all read and gave advice on a version of the text. I owe a special debt to my parents, John and Charlotte Mundy, who have helped at all stages of the work. Lastly, Michael Gilsenan and Anna Enayat encouraged publication of this book; and Ewan Smith, Anne Le Fur, Philip Armstrong and Richard Saumarez Smith gave form to its various parts. I am deeply grateful to all. None, however, has any part in the shortcomings of my work: for those, and for the interpretations offered, I alone bear responsibility.

The conditions of field research and the documentary sources for this study are described in Appendix 1.

To Sayyida, Sharifa and 'Abd as-Salam

دار أبوك معمور على حيد
والجمل تطلع رويد
دار أبوك معمور بمرمر
والعرس مرقح دخل
دار أبوك معمور على الماء
والمناظر في الهواء
دار أبوك معمور بياجور
والحمام فيها تدور
دار أبوك ليّة بليّة
والحرس والدورية
دار أبوك أعلى من الطيور
شامخة في عرض الحيود
مال أبوك شرقي وغربي
كم تطاوف يا غبي
مال أبوك شرقي وغربي
والسواقي قد التقين

Your father's house is built on a mountain
The camels climb slowly
Your father's house is built in marble
The wedding party enters joyously
Your father's house is built over water
Its high rooms are in the sky
Your father's house is built of brick
Doves circle about in it
Round round your father's house
The guards and night watch
Your father's house is higher than the birds
Haughty on the cliffs above
Your father's land lies east and west
How far you do not know
Your father's land lies east and west
Its water channels flow one into the next

Verses from the women's wedding songs
in honour of the bridegroom

I

Introduction

It is not easy, even in Europe, to obtain a thorough knowledge of the principles of any political constitution; but, among the mistrustful, suspicious inhabitants of the east, such a thing is almost impossible. I could not learn upon what laws and conditions the confederation of Hascid-u-Bekil is maintained. All I know is, that they choose a certain number as chiefs, and, in war, so many generals, to command their united forces.

Carsten Niebuhr, *Travels through Arabia and Other Countries of the East*, 1792, vol. 2, p. 51.

Unfortunately, the relationships between kin group, village, the "commune" of villages (Markgenossenschaft) and political association belong to the most obscure and least investigated areas of ethnography and economic history.

Max Weber, *Economy and Society* [1918–20], vol. 1, p. 370.

Themes of study

Yemen is justly renowned for the architecture of its houses, an art which is as much of the village as of the town.[1] In a village wedding song the bridegroom will be praised for his father's house, tall, perched high on the slopes, with windows like decorated eyes. Yet if the houses of Yemen have impressed every visitor, the form of organization within these structures has found little place in scholarly discourse on Yemeni society. Domestic government has scarcely been addressed. Instead, the articulation between the local and the national has been seen in terms either of status groups or of tribes, with scant attention to the nature of local formations. This work is an attempt to look at the relation between domestic government and the wider polity in a different light.

In order to document the articulation of household and house with this wider polity, we need to work at an intimate scale. The present study concerns one community, a valley of irrigated agriculture on the Ṣan'ā' plateau. By its proximity to the capital the area looks to the city, but by its agriculture and political alliances it belongs to the rural world. The character of the locality does not prompt one to evoke a dichotomy of city and tribe, but rather to explore the complexity of social form on its own terms and to build up a reading from first elements.

Our analysis of the integration of house within community and polity will follow a double movement, starting first from the wider polity, through the articulation of house to community, down to the internal structure of the house, and second, back upward through the nets of alliance linking the houses of the community to the wider whole. More exactly, after a sketch of the national polity, we go on to consider in Chapter 2 the idioms in which men and women speak of the locality: interpretations of landscape, local history, political allegiance and social rank. In Chapter 3 we turn to law and justice in the community, the social framework of disputes and their resolution. The character of most litigation will not appear exotic; property is the rub. And so Chapter 4 addresses the imagined forms and everyday employment of property. This sketch of the economy will serve as backdrop to an examination in Chapter 5 of the morphology of social associations – house, household and family across the groups of the community. Behind form lies process: Chapter 6 considers the imagined and tangible exchanges binding men and women into the patterns of social cooperation outlined. These dynamic exchanges, built in terms of individual and collectivity, at one and the same time relations of conflict and of cooperation, create the associations of daily life. From here the movement of analysis is reversed, back from smaller to larger associations, from the cycles of family to – in Chapter 7 – the skeins of connubium that knit together the community. And in closing we shall return to reflect on the questions with which we began: on the place of house and community in the wider social and legal order and on the nature of rural political tradition in North Yemen.[2]

In the early 1970s, when the research for this study began, the outlines of an older political order were still evident. Not only in architecture did the house appear central: it still served as site and organizing model not only of production but also of rule. The 1970s marked a time of rapid "institution building", as political scientists put it. And, contrary to what the political rhetoric of the time would have us believe, such institutions were in fact erected on the earlier introduction of printing and the modern arts of government.[3] But these institutions of the Republic did not as yet obscure just how limited bureaucratic development had been prior to 1962, the date of the overthrow of the Imamate, when even at the pinnacle of government the model of rule had been that of a dynastic house (*daulah* in Yemeni dialectal usage).[4] Brothers, sons and cousins of the Imam served as ministers and commanders; foreign trade was essentially a family monopoly; the court, not the administrative department, was the site of Imamic legal judgement. True, the Imam's domestic space was grand: unlike the households of most other men it contained both slaves and servants. So too, the houses of powerful political figures might include an independent reception room, with an entrance separate from the house, known as a *maḥkamah* or *ḥukūmah*, a place of judgement. In the later years of the Imamate, modernist jurists deplored the way justice was administered: judges, who were paid at best a scant salary, accepted monies directly from the litigants; court was held early in the day by the door of the judge's home and later in the afternoon in his reception rooms.[5] If this was true of state office-holders, it was all the more so in the case of shaikhly government. A shaikh governed from his house. In the mountains of North Yemen there was little tradition of clan or village guest-houses:[6] the only public institutional spaces were markets and mosques, which served as meeting places for political deliberations in rural areas. In the city, too, private houses were imposing institutions. Yemeni authors from al-Wāsi'ī to al-Jāwī, addressing a wider Arab audience, stressed the autonomy of the Ṣan'ānī house: the ground floor contained the stalls of animals, a well, and grinding stones; each house baked its own bread every day.[7] The resilience, even the combativeness, of the urban population is nowhere as striking as in the nineteenth-century chronicles,[8] which portray Ṣan'ānīs responding in kind to the aggression of outside groups. Under the leadership of their quarter or market headmen (*'uqqāl*), Ṣan'ānīs could mount common defence or even take revenge on groups outside in a manner not so different from the "tribes".[9] The image of greatest desolation in nineteenth-century chronicles was that of a ruling house of the city with its door and shutters torn away: in the city and the country the inviolable house towered as the figure of political order.

We need to build our models of Yemeni society from such basic structures, from households and houses as the first level of economic and political institution, not from a notional tribesman[10] or from abstract actors such as tribe or city.[11] It is in the development of a division of labour between households that agricultural areas differ one from the next. In landlord areas – in the irrigation zones of the Tihāmah, for example – households form part of an elaborate division of labour; by contrast, much of what underlies the "segmentation"[12] of "tribal" areas is the very limited division of labour between agricultural households.[13]

To say this is not to plead for a return to an Aristotelian vision where the household forms an auto-generative kernel and natural model for rule.[14] Nor is it to argue for an eighteenth-century dreamland wherein all of society in this corner of the Orient forms but the domestic arena of a despot.[15] At issue is the manner of the political association of households, through economic coercion in the landlord areas or through contractual political arrangements in the areas deemed "tribal". If we accept that the household forms the first unit of politics, two observations follow. First, the domestic group is not just an affair of "women". The division in the anthropology of the Arabs between what Abu-Lughod has termed studies of the "harem" and those of "segmentary society" is pernicious:[16] any systematic analysis of the social forms included under the latter category requires dissection of the relations veiled behind the first. Second, if the household is the smallest unit of politics it stands within wider patterns of legal domination in society. Contrary to models of tribe versus state, household government in this complex society is moulded by textual traditions purveyed in both country and city by legal specialists. The regional systems of Yemen were bound both by trade and by the networks of literate specialists who served state and local powers. Such literati studied not only at the institutions attached to mosques[17] but also in the houses of learned families, themselves quasi-domestic institutions, recognized as *hijrah*[18] in different regions.[19]

The rural tribes do not stand apart with their secular orality – as in a Gellnerian model – from the scriptural Islam of the city.[20] In a society possessing the written word, oral tradition is cognizant of writing.[21] What is of interest is the interpenetration of the oral and the written, the structuring of traditions principally written or principally oral, and the social site of specialized literate traditions. A sociology takes as starting point not only what people write but what they do. Consider religion, the central domain of the written tradition, where definitions of orthodoxy are composed. In the religion of village women, for example, we see written traditions recited and the rare literate woman specialist, but within systems of meaning that find little expression in written genres. This is not only because religious virtuosi are men but also because the relationship between practice and written genre is never simple. Orthodoxy is by definition a contested notion: we should allow the testimony of practice, and not only the sermons of the bearers of orthodoxy, to guide our understanding of the religious sphere. If anthropology has any *raison d'être* in the late twentieth century, it is to allow us to confront the written schemas of the intellectuals with the richer and untidy welter of living practice.

As the smallest unit of political society, the household is inscribed in relations not only of violence (of feud) but also of legal domination. In the country as in the city a household does not – as in so many models of segmentary society – rule itself; its internal configuration is also structured by law. This is not to suggest, following the fantasies of islamicist writings on "the Muslim Family", that people simply live out the Law. Rather, the members of a house appeal to legal agency in the case of disputes not only with those outside but above all between those within. It is not only in the modern European state that we observe a dialectic between forms of state and domestic rule. True, the forms change: from litigation to discipline, from the state as legal authority (before which members of domestic units fight out their contests) to regulatory agencies that knit the domestic domain to the project of the state's discipline.[22] But a unity in the diverse forms of rule, from state to family, is not unique to modernity.

The approach of this study is thus monographic: it attempts to build, by the most orthodox techniques of ethnography and social history, a vision of social process and structure in one community. Its aim is not novelty of method but care and quality of documentation. The locality so documented represents not a cell, identical to its neighbours, in a segmentary system (the Durkheimian tapeworm) but an object historically particular, defined by its internal patterns of cooperation and exchange as well as by its links with the outside. It belongs to a wider system, albeit one little centralized.[23] Thus, on the one hand, careful documentation of this part does shed light on the character of relations in the whole. And on the other, the non-centralized nature of political relations will require that we link this study to others of similarly small scale if we are to compose, in time, a social history of Yemen. We need to build a corpus of documentation in terms other than the segmentary problematic, in terms not of tribes against the state but of village alliances, regional systems and national leadership. This history requires documentation of the component elements of local government: forms of cooperation (family, household and house) and exchange (marriage, market, law and political leadership) as these extend from smaller to larger networks and groups. Armed with a morphological representation of social practice, we will be less tempted to treat the abstract or symbolic idioms of honour, law or ritual as the summary of an otherwise unintelligible practice.[24] Rather, the abstraction and symbolic resonance of such discourses and the social site of their performance become questions that we can then explore. With a set of such studies, we shall be able to grasp the interrelations between local, regional and national systems at particular moments of time. And far from leaving the tribes of Yemen in the ghetto of the segmentarist problematic, we will then see that their agriculturalists belong also to a world of "peasant production" and its comparative themes.[25]

Method is not a neutral matter: this book seeks to break with two traditions, or procedures, that have marked studies of Yemeni society. First, such studies generally eschewed statistical analysis, and second, they adopted formal models, drawn from cultural categories or sociological typologies, whenever they attempted a description of society as a whole. The reasons for the dearth of figures should be obvious. Statistical representation of a population, which makes possible a bird's-eye-view of social morphology, rests on centralized procedures of registration; its deployment in the form of reports belongs to the administrative rule of the modern state.[26] As we have seen, the state in North Yemen retained a more archaic quality well into this century, and such techniques were just appearing in the Yemen of the 1970s.

The models that have guided interpretation of North Yemeni society have been essentially of two kinds. Until the late 1970s the dominant image of Yemeni society was that of a hierarchy of social statuses and the central object of debate the nature of stratification, whereas from the early 1980s the categories of interpretation shifted to tribe and state and debate came to focus on the nature of the Yemeni tribe. With a little hindsight, what is striking is the manner in which the shift in these images appears to mirror not only the areas privileged by research, largely urban in earlier decades and rural from the 1970s, but also a shift in the ideology and structure of the state.

Although its formal doctrinal basis was insecure, status rank lay at the heart of the legitimacy of the Imamic state.[27] In the high written tradition, justice was seen as a question of hierarchical order.[28] Explicit marking of social orders by dress and sumptuary regulations impressed European observers: from Glazer to Gerholm, European authors gave pride of place to status hierarchy in their interpretation of Yemeni society.[29] The British authorities in the Aden Protectorate, and even more so in the Hadramaut, respected notions of status rank in their "protection" of the indigenous social order.[30] From the 1960s, with the instauration of the Republic in the North and revolutionary movements in the South, Yemeni authors too began to write of status rank as characteristic of the *ancien régime*.[31] For the Marxists, the issue was the class character of Yemeni society;[32] for the non-Marxists the Republic would, by destroying the Imamate, the *clef de voûte* of the system, undo the status order of traditional society.[33] Most, but not all, of this sociology was written from the vantage point of towns.

From the 1980s, however, interpretation and debate came to centre around the tribe as the key to understanding North Yemeni society. In part this reflects the fruit of research in rural areas and the contribution of anthropologists, with their disciplinary tradition of discourse on tribes and "segmentary society". But only in part: the period was also one of change in the forms and ideology of state in Yemen. In the Southern People's Democratic Republic of Yemen, a rhetoric of radicalism and an effective commitment to strong central government won the day; in the Northern Yemen Arab Republic the radical populist movements of the 1960s, directed against a dynastic Imamate that had ruled in the name of Islam, gave way to national reconciliation but with a continuing unshakeable commitment to republicanism. Throughout the 1970s, Islamic political movements in the Yemen Arab Republic retained a marked elitist character. The populist drive of the 1960s was domesticated politically by redefining the people (*sha'b*),[34] as not exclusively a body of citizens (*muwāṭinīn*, the term never disappearing from political discourse) but equally as a collection of tribes (*qabā'il*). Two authors have noted that in 1986 no less a person than the head of state, when asked by a journalist whether Yemen had passed beyond the "stage of tribalism", responded that in Yemen the state belongs to the *qabā'il*.[35] The president's answer plays on ambiguities in the term *qabā'il* which can mean anything from country-folk to men of the tribes (the arms-bearing groups of the North) as opposed to the peasants (*ra'āyā*) of Tihāmah, the Western foothills and Lower Yemen. The definition of the population as *qabā'il* was coherent with central characteristics of Republican government: a recognition of the social equality of men, the entry of the major Northern shaikhs and other regional rural elites into key positions of the central government, an increasing reliance on men from the Northern tribes, particularly those of Ḥāshid, in the army and agencies of security, and a continuing ambivalence concerning the development of effective bureaucratic structures of rule in the central state.[36] As one author puts it, it is in the nature of tribal society that, on behalf of their tribes, shaikhs deal with foreign governments as equals.[37]

In anthropology this political conjuncture has found expression in studies in both Arabic and English. For example, the work of Abū Ghānim and Dresch of the 1980s shares a common objective:[38] to interpret the tribes of Ḥāshid and Bakīl (to which the citation from Niebuhr refers and whose territories lie around and north of the city of Ṣan'ā')[39] in the light of anthropological traditions for the analysis of "segmentary societies". Both authors refuse, moreover, to be restricted to documentation of a single community but aim instead to grasp the logic of the wider system – from the vantage point of the company of shaikhs.[40] Both agree on the irrelevance of economy for an understanding of tribal society: Abū Ghānim finds the sinews of this society to be those of kinship, which in his view is a principle divorced from economy;[41] Dresch treats segmentation as an *état d'esprit* in the mind of every tribesman, impossible to locate in either economic or ecological space.[42] Whereas earlier readings, by the very order in which they listed status categories, gave pride of place to the cream of urbanity or to the religious "aristocracy", the models of Abū Ghānim and Dresch place all other estates of society, both the genealogically distinct religious groups and those associated with the market, under the protection of the tribes, "within", as Dresch puts it, "the tribal peace".[43]

The power of this social vision is its construction of unity. In spite of the ideological antipathy, underscored by Dresch, between *sayyid* historiography (that of the Zaidī[44] religious literati) and the histories of tribesmen, society in this model forms a whole and is not composed of two distinct social forms, tribe and city, as in Gellner's Khaldunian vision of "Muslim society".[45] The dominance of the tribes binds society into a whole. Nor is the model disturbed by what another author, al-Maqramī, in recognition of the undisputed fact that over half the population of North Yemen lives in "peasant" not "tribal" communities, introduces as third term alongside tribe and city – the village.[46] The formalism of al-Maqramī's analysis, which proceeds from ideal-types but without the Weberian historical tradition, proves unsatisfying when set beside the more powerfully integrated visions of "segmentary society". But it has the cardinal virtue of reminding us that a model of society in North Yemen cannot stop at Ḥāshid and Bakīl, however powerful the leadership of these groups may be, but must take account of the economically central if sometimes politically marginal populations of Tihāmah, the Western mountains and Lower Yemen, that is to say, must take account of fundamental economic and social diversity. Since the seventeenth century, Imamic state formations have built on alliances with leaders from Ḥāshid and Bakīl to rule over peasant areas; this basic political orientation did not change radically with the coming of the Republic. "Segmentary society" in the North does not stand isolated – let alone in the late twentieth century – from this wider context.

The image of segmentation, although it captures the intensely local allegiances of rural and urban communities, belongs to a Durkheimian legacy of mechanical solidarity, where each segment resembles the next:[47] it suggests neither the diversity of local conditions nor the criss-crossing networks which made for the unity of the whole. An understanding of this non-centralized yet complex political economy requires recognition of both unity and diversity: of fundamental structures common throughout, of regional diversity, and of the networks of trade, learning and legal domination which bound the regional systems together. Common structures are so evident as often to be overlooked, not least if we forget the economy. Until the 1970s more than four-fifths of the population of North Yemen lived dispersed in small villages; only in the 1960s did the population of the capital Ṣan'ā' start to grow beyond the 50,000 souls of the city *intra muros*.[48] Slow population growth over the reigns of Imams Yaḥyā and Aḥmad Ḥamīd al-Dīn (1918–62) rendered emigration the preferred solution to any shortfall in income for many village families in what remained a poor and marginal agrarian economy.[49] Although, from mid-century, and particularly after 1962, imported technology and a freeing of the market permitted a tremendous increase in market exchange, the growing dependence of the economy as a whole on oil rent – through migrant labour, direct subsidies and, from the late 1980s, national oil production – has led to vertiginous growth in imports of finished products and a highly uneven growth in productive capacity, even to declines in certain sectors of agriculture and crafts. This wider economic history has marked political transformation not only at the national level but in the most remote rural communities.[50]

It is this political and economic context that, after the unification of the two Yemens in 1990 and the legalization of more overtly ideological party politics, appears set today to expose the limits of an unstructured "tribal" populism.[51] This is not to say that the Saudi model of an islamicist ideology of state and a vision of political society as composed of tribes[52] will vanish overnight, but that the increased diversity of the whole will render less plausible any unitary model of Yemeni society which takes the tribe as first principle. Although the results of this sea-change in politics are only just beginning to surface in scholarship, anthropologists are already reworking their material to interpret contemporary national (and nationalist) political culture.[53] It is not our brief to pursue these developments, as they would take us far beyond the years with which we are concerned: they may serve as a warning, however, of the political contingency of unitary models such as "segmentary society" and of the simple need for painstaking documentation if we are to advance very far in an understanding of Yemeni social history. In the present contribution to that project, let us begin by considering something of economic history.

The national context: geography and history

Prior to the integration of the Yemen, during the 1970s, within the wider Arabian *rentier* economy of petrol production, the mainstay of the Yemeni economy had been agriculture.[54] The heart of North Yemen is a mountain range with peaks over 3,000 metres above sea level (see Map 1). Rainfall varies sharply over the mountains from the wetter southern and western areas to the drier northern and eastern. This division reflects the close relation between altitude and precipitation. Whereas in large areas of the southern and western mountains spring and summer rains are sufficient to assure one or more grain crops a year, in the coastal plain of the Red Sea (the Tihāmah), in the central mountains to the north of the town of Dhamār, and in areas east of the high plateau, the summer rain-fed grain crop fails in poor years and in the best produces only a modest crop of sorghum or millet. Throughout the highlands, agriculture requires high investment in terraces, in the careful levelling of fields,

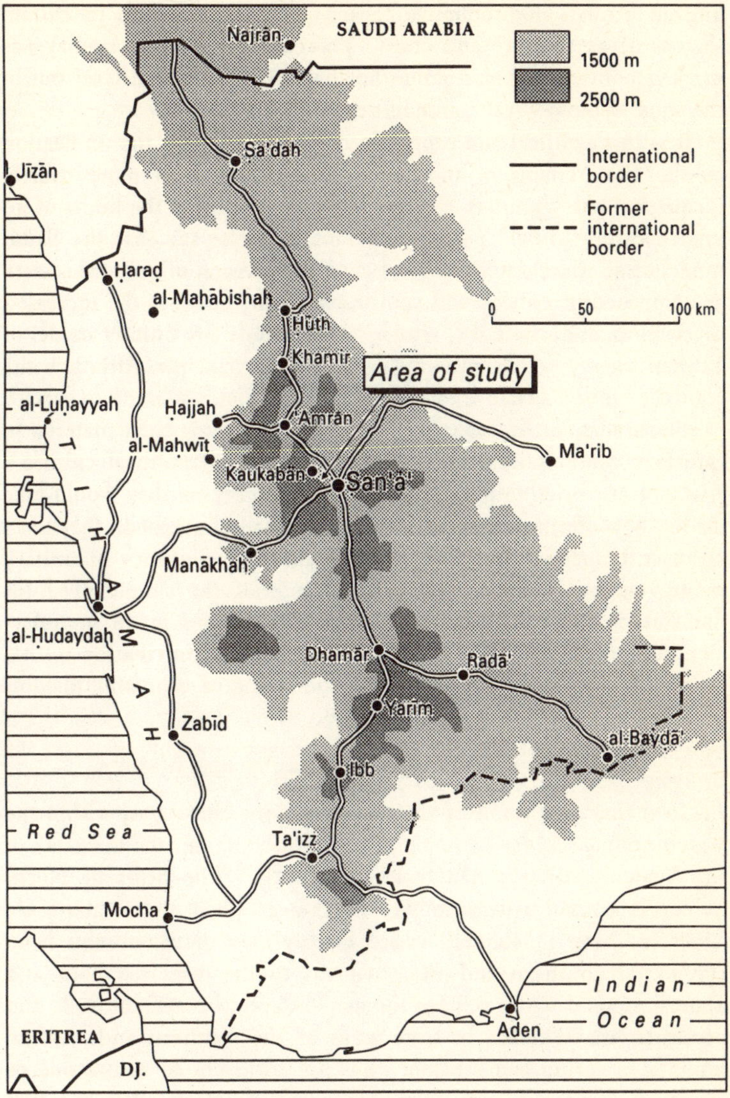

Map 1 The northern and western parts of the Republic of Yemen

and in catchment systems for local run-off. Even after such investment the yields from rain-fed grain agriculture are unreliable in most northern areas and along the coast. These zones are broken by strips of more intensive, heavily capitalized irrigated agriculture, the greatest being the extensive areas of spate-irrigated land along the wadis of the Tihāmah, but much smaller pockets of wadi and *qanāt*[55] irrigated land also exist in the high mountains.[56] Wadi Ḍahr, the community with which this study is concerned, occupies part of one such small-scale, intensively irrigated system. Abutting the Ṣan'ā' plateau, it lies more than 2,000 metres above sea level.

This mountainous land was hard to govern. During much of the nineteenth and early twentieth centuries, government authority – and, for that matter, urban traders – found it difficult to centralize agricultural surplus. In 1884 the Ottomans, short of grain, looted the homes of rural people in the vicinity of Ṣan'ā' and in 1904 Imam Yaḥyā and his supporters raided the houses of Ṣan'ānīs for grain.[57] And much later, in the early years of the Republican regime, the first priority for the central government was the building of adequate grain storage facilities.[58] During the late 1960s, as often in the past, the threat of famine was a real one and government storehouses were drastically inadequate. This did not mean that cultivators were everywhere left with their surplus, but rather that relations of domination and tax collection were not centralized throughout much of the last two centuries. The farming out of taxes was as common as regular assessment by the central government. Effective coercive power often lay in the hands of rural landlords and leaders, especially the northern shaikhs.[59]

The advance of the Ottomans to the main towns of the mountains in the 1860s had marked a move towards greater central power. The Ottomans firmly held the coastal Tihāmah and large areas of lower Yemen. On the coast some of their governors came to acquire large estates, and in parts of lower Yemen their rule permitted the peasantry to weaken the hold of landlords of northern origin.[60] By contrast, the Ottomans met severe resistance in northern rural areas and were not able to extend tax and census procedures there. Nevertheless, when the Ottomans finally withdrew, their army provided the model for the small force built by Imam Yaḥyā. So too the schools, courts, forts and communications networks (notably the telegraph) of the Ottoman state were taken over by Imam Yaḥyā at the end of the First World War.[61]

The regime which supplanted the Ottoman garrisons in Ṣan'ā' was by contrast deeply rooted in the history of North Yemen. Imam Yaḥyā Ḥamīd al-Dīn established a regime exemplary in its duration and in the extent of its control, yet the traditions on which it drew were very old indeed. The first Zaidī Imam, Yaḥyā b. al-Ḥusain, titled *al-imām al-hādī ilā 'l-ḥaqq*, had entered Yemen at the end of the ninth century and founded the religious centre of the Zaidīs in Ṣa'dah.[62] Although differing little in legal practice from Sunnite schools, Zaidism advocated an active political role for the Alid descendants of the Prophet in the person of an Imam who should rule with justice, applying his exemplary knowledge of Islamic law.[63] For long periods the rule of the Zaidī Imams was restricted to the far north about the town of Ṣa'dah, but from the seventeenth century onwards their rule again extended more widely over the country.[64]

Imamic government was of a religious character, sharing power with and at times dominating, but never entirely restructuring or supplanting, rural political, military and legal structures. Its rule rested on an uneasy pact with northern leaders and groups. The allegiance of the prominent shaikhs was rewarded by alliance and simultaneously controlled by a system of holding (and educating) young hostages from their families. During the reign of Imam Yaḥyā, the developing administration of the Imamic state moved to institutionalize status differences.[65] The cadre of the Imamic administration proclaimed themselves the bearers of the civilizing tradition of Islamic learning and law. Under the Imamate Islamic *sharī'ah* was to conquer divisive tribal custom and the ulema (the scholars) would rule and not merely serve the shaikhs.[66]

But the ideological power of the Imamic state did not erase rural political idioms and leadership. During the nineteenth and early twentieth centuries the economic power of urban forces remained circumscribed. Craft production and trade remained small-scale, and specialists were divided in status between those who ruled (families with literate and religious specialities or engaged in long-distance trading) and those who served (the craftsmen and market-service families). In the countryside arms-bearing farmers regarded the groups who worked in craft production, petty trading and market services as a dependent service class attached to their local political communities. Even in large towns the men who performed such occupations were distinguished as Jews or as Muslim strata (*mazāyinah, banī 'l-khums, nuqqāṣ*) marked by sumptuary customs or regulations.[67] Literate specialists, who sought to govern, to regulate the market, and to control long-distance trade, distinguished themselves from the labouring specialists of the market.

The Zaidī Imamate could not build its power solely upon a union of non-agricultural specialists: it required the support of the militarily powerful northern landowning shaikhs and the groups of fighting men that they could muster, usually from the poorer village families. The development of shaikhly constellations of power, in the manner described by Montagne for the Moroccan Berbers,[68] was curtailed by exporting shaikhly leaders to tax prebends in richer areas.[69] In this way the tribe was sanctioned as a status group within the state. The Imamic state rested on an alliance of the farmer (the fighter) with the preacher (the judge) and on the symbolic and political suppression of mercantile and craft interests more generally.[70] The union of religious leaders and martial farmers from agriculturally marginal areas formed a loose prebendal dominion over the more productive, largely Shāfi'ī, peasant areas of the west and south.[71] Whether collected by regular employees of the government or by irregulars from the north, taxes were paid by those who produced most, by the peasants of the richer areas. For example, Goitein reports that the Jewish villagers of al-Gades in lower Yemen called the local landlord *'askarī*, "soldier", noting, however, that he and his like came from the eastern pastoral region and should be distinguished from the regular *'askarī* who accompanied the local government officer on his tax levies.[72]

The long reign of Imam Yaḥyā (1918–48) appears as a period of relative prosperity, especially when compared to the famines and ravages of the first decade of the century and the years of the First World War.[73] But local artisanal production began to suffer as imports from industrial Europe increased steadily after the opening of the Suez Canal in 1869. The eventual departure of the bulk of the Jewish community in 1949–50 reflected not only the establishment of the state of Israel and the organization of "Operation Magic Carpet", and not only the fears engendered by the assassination of Imam Yaḥyā in 1948 and the ensuing conflicts culminating in the sack of Ṣan'ā', but also the difficulties encountered by craftsmen, a great many of whom were Jewish, throughout the early twentieth century.[74] The decline in local craft production may have strengthened the hand of the central government by permitting monopoly concessions and taxation of growing imports. But it also entailed further ties with the outside. By the late 1940s and 1950s traders and Yemenis from the North established in the port city of Aden expressed their political opposition to the Zaidī Imamate. The Free Yemeni movement was to call for the opening of Yemen and the overthrow of the Imamate.[75]

This came about in 1962, when a small group of army officers stormed the Imam's palace. They soon received support from Nasserite Egypt. Egyptian forces were to remain in Yemen for five years and to leave only after defeat in the 1967 June War with Israel. On the other side, the Saudis, with the tacit assent of the British and the Jordanian governments, supported the Imamic, or "Royalist", resistance and established links of clientship with major shaikhs which were to last long beyond the termination of open conflict. In the ensuing civil war, which flickered and flared for seven years, Yemen became the stage for a political contest that went far beyond its borders. After Egyptian troops withdrew in 1967, Royalist forces appeared for a time to be ready to close in on the Republic. In 1968 the Royalists besieged Ṣan'ā' for seventy days but failed to take the city. The failure of the Royalists to take Ṣan'ā' and the simultaneous elimination inside the Republican camp of the most orthodox leftist and anti-shaikhly elements set the stage for national reconciliation.[76] By contrast, in Aden, the left was to assume power.[77]

Following the siege of Ṣan'ā', the Yemen Arab Republic witnessed something of a political restoration, although the North Yemeni economy was already very different from that of 1962. The subsidies provided to the major shaikhs by the Saudis, and at times by the Egyptians, had greatly strengthened the hand of rural, largely northern, leaders. Thus, following the 1970 Khartoum reconciliation, not only moderate Royalists but shaikhs of various persuasions entered the central government. In 1971 the *majlis al-shūrā* was formed and rural leaders held the majority of the seats. The speaker, 'Abdullāh b. Ḥusain al-Aḥmar, was the paramount shaikh of Ḥāshid, one of the two great political leagues of the north, unchanged in name, if not in substance, for centuries;[78] and he himself was arguably the most powerful individual in the Yemen Arab Republic.[79]

The years of the civil war had also been years of drought; local agriculture was no longer the mainstay it had been in 1962. Under the presidency of Qāḍī 'Abd al-Raḥmān al-Iryānī (1967–74) successive governments rested on the politics of compromise. Severe budgetary deficits, attributable as much to the growth in the institutions of government as to declines in tax revenue, mismanagement and the filling of private pockets, tied the hands of the central government. The financial resources of the government were as yet limited. Only after 1970 did Saudi Arabia begin to lift restrictions on the immigration of Yemeni labourers; and only after 1975 did the building boom of the oil states begin in earnest and come to employ as many as a million Yemenis.[80]

In 1973 Prime Minister al-Ḥajrī secured an agreement whereby Saudi Arabia undertook to cover the government budgetary deficit directly. From 1975 the Saudis were also to cover important military purchases by the Yemeni state.[81] In 1974 a bloodless military *coup d'état* led by Lieutenant-Colonel Ibrāhīm al-Ḥamdī ousted the Iryānī government. Al-Ḥamdī was to prove an astute politician. In 1975 he moved successfully against his major competitors for power in the centre and against the major shaikhs of the north. In the same year he dissolved the *majlis al-shūrā*, and 'Abdullāh al-Aḥmar declared the government invalid. For a time the centralizing momentum appeared stronger than ever before. Yet there was a looming contradiction between the centralizing nationalism of the regime and its financial dependence upon outside aid and remittances, above all from Saudi Arabia. Al-Ḥamdī was assassinated on 11 October 1977, the day before he was due to travel to Aden for discussions on the unity of the two Yemens.

This study, conducted between July 1973 and April 1977, belongs to this period. Swept along by the swift rise in oil production and revenue in neighbouring countries, the Yemen Arab Republic was moving from a poor agricultural economy with limited, long-term, long-distance migration to a booming market economy fuelled by the remittances of short-term mass migration and by direct subsidies to the central government and to major rural shaikhs.[82] The bases of the older class structure (landownership, local agricultural tax revenue and limited export-import trade) were being supplanted by new sources of wealth: government salaries and bribes, labour in the oil-producing states and a booming import trade. On these bases began to rise the three classes characteristic of so many poorer economies today: state employees, migrant proletariat and import traders. Aided from the late 1970s by internationally funded projects for the "development" of agriculture and of government bureaucracy, the three classes swept before them the remnants of the older agrarian order.[83]

Yet the decline in the power of rural society and its leaders, consequent on such transformations, was cushioned not only by the national proclivity for *qāt*,[84] the sole locally grown crop without a foreign competitor, but also by the wider political value of the shaikhs to Saudi Arabia, the state most fearful of Yemen's potential power in the Peninsula.[85] In the years following al-Ḥamdī's death, after the time covered by this study, the central government was to lose such control as it had over the economy in large areas of the east and the north (including the Tihāmah). This continuity of "tribal independence" was itself the child of historical circumstance: the overall political and economic importance to Saudi Arabia of decentralized political relations in North Yemen.

Turning to the community of our study, we find that it too presents a series of contrasts. Occupying the central portion of a wadi system flowing onto the high plateau on which Ṣan'ā' stands, Wadi Ḍahr forms part of the immediate agricultural hinterland of the city.[86] Internally, and in line with the intensive irrigated agriculture of the area, men of the community differ markedly in wealth and occupation. At the same time, the village forms part of the political associations of rural North Yemen, of the *qabīlah* or tribe of Hamdān and thereby of the league known as *qabā'il* Ḥāshid, the tribes of Ḥāshid. These tribal divisions have long been bound up with the administrative divisions of the central state. The territory of Hamdān is both a "tribe" and an administrative unit for which the central government appoints an Islamic judge (*ḥākim*) and a governor (*'āmil*). Central government recognition of the men chosen as shaikhs, both for the area as a whole and in every village, is required for such figures to represent their communities effectively in dealings with agencies of the state.

There are other contrasts. Even in the mid-1970s Wadi Ḍahr appeared still to live by an older economic order. This illusive continuity owed much to the returns fetched by the community's agricultural products in the city markets and to its consequently low rates of labour migration. The area produced a fine quality of *qāt*,[87] the profits from which cushioned Wadi Ḍahr from a radical break with economic strategies of an older kind, a break such as was experienced in many grain-growing, dry-farming villages. Yet, and particularly so in the case of this community close by the capital city, the dramatic economic changes brought about in the 1970s by the mass migration of labour to the oil economies should not obscure the slower transformations of the earlier part of the century. Yemen did not, as journalism would have it, step only today from the Middle Ages into the modern world.[88]

From the vantage of the 1990s the 1970s appear almost as a lull between two storms: between the years of civil war (1962–70) and those of the structural incorporation of Yemen in the oil economy of the Peninsula (1978 onwards). The impression given by this study, that of observing the very end of an *ancien régime*, is heightened by the attention it gives to domestic structures and marital alliances. These reflect the choices of an older generation: nostalgia is there in the material.

2

The locality: images of place and political order

Ṭauq ibn Aḥmad al-Ḥabashī al-Naḥawī, the companion of Abū al-Ḥaṣīf, who was from Egypt, looked down on the wadi [Ḍahr] ... and said "I have entered the lands of Egypt, Iraq and Syria and I have never seen the like of this valley".

Al-Ḥasan ibn Aḥmad al-Hamdānī (b. 280 AH/893 AD), *al-Iklīl VIII*, pp. 77–8.

The locality of Ḍahr is known for its landscape; it is a place of memory and ancient settlement. Outward form and inward memory, political community and social imagination: such are the topics of this chapter.

Landscape observed

A map reveals something of the geography: an incised canyon widening into a small flood plain, a winding walk of some ten kilometres in length. (See Maps 2 and 3.) The canyon has been cut by several sources: by a perennial stream which arises from ten springs in Bait Na'am; by runoff from spring and summer rains converging as five local watercourses (*sails*); and more infrequently by floods which converge far above in the mountains and sweep down along the valleys above Wadi Ḍahr. In August 1975 a torrential flood, such as had not been seen for almost a century, destroyed lives, houses and orchards throughout Bait Na'am and Wadi Ḍahr. Its waters reached the Ṣan'ā' plain.

The irrigated floor of the canyon is cultivated in small, often walled, plots. On the lands above the valley lie larger, carefully levelled fields where sorghum, barley and pulses are planted following the spring or summer rains. The areas of dry farming extend back west towards the grain-farming lands of the mountains where rainfall is greater. Settlement follows the line of the stream. At the head of the

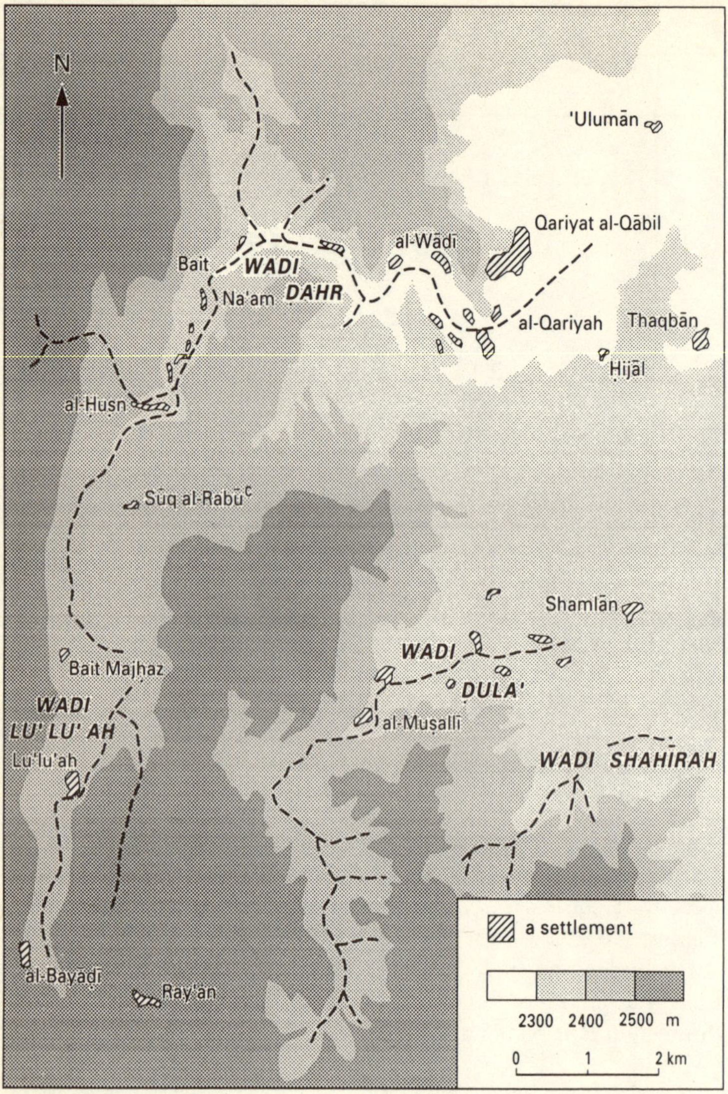

Map 2 Flood ways of the Wadis Ḍahr, Ḍula' and Lu'lu'ah

Note: Before the introduction of motorized pumps, perennial irrigation was assured by the water of springs in Wadis Ḍahr and Lu'lu'ah and of underground *qanāt*s in Wadi Ḍula'.

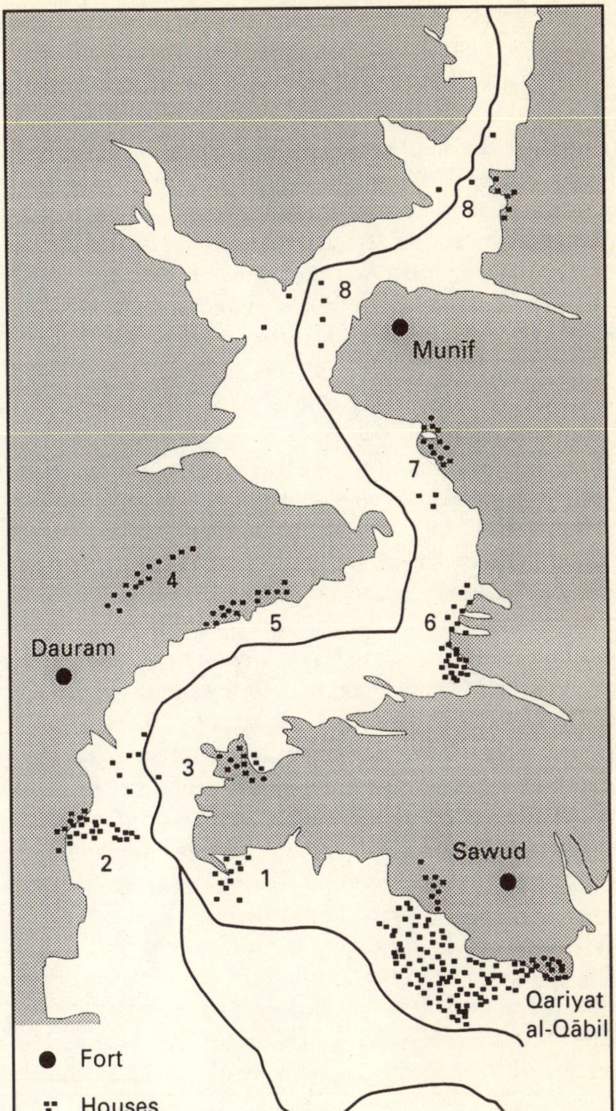

Map 3 Qariyat al-Qābil and wards of al-Wādī

canyon on a natural fortress stands the only substantial agglomeration in the upper section, Bait Na'am. The settlements there, Balad Bait Na'am and al-Ḥuṣn, command not only the narrow irrigated area below but also more extensive upland rain-fed grain lands. In the open lands behind al-Ḥusn, a regional market (Sūq al-Rabū') is held every Wednesday, and produce from the irrigated gardens is sold to men and women from the grain-growing lands up-country. Butchers from Wadi Ḍahr, who on Sundays and Tuesdays may attend markets further east, sell meat and buy animals. And the Shaikh of Hamdān, who has for much of the century come from the adjoining wadi of Ḍula', may attend to adjudicate disputes. Settlement below Balad Bait Na'am takes a different form: clusters of two or three tower houses, most known by family names, balance like small fortresses on the cliffs. Somewhat more than half-way down the canyon tower the ruins of a fort (Munīf). Below this in the wadi lies an ancient flood-break (al-Maradd) which marks the boundary between the communities of Bait Na'am and Wadi Ḍahr.

Below al-Maradd, houses are built in the canyon, first close along the sandstone cliffs and, gradually, just before the canyon widens, on the irrigated floor. On the heights above stand towers, and the only settlement on the cliffs, Ṭaibah (Ward 4 on Map 3), contains elements of what were once more important fortifications. Overlooking the canyon, Ṭaibah consists today of only scattered houses, but a great mosque and large cisterns carved in the rock reveal that the village was once a local centre. From the upper wadi near the flood-break there is an easy ascent to the back of this ward. Overlooking the lower canyon, it commands a way into the wadi, today the modern road from Ṣan'ā' to Wadi Ḍahr, as well as a path up-country to the Wednesday market and beyond, still used by local people. A black volcanic outcrop (Fidah), overhanging the present road from Ṣan'ā', also hides the remains of old fortification.

Settlement is most dense in the lower wadi. A few shops cluster about the great old tree under which, on Fridays, local butchers and peddlers ply their trade in memory of what is said once to have been the market day. At the lower corner of the canyon, on a towering sandstone outcrop, stands the summer palace of the former Imams, Dār al-Ḥajar. The 1975 floods uncovered the remains of an ancient flood-break in the wadi below the palace, close by the present division between the community of Wadi Ḍahr and that of Qariyat al-Qābil. A more urban settlement, with a great mosque, permanent shops, and a little "women's market" tucked away in the back streets, al-Qariyah has a population greater than that of all the wards of Wadi Ḍahr. Crowned by the ruins of a small fort, Qariyat al-Qābil lies crescent-shaped before its walled gardens.

Except for days in spring or summer when, after heavy rains, flash-floods rush down the canyon from the heights above, agriculture depends on the serial extraction of water from the stream. Both settlement and access to water follow the line of the stream, inviting tension between upstream and downstream communities. Customs have long been established to contain this tension. Rights to irrigation water from the stream are divided exactly in half between Qariyat al-Qābil and the upper communities. Of every thirty days, fifteen belong to the upper lands inside the canyon and fifteen to the gardens of al-Qariyah. Along the divide between al-Qariyah and al-Wādī runs that of the great rural political alliances of the North, Ḥāshid and Bakīl. The upper section comprises two communities, Bait Na'am, with rights to four and a half days of water, and Wadi Ḍahr, with ten and a half days, or respectively five and ten once the transfer for a small channel of drinking water is taken into consideration. On closer inspection these secondary divisions again correspond to geography: in Bait Na'am the stream flows in its natural bed, whereas in Wadi Ḍahr it is lifted and canalized. In Bait Na'am the houses stand like fortresses on the heights above, whereas in al-Wādī they are built down in the canyon, first along the sides and gradually venturing to occupy the wider floor.

Within al-Wādī, the community of our study, settlement, irrigation, and even politics take linear form. There are eight wards in the community: seven strung along the stream in the canyon and only one, Ward 4, on the cliffs above.[1] Two supervisors (or literally "turn-keepers") chosen respectively by the leaders of the upper wards and by those of the lower, oversee the distribution of water to the fields. And although the central government officially recognized only one shaikh for the area, during fifteen years in the 1960s and 1970s there were effectively two shaikhs in al-Wādī, one from the upper wards and the other from the lower.[2] At first glance geography appears effortlessly translated into social practice in the manner of the slow fusion of tradition. But this landscape belongs also to a common memory and an imagination of community.

History remembered

Oral tradition tells of three histories: an ancient history of place, a medieval history of contest, and a modern history of politics. Landscape is the subject of ancient history; place derives not only from God's work but also from the civilizing labour of men, when men were giants (*'amālika*).[3] It is said that long before the coming of Islam, Sultan Ḍahr, who gave his name to the area, oversaw the construction of the great stonework flood-breaks that today mark the boundaries between the three communities.[4] The canyon then formed part of an single irrigation system, utilizing the floodwaters draining from the Jabal Ḥaḍūr: through the area flowed a river much greater than the stream of today.[5] The great walls of Ṭaibah bear witness to what was once his fortress.[6] The coming of Islam is also written in the land. The son-in-law of the Prophet, 'Alī ibn Abī Ṭālib clove the passage in the sandstone rock along the road from Ṣan'ā'. This bears his mark.

The history, not of landscape, but of men in the time beyond documents, takes the form of short tales of raids and heroic conflict. The men of the area defend a woman who comes to them seeking justice against her own people. A war-lord from the eastern tribes, envious of the lush wealth of the wadi, comes to plunder and lay waste; the men of Ḍahr defend their land, renowned as one of the gardens of Yemen, against the rough men from the east.[7]

Closer to the present, the heroes recede. Events and men belong to the politics of a world more clearly etched. A house marks the place where a man of a prominent family of the lower wards murdered the Imam al-Nāṣir; chronicles record the death in the year 1840.[8] The murder is not a matter of pride today, but neither is it denied. It is explained in terms of the alliance of Ḍahr with the Ṭayyibī Fāṭimīs of Ṭaibah against the Zaidī Imam.

The modern history of the community has been elaborated by the leaders of al-Wādī in a practical context: a series of legal battles over the division of irrigation water between the three communities of the wadi. Law is everywhere the mother of history:[9] whatever Islamic or customary legal theory may allege, documents establish right[10] and, in so doing, they engender a far more modern historicism.

The contest over water concerned not only the three communities strung along the stream but also central authority. The ruling dynasties, the religious sects and the three communities represented by their leaders all play a role.[11] The earliest extant document dates from the seventeenth century; a judgement of the conquering Imam al-Mu'ayyad, it concerns the overall allocation of water. The last of the major legal documents derives from a court case in 1970. The shaikhs represent (as *wakīls*) their communities in such legal contests. If the recurrent character of such contests seems at first to support a segmentarist interpretation of the conflict – the evenly balanced communities ritually reasserting their opposition in law as in feud – the involvement of the state and the shifts in the terms of the documents themselves do not support such a vision of stasis.

Meeting through their leaders in the court, the contending communities do not agree on the interpretation of the past. The aggrieved party appears to possess the more acute sense of history; by contrast, the community defending acquired right counters by declaring present arrangements immemorial tradition. But the defendant's invocation of golden custom is vitiated by the changing terms of the documents surviving. The dialectical contest of the court encourages the construction of political histories, registered for posterity by the scribe of the court and reviewed by the parties concerned in every subsequent case.

As told by the leaders of Ḍahr, the aggrieved party for much of the twentieth century, the history falls into three periods: the seventeenth and eighteenth century when forces – not figures – meet, the nineteenth century when scholars reach reasoned judgements, and the twentieth century when political figures act according to well-delineated interests. The documents of the seventeenth and eighteenth centuries belong to a history painted in broad strokes in which neither the men of the state nor those of the locality possess detailed biographies. The right of the state treasury to a time-share in the irrigation water is interpreted as a payment which the disputing communities gave the ruling Sharaf al-Dīn Imams.[12] This reading casts the local communities, not the Imams, as primary actors and holders of right. The lengthening of the turn-round period of irrigation which can be discerned in the documents is explained in a similar spirit. The communities, it is said, agreed on occasion to lengthen the cycle of irrigation so as to reduce the proportional value of the days held by the state treasury (e.g. three days out of eighteen shrinking to three of twenty-one and finally of twenty-eight). The interested engagement of the Imams evident in the last acts of the history encourages scepticism before an interpretation of the more distant past in which the local communities acted but the Imams merely arbitrated. Such a construction serves to play down the claim of the descendants of the Sharaf al-Dīn Imams to a share in the water and to set the scene for the drama of injustice represented in the biased rulings of the twentieth-century Ḥamīd al-Dīn Imams.

According to the leaders of Ḍahr, the nineteenth century was the period when al-Wādī's rights were justly honoured in law. In their interpretation of the documents from the nineteenth century, penned by Islamic scholars rather than ruling Imams, other themes emerge: the relations of the communities with the people of the city of Ṣan'ā' and with the Ottomans in Ṣan'ā'. Arguing from principles of law, senior Islamic scholars recognized the priority of the upstream communities (*al-a'lā fa-'l-a'lā*) and overrode the allotment once enjoyed, with little justification in Islamic law, by the Sharaf al-Dīn Imams. The political context of this scholarly impartiality remains obscure: there is a nervous admission of the support given by the area to the Makārimah in their contest with the Zaidī Imams, but little local recognition of what published chronicles suggest to have been the good relations with the Ottomans enjoyed by Hamdān (the tribal group to which al-Wādī belongs). The history of the leaders focuses rather on the justice of the nineteenth-century scholarly judgements favourable to the interest of al-Wādī.

By contrast, in documents from the twentieth century all figures are said to have defined political interests. The Ḥamīd al-Dīn crush the Makārimah and impound their lands as a state *waqf*. The Imam imprisons the shaikhs from Wadi Ḍahr until the community agrees to a less favourable division of the stream waters. The support of the Ḥamīd al-Dīn for the people of al-Qariyah is grounded in economic interest, as the ruling family and several of its major *sayyid* supporters own houses and land in Qariyat al-Qābil. Although over the long reign of Imam Yaḥyā relations between the community and the regime were gradually to improve, it was only in the reign of al-Imām Aḥmad (1948–62) that they are ever described as good. Even today, it remains a matter of pride that no member of the Ḥamīd al-Dīn came to own land in the community and that the summer houses of the leading *sayyid* families of the regime are clustered in al-Qariyah, not al-Wādī. The colouring put on this history depends upon the speaker and the time. In a lawsuit in 1967 the leaders of al-Wādī spoke scathingly of the former Imamic family and the associated *sayyid* houses, but only three years later, in a subsequent legal battle, they employed a language more subdued, echoing political change both national and local.

This is a political history in which written documents are central and the rural communities appear clearly differentiated by social composition and political allegiance. And it is a history of the relations of local communities – to each other, to sect and to state. Its time is structured by the sequential dates of the documents and by the bunching of time about the punctual judgements recasting the terms of community right.

Three kinds of history: the first concerns the antiquities of origin, the second tales of heroic combat and regional contest, and the third a political history of legal right. Each, in a different mode, states something of the distinct nature of the community. The tale of origin points to regional links still evident today;[13] the tribal stories contrast the wealth of the irrigated lands about Ṣan'ā' with the dry lands and their harsh inhabitants only a little way to the east; and the modern history concerns the changing terms and political context of local community right. Each, as remembered today, bears some relation to a written form: respectively, to the antiquities of al-Hamdānī;[14] to the gestes of al-Hamdānī[15] (and the brief notices of conflicts between rural groups in chronicles such as al-Wāsi'ī); and to the many documents kept as heirlooms that make possible a history of right.

These histories express a certain regionalism, the antithesis of what Dresch judges to be the Yemeni tribal imagination of society and history. He writes:

> The world of most tribesmen's imaginations ... extends usually in a single dimension ... formed of persons whose characters are serial: everyone's faults and virtues are potentially the same as everyone else's, and the tales that we tell of them may well be the tales they tell of us. "Regionalism" is not the mode in which tribesmen conceive their differences.[16]

This conclusion follows from Dresch's privileging the genre of heroics in constructing a "tribal history" as a foil to dynastic, Islamic history. But such abstraction from the social site where any "tribal history" is constructed runs counter to the experience of rural leaders. Just as the writing of al-Hamdānī also contains the antiquities (the tales of the origin of place where sultans, not tribes, loom large), so men of today also possess myths of the origin of place. And if we are not to exoticize the "tribesmen" of today, we must also consider their more "modern" histories which embrace both Imams and shaikhs, both state and tribe, constructed from the point of view of the locality and its interests today.

Community imagined

AN EXCHANGE

It is recounted that following the conflict over the division of the stream, Imam Yaḥyā imprisoned the shaikh and leaders of Wadi Ḍahr. The Imam summoned the shaikh to his presence. After the shaikh had been led in, the Imam turned to him and asked with disdain: "Who made you shaikh? (*man alladhī mashayya(kh)-k?*)" The shaikh replied: "those who made you Imam (*hum alladhī[na] 'ammam-ak*)".[17]

This exchange plays on images of political legitimacy. The Imam's question to the shaikh derides the pretensions of a rural leader whose support comes only from a rough crowd of villagers. But, turning the matter round, the reply of the shaikh undercuts the claims of religious leadership. It points to the source of political leadership, not the pretences of legitimacy. Whereas the Imam evokes an elitist image of the religious deputy, the shaikh counters with the principle of direct representation: *they* select us both, shaikh and imam. The shaikh's response refers implicitly to both the popular basis of all leadership and the institutional relationship between rural political leadership and the Imamate.[18]

A CORPSE

One morning in 1977 the body of a murdered man was found lying in the lands of the community. The government demanded blood-money from the community for the murdered man, who later proved to have lived in the suburbs to the north of Ṣan'ā'.[19] The community refused to pay, arguing that the corpse had been taken out at night and dropped over the cliffs above where it had been found. When the community refused to pay blood-money the government imprisoned the shaikhs. The men of the community then closed the road, or as they put it, the borders, and posted a watch day and night. Three days later the police arrested a suspect; the government retracted, and the shaikhs went free.

In this case, as in the conflict in the days of Imam Yaḥyā, the government imprisoned the shaikh; the shaikh stands for the community before the outside and the state. In the first contest the government alienated a part of the common property of the community (the share of the community in irrigation water); in the second it demanded blood-money from the community as a corporation. In the first case the government enforced its legal ruling on the recalcitrant community by billeting soldiers in the community; in the second the men closed the borders. Let us explore further the images of membership, territory and leadership by which the community is imagined.

If one asks a local man directly about the principles of membership, he responds in an older political idiom, there being as yet no language to capture the intermediate solutions of the day. Three principles emerge in the discussion of the principles for membership: the exclusion of figures attached to the state, the notion of protection (*man'ah*), and the responsibility to pay common contributions. Excluded from membership are figures such as a government soldier (*'askarī*), the keeper of a mosque, or a man of religious learning (*faqīh*) who has been given *hijrah* status.[20] This term refers to the protection offered to a man (or family) of religious status by a community, allowing him to reside in the area, to be protected by the community and yet to be exempt from contribution to the common fund of the community. In the early 1970s a government official, army officer, visiting teacher or other person coming to reside in the community did not for that reason share in the decisions and responsibilities of the local polity. But the few men from families of the area who entered government employment were not excluded from participation in local political life.

A labourer from another area who came to work in the community equally did not by mere residence become a member of the community. Should a man of the community take objection to such a figure, he could appeal to the shaikh, who would tell the man to leave. In 1976 a worker and his wife from the poor region of Arḥab, who had lived in al-Wādī for four years, began to lay the foundations of a tiny house against the side of the cliff in Ward 2. An established farmer of the community complained to the shaikh, claiming that the house would obstruct irrigation channels. As if to give the man from Arḥab the means to go packing, the local farmer bought the pile of rocks from him for a high price. The man and his wife left quickly to find another market for their labour. The objection was generally seen to be false since two poor men of the community had already built small houses nearby. Some people regretted that the poor man and his wife had been so rudely driven out, but the worker had no patron and no one felt compelled to take up his cause.[21]

The position of a labourer from another community is distinct from that of families traditionally attached to the community as "servants" (butchers, vegetable growers, barbers, marriage dressers, grain measurers, innkeepers). In the past the protection of the labourer was an individual relationship of patron to hireling,[22] whereas the latter were considered, in a manner parallel but distinct from the protection of the man of religion, as under the corporate protection of the community. Today this erstwhile subordination is a topic of some embarrassment; the dress of younger men, who sport the same dagger as the farmers, does not announce their inherited status.[23] But continuity of occupation, property, and marriage closure means that such distinctions are not easily forgotten. And in the 1970s the government might itself still treat the butchers of the community corporately, as if they formed a kind of guild.

GOVERNMENT AND THE BUTCHERS

One Friday morning in 1975 an employee of the Ministry of Supply came from Ṣan'ā' to buy meat from a local butcher. The butcher gave the man three measures of meat, but told him it was four and charged him accordingly. The employee informed the ministry. Later in the day the governor dispatched soldiers to discipline the butchers. All went to jail save two who were judged too miserable to punish; held in two jails, the butchers were released only on the Sunday afternoon. The costs of the episode were divided among all, including the two butchers who had not been arrested.

On their release the butchers went to the leader of the upper wards, at that time officially recognised as shaikh, and asked him to take action against the collective punishment. The leading butcher pledged to follow the shaikh's advice (*qad niḥnā ba'd qaul-ak*). But the shaikh merely hemmed and hawed. Before they left, the leading butcher – or so his wife alleged – challenged the shaikh in anger: "Are you a man? (*aw ant rajjāl?*)" A man should not stand by while all the butchers were punished for the fault of one.

The butchers then approached the former shaikh, unofficially still shaikh in the lower wards and the market quarter. At this point the leader of the butchers adopted a traditional idiom, emphasizing the position of the butchers as servants of the community and the duty of the shaikh to protect them. The shaikh supported them and tore up the order that had come from the government requiring them to use kilogram weights and to charge the same prices as butchers in the Ṣan'ā' market.[24] The old mother of the leading butcher boasted that she had said to the shaikh, "Are you going to stand for their treating your servants (*ḥaqqa-kum al-khadam*) so?" The shaikh, she said, had replied: "You are the older and wiser of us and so already know that all they want in Ṣan'ā' is money."

The government here punished all the butchers for the misdemeanour of one and then sought to impose on them rules issued for the butchers of Ṣan'ā'. With the more educated shaikh of the upper wards the spokesman of the butchers had simply stressed the injustice of the collective punishment, but the shaikh did not take up the case. With the more traditional shaikh of the lower wards, whose constituency was based in part in the market quarter of the community, the leading butcher (who would never describe his daily work as service as he owned land and houses and received no part of the harvest but rather paid taxes), appealed to the shaikh's duty to protect the community's servants. By tearing up the order which imposed the regulations of the Ṣan'ā' market on the community's butchers, the shaikh affirmed the will of the community to administer its affairs, even its market, internally.

As the resolution of this dispute reveals, the community traditionally had jurisdiction over common resources within its territory. In the case of irrigation water, the total allocation is ten and a half days, ten distributed between the landholders of Wadi Ḍahr according to the area of land each owns, and one half-day given to Bait Na'am in return for continuous rights to domestic water throughout the month, including the days when the main part of the stream is used for irrigation upstream. The land of the village is similarly a common territory and privately owned. The pasture lands surrounding the private holdings of agricultural land are open to all of the community.[25] Local tradition recognizes that such uncultivated land belongs to the community, not the state.[26]

The local community controls who may reside within its borders. The older idiom was that of protection; that is to say, the men of the area were in some measure responsible for those in their charge. Today it is rarely a matter of common defence of men and territory, although as the case concerning the corpse reveals, the notion of territory had not vanished, and moreover, the state and not only the locality continued to require corporate responsibility for the payment of blood-money. The term *mukhuwwah*, brotherhood, is evoked in relation to fiscal co-responsibility for blood-money.[27] In contrast to the provisions of Islamic law, blood-money paid between members of the community is a third lower than that paid for outsiders:[28] members should contribute to the blood-money owed by any one of them to a man of another community; they must cover the blood-money due for the accidental or unresolved manslaughter of one of their own. In terms of blood-money members have rights in one another (*la-hu al-ḥaqq fī-h[i]*).

Blood-money is paid in cash. So too the defence of community interest, in the form of litigation over irrigation rights or payments in the event of contest with the government, usually takes monetary form. The community possesses a common fund. Contributions are collected on two bases: person and property (*al-ḥāl wa-'l-māl*).[29] By the first criterion, harking back to notions of physical protection, a severely disabled man is excluded from contribution and thereby from full political membership. In the case of a small sum, collection is most often made by head count; but in the case of major expenses, agricultural land forms the basis of assessment.[30]

Such collections are managed by the shaikh in the name of the community. The shaikh is both leader and legal representative of the community; he is responsible to the community that selected him. His is not the only political office in the community. Each of the wards of the community has a head (*'āqil*) and these men participate in any important decision concerning the community at large. Equally, the community selects supervisors for the distribution of irrigation water on principles quite independent from those of the shaikhdom. And lastly the community recognizes a document writer (*amīn*), who produces legal documents for the shaikh and for individuals in the community.

The shaikh is something of a ruler: as we shall see in the next chapter, he sits in legal judgement of cases, may impose fines, and can imprison men who have disturbed the peace. But the ultimate power of rule-making or legislation belongs to the community and the shaikh's legitimate role in law-making is to represent the collectivity. The tension between the rule of the shaikh and his simultaneous submission to the law-making of the community and to the law of the government may be explored in a case that occurred in 1974.

MURDER OF A MAN FOUND STEALING *QĀT*

On the morning of 18 Muharram 1394 AH (11 February 1974) Muḥsin al-ʻIzzī Ḥātim, a carpenter, lay dead at the door of his house, his mouth stuffed full of *qāt*. This man and his brother, also a carpenter, had long been suspected of theft.[31] In the course of negotiations concerning the payment of blood-money, the *amīn* drew up a document summarizing the legal hearing and the settlement.[32] Its main clauses were as follows:

> The local shaikh advanced a plea on behalf of the mother, widow and minor son of the murdered man. In this he stated that the man was found dead with two stab wounds. The body had been transported from a plot in the irrigated lands that belonged to Bait Rukaim. The governor (*ʻāmil*) of the area then arrived to attend the meeting in his capacity as government inspector, followed shortly by the regional shaikh. They proceeded to inspect the blood at the place of the murder and to question the men who owned the plot. The men admitted that the carpenter had come at night and had stolen *qāt* from the plot, and that one of them had murdered him. They then went on to describe how the thief had fought back when accosted and how Ḥamūd Ḥusain Rukaim had struck only in self-defence. After hearing this statement, the regional shaikh sent Ḥamūd Ḥusain to jail in Ṣanʻā'.
>
> When the leader of Bait Rukaim, Muḥsin Muḥsin Rukaim, heard of this, he replied that since the men of Bait Rukaim were of the locality, the death was the jural responsibility of the shaikh and the notables of the community. All the notables[33] were then summoned; they replied that the matter concerned only the two parties and that they were not legally responsible. Muḥsin Rukaim then said that the response of the leaders avoided reality: earlier rulings stipulated that no blood-money would be due for a man found stealing and there were also specific rulings concerning the man now dead stating that no blood-money would be due if he were found aggressing against anyone. The shaikh of the community denied the existence of such rulings; the men of Bait Rukaim replied that the shaikh was obliged to produce the rulings, both the general rulings and those specific to the man who now lay dead.
>
> The shaikh of the community brought forth a document signed by the ward heads, notables and individuals of the community. This stated

> that since theft, damage to *qāt*, and violation of property had become commonplace and yet no one prevented wrong or brought people to the right path, the signatories had agreed that no blood-money would be due for anyone found stealing *qāt* or other property in Wadi Ḍahr. A property owner who killed a thief caught in the act would not bear legal responsibility for the thief's blood; this was affirmed by the mutual agreement of all the men of the community, each by his signature. If the thief were from al-Wādī, there would be no blood-money; if he were from outside the area, all the men of the community were to contribute to the payment of *diyah*. Any man who tried to force entry or was found wandering about after ten o'clock at night was to be fined fifty riyals and to be imprisoned for one week. Written in hand of the *amīn*, the ruling was dated 1288 AH (1968); most of the men of the Wadi had penned their signatures to the document.
>
> After the document had been read out, the two brothers of the murdered man admitted that their brother had been caught stealing on previous occasions. Muḥsin Muḥsin Rukaim noted that Bait Rukaim had informed the regional shaikh when on a previous occasion the man now dead had been apprehended stealing *qāt* in the same area. Then Muḥsin Rukaim again described how Ḥamūd Ḥusain had killed the thief only in self-defence. And he ended by appealing to the maxim: people are guarantors of their rulings (*al-nās 'alā qawā'id ḍawābiṭ*).
>
> And after this was all written down, the regional shaikh judged that, out of compassion, the Islamic blood-money should be paid to the heirs of the deceased, that is, the mother, widow and minor child. The two brothers of the deceased then forswore one-quarter of the blood-money for the sake of brotherhood. The leaders of the community agreed to this in spite of the fact that the man was a recognized thief.

Such were the clauses of the document. In accordance with the judgement, the local shaikh proceeded to collect the blood-money from the community. The *shar'ī* blood-money was then 770 Maria Theresa silver riyals, a total of 8,000 paper riyals in 1974.[34] When the governor (*'āmil*) had come out as inspector, Bait Rukaim had given him 1,000 riyals. Of the 8,000 riyals *diyah*, another 1,000 was said to have gone to the governor, while the rest (7,000YR) was divided among the heirs of the deceased according to their Islamic quota shares. The shaikh and document writer (*amīn*) visited the widow's house twice. First the *amīn* drew up an inventory of the belongings in the house; this was required under Islamic law since the deceased left only a minor male child.[35] The second time they went to deliver the blood-money to the widow, mother and son of the deceased.

A month later the upper wards, to which Bait Rukaim belonged, withdrew their support from the shaikh. They maintained that he had collected too much of the blood-money from them, sparing his supporters in the lower wards. A man of Bait Rukaim was then selected as shaikh; he was to retain the post for only a few months before it reverted once again to the former shaikh. The transfer of the shaikhdom was interpreted as financial and moral recompense for what Bait Rukaim had had to pay in contravention of community rulings, but it was generally acknowleged that the man selected did not really cut the figure to continue as shaikh.

In this case the local shaikh acted as legal representative of persons of the community who had been harmed. He argued in their defence, in a manner consonant both with his responsibility towards them and with his role before the representative of the central state, the governor, who came to inspect immediately after the murder. The shaikh's role in defence of jural minors (two women and the young boy) of the community was compatible with his being party to the ruling of the regional shaikh, which stipulated that the *shar'ī diyah* be paid, but not with his role as defender of community interest in general. After all, the ruling of the regional shaikh contravened local legislation. Unlike the regional shaikh, who clearly had one foot in the locality and the other in the central government, the local shaikh remained more firmly identified with the locality. But in practice it was he who actually carried out the judgement. In spite of his formal denial the local shaikh knew very well of the ruling that no blood-money was due for a man from the community found stealing. This ruling was binding upon all. He also knew that this ruling was incompatible with the provisions concerning blood-money in Islamic law, even if the ruling was not unique to the community nor without historical precedent.[36] The settlement was a compromise: between community ruling and the Islamic law of the state concerning blood-money, between the control of theft and the drama of a widow (albeit herself a well-known petty thief) and a child left without supporter. The settlement did not contravene community rulings: the *shar'ī* blood-money was paid out of compassion for the family of the robber, not because it was legally required. Indeed, the assembled leaders stated that they agreed to the payment of blood-money in spite of the fact that the man was a known thief. And lastly the blood-money was collected from all the men of the community, and not simply from the relatives of the man who had killed the carpenter.

The notion of jural contract, which we find here in the practice of legislation by a community composed of assenting individuals, extends to the very existence of the local political community. Just as men must give their assent to the leadership of the shaikh, so they may rewrite the contracts of their political allegiances. In imagination the local polity is ultimately a product of contract.[37] But a restructuring of wider political affiliation is a much rarer event than a mere change of leader.[38] Ordinarily the bases of men's cooperation pass unspoken and unquestioned. In the early 1970s, however, technical change in the provisioning of irrigation water threatened the bases of everyday communality in this agricultural community. This led to political moves which further expose the presumptions concerning membership and leadership – and the tension between the two terms – in the community.

THE COMMUNITY DIVIDES

The 1970 legal contest over irrigation water was fought for reasons different from those of earlier cases. The same protagonists met: the two communities upstream opposed the community downstream, and all the old documents and arguments were paraded. But the terms of irrigation had changed. In the four years after the lawsuit of 1967, sixteen motorized pumps had been mounted on wells in Bait Na'am and five in the uppermost quarter of al-Wādī. This time, unlike 1967, it was the downstream community, Qariyat al-Qābil, that filed suit, charging that the pumps had reduced the flow of the stream, causing damage to those downstream. Representing al-Wādī in the court case were the shaikh of the upper wards, himself a pump-owner, and a ward head of quarter 5, who was allied by marriage to both the shaikhs. The shaikh of the lower wards played no part in this lawsuit. Only after the expensive court case came to an end, without any restrictions on the pumping of water, did the internal contradiction in interest between the pump-owners in the upper wards and the men in the lower wards come to the fore. The latter felt that they had paid twice: first for the court case and, second, in water loss.

The men of the lower wards moved to contest the leadership of the shaikh of the upper wards who had represented them in the case, himself a pump-owner and a wealthy man. Led by a young man of modest means from a wealthy patronymic group of the lower wards, a movement of "youths" gathered momentum; a few younger men of the upper wards also adhered to the "youths" of the lower wards.[39] The leader had entered the Republican army early in the civil war and, although a paratrooper of some distinction, continued to live in the village and remained involved in its politics. His vision was that of a community of direct self-rule, with membership, rather than leadership, its first principle. In this vision the shaikhs appeared almost as usurpers. Later, in 1977, he reflected on political life in the community:

> Today people have become weak and fearful even though they have in fact nothing to fear. In 1973 we fired a shot right into the house of the shaikh of the upper wards, and for a time he did not dare to walk outside. To those who were afraid, I had said: "But what do you fear? You are a good number, armed, and can take to the mountains, leaving the old men at home if the state pursues you. You are as numerous as those who rule in the government."
>
> The standard practice of the shaikhs is to develop some latent source of dispute and to encourage one party, either verbally or by money, to take the issue to court so that the shaikh's real enemies become embroiled in expensive litigation. The shaikhs move as if in international politics. This is more deceitful and harder to uncover than direct exploitation. In such indirect intrigue no one can bear witness against them.
>
> The shaikhs cooperate with each other and if they have personal differences they try to make them appear like general issues. People are fools to be taken in by the shaikhs: they are like sheep but with one difference. When they are sold, sheep go with the buyer, but here, after being sold, people return to the pen to be sold again.

His bitterness reflects the failure of the revolt he had led. Soon after the move against the shaikh of the upper wards, the paratrooper was sent abroad for further military training. In his absence the men of the lower wards challenged not their leaders but their wider political affiliation. Led by the shaikh of the lower wards, whom the paratrooper suspected of deliberate deceit in this manoeuvre, the lower wards of the community applied to join al-Qariyah. In fact this was too major a realignment for the downstream community and the higher shaikhs of Bakīl, crossing as it did the fault lines of the political alliances of the North, Ḥāshid and Bakīl.[40] In the end the lower wards joined the group of the paramount shaikh of Ḥāshid, ʿAbdullāh al-Aḥmar. But it soon became apparent that just as he had not done so when a member of the committee of judgement in 1970, al-Aḥmar had in fact no intention of opposing the pump-owners.

The transfer of allegiance rapidly emptied of content: the men of the lower wards belonged to a group miles away, but at home nothing had been effected. Quietly, however, everything continued to change: in the four years after 1970 wealthy farmers throughout the lower wards purchased pumps. The spread of the technology began to render absurd the political moves adopted to contain it. In 1974, less than a year after their secession, the regional shaikh was able to convince the breakaway wards to return to the fold. The new technology restored a kind of unity at the same time as it irreversibly diminished the flow of the common water of the village. By 1980 the area was to come to depend entirely on private pump irrigation, but the resentment of those without pumps did not blossom again in the period of this study. In the 1970s the pumps were providing the community with more water than ever before. The price of oil escalated, Yemeni labour left for Saudi Arabia in great numbers, and cash income from the prized, long-stem *qāt* of the area soared. Even the poor of the community could afford to purchase water from the pump-owners, supplementing their income from agriculture by trading *qāt*.

The central importance of local politics slowly receded with the stream. Never after 1974 did the men gather before the house of the shaikh in the nights of the holiday (*ʿīd*) to chorus mocking but affectionate ditties composed in his honour. By 1980 the contest between the shaikhs of the upper and lower wards would be over. Leadership would pass to the head of Ward 5, who in 1975 had started to built a fine house in Ṣanʿāʾ from, it was said, the aid donated to the area after the devastating floods of that year. By the end of the 1970s young men were beginning to turn to the capital and its networks for work.

The erosion of a central element of village self-government, its common irrigation water, led to political resistance as men contested the leaders associated with the new private technology of irrigation and then sought to restructure their political alliances in line with the emerging divide between those retaining a common interest in the stream and those upstream who owned pumps. The translation of such divisions into the institutions of village government prompts one to examine further the terms under which the local community was built. The tension between membership and leadership, or the jural power of all members and the unequal power of men to lead and represent each other before similarly constituted local groups or before the government, is inscribed in the terms in which the local polity is imagined. The circumscribed self-government of the community rests on both economic and moral bases. Other communities will differ from that under study both in their relation to the state and in the balance they exhibit between an egalitarianism of membership and a hegemony of leadership. Our task here is to explore the elements underlying the balance evolving in this one community over a period of a few years. This requires that we look closely at the constituent elements and processes of village life. But before we leave the place of the community in society at large there is yet one more common idiom for imagining society, to which we have as yet only alluded.

Status and community

Images of status

In sumptuary regulations, in historical and legal writing[41] and in the oral culture of the religious elites of the Imamate,[42] we find a vision of social order as a hierarchy of ranks. In the speech of older women the vision of social order takes the form of a tripartite division: men of religion, men of the sword and the plough, and men of service. Images of rank are cast in terms of origins. Houses (*bait*, pl. *buyūt*) possess origins; men are known and ranked as members of houses. The charters of origin of the three major categories reflect the organic institutions with which such identities were bound up: the networks of religious learning and central rule, the rural political communities of agriculturalists, and the market (or, in economic jargon but truer to the older terms, the service sector).

Men of houses of religious status trace their origins through individuals back to the founders of the faith: in the case of the *sayyids* to the sons of al-Ḥasan and al-Ḥusain,[43] in the case of several distinguished families to Quraish, and in the case of other families to the founders of centres of religious learning (*hijrah*) within Yemen. Prominent members of the latter two groups are known by the title *qāḍī*.[44]

Genealogy is a written art.[45] Families of religious learning, be they *sayyid* or *qāḍī*, cultivated elaborate genealogies. A central genre of historical writing was the biography of scholars, *ṭabaqāt*, each individual biography preceded by a long genealogical identification of the distinguished scholar and by a genealogy of his scholarly studies.[46] In the reign of Imam Yaḥyā, Muḥammad Muḥammad al-Zabārah composed not only grand compilations of such biographies but also a handbook of *sayyid* houses, which included all the major *sayyid* and a number of the important *qāḍī* houses of his time, arranged alphabetically under family name.[47] Those *sayyids* or *qāḍīs* whose poverty or farming way of life excluded them from the ranks of the learned or ruling houses did not keep such written genealogies, nor did their names necessarily appear in the handbook of al-Zabārah.

Among the majority of men, the *'arab* of the towns or the *qabīlīs* of the countryside, no such elaborate genealogies are cultivated. Rather a person traces his origin back to a particular place where his patronymic house is known for its relation to the land, its honourable occupations and its marriage alliances. There exist representations of the relations between the major tribes of Ḥāshid or Bakīl. These take the form of a tree, a net of branching relationships, rather than the string of individuals as in the learned pedigree. But as Abū Ghānim notes, this literary form bears little relation to contemporary relations.[48] Ordinary farmers do not attempt to relate individual family histories to such written lore. Origins are discussed not so much to validate a person's positive claim to status as to discredit the pretensions of someone else, usually the rich. Some families know well that their name has been bound to an area for generations, others, whose patronym occurs in early histories, for centuries.[49] Families may proudly mention that their forefathers were shaikhs. Most can give a place of origin, although many have moved several times before coming into the community where they now reside. A place is simultaneously a territory and a community of men. For the *qabīlī*, membership of a community ultimately guarantees origin. Honour is essentially a question of occupation and alliance.

The origins of men of religion are constructed by a scriptural pedigree; those of the men of the sword and the plough by the witness of community; but those of the men of service by an unworldly myth.[50] The origin of the *banī 'l-khums* goes back to the mists of time, when mankind travelled across the rivers at the end of the world to the land of darkness (*arḍ al-ẓulūmāt*).[51] On this journey men had only a white rooster to tell them the time of day and a nursing she-ass (*bahīmah muʿjiyah*, hell-bent to return to her foal) to guide them back. Once they had reached deep inside the land of darkness, they were told to collect some of the earth (*turāb*). This felt very powdery, not at all like clay. Some men, refusing to obey, did not gather any dirt. When at last they returned from the rivers and came into the land of daylight, they found the soil to be gold. Those who failed to collect any gold then asked for a share. They were given a fifth, whence their name, "sons of the fifth".

Those who recounted the story found it puzzling. For the religious scholar (*ʿālim*) it seemed a curious item of tradition, but for the bath-keeper the mythical, ahistorical tone of the charter irritated her. She was fond of story-telling herself, brilliant in her rendition of tales of spirits, Jewish wizards and sexual dalliance – all for her mere fables ("*hī ghair ḥizwīyah*"). But she dismissed the story of the *banī 'l-khums* because it purported to be a history – of her own origin – and yet its character was but that of a fabulous tale.

Of the three genealogies, the first is elegantly historical, individually documented, passing back from name to name to the revered founders of the faith and of high law. The second is bound to the living memory of men, to the political charters of larger units, to those whose ancestors were fighters and leaders, rooted in the soil. The third is a tale set out of time in a land of darkness, a tale unwritten about a people dependent on others, without origin (*bi-lā 'aṣl*). The first two rest on quite distinct conceptions of honour and thereby register, in veiled terms, the contest of status between the two great institutions of traditional political life, the rural communities of farmers and the religious state, the latter embodied in the networks of the great scholarly families. The third story of origin, in every sense a foil to the others, evokes images of a nether world, of alchemy, of the power of gold, and of the origins of servile dependence.

Such charters of status are not mechanically bound up with occupation or economy, however much they implicitly associate rank to institutions of the political economy. Indeed, the market is nowhere alluded to: the surreal tale of origin of the *banī 'l-khums* is set far from this world. The market is not a place of origin according to this status ideology. By contrast, the development of the market brings about, as in the society of the city of Ṣanʿā', a blurring of such rustic moral notions as are embodied in the threefold ordering of rank.[52] The ideological construction of status eschews the notion of a direct correspondence of status to occupation and wealth. Yet it suggests both the institutional associations of the three status categories and the limits to the social development of these institutions. The centrality of the notion of descent in determining status is eloquent of the mixed forms of religious state, of rural community and of the market in which kin and domestic units form central organizational units within emerging structures of the political economy.

By the 1970s it was apparent to men and women that the market (and marketable labour) was set to be the dominant institution in the new Yemen. It was thus rare to hear the three ranks set side by side. Only occasionally would a woman of the older religious families or of an old-fashioned culture of piety proffer a vision of social order as the tripartite ranking of men. In a gathering of any size such remarks would rarely be left unchallenged. But the organic relationship between the system of ranking and the central institutions of pre-revolution society – the networks of the religious state, the rural community, and the market – were still discernible in the composition of the community that we are studying, and in its relations with wider systems of economy and government.

Community and status order

As we have seen, the community of Wadi Ḍahr occupies the middle portion of a small wadi system stretching from the foothills to the Ṣan'ā' plain. It lies in the middle of the continuum of this small system not only physically but also socially and economically. This is made clear if we briefly contrast the two communities on either side of al-Wādī. Prior to the introduction of motorized pumps in the late 1960s, the household economy in the upstream community, Bait Na'am was built around grain production, with cultivation of tree fruit and *qāt* only secondary. By contrast, in Qariyat al-Qābil downstream, farmers gave their land to growing *qāt* and fruit, especially grapes, for the city market and purchased much of the grain they consumed. Traditionally, irrigation in Bait Na'am had been organized according to a communal schedule for the cultivation of winter and spring grain crops; in al-Wādī and al-Qariyah the distribution of water followed a more individualized rota according to the size and location of fields.

The patterns of landownership also differ from upstream to downstream. The farmers in Bait Na'am own the irrigated lands they farm, and many also possess grain-producing land back-country where they maintain close ties and marriage relations. In so far as these families served the Imamic government, they did so as soldiers or tax collectors in other areas. Thus, two of the largest families of Bait Na'am had branches that had become landlords in lower Yemen. By contrast, the resident farmers of al-Qariyah had long been closely tied to the ruling families of the Imamate. Several major *sayyid* houses, among them a branch of the Ḥamīd al-Dīn, resided in al-Qariyah where they owned orchards and vineyards tended by local share-croppers.

Al-Wādī lay in the middle. For hundreds of years farmers in Ḍahr had devoted a large part of their irrigated lands to orchards and so to production oriented to market sale. Although until the early 1960s considerable areas of the irrigated lands were given over to winter grain and fodder crops, even then it seems that only a minority of households were able to produce enough grain to cover their needs in any but the best of years. To supplement their own production, most relied on market purchases and on grain from lands cultivated by share-croppers back-country.

In the lowest ward of Ḍahr stands a summer palace of the former Imams, Dār al-Ḥajar; several other families prominent in politics or intellectual life during the Imamate also have summer homes in this ward. The twelve houses of urbanites, including one of a prosperous Ṣan'ānī trader, stand close by one another.[53] (See Table A.1 in Appendix 4.) The shaikh of the upper wards once expressed pride in the community's refusal to sell land to the *sayyids*, by whom he meant the Ḥamīd al-Dīn themselves. In spite of the cluster of summer homes in the lowest wards, his pride is largely borne out by the figures on rights in the land irrigated from the stream. Under 5 per cent of this land is owned by men resident outside the community and more than half of this belongs to men of the community who have moved outside – in the two most important cases, for political reasons. Almost all the holdings of outsiders are tiny, a single garden or two. (See Table A.2 in Appendix 4.)[a]

The small proportion of land owned by people from outside the community belies the historical involvement of the state and the city in the land of the community. It excludes the area, perhaps some 5

[a]Tables with the prefix "A" are all in Appendix 4. In the rest of this book reference to the appendix is to be omitted.

per cent of the irrigated lands and 10 per cent of the rain-fed fields, that belongs to the *waqf* of the *madrasah 'ilmīyah*.[54] As discussed above, this *waqf* was created out of the lands impounded from the Makārimah early in the century. Overall, although the lower wards were more closely bound to both the market and urban families, the community retained control of its lands. The bulk of community land is owned by men and women born and resident in the community.

No major change occurred in the holdings of Ṣan'ānī families after 1962. Today relations between landowner and local cultivator are formal, at times hostile, since there is little a non-resident can do to oblige a farmer to give up the proportion of the produce claimed under the old regime. When they stay in their homes in the community, the men and women of such families generally do not attend the afternoon gatherings of the local people. But a few families, old Ṣan'ānīs with long ties in the area, particularly those no longer so prominent in the halls of power, are more closely linked to the families who tend their land and watch over their homes. Three households, a wife and children avoiding a crowded house in the city, a family profiting from the explosion in house prices there to rent their city house to a foreign company, and a childless woman fleeing an unhappy marriage, moved year-round to their houses in Wadi Ḍahr. Two women had in years past married their share-croppers. One belonged to a distinguished *qāḍī* family with a house in Ward 1. She had inherited land in the community from her mother, daughter of a shaikh of the community, and her husband was in fact her mother's sister's son.[55] The other woman, Kātibah, was herself from a rural background, but had been married young as third wife to an elderly *qāḍī*. After the death of her husband she settled with her young children in their house in the area, leaving the two senior co-wives in the grander city house. Some years later she married the family's share-cropper. Unlike the first woman, who never bore her husband any children and eventually won – at great expense – a divorce from him, Kātibah became fully integrated into local society. The children from her first marriage all married into Ṣan'ānī families, but the three from her second husband found spouses within the community. Kātibah's marriage to a man some years her junior, who had not had the means to marry before and had moved into her home, was celebrated with a ditty: "Whoever walks by the door, consider how the judge has been replaced by a flea."[56]

As this ditty suggests, these marriages may reflect a change in the balance of power since 1962. In 1962 the state administrator was withdrawn from the area, never to return. A number of strategic marriages, where the daughters of prominent families of Ḍahr had married into Ṣan'ānī families, have not been repeated. In 1975 a wealthy Ṣan'ānī family sold their house to the most prosperous local family of butchers after the community refused to allow its sale to the regional shaikh. The area was no longer a meeting place of the elite, and political links with this part of the countryside now counted for little. Certain of the Ṣan'ānī families, able to play roles in government on a national scale, stood increasingly aloof, a class above the farmers. But others, whose religious status had once assured them a certain distinction in the Imamic polity, now lived quite unpretentiously from limited agricultural holdings, minor government service or small trading enterprises, in a manner that drew them closer to their neighbours in al-Wādī.

In the main the outsiders with summer homes in the community belong to houses of religious descent status: 38 per cent are of *sayyid*, 37 per cent of *qāḍī* and 25 per cent of *'arab* status. A few local families also belong to houses of *sayyid* (3 per cent) or *qāḍī* descent (4 per cent); most live in the lower wards of the community where over time several *qāḍī* families have settled and married into local families. But whereas certain of the Ṣan'ānī families continue to enjoy both learning and wealth, there is little congruence between descent status and wealth among most of the local families.

Land, occupation and status

If we consider the distribution of landownership, we find that households of *qabīlī* status have the highest average landholdings (Table 2.1). The few local *sayyid* and *qāḍī* houses are not distinguished by the size of their landholding. On the other hand, the *mazāyinah* stand out by the paucity of their landholdings. True, some *mazāyinah* do own land, and this is conceptually important. But whereas only 20 per cent of *mazāyinah* households own land, 79 per cent of the *qabīlīs* do so, and the average holding of the former is tiny compared to that of other status categories.

The *mazāyinah* feel that their traditional status was bound to their landlessness. The wife of a prosperous butcher,[57] herself the daughter of the Imam's butcher in Ṣan'ā', never forgot an incident that occurred some twenty years before when she had gone with her sister

Table 2.1 Landownership by status category of head of household

Status category	No. of households (hhlds)	No. of landed hhlds	% of total land	Mean per total hhlds	Mean per landed hhlds
Sayyid	8	5	2	59	94
Qabīlī	241	194	94	83	104
Muzayyin	32	8	1	4	18
Qāḍī	11	10	3	51	56
Total	292	217	100 n=21257	73	98
Status unknown	32	7	n=339		

and mother to a wedding party in Wadi Ḍahr. Her sister, who was very pretty, rose to dance with another woman. The singer, a *muzayyinah*, praised the girl as *khādimat al-duwal*, the servant of rulers.[58] The girl's mother turned on the singer: "You may serve, but we do not need to serve." This, she explained, was because their family had land (*māl*). But from that day on her sister never rose to dance again, fearing what the singer, the most popular *muzayyinah* in the community, might say of her.[59]

No *muzayyin* of the community makes his living solely as a farmer whereas several of the *sayyids* and *qāḍīs* do so (Table 2.2). The eight locally resident *sayyid* households differ little in their occupations from the *qabīlī* households. They belong to two types. The first are long-established local landed households, the second landless newcomers to the community. Five households belong to the two landed *sayyid* families of long standing in the community. Although these households do not stand out from those of other farmers in terms of their landholding, the larger of these two families is mentioned in Zabārah's handbook and before 1962 it had closer links than other farmers with important families in the Imamic regime.[60] Today two brothers of the family who continue to own land in the community live in Ṣan'ā'; one works in commerce and the other in government. For those remaining in the community, however, links to other families of religious descent are no longer much emphasized. Although the leading man of the family, the ward head of the market quarter, is a man with some education and sometimes represents

Table 2.2 Occupation by status category of head of household (per cent)

Occupation	*Sayyid*	*Qabīlī*	*Muzayyin*	*Qāḍī*	Total	Status Unknown
Landed	3	95	–	2	100	n=4
farmer	62	75		37	65	
					(n=189)	
Landless	3	91	6	–	100	n=19
labourer	13	13	6		12	
					(n=34)	
Trading	18	64	–	18	100	n=0
	25	3		18	4	
					(n=11)	
Market	–	–	100	–	100	n=1
services			69		7	
					(n=22)	
Craft, not	–	–	100	–	100	n=1
building			6		1	
					(n=2)	
Mechanic	–	44	44	12	100	n=0
& driver		2	13	9	3	
					(n=9)	
Building	–	92	8	–	100	n=2
		4	3		4	
					(n=12)	
Literate	–	33	–	67	100	n=3
specialist		<1		18	1	
					(n=3)	
Government	–	70	10	20	100	n=2
service & guard		3	3	18	3	
					(n=10)	
Total	3	82	11	4	100	
	100	100	100	100	100	
	n=8	n=241	n=32	n=11	n=292	

Note: The percentages in the tables have been rounded arithmetically: thus on ocasion row or column per cent totals may add up to 99 or 101, not the 100 per cent shown uniformly as the actual total.

people in court cases as a *wakīl sharī'ah*, no one in the family is particularly known for his learning or marks himself off in dress or manners from other farmers.

The other type of *sayyid* household is that of poor families who have moved into the area in search of a living. One old couple and their married daughter make ends meet by serving in the homes of the Ṣan'ānīs, by reading the Koran, and by occasional work in the fields. The daughter's husband sells old clothes on a pushcart in the Ṣan'ā' market. Despite their humble occupations the *sayyid* identity of the family played a role in the marriage of their granddaughter. Her father had divorced her mother and gone to work with his elder son in Saudi Arabia. Through an intermediary a marriage was arranged for the girl with an minor army officer from a *sayyid* house of famous name. The celebrations for the bride were held in the shaikh's house, as her father's home was not considered presentable. The second poor *sayyid* family sells vegetables in the local market place. And the third household is composed of a *sayyidah* who makes her living as a petty trader married to a non-*sayyid* soldier.

Local *qāḍī* families comprise a number of farming households hardly distinguishable from, and intermarried with, *qabīlī* farmers. The daughter of one such family remarked that they were *qāḍīs* in name only, no different really from other *qabīlīs*. But among households of *qāḍī* status there are also several families with less deep ties to the area, for whom a tradition of literate education rather than landholding has determined occupation. These families have sought to educate their sons and to secure them work in the government bureaucracy in Ṣan'ā'.

For the *mazāyinah*, too, modern education promises new opportunities. Most of these modest households, whose heads work in butchering or other market services, cannot proceed very far in such aspirations but they do have as model a major figure in the government. The most prominent man of the community to enter the Republican government came from one of these families. His father died when he was a boy and as an orphan he entered military training. He rose to the rank of officer and participated in the revolt against the Imam. In the early years of the Republic he acted as the primary link between the community and the central government and, as a supporter of the "youths", he played a part in securing government recognition for the shaikh of the lower wards against the shaikh of the upper wards. One of the Free Officers and several times a minister, he was a political figure of national stature: labourer, shaikh and *faqīh* all approached him when they needed a friend in government.

It is when we turn to the *qabīlī* families, over four-fifths of the households of the community, that we appreciate the dominance of agriculture in the local economy and of landed farmers in the local polity. True, the area has long had an important number of craft and market specialists; and there are a number of literate specialists and men working for the government. But the heart of this local community lies in the production and politics of agriculturalists.

This chapter has considered the principal idioms governing local political order: interpretation of the past, notions of social status, and constitution of the local political community. In the shape of all of these we have seen the mark of writing. Even that hoary genre of oral tradition, myths of origin, proved to have its written equivalent; and when we came to more modern histories, their very construction rested on documents. We have noted differences in the genealogies of the three status categories. Those of the *sādah* and the *quḍāh* were scriptural and centrally sanctioned, those of the *qabā'il* collectively attested and locally referent, and those of the *banī 'l-khums* inversions in the idiom of story-telling. Taken together the three embrace the structural repertoire of social knowledge from sacred script to collective attestation to profane story-telling. And, lastly, in the constitution of the "tribal" community itself, a domain where ethnology leads us to expect an ideology of substance, we found that descent was not the primary idiom for political solidarity and that the contractual character of local association was underscored by the casting of local law-making in written form. Men invoked brotherhood when negotiating blood-money, but such payments were also the object of haggling and of precise agreements concerning fiscal co-responsibility. The written undertakings of "tribal" association were hidden from the gaze of outsiders, but this was not due simply to their shadowy legitimacy in the view of the *sharī'ah* and the state. Families also lock away their thoroughly Islamic documents, in a world that hides rather than advertises what it most values.

3

Law in the locality

As the cases of the last chapter revealed, different legal traditions and agencies come together in the settlement of disputes. Both scholarly commentary and local knowledge distinguish between Islamic jurisprudence (*fiqh*) and common law, although the two traditions have met over so many centuries as to have produced, in living practice, many intermediate forms and common progeny. During the 1970s the specialists of Islamic *fiqh* were men who had been trained before 1962. The codification of Islamic *fiqh*, reform of its training and introduction of civil commercial law were all just beginning during those years.[1] The tradition of *fiqh*, as it could still be observed in the 1970s, is best understood as an educative project, rather than a code imposed by a state.[2] In the traditional cursus of study, *fiqh* formed the backbone of all advanced education. After completing the Koran, a student would turn immediately to a primer of Zaidī *fiqh*, usually *Kitāb al-azhār*.

As sacred law the *sharī'ah* was universalist, both structurally – in contrast to the particularism of common law – and in content – the breadth of the domains which it covered. This educational project, which in a society of restricted literacy worked to unify the practice of the ruling groups, extended from the most intimate ritual disciplines of the body to dustier questions of economic contract. And it was incumbent upon the literate specialists of the tradition to disseminate its teaching more widely by sermons and oral teaching in the mosques.[3] Common law was, by contrast, particularist and, while it often took written expression, was acquired by practice, not scriptural study.

In the course of everyday life, local communities, like "semi-autonomous groups" the world over,[4] established their own rules and common ways of doing things. Thus, Wadi Ḍahr possessed detailed conventions to govern the distribution of irrigation water both internally and with adjoining communities; and the ward heads appointed and empowered supervisors to oversee those rules. From a comparative perspective what distinguishes this community – and perhaps "tribal" communities of North Yemen generally – is not that they produce such rules but that, in line with their overtly contractual political organization, they also formally restate or revise rules binding on all and may put into writing the process of local law-making.[5] The case of the murdered carpenter exemplified this process.

Beside local custom and formal law-making there is also what one might call the ground rules of place.[6] The core of common law is considered to lie in principles of restitutory justice, a matter of laying out moral order in space, known in manuscripts as *man'* or *man'ah*.[7] Restitution is due for encroachment on the individual moral and physical space of a man or a woman and on the precincts of delimited places: in such cases a sheep or bull should be offered and its blood let.[8] Shedding blood, sacrifice in that sense, is a sign of liminality common in the symbolic repertoire. It is only in the case of a man having offended a woman that a different liminal idiom is used, when the man has to give the woman a covering garment (*maṣwan* or "protection" in the local idiom.) This is not to suggest that reparation for physical injury is unique to *man'ah*. It is also a principle in *fiqh*; indeed, locally, payments for minor injuries follow the schedule for compensation in *fiqh*.[9] But *man'ah* goes beyond Islamic provisions in the attention given to insults impugning a person's reputation, and this is something borne in mind whenever people take to quarrelling.

In terms of legal agency we have already met all the major figures. The state appoints two officials, not to the locality but to the wider administrative area of Hamdān: a judge trained in Islamic law (*ḥākim*) and a civil governor (*'āmil*) who has general responsibility for order in the region.[10] The first is responsible to the Ministry of Justice, the second to the Ministry of the Interior. Shaikhs, on the other hand, are figures of legal authority whose selection lies ultimately in the hands of rural political associations. This said, the government is not indifferent to the character of such men and, in the case of a local shaikh, may be able to refuse to recognize the man selected by the community. Besides the shaikh, the other figures of legal authority in the locality are the irrigation supervisors, the ward heads and the document writer.

Of the shaikhs it is the local and the regional shaikhs who play the greatest part in local litigation. The shaikhs of national stature, ʻAbdullāh Ḥusain al-Aḥmar of Ḥāshid and Aḥmad al-Maṭarī of Bakīl, appeared, we have seen, only in the cases of conflict between communities. (See cases 56a, 56b in Appendix 2.)[a] Just as the national shaikh is a figure both within and without the state, so the regional shaikh of Hamdān collaborates closely with the governor in the settlement of many disputes. The personal power of the shaikh of Hamdān was doubled by the role of his brother, who was, by the late 1970s, head of the armed forces.[11] Such a man was thus himself not entirely outside the state.

The relationship between legal tradition and legal agency observable in dispute settlement does not correspond to the dichotomous structure propounded at times in the polemic of Zaidī ulema[12] and, in the case of anthropology, enshrined in models, most notably that of Ernest Gellner, of segmentary society facing a city state.[13] As Gellner's model, with its forceful synthesis of intellectual traditions, remains of importance in studies of the Middle East, we should recall the oppositions which it proposes for the field of law.[14] Its agonistic sociology contrasts justice in the rural tribe to justice in the urban state by a series of memorable oppositions: secular custom/sacred law; orality/literacy; feud/domination; arbitration/judgement; equality/hierarchy. Our analysis of local-level law will proceed in such a way as to expose the irrelevance of such elegant oppositions.

The segmentary model is concerned with feud or litigation between the component units of society, houses, lineages or tribal segments. But aside from reference to the compulsive force of the honour code, the internal structure of the smallest units remains of little interest to segmentary analysis.[15] Yet, if we examine disputes and their settlement in the community, we find that half of all disputes, and several of the most serious, concern close relatives or members of the same household (cases 4 through 27). Conflict is, if anything, more intense within the smallest social units than between them. And written documentation (of marriage, inheritance, sale and gift) is of great prominence in transactions between close kin.[16] Disputes between close kin form the bulk of the cases adjudicated

---

[a]All numbered cases are found in Appendix 2. In the rest of this book reference will be made simply to case number without repetition of reference to the appendix.

before an Islamic court of the state (marital cases 21a and 27 and inheritance cases 11a, 16, 23, 24, 28), the only other type of dispute so adjudicated being disputes between the communities over the division of the waters of the stream. Cases between close kin also come before the local shaikh, but the character of the disputes is different. In the cases where persons appeal to Islamic authority, one party seeks a radical restructuring of relations within the domestic corporation. This usually pits a weaker claimant, and not infrequently a woman, against the dominant manager of the domestic corporation. By contrast, the cases before the shaikh concern keeping the peace between relatives or in-laws, sometimes at the behest of the dominant manager (cases 4, 11b, 12b, 13, 15, 17, 20, 21b and 29) or settling the terms for a divorce when both parties are agreed in principle (cases 19 and 25). We shall return to the character of the shaikh's justice below, but first we should reflect on these disputes between kin.

Kin fight above all over property; more than among strangers conflicts between kin or spouses arise from concrete interests and not from an allegedly "particularly ticklish sense of honour" in this society.[17] Thus women appear frequently as parties in such disputes. Where women challenge men, the cases concern marriage or inheritance and are fought primarily before Islamic legal authority.[18] It may be noted that the political architecture of houses allows women access to the legal figures of society through domestic space, from *bait al-imām* to *bait al-shaikh*. When a woman seeks redress or refuge, she can pass into the domestic space of the religious judge, either physically[19] or simply metaphorically.[20] This promises to change with the increasing institutionalization of the courts, but was still the case in the early 1970s. And although a woman of the community rarely appeals to the shaikh in a marital dispute,[21] she may be taken in by a trusted but unrelated man of the quarter who will then negotiate her case (cases 7 and 18).

What does this mean? The most intimate of social groups, the building blocks in a segmentary model of society, do not always govern themselves. The internal order of intimate kin (where relations of authority between generations and sexes are criss-crossed by the tension between individual right and corporate management) is not magically assured by the honour code.[22] Such fundamental blocks of society may be the scene of wrongs ungovernable within their walls: a protector (father or brother) may abuse his wards; a son may kill his father.[23] Government does not begin at the higher-level boundaries between groups, but at home. It is the family that contains the seeds of everyday legal domination.[24]

The justice of the local shaikh goes beyond the role of arbiter in a "segmentary society" formed from the juxtaposition of lineages, the relations of which the shaikh brokers. Rather, the community is composed of its houses but is more than their sum.[25] It is only at the level of the community that men meet solemnly to choose a leader (the shaikh) and to legislate the terms of their association.[26] It is immaterial that many of the rules, for example with regard to irrigation or to blood-money, are not new;[27] what matters is that men believe them to be the result of their deliberations and to be binding through their publicly given assent. For example, the power that the community assigns to the irrigation managers is in no sense simply an extension of the rule internal to a house. In performing his duties, the irrigation manager, chosen from the men of the community, is as inviolate as any figure of religion in Gellner's model. He is invested with particular powers by the community as a whole.[28]

The reduction of local legal institutions in the segmentary model to arbitration (and feud) hardly does justice to what we observe.[29] The community controls feud within its bounds: any murder must be sealed with blood-money, the payment of which is negotiated through the shaikh. In cases of inadvertent manslaughter or where the murderer is judged unknown or not legally responsible, all the houses of the community contribute to the blood-money (cases 13 and 41). The office of the shaikh possesses a sacrality that empowers him not only to arbitrate but also, within certain limits, to judge and to police. True, the shaikh often serves as arbiter for settlements following quarrels or brawls of one kind or another; in the honour code, in the tradition of *man'*, violation of a reputation, person or place requires a payment (symbolically in the form of a sacrifice) to restore the honour violated.[30] But such conflicts are not a matter that concerns only the individuals engaged. The shaikh acts to check the repetition or spread of violence. In order to keep peace in the community the shaikh may impose fines on both men and women to be paid to the community chest (cases 4, 32, 34 and 43); he can imprison offenders for short periods (cases 2, 34, 35a and 38) or, quite exceptionally, he may participate in the physical chastisement of a thief (case 37). On behalf of the community, the shaikh can exile a man (case 15). And the notion of inviolability which, in the Gellnerian segmentary model, adheres exceptionally to the figure of religion, is ubiquitous: it covers all private, walled places (cases 4, 31 and 42); public spaces such as the market and bathhouse (cases 33b, 50 and 51); and the honour and persons of all men and women (cases 19, 21b, 22, 28, 31, 32, 33, 34, 39, 42, 44 and 51). People and places enjoy different degrees, rather than fundamentally different kinds, of inviolability.[31]

The notion of degrees of honour (and inviolability) invites us to reconsider the characterization of rural tribal organization as egalitarian in contrast to the hierarchical elitism of the scriptural state. The segmentary model concerns not economy but political ethos or ideology, so let us start with that. Even at the first level of rural political organization, where members of the local community can, and sometimes do, meet face-to-face to make important decisions, we have observed a dialectic in political ethos: a tension between radical representativeness and routine leadership.[32] In the early 1970s the issue of what should be the nature of local political organization was not hermetically sealed from wider debates about the structures of the emerging polity: how directly participatory should tribal government be, and who exactly should count as a member? At higher levels, where men rarely if ever met to replace their representatives, this tension cast a pall over the legitimacy of national shaikhs. The wealth of these major shaikhs, following the years of the civil war, was as yet egregious. Moreover, the particular form of integration of a national labour market, so characteristic of Yemen from the 1980s – in which the national shaikh secures the employment of his followers in the army or agencies of security – was only just beginning. Thus, a shaikh of national prominence could find it difficult to justify his wealth in terms of his brokerage of regional interests in the national polity at large. And at lower levels, given that the 1962 revolution owed much to the men of the market, by what logic were such men to remain "under protection" and outside participation in the local political community?

Such debates parallel differences in academic readings of North Yemeni rural society. On the one hand, the ideologues of the 1962 revolution stress the inegalitarian ethos of the old order;[33] for them rural society forms an indivisible part of a wider inegalitarian whole. On the other hand, segmentary readings consider the structure of society to be tribal and those "under protection" – religious and market groups and all women – as subordinate to that basic architecture.[34] Only in this manner is it possible to retain the characterization of the political ethos of this society as egalitarian. And whereas the first reading often assumes a falsely mechanical correspondence between the distribution of wealth and status,[35] the second, equally, exhibits a sublime indifference to the power of the wealthy and the frailty of the poor.[36]

Let us return to the case at hand. The community under study exhibits both economic inequality and social complexity. At the level of political ethos, tension was manifest between the political equality of members of the community and the economic inequality of houses. This complexity can be observed in the justice of the shaikh. We have noted that the shaikh both serves as arbiter in cases governed by *man'* (the restitutory justice of the honour code) and oversees the policing of the community – jailing, fining, exiling and imposing judgement. The shaikh's power to police, as opposed merely to arbitrate, depends not only on the gravity of the case but also on its social site. The local shaikh rarely polices relations within the inner circle of kin (siblings, parents and children, members of one household). The exceptions to this are revealing. In case 4 the shaikh is invited by two husbands (brothers) to enforce peace on their warring wives (two sisters); so invited the shaikh imposes fines on the women in the name of the peace of the house. In case 45 the shaikh jails two brothers who have clashed and draws up a document stating that all rights in the house rebuilt on the site of their father's home belong to the resident brother. This is exceptional: to explain the shaikh's ability to so rule between brothers, we should note that the men concerned are poor butchers and that the brother judged to have no rights lives outside the community altogether. In all other cases where kin fight over real property the legal authority consulted is a figure of the state[37] and in such cases, should the shaikh fear that a dispute may lead to murderous violence, he appeals to the state for policing (case 11b). Only in the case of murder within the family does the local shaikh, usually in consultation with the regional shaikh and the state governor, impose a settlement. Otherwise, and particularly among the wealthy, the inner family forms a circle within which the shaikh neither arbitrates nor polices. The house is the first level of government, closed to the shaikh's policing, save in the case of murder;[38] but a murder destroys that government (even in the richest houses) and invites outside authority inside. Otherwise, to enter the walls of a house the shaikh must be invited, or must appeal to the authority of the state, or must covertly support one party, in the shadows and out of view.

Outside the house the character of the shaikh's justice again reflects its practical context. Whereas in principle the shaikh works to keep the peace at all levels of the community, the means at his disposal depend also on the stature of those disputing. Among men who are full members of the community, much of the shaikh's justice does indeed take the form of arbitrated settlements (cases 19, 21b, 29 and 33). The institution of guarantors, engaging wider circles of the community, enforces the settlements agreed.[39] But in cases of theft – where the thief is almost always of a lesser stature than the man whose property he purloins – the shaikh imposes judgement; in this he has the community firmly behind him (cases 37, 38, 40 and 42). The shaikh's power to police, rather than merely to arbitrate, is most apparent in cases involving persons "under protection": juveniles, the insane, labourers from outside, women and market folk. The fights of children and youths come before the shaikh; boys learn early to proceed to the shaikh should a fight lead to injury. Such policing is quite directly paternalist: in one case the shaikh delegated punishment to paternal authority (cases 1, 2 and 3). So too it is the shaikh who orders a madman to wear irons should he prove violent. And pity the migrant labourer: if he (or she) comes into conflict with a person of the locality, the shaikh will expel him (cases 46, 47 and 48).

The disputes between women appear at first much like those of men. Women are moral and legal persons and in settlements they too give restitutory payment (and offer animals for sacrifice) to persons and places (cases 4, 31 and 51). But women pay fines to the community chest (cases 4, 32 and 34) far more often than do men (cases 34 and 43).[40] And, in a way quite unthinkable among men, who must agree publicly to the rules that govern them, the quarrel of an individual woman may lead the shaikh to pronounce regulations governing all women (cases 17, 31 and 51).[41] In fact, this paternalist rule-making meets with a classic response from the subjects: no woman contests the rulings but all soon begin to ignore them. Not without parallel are the cases involving the butchers: legal authority (of the state) may punish them collectively for the fault of one (case 54a) and when the shaikh fails to defend one of them, they protest as a corporation (case 35b). As this case makes clear, their "protected" status does not always mean that honour is done to everyone of them in practice.[42] The legal corporatism observed in cases involving women and butchers contrasts with the vaunted individualism of tribal legal institutions.

Lastly, the location of orality and literacy and of secular custom and sacred law do not respect the clear oppositions of the segmentary model. In several of the cases, we observe the shaikh of the community ruling in terms close to those of Islamic *fiqh* and cooperating closely with central legal authority (cases 11, 28, 41 and 44 and the divorce case discussed in Appendix 3). Local justice does not appear simply as the product of secular custom, opposed to the sacred law of the men of religion. In content and in form, local law appears more complementary than contradictory to the law of the state (cases 12b, 20, 25 and 41).[43] Documents, rich in the formulae of Islamic law, are everywhere; the shaikh's justice itself takes written form, as the *amīn* pens his decisions.[44] Common law is not purely a matter of learned orality, untouched by a scriptural legal tradition.[45] At the level of practice a marriage of the two traditions has long characterized local law.[46]

This is not to argue that the justice of the local shaikh is identical to that of a judge trained in *fiqh*. A plurality of legal agency and tradition is manifest; we observe both occasional contests over jurisdiction between shaikhly and state authority and their everyday cooperation in the resolution of disputes (cases 5, 11b, 21, 25, 40, 41, 43, 49 and 51).[47] Just as the documents of the *amīn* vouchsafe an Islamic character to the shaikh's rulings, so too legal authorities of the state may in practice accept the settlements of the shaikhs (cases 25, 28, 41, 44 and 51).[48] Such collaboration distinguishes the legal settlement of the most common of disputes: those between kin or spouses. Given the intimate relation between domestic government and the stature of a house in the local polity, major conflicts within a domestic corporation go before the religious courts of the state rather than the court of the shaikh. But the enforcement – within the walls of a house – of a ruling from a religious judge involves both local and central authority. The legal order begins in the family, not only in the sense that in the pre-bureaucratic state domestic relations provided a model for dominion, but also in the sense that domestic government is ultimately not autarchic. *Oikonomia*[49] belongs to a wider legal order.

4

The village economy: agriculture and the market

Il faut se ressouvenir ici que le fondement du pacte social est la propriété; et sa première condition, que chacun soit maintenu dans la paisible jouissance de ce qui lui appartient. [It should be remembered here that the basis of the social contract is property, and its first condition, that everyone peacefully enjoys what belongs to him.]

Jean-Jacques Rousseau, "Economie politique", in Diderot and d'Alembert, *Encyclopédie*, Vol. 5, 1755, p. 346.

An introduction: the division of labour

In Chapter 2 we observed that almost a quarter of the heads of households (or 15 per cent of all married men in the community) worked in crafts or non-agricultural services. This diversification is not a recent development; most such specialists have traditional occupations and as yet very few men (4 per cent of heads of households, including soldiers and the two old guards on the former summer palace of the Imam) are employed by the central government. For a small community, close by the major craft and market centre of Ṣan'ā', the proportion of specialists appears high – if not in comparison with villages in India, certainly in comparison with villages of Greater Syria prior to the recent development of government employment.

Although seemingly farfetched, this double comparison is not without some utility.[1] In an early ethnography Abdalla Bujra compared Yemeni status categories (as observed in the small town of Ḥuraiḍah in the Hadramaut) to Indian concepts of caste.[2] To evoke Bujra's attempt is not to enter into sterile discussion of definitions of caste but simply to emphasize that Yemeni society embodies a concern with diversification of occupational structure *within* the village, that is certainly no more distant from Indian village hierarchies than it is from North Arabian tribalism or the social homogeneity of village communities in Greater Syria.

Table 4.1 Occupation by landholding of head of household

Occupation	Total hhlds	Landed hhlds	% hhlds landed	Total land	Mean land per hhld	Mean per landed hhld
Farming	246 76%	193 86%	78	20,685 95.8%	84	107
Trading	11 3%	7 3%	64	190 0.8%	17	27
Market services	23 7%	7 3%	30	160 0.7%	7	23
Craft, not building	3 1%	–	–	–	–	–
Mechanic & driver	9 3%	5 2%	56	203 0.9%	23	41
Building	14 4%	2 1%	14	84 0.3%	6	42
Literate specialist	6 2%	3 1%	50	108 0.5%	18	36
Government service & guard	12 4%	7 3%	58	166 0.8%	14	24
Total	324 100%	224 100%	69	21,596 100%	67	96

Specialists were dispersed throughout the rural landscape of North Yemen; they exchanged their products with agriculturalists directly in the villages, not only in city markets, and through the dense net of periodic rural markets. By contrast, in the Syrian plains, craftsmen and traders concentrated in the cities, periodic markets were rare, villagers or bedouin at times came from great distances to visit the urban markets, and itinerant pedlars took the products of the city out to the villages. The social geography of North Arabia and the plains of Syria is one of Khaldunian contrasts: of *ḥaḍārah*, the appurtenance of the city, and *badāwah*, a country ethos essentially agricultural and pastoral.[3] The clarity of the contrasts in the social geography of *bilād al-shām* is very different from the interlacing networks of specialists spread throughout the countryside of *bilād al-yaman*.

Table 4.2 Landownership by birthplace of head of household (per cent)

	Born inside	Born outside	Total	
Landed	97	3	100	(n=224)
	79	14	69	
Landless	57	43	100	(n=100)
	21	86	31	
Total	85	15	100	
	100	100	100	
	n=274	n=50	n=324	

Note: Corrected Chi Square=80.1, significance level=0.0000

In North Arabia the steppes belong to bedouin, while trade and craft huddle in the oasis towns; in the great Syrian plains villages are home to agriculturalists and rarely to craftsmen. The sociology of such communities, the way men think their relations, belongs to a Khaldunian tribalism which emphasizes common descent over territory as the primary social bond. By contrast, in Yemen the presence of specialists inside the agricultural community renders the question of rank and differentiation more central to the political constitution of rural groups and the principle of common descent less prominent in the identity of rural communities.[4] The character of local descent structures and their relation to the political structure of the community under study is something to which we shall return in the next chapter.

As we have already seen, the existence of an idiom of status does not in practice entail rigid correspondence between status and occupation, or status and landownership, or occupation and landownership, especially not in this comparatively rich community close to the city of San'ā'.[5] Rather the correspondence is very broad: 57 per cent of specialists belong to status groups other than *qabīlī* as opposed to 5 per cent of agriculturalists;[6] and *sayyids*, *qāḍīs* and *mazāyinah*, or specialists in general, do own land, although less on average than *qabīlīs* and agriculturalists (Table 4.1).

The processes whereby a man (or a woman) come to control rights to land and water are long-term and central to membership (and social reproduction) in the community. Aside from the Ṣan'ānī elite with small gardens adjoining their summer homes, it is scarcely an exaggeration to say that one had to be born in the community to own land there. It is the landless who move, be they specialists or simple labourers (Table 4.2 and Table A.3).[7]

The baldness of this fact points beyond occupation and status to the other great source of social solidarity and division – property.

Agriculture

The character of property

Although, as we have already seen, the community has a territory and a collective time-share in the waters of the stream, this is paradoxically a village economy practically without commons. Community lands include large areas of uncultivated land, available for pasture on what little vegetation there may be. These lands are termed *maḥjar*. The resonating etymology of this term denotes an area ritually marked and off bounds to others, and so indeed the community could in principle close access and pasture to outsiders. But within the village, this marginal land scarcely forms a very valuable commons. All cultivated land is privately owned.

In the case of irrigation water, there is a more complex play between the common right of the community and individual right.[8] The community possesses a global allotment of water, a collective right jealously defended against other communities and the state. And the practical management of irrigation, overseen by local irrigation supervisors, not the shaikh, itself creates an important sense of community. Maintenance of the main channel is a common responsibility of all landholders. There are two irrigation supervisors, chosen by the leaders of the community, one from the lower wards and the other from the upper wards. They supervise irrigation, keep the registers of entitlement and transfers, evaluate water theft, and impose fines for water wrongly diverted.[9] But here again virtually all irrigation rights, along with the land to which they adhere, belong to individuals. In the mid-1970s disposal by sale of the slight margin of excess water was a right enjoyed by the shaikh, even if in theory the revenue belonged to the community chest. And the introduction of lift-pump irrigation during the period of this study worked to erode further the common in favour of private interest.

In legal terms, all cultivated land is *mulk* (private land according to the categories of *fiqh*), or *waqf* (land endowed to charitable purpose), or state domain (termed *ṣāfiyah*, *ṣawāfī* locally).[10] Although the latter two are of importance in al-Qariyah downstream, in Wadi Ḍahr the only important *waqf* is that of *al-madrasah al-'ilmīyah* and the only state domain a garden adjoining the summer palace of the Imam.[11] It is the first category that dominates land tenure in the community. Both rain-fed land on the heights above and irrigated land in the valley below are held as *mulk*. This legal status ties the land of the community into a much wider field – that of Islamic law and its specialists. Documentation of property employs the formulae of *fiqh* for sale, for lease,[12] for gift, and above all for inheritance. Through their production of this documentation and its certification, Islamic legal specialists (and the political forces with which they were associated) were involved in the most intimate transactions of daily life. As we shall see, the terms of the law, where property rights belong to individuals and indiscriminately to both sexes, are in constant play with the practical organization of cultivation in households.

Although the abstract legal definition of *mulk* tenure is the same for both rain-fed and irrigated land, there are differences in the type of right and in the mode of attestation of property right between the two types of land. In rain-fed land, planted in field crops and only very rarely in *qāt*, rights concern the soil of the plot and the ancillary areas where run-off water gathers before being channelled onto a plot,[13] as even in rain-fed areas the fields are meticulously levelled and surface runoff carefully directed onto the field. In the irrigated lands, rights concern not only the soil of the plot itself, but also stream water, channels, plantings (i.e. vines, *qāt* or fruit trees) and ancillary structures (i.e. mud walls and guard room).

There has never been a cadaster in North Yemen. Central government involvement in land came through the courts, in the course of litigation by individuals over land and communities over irrigation water, not through the certification of property by a trigonometric cadaster. On two occasions, however, a full register of the lands entitled to irrigation in the communities sharing the stream was drawn up under the aegis of central authority, with all plots defined by size, by owner, and by serial location on a channel. The first such register (*miswaddah*) is said to have been compiled in the nineteenth century; the extant register dates from 1927 in the reign of Imam Yaḥyā.

The boundaries of plots in the irrigated belt are rarely the subject of dispute between neighbours. Plots are walled, demarcated in practice by irrigation channels, and their size monitored (and publicly known) by the continual process of distribution and registration of irrigation water (the time-share of a plot corresponding to its area). In the rain-fed lands, by contrast, piles of stone mark boundaries and plots are almost never walled. There is no central register of holdings in the rain-fed lands; and long stretches of time pass without even local political authority reviewing the boundaries of one field or the next. Attestation of property rests on documents penned in the formulae of *fiqh* and on local authority embodied in the leaders of the community. A legal case of 1974 may illustrate this process.

A BOUNDARY STONE DISPLACED

A landholder went to the shaikh and accused the owner of the adjoining plot of having moved the boundary marker between their two plots and of deflecting the water flow of the spate course to the benefit of the defendant's field. The first step was to appoint a guarantor (*ḍāmin*) for each party.[14] Guarantors are men of standing in the community who undertake to hold both parties to the peaceful prosecution of a settlement and to fulfilment of its terms. Documents stating the identity of the guarantor, the parties to the dispute, the nature of the legal action to be guaranteed, the person of the judges, and the names of four witnesses to the guarantee were given to each guarantor.[15]

At the appointed time a party consisting of the two shaikhs of the community, the *amīn*, a local surveyor, and other quarter heads and witnesses proceeded to the plots in question. The *amīn* read the documents (*baṣā'ir*) aloud. These stated the rough location and area of the plot and the manner of its acquisition, by inheritance in the case of the claimant and by purchase (from the claimant) in the case of the defendant. The surveyor then measured the plots and it appeared that the claimant was in the right. The boundary marker was restored to its original place so that the areas of the plots again corresponded to those given in the documents. The shaikhs ruled that if in future either party were to attempt to change the path of the water channel, he was to pay YR1,000 as fine to the community chest and was to give a bull in amends to the other party.[16]

In other words, the source attesting property right consists of privately held documents composed according to the formulae of *fiqh*. These are made public by the *amīn* reading them aloud before an assembly of local figures, some of whom have only partial literacy or none at all[17] but all of whom constantly deal with like documents and so are familiar with the terms of the law. As we have seen, the *amīn* possesses basic training in *fiqh* and serves the shaikh and other men and women of the community as document writer. The judgement of the shaikhs is backed by the power to impose fines in the case of any further misdemeanour. The fines have a double structure: a sum to the community chest and amends to the party wronged. This first payment indicates that the "peace" of the community is in no sense reducible simply to the absence of feud but rests upon institutional engagement in the order of relations and properties between houses of the community. Lastly we should note that the measure of land is a local one: *al-libnah al-ḍahrīyah*. The metrical expression of local knowledge, this small unit is used only in Ḍahr and the neighbouring wadis of Ḍula' and Lu'lu'ah.[18]

The rights attached to land in the irrigated belt are more complex; they concern stream water, soil, and all that stands on the land, i.e. plantings and structures. An owner usually holds all three, but the first and last can be transacted independently from the land, punctually in the case of stream water, and for defined or unlimited periods in the case of plantings and structures.[19] Let us consider the conception of these rights, each in turn.

Rights to irrigation water Rights to stream water follow landownership: for every hundred *libnah ḍahrīyah* a man has one *ṭāsah* of water a month.[20] These rights cannot be permanently alienated from the land to which they correspond. A man may, however, apply his irrigation allotment to any of his different plots, according to the needs of its plantings. And from the early 1960s holders have been free to trade and sell water, and within limits, even to take an advance or to accumulate credit on the overall irrigation budget of the community. The greater flexibility in water distribution corresponds to the increasing importance of *qāt* during this period. Under irrigation, *qāt* can be made to bud during any but the two coldest months of the year; and prices are highest in the winter months when rain-fed *qāt* is not available in quantity in the market. But the easing of exchange of water also prefigures a process of freeing water from land that developed rapidly from the mid-1960s following the introduction of mechanical water-pumps. In the 1970s, with both the stream and the pumps, water was available in greater quantities than ever before; many areas in the wadi formerly sown with annual crops were planted with *qāt*. But there were signs that the new technology promised only a brief respite from the scarcity of water.[21] From the mid-1970s the ground water-table began to decline every year. In the long term, the reliance on pump irrigation, for which small-holders have to pay cash and not simply offer their own labour as in the case of irrigation from the stream, promised to bring new forms of inequality. But this was yet for the future; for the moment water was available as never before.

Land rights Rights to stream water are tied to land, although in any one turn water can be exchanged independently from land. Permanent transfer of rights to water can occur only through the alienation of land. Although sales of rain-fed land have not been uncommon in recent years, farmers do their utmost to avoid selling land in the valuable gardens of the wadi.[22] If desperate to raise money, a farmer would sell rights to the plantings, thereby transferring cultivation rights to the purchaser of the stock but retaining for himself a proportion of the produce and the possibility of buying back the stock and cultivation rights at a later time. Rights to irrigated land pass primarily through inheritance, not sale; sales are most common between co-heirs.

Men and women conceive of land rights very much in the terms of inheritance. Rights belong to individuals; men and women hold rights that differ not in quality but merely in quantity (a female being entitled to half a competing male heir's share); and land rights are eminently partible.[23] All children, spouses and surviving parents are entitled to a part in an estate; in the case of only female children surviving, siblings and cousins may also enter the succession. Such rights are ordered by the principle of family relations, both filial and marital, and not according to the particular relations of management and cultivation within and between households. Such a vision of property encourages long-term strategies whereby managers of households anticipate and adapt relations within the household to assure succession to land. Local society is marked by a fertile tension between the criss-crossing claims arising from ownership and the more visible day-to-day organization of cultivation. This is not to say that such notions of a private property gone mad are somehow imposed by the terms of a law at odds with the working of this, or any, peasant agricultural system.[24] On the contrary, the law with all its tensions seems strangely at home here. How do we explain this?

The land of the gardens is eminently subdivisible: a farmer works a garden with a hoe, not a plough, and a plot may be subdivided into tiny basins so that its various plantings and crops can be irrigated at different frequencies. Whether or not the shares of co-owners are delineated on the ground, these gardens produce cash crops, the revenue of which can be divided among many claimants. Irrigated land is far from equally distributed among agriculturalists of the community; thus, a variety of arrangements for cultivation are available to the owner of a property, as those who have less land, or none at all, seek to work the land of others. But beyond, or underneath all this, are the labour processes of cultivation in the gardens.

We have just noted that cultivation in the gardens is done with a hoe; no plough teams enter the walled enclosures. Little cooperation is required in such work. The hoe is also the tool used for irrigating. Day-to-day delivery of water to the fields does not require large groups of men simply to turn the stream or to maintain the channels: two men can direct the water, and all side channels can be maintained with only limited coordination between the holders along a channel. The stream flows gently and major repair of the main channel is required only after destruction by large flash-floods (*sail*). In the floods that swept through the area in 1975, fourteen persons died and a number of houses were destroyed. Only then did all the men of al-Wādī join with those of al-Qariyah for several days' work to rebuild the entire channel. This is not a system characterized by large-scale coordination of human and animal labour, where political control and indeed property in land are bound up with irrigation management.[25] The labour process of cultivation verges on the individual; it requires no animal power and only simple tools.

Quite as important as the cultivation of the soil or the labour of irrigation is the care of plantings: their establishment, pruning, dusting, and the renewal of the wooden trellises for vines. The division of labour in garden cultivation is usually built around a household, but the allocation of tasks by sex is not inviolable. Women landowners without a man at home may employ a labourer. Lastly, of all the tasks in cultivation perhaps most time goes to guarding valuable crops when close to picking. This is is not a matter of strength but of social relations: at night only men sleep out in guard houses, armed with a knife or a rifle, but during the day an old grandmother, supplanted in the kitchen by her sons' wives, or in the afternoons even children, may be sent to guard. In the daytime sounding the alarm is all that is required.[26]

The individuality of many labour tasks, the participation of both men and women in the care of gardens, the availability of hired labour, the importance of social relations as opposed to brute labour (evident in the time spent guarding) and the investment in the plantings of a plot all render reasonable the individualist ethos of property invited by the terms of *farā'iḍ* law.

Rights to plantings and structures In most cases, rights to plantings and structures belong to the landholder, who also cultivates the garden. One woman noted wryly that if one wanted to have a good laugh, one should go to see her part in her father's estate; every time the party dividing the land had come to a large tree, they had swung the rope towards her side leaving the tree in her brothers' portion. Tree stock is in itself valuable.

Plantings may also be held independently of the land, and in such cases cultivation rights follow ownership of the stock, not the land. If the term for land, *māl*, connotes wealth and possession, that for rights to the stock and to cultivation, *shaqīyah*, points instead to labour invested. In the most important form of agricultural contract in the gardens, called locally *mushārakah* or simply *shirk*, the labour embodied in the stock is carefully evaluated. Both at the start of the contract and at its termination an experienced third party estimates the value of the *shaqīyah*. In the case of fields with good plantings, the *shaqīyah* will be high: it may reach one-quarter of the value of the land. In the case of fields without plantings or with poor stands, the share-cropper acquires anywhere from half to all the value of plantings, guard walls and other improvements which he introduces. Such an agreement both indemnifies the owner against damage to the plantings and protects the cultivator against sudden expropriation or loss of his accumulated labour. The form of the contract presupposes that the share-cropper possesses some capital, which he will use either to make a down payment, or, in the case of a plot without plantings, to exploit in improvement of the stock until the plot begins to bear a return. The form of the *mushārakah* contract means that the share-cropper must be an established farmer, not a simple labourer. In the local phrase, *man sharik malak*, "he who share-crops, owns".

Traditionally the division of net returns in such a contract gives half to the share-cropper (*sharīk*, literally partner) and half to the landowner. Save the tax which comes off the top, all costs are borne by the share-cropper. In the 1970s the share of the cultivator was often greater, particularly when the landowner was a female relative or someone resident outside the community. In the first instance the contract is usually written in a so-called "*waraqat al-ījārah*", rental document – something of a misnomer, as people point out. This is in principle renewed verbally every year. By their nature these contracts tend to be long-term, although the landholder retains the right to buy back the *shaqīyah* and reclaim cultivation rights to his plot. Sometimes a father lets a son take on a field that had been neglected; in such a case all improvements made become the son's property. Or a mother may favour the son with whom she lives by giving him cultivation rights to the plot she has inherited; this in turn gives him a claim against the joint estate (both the *shaqīyah* and a sum, the *shaqā'*, an indemnity, again conceived in terms of labour, allowed the cultivating heir). Or a young man in a landed household with several men will take on cultivation of a plot from a household short of labour.

It is said that prior to the recent growth of cash income from *qāt* a far larger proportion of the irrigated land was cultivated under such *mushārakah* agreements. When families needed cash for some purpose – for marrying a son, building a house, or in hard times for purchasing grain – they would sell rights to share-crop a small plot of land to another household in return for the needed capital. Or a family might mortgage or sell a plot of land while retaining rights to share-crop it. Because few households had large cash incomes, families would find themselves unable to buy back share-cropping rights from their neighbours, often their relatives, or to buy back title to their land from those who had acquired it in bad years. Only with the leap in cash income from *qāt* have households reclaimed cultivation rights held by other households and has the dense criss-crossing of rights between households been reduced.

There are other, less common, forms of agricultural contract. If the share-cropper does not advance cash and "has only the key" with no right to the stock, the contract is simply termed "guarding" (*ḥamā'*). In this contract the share of the cultivator (the *ḥāmī* or "guard") is less than in *shirk* agreements and the owner retains a direct interest in cultivation, sharing in some of the costs. On irrigated fields the "guard" traditionally takes a fifth of the net return, but here again in practice contracts usually give the cultivator a larger share. Some 2 per cent of the lands with rights to stream irrigation is cultivated in *ḥamā'* contracts.[27] All the plots lie in the lower wards, and most are tiny gardens of Ṣan'ānīs. On rain-fed fields, where stock (and *shaqīyah*) is not at issue, the cultivator's share would be a half or even more. Lastly, land may be rented in exchange for a flat sum (*taqabbul*), but this contract is rare except between relatives, especially between the cultivator and a female relative living in another household who, unable to obtain a full return on her share in a jointly-owned plot, is willing to settle for a small sum annually.

The distribution of rights to land

The conceptions of right sketched above, where land is imagined in terms of wealth and possession (*māl*) and stock in terms of labour (*shaqīyah*), are bound up not only with the wider terms of the law but more immediately with local processes of production and the social distribution of rights. Given the plurality of types of right, one would like to be able to sketch the distribution of all such forms – rights to rain-fed land, to land with rights to stream irrigation, to land in the wadi newly developed under pump irrigation, and to cultivation and stock independent from land. But, short of a survey which would have been difficult and unlikely to have produced reliable results, such an overview is possible only for those rights registered, that is, rights to stream water corresponding to ownership of irrigated land in the central wadi lands. It should be remembered, however, that this is but one form of right, albeit overwhelmingly the most valuable, and that if we could also measure the distribution of other types of land right in the community, the overall inequalities of wealth might appear rather less harsh.

The present discussion is confined to the distribution of land (and stream water) among agriculturalists, about three-quarters of the households of the community. If we were to include specialists in our examination, the distribution of land would appear far more unequal, but we would then be comparing those who depended on land for their livelihood with those who did not. (See Figure B.1 in Appendix 4.)[a] The definition of agriculturalist adopted here does include, however, landless labourers, regardless of how long they have been in the community, and those men who make their living by trading *qāt*.

---

[a]All figures beginning with the prefix "B" are to be found in Appendix 4. In the rest of this book, the diagram will be cited without reference to the appendix.

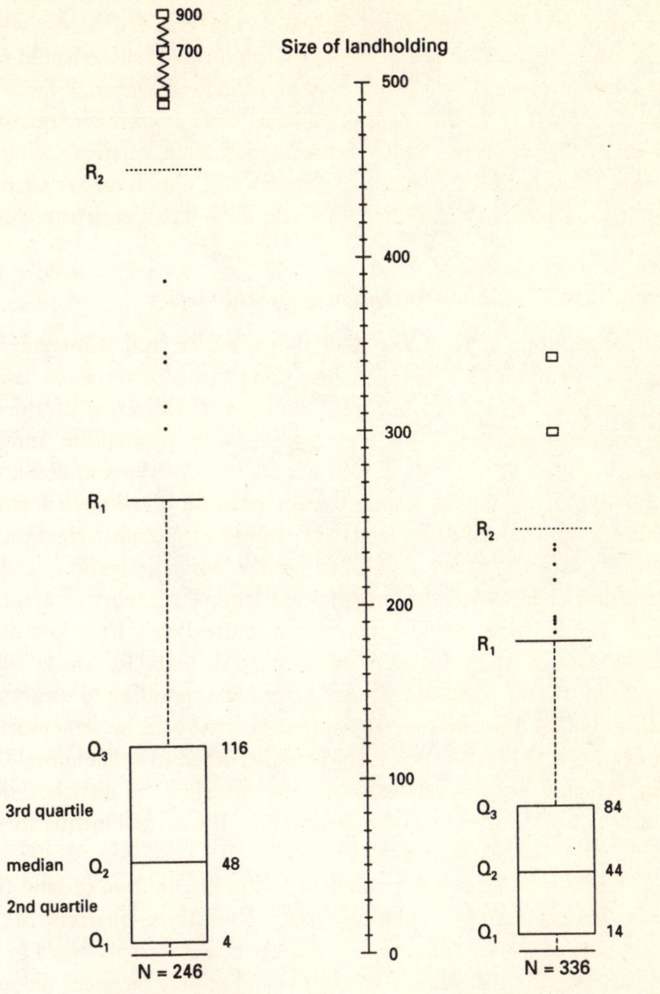

A. By household

B. By married man

Q1 marks the first quartile, Q2 the second or median value and Q3 the third. The distribution of exceptional outlying values is depicted by R1 and R2, the first being the nearest value to one "step" (i.e. 1½ times the "mid-spread" of Q3 minus Q1) and the second the value closest to two "steps" (i.e. 3 times the "mid-spread") above Q3, the upper quartile. Any values beyond R2 are indicated by small boxes, joined by jagged lines for those lying outside the scale running between the box-and-dot plots.

Figure 4.1 Distribution of landholdings by household total and by married man

A "box and dot" diagram (Figure 4.1A) shows the distribution of household landholdings by quartile rank. Divided in this manner, the bottom quartile of households working in agriculture own no land, the second quartile 8 per cent, the third quartile 24 per cent, and the top quartile 68 per cent of the land. In short the bottom half of households are virtually landless and over two-thirds of the community's best land is held by the top quarter of households.

But what are the implications of the base used, the household, when the average size of the unit in the lowest quartile is below four persons and in the top quartile above ten?[28] Perhaps it is merely variation in household size, and hence in cumulative landholding, that gives a spurious impression of sharp inequality?

The ranking of households according to landholding by married man produces a distribution considerably less sharply skewed (Figure 4.1B). Again, the first quartile of households own virtually no land (1 per cent of the total), the second quartile 12 per cent, the third 25 per cent, and the top quartile 61 per cent (with the top 5 per cent of households holding 21 per cent of the land). In fact any married man with less than 25 measures would find it hard to make ends meet. This means that just over a third of all married men in farming would require some other source of income beside their own landholding.

There is considerable coincidence between the two distributions. Of the top quartile of households by total landholding some 70 per cent are also in the top quartile of households by land per married man. Only two of the very big households prove to have low holdings per married man, and a few individuals heading small households have relatively large holdings. There are two processes behind the distributions: the developmental cycle of the domestic group and the long-term structures of inequality in family wealth. The latter is the most powerful in structuring the distribution analysed above. Yet, since the reproduction of the latter also passes through the former, two facts should be noted: 30 per cent of the households in the top quarter by total landholding fall into the third or second quartile by landholding according to married man; and while the men in the top quartile according to landholding per married man hold at least twice the median of landholding, it is only men in the top 15 per cent who hold at least twice the mean landholding per married man. In short, the reproduction of the relative wealth of those at the top, as it intersects with the development of the domestic group, is by no means always assured.

Down at the bottom, differences appear more stark. Although some of the landless labourers are simply seasonal migrant labourers,[29] over half of the landless heads of household were born in the community. About a third of the labourers work primarily for one landed household. The rest work for any farmer who needs them, day by day or week by week. Those seeking work gather early in the morning in the marketplace, offering their labour for such tasks as hoeing, weeding, repairing walls and house-building. Contradictory trends were affecting the position of labourers. On the one hand, share-cropping rights were becoming more difficult to obtain as households reclaimed their land. On the other hand, with employment open in the oil states, labourers now belonged to an international market. From 1973 to 1977 daily wages rose about fourfold from 4–5 riyāls to 20–25 riyāls plus lunch for a day's labour from 7 a.m. to 2 p.m. The increase more than kept pace with the rise in the price of staples. By the late 1970s farmers complained of the cost of hiring labour and the difficulty of retaining labourers in the face of growing urban employment and labour migration to Saudi Arabia. But the status attached to labouring was such that although many smallholders in the community were relatively underemployed, they resisted working for a daily wage. For, unlike share-cropping agreements in the gardens, where both parties own some capital and share the profit, the relation between landowning farmer and hired hand is of another order. If in the idiom of community – of *qabyalah*[30] – the possession of land secures brotherhood, landlessness just as surely marks its absence.

Patterns of production

In accordance with this distribution of landownership, the household forms the basic unit of co-cultivation, supplemented by longer-term share-cropping contracts with other households and by short-term hire of wage labour. The continuity of household production, of the area's involvement in the market, and of valuable garden production might have suggested to the casual visitor that in the mid-1970s little, save the pumps, had changed in local agriculture. The erosion of the grain economy marked Ḍahr far less than it did more isolated villages, in which grain production suddenly no longer represented the mainstay of family budgets but simply a poor supplement to wages sent home from labourers abroad or in the towns.[31] But if the land of Ḍahr has largely retained its farmers by rewarding them incomes comparable to wage labour elsewhere, this is not because the patterns of farming remained static but rather because they changed.

Farmers traditionally combined irrigated crops in the canyon with rain-fed grain and legume crops on the heights above. In the irrigated belt there were three types of field: gardens of *qāt*, fruit and nut trees (pomegranate, orange and quince were often planted a little apart because of their special requirements in irrigation, but other fruit trees were generally interplanted); arable fields where alfalfa, fenugreek, legumes, winter barley or summer wheat were planted; and, in the lower sections of the canyon (al-Qariyah and the lower wards of al-Wādī), vineyards, sometimes interplanted with *qāt*. Producing from late February to December the fruit includes, in order of ripening, two types of apricot, peach, apple, pear, fig, pomegranate, prickly pear, two kinds of quince, walnut, winter citron and orange. The vineyards of the lower reaches of the community contain five kinds of grape, ripening successively.

Such mixed production entails a staggered but almost continuous demand for labour; only two months, from mid-December to mid-February, when the temperature sometimes falls below freezing just before dawn, are slack months. As well as providing fruit for household consumption the mixture of trees reduces the impact of failure in any one type of fruit. Fruit yields vary greatly from one year to the next, depending on the yield the year before, on the frost, on the rains, and on the timing of irrigation. The yields of especially fickle fruit such as pears and pomegranates can vary by as much as ten to one from good year to bad.

Qāt, by contrast, has proved to have more reliable yields, and as an evergreen can be induced under irrigation to bud at any time save the two coldest months of the year. Its labour requirements are well below those of grapes, if slightly above those of other tree crops. It is therefore a good crop from the farmer's point of view and the demand and price of *qāt* continued to soar during the 1970s as *qāt*-chewing became an indispensable form of conspicuous consumption in North Yemen.

Qāt has been grown in Yemen for several hundred years.[32] Its plantations can produce for many years; the oldest existing stand in al-Wādī was said to be eighty years old. But local men maintain that significant commercial planting of *qāt* dates only from the reign of Imam Yaḥyā. Its cultivation accelerated after the 1962 revolution, limited only by the plant's sensitivity to frost. By the middle 1970s *qāt* had been planted in any plot where it would prosper – in between fruit trees or in lieu of grain fields. Where *qāt* replaced grain fields, farmers could plant it in regular rows which allowed controlled application of irrigation water. But in plots with valuable stands of fruit trees, where trees might in some cases be owned by different members of a single family, farmers would not destroy established trees to plant *qāt*. The value of produce from mature fruit trees continues to outstrip that from young *qāt* shrubs for several years.[33] Thus *qāt* plantings were introduced alongside and in the midst of older mixed forms of cultivation. *Qāt* occupies somewhat less than a tenth of the rain-fed land. It is planted alone on some 25 per cent of the irrigated land and is interplanted with fruit on another 40 per cent. The rest of the irrigated belt is divided between orchards (about 10 per cent of the total), vineyards (10 per cent) and arable fields (15 per cent).[34] Overall, the spread of *qāt* represents an intensification of cultivation; *qāt* has been added to existing stands of fruit trees and has replaced former grain fields. Lift-pump irrigation has permitted this development.

The introduction of pump irrigation meant that water was fast becoming a cost paid in cash. Few of the other inputs in cultivation of the gardens were as yet purchased,[35] the exceptions being the wooden poles used in the annual renewal of grape trellises and a powdery dirt brought from collection points within a radius of forty kilometres and applied as fertilizer, preservative and pesticide for *qāt* and grapes. Vines are the most demanding of all plantings. The trellises must be repaired every year. Grapes are "dusted" up to ten times before picking, *qāt* three or four times, other fruit trees not at all. Overall there has been little change in types of fruit or grafting techniques. The Ottoman Turks are said to have introduced new types of fruit, but in the 1970s the only new tree stock planted was oranges.

In the arable rain-fed fields, tractors hired from outside have become a common sight at ploughing time. Most farmers, however, continue to work their fields with a scratch plough drawn by a pair of donkeys or even a lone donkey. In the 1970s oxen or mules were rarely seen on the fields. Harvesting and threshing of sorghum, often interplanted with beans (*dijrah*), is done by hand. Farmers may hire a pick-up truck to carry the sorghum stacks home from the fields above, but most simply continue to use a donkey for this task.

In short, the most important element in farming is still human labour. The basic unit of labour is the household, but to put the matter this way obscures the fact that not only may the household have recourse to the labour of members of other households but also that the structure of households is itself not uniform. The very mixed cropping pattern entails sequential labour demands; this permits a small household composed of a man, his wife and children (and perhaps an unmarried brother when a married man's children are young) to cultivate a mixed plot or two in the irrigated belt and a plot in the heights above, and also from time to time to do a little work, often in the guise of *entre-aide* in kind, for a more wealthy family. By contrast, households rich in land may develop a complex division of labour. The more land a household owns, the greater range of crops it cultivates (and in the case of *qāt* the more complex the staggering of budding and cutting). A sense of this can be grasped from the schedule of irrigation in one ten-day period of irrigation in 1972.

Of the 180 holders of water rights (persons or groups of persons) three failed to claim their share and so it was given to a wealthy landholder. This arrangement allowed the farmers in question to claim their shares from the water allotment of this farmer in the next turn. Twenty-seven holders sold all their water or otherwise repaid water owed from an earlier turn. By and large, those who sold all their rights were smallholders, but one of the richest of all households, which owned a pump well, also put its stream allotment on sale through a local shopkeeper. Of the remaining 150 holders, 14 were specialists or Ṣan'ānīs with local cultivators, who each irrigated only one plot. Among the 136 agriculturalists who used part or all of their allotment, 45 (33 per cent) irrigated only one plot. Among all farmers sale and exchange of water were common, and so a man who irrigated only one plot in this cycle might in fact hold two or three plots. Another 43 holders (31 per cent) irrigated two or three plots. Forty-eight holders (36 per cent) irrigated four or more plots and, of these, 17 (13 per cent of all holders) irrigated more than seven plots. It should be remembered that irrigation was now available from the pumps as well as the stream, and so actual schedules of irrigation were yet more complex.

Differences in household size, which we shall examine in the next chapter, do not arise solely from considerations of labour organization. The developmental cycle of the domestic group, vagaries of reproduction, the political value of a large household and long-term considerations of succession to land also play their part. Yet it is evident that in households with sizeable landholdings a complex division of labour can be supported, not least when we recall the importance of guarding crops when near to ripening.

The first principles of this division of labour are sex, wealth and age, in roughly that order of importance. Even in households rich in land women usually work in agriculture. While not inflexible in all details, the sexual division of labour creates the coercive bonds at the heart of the household. Households without an adult man, notably those headed by a widow, may establish long-term share-cropping contracts with a man of another household, contracts sometimes translated with time into marriage with the young widow or in one case of an older widow and her unmarried daughter into virtual adoption of the share-cropper's child.[36]

Although the changes in agriculture, technology and economy have transformed much of the internal content of the work of the two sexes, the formal external lines of the division of labour appear stable. In a classic manner these structures assign to men the tasks considered "heavy" and more "dangerous" and to women their opposite; or considered more closely, they grant men the initial, punctual, externally political and commercial tasks and women the secondary, repetitive, internally managerial and domestic tasks. But to say this is not to suggest, in the manner of Bourdieu's classic structuralist essay on the Kabyle house, that the sexual division of labour at all points recapitulates the division of sexual labour – men plough and women grind? – nor that it corresponds to a rigid dichotomy of field and home.[37]

Men work with the hoe and irrigate the gardens. Only they go out alone to guard the fields at night. At the coming of a flash-flood they open channels to the fields with their hoes, while women stay at home with an eye on children and on potential leaks in the mud-packed roofs. Men maintain the irrigation channels, the walls and guard structures of the fields. And men dominate all aspects of *qāt* production, the major cash crop of the day.

On the rain-fed fields men hold the plough but women broadcast the seed. Women often work long hours in the cultivation of grain; they sow the seed, weed, guard crops in the daytime, tend the beans or tomatoes interplanted with the grain, and work in the harvesting or threshing of sorghum. Women of poorer families may also work as labourers for other families at harvest time.

By contrast, *qāt*, particularly when planted alone, is distinctly a man's crop. Men work the soil about the *qāt* plantings, supervise irrigation, dust the *qāt*, and above all cut and market the *qāt*. With the exception of a few towering pear trees, which only a young man will climb, men or women may pick fruit crops. But in the case of *qāt*, only men inch up the thin shrubs which under irrigation grow as tall as trees – "too dangerous" for women. Only men trade *qāt*. Women who own *qāt* fields, and who may supervise or even work alongside a son, husband or share-cropper in its cultivation, do not sell it to runners in open auction although they may arrange privately for its sale. Men's dominance in the production and marketing of the primary cash crop will surprise no one familiar with the modern transformations of peasant agriculture, where in many a society the less lucrative crops, part of which continue to be processed and consumed at home, become more firmly identified with women's domestic sphere. But the male character of *qāt* does not appear to be a new phenomenon. Its consumption was long a male prerogative, as was the smoking of tobacco. Or so people maintain today: before the revolution women rarely chewed *qāt* or smoked tobacco. One might question whether only women were so abstemious and not also many poorer men. Women chew *qāt* quite as regularly as men but in much smaller quantities. But there are exceptions; two women in the lower wards chewed large amounts. They were both landowners (heiresses with no brothers), experienced farmers and, in fact if not in name, heads of their households. The quantity of *qāt* these women took to a women's gathering was not interpreted as a sign of a husband's affection as it was with other women.

If in most households women take little part in cultivating *qāt*, this is not true of fruit, which is integrated into the domestic processing that forms the core of women's work. Women and children often guard fields in the daytime, help prune, dust, weed and harvest grapes, and pick a good part of the fruit from the apricot, apple, peach, walnut and other trees. Women are particularly fond of the vineyards in the lower wards, where the grapes grow on raised trellises, forming in summer a kind of magical cover to an enclosed garden. In summer women go each day to the gardens, to collect vine leaves and other fodder for household animals, to pasture sheep under the vines, and to deliver food to husband or labourer. When the grapes are ripening the senior woman of the household rises early to pick the fruit before the sun is strong and before men are out in the fields. She may close off a room in which to dry grapes for raisins, fencing the open windows with thorns. On the roof she may dry some of the season's apricots and quinces: the apricots for Ramadan, the quinces in a large earthenware bowl for vinegar.

Animals are also in women's care and are often their property. Households do not keep large herds of animals: a donkey (usually men's property), sometimes a cow, a few sheep or goats, and chickens. In the summer women may take sheep to pasture under the vines but most of the year the few animals go with one of two herders in the community, who gather them in the early morning and return them in the late afternoon. Since powdered milk has entered the market, fewer families keep a cow. The cow is an intimate of the house, with a stall on the ground floor. An older woman often owns and cares for the cow, which she feeds by hand, wrapping each stalk of sorghum round with alfalfa. Poorer women who own a cow may sell some of the milk, but other households keep a cow only for domestic consumption. When the cow bears a calf, the first milk is prepared as a delicacy known as *al-ḥarīwah*, the bride.

If, over the last generation, the balance of agricultural work has tilted towards male-dominated cultivation of a primary cash crop, women's domestic tasks have changed even more dramatically. Flour mills appeared a decade before water pumps, relieving women of one of their most relentless chores.[38] The decline in the local grain economy, whereby households now purchase imported grain from the market, has transformed relations within the household. The senior woman, who by agreement with the senior man held the key to the stores, ruled over all junior women and men. The bypassing of this harsh internal economy reduces the power of senior women, who in larger households may have a cathedral presence. The decline in their authority appears to surpass the erosion of control by senior over younger men resulting from the latter's role in the marketing of *qāt*, which allows them to pocket a little money on the sly.[39] Changes in the domestic economy have also diminished employment for poorer women: grinding grain (and carrying water) for the more prosperous households. By 1977 small pipes carried water from the wells to all of the prosperous households. Water flowed to the yards only briefly every day, but a tap in the yard greatly eased another constant chore of women. Other services long performed by women have to be purchased: wood is now scarce and expensive, and although women continue to collect wood from the orchards and make dung-cakes in the yard, families purchase wood brought by truck over great distances and primus stoves are found in every kitchen. It is only a matter of time before butane gas stoves enter local kitchens. Fewer families keep a cow and mothers purchase tins of imported powdered milk, weaning their infants young. Yet, as the absolute burden of women's domestic processing (the sphere where women traded and exchanged services with other women) has decreased, women's investment in child care has increased. The demise of the old economy of householding is but part of much greater changes that allow the survival of children in numbers startling to older women. As one put it: "In our day we were always giving birth but raised only a few children; today's women – it is as if they were hens hatching eggs."

The market

Agriculture and the market

In spite of the rising cost of the extraction of water and the small holdings of many farmers, local agriculture has allowed men to remain on the land and to obtain incomes comparable to the wages of labourers working in the oil economies. This is reflected in the exceptionally low number of men working abroad: in 1975 there were only fifteen young men employed outside Yemen. The relative continuity and even prosperity of local agriculture is bound to the conditions of exchange for its produce.

The marketing of fruit and *qāt* has always been small in scale. In years past farmers took their produce to market themselves by donkey or sold it to petty traders who carried it to various rural markets. In Ṣan'ā' the farmer sold his produce in open bidding to a Ṣan'ānī fruit seller. The fruit seller or *muṣliḥ* in principle made a profit of 10 per cent on the sale, but however successful, he remained more a broker than a merchant. He did not control the transport of produce, nor could he store the fresh fruit so as to speculate on shortages or gluts, in the manner that traders do with grain or even raisins. There are few ways to capitalize on spoiling produce: one prosperous fruit seller kept a flock of forty to fifty sheep and goats on the ground floor of his house just beside Bāb al-Ṣabāḥ, the busiest produce market in Ṣan'ā'. A herder took them daily to pasture among the growing refuse heaps of the city. Ṣan'ānī dealers do not seem to have intervened in local production nor to have entered into long-term agreements with farmers to purchase produce, although some developed close individual relations with particular farmers over the years. For example, one woman of a small trading family in al-Wādī was married to an established *qāt* dealer of Ṣan'ā'.

Fruit marketing did not appear to have changed greatly in the 1970s. The farmer or his son takes his fruit into Ṣan'ā' by car, or occasionally to another rural market, or sells it to a dealer at home. No promises are made before the harvest. Prices depend upon yields and quality. By 1976 the growth of the urban market and of cash income throughout the country had driven demand for fruit high enough that the return on some fruit began to approach that on *qāt*.

As *qāt* marketing expanded in the 1970s, it became more decentralized and competitive.[40] Farmers say that until the 1960s most families sold both *qāt* and fruit to established shopkeepers of Ṣan'ā'. Some Ṣan'ā'nī fruit sellers also dealt in *qāt*. *Qāt* is even more perishable than fruit. Its chemical content begins to change after twenty-four hours and so it is very difficult to sell more than thirty-six hours after it has been picked. *Qāt* is best consumed on the day it is cut.

As the market for *qāt* grew, men began to specialize as brokers (*mufāwitūn*) or "runners". By the mid-1970s two of the *mufāwitīn* of the community had also rented small shops in the city, to which they commuted daily. These men joined other villagers who opened shops for *qāt* outside the old markets, in which Ṣan'ānī brokers of fruit and *qāt* predominate.[41] In the 1975 census, eighteen men of the community stated that they traded *qāt* full- or part-time. Many go into the capital almost daily, staying at home only during the few months of the year when little *qāt* is cut in the area: in the late summer when large amounts of rain-fed *qāt* flood the market or in the two coldest months of the year, December and January, when no *qāt* is cut in the area. Others, who combine *qāt*-running with farming, trade only when they consider that prices are advantageous. A runner decides on his purchase depending on supply, the market price and what he can transport. When prices look good, a runner may buy some twenty bundles in open bidding at the field or at the collection points to which farmers bring *qāt*.[42] After washing and wrapping the *qāt*, the *mufāwit* adds his bundle to that of others riding together on the share-taxis and small trucks going to the capital. Although most of the runners live in the area, outside runners also join them. Farmers say that they prefer open competition between runners and that they do not reserve *qāt* for a friend nor enter into any long-term arrangements with a dealer.

Although a farmer might on occasion get a better price if he took his own *qāt* into Ṣan'ā', it is in general the *mufāwit* who bears the risk. Not infrequently, the *qāt*-runner barely covers the cost of his travel. It is a trade where a few windfalls make days of small returns worthwhile. Men of quite diverse backgrounds have made their name as runners. Three are younger sons of large landed families, who, not having come into any land themselves, have chosen in this way to be somewhat independent of the family head. Some of the most successful runners own a little land and so fall back on farming in periods when the market price of *qāt* is low compared to that sought by farmers. Yet others are landless men (one of *muzayyin* origin), as are the two who now commute to their stalls in Ṣan'ā'. Only the very poor agricultural worker without any capital beyond his daily wage and without long-standing contacts in the local community seems excluded from *qāt*-running. The runners make a better living than that of the average agricultural labourer, but the margin is a narrow one for a landless *qāt*-runner with nothing to fall back on in slack times and with limited cash for speculating when prices are good. The trading networks to which such men belong are labour-intensive, flexible, decentralized and rapid in delivery, but not without risks for the runner.

Specialists

Tradesmen In contrast to the market services, by tradition occupations carried out by *mazāyinah* families, men of farming families view trading and shopkeeping favourably. Farmers have always taken their produce individually to Ṣan'ā' and rural markets and they are conversant with the ways of the market. There are seven little shops in the market quarter, four or five of which are usually open at the same time. These stock daily staples and a common range of goods from Chinese soap powder to local henna, from kerosene to Lyle's golden syrup (the civil war is said to have spelt the end of most beekeeping in the North), from tins of Malaysian pineapples to Indian hair-oil. There are also two mills in the area, one in the upper wards and the other in the market quarter. The latter belongs to the most prosperous trader of al-Wādī, but many of the women prefer to use the larger and better mill in al-Qariyah some twenty minutes' walk away.

Several of the shopkeepers had moved into the community from outside. One, a *sayyid*, is more a petty pedlar than a regular shopkeeper. A second, however, one of the two most successful shopkeepers of the community, settled in the area only twelve years before and retains ties with his home community, from where his wife and his two sons' wives also come. And the third hails from a Ṣan'ānī family, traditionally craftsmen and shopkeepers, which had settled in the area a generation or two earlier; they acquired some land in the community by marriage and purchase.[43] The other four shopkeepers are of local families. Two belong to a small family, specialized in trading. The third man had in the old days traded raisins for *qishr* (the dried fruit of the coffee bean, used to make a hot beverage). The fourth is of a landed family who had moved out of his father's house and left the cultivation of the family land to his son, father and brother.

Of the shopkeepers, two have no land at all and the amount of land owned by the others is modest. Overall, none of the men in trading can be counted among the most wealthy or politically powerful men of the community. In the first years of the revolution, the Sallāl government recognized as shaikh the most successful shopkeeper of the market quarter. This is revealing – of more than the personal relations between this trader and 'Abdullāh Sallāl – but his leadership had little legitimacy in the eyes of men of the community. In the early years of the Republic, the community had split, with only the lower wards about the market quarter being in any sense pro-Republican. But it was not long before the government had to accept the much stronger candidate from the lower wards, a wealthy farmer, whom we have already met on more than one occasion.

The more successful shopkeepers prosper well enough, but the margin of profit is held down by the high prices a shopkeeper must pay on his small wholesale purchases. For centuries farmers have been bound into a monetary economy, and their proximity to Ṣan'ā' has long allowed them alternatives to the prices and goods offered in rural markets or local shops. With automotive transport, prosperous farmers buy staples in bulk from Ṣan'ā'. Thus the profits of shopkeepers come primarily from occasional small sales and from supplying the poorer households, which cannot afford to buy in bulk. Two shopkeepers went bankrupt during the 1970s. One, who still keeps a shop under his home, had tried to expand into long-range trading as well. Before the revolution he had followed in the steps of his father and traded raisins (and other fruit in season) for *qishr* in Manākhah.

On the strength of this, he and his brother were able to purchase a small plot of land, and in about 1970 the brothers decided to try to bypass the Ṣan'ā' middlemen and to carry fruit directly by truck to a shop in al-Ḥudaydah. After borrowing considerable sums from several prosperous farmers of the ward, the brothers eventually went bankrupt in 1975 and were still struggling to acquit themselves of their debts two years later. On the whole, the shopkeepers do not have much of a role in the sale of produce from the area, do not have a monopoly upon the provision of imported staples, and are not distinguished as moneylenders. As noted, the traders who went bankrupt had themselves raised finance from wealthy farmers. When men need money they usually borrow from relatives or neighbours. Women may raise money by pawning their jewellery with one of several women, sometimes but not exclusively with the wife of the most successful shopkeeper.[44]

Craftsmen Most of the traditional rural crafts and services are represented in the community: the butcher, marriage-dresser, innkeeper, tea-seller, tanner, dyer, tailor, mason, white-washer and carpenter. There is also a more urban speciality: a family of bath-keepers serves in the bath house attached to the former Imam's summer palace. The elder woman of the family of bath-keepers, who used to dress brides when she was young, also does cupping for blood-letting and prepares the dead, a service performed among men by the local document writer, himself a religious specialist in the wider sense. By and large these craftsmen enjoy long-standing ties with the community: 87 per cent were born in the community and the same proportion own the homes in which they lived. Few of these men own land but in their midst two groups stand out: building craftsmen (masons and carpenters) and butchers. Almost all these men were born in the area and a number own some land.

A good mason is a respected man, the demand for whose skills has stood up well. Whereas the demand for specialists in building, such as the mason or white-washer, has if anything expanded, that for the carpenter has been undercut by the cheaper prices offered on ready-made windows and doors in the burgeoning workshops of Ṣan'ā'. As we have seen, the two carpenters were believed to have turned to theft to bolster their flagging trade, with tragic consequences for the man left lying at the door of his house, his mouth full of *qāt*. All the crafts have confronted change yet more dramatic than that faced by farmers. Change is not new: local craft products have been undercut for many years by imports of industrially produced goods and by the unification of the national market through automotive transport. Twenty-five years earlier there were also potters in the community: one of the two Jewish families of the community, who left with the bulk of Yemeni Jewry in 1949–50, were potters. The tanner, who keeps to himself, does a small trade. He is said to be a *muhtadī*, a Jew who converted to Islam.

Some butchers are very prosperous. But with automotive transport, much of the labour of butchers, the long cycles of visits to markets and villages to collect animals, has been transformed, leaving the fourteen households of butchers, the largest single craft group in the village, underemployed. One man quietly tried his hand at wine-making, again a craft vacated with the departure of Yemeni Jewry.[45] True, the old traditions persist, whereby households employ a butcher to kill any animal larger than a chicken, and add to the earnings of butchers; larger cash incomes among prosperous farmers have raised the demand for meat; and on Fridays Ṣan'ānīs now drive out to buy the more expensive but preferred local meat slaughtered in Ḍahr. One or two butchers who have extended their network of supply to the markets of Tihāmah prosper; but others only just eke out a slim living. And the long-term effect of the national market promises further change in the corporation of butchering.[46]

For economic and, in the case of the *mazāyinah*, also for social reasons, families of craftsmen have begun to seek new forms of employment for their sons. Many go for a time to work abroad, and some, returning with a little capital, purchase cars and work as drivers. And far more than the farmers, who evince at times a time-honoured disrespect for the disciplines of school,[47] these families aim to invest in the schooling of their children and to place them in government service. They have as model the man of the *mazāyinah* who rose through the officer corps to be the only prominent figure in the government hailing from the community.[48] Two paths lead to government employment: schooling and military training. This leads us to the last set of specialists in the community: literate specialists and government employees.

Literacy: the religious specialist and the government employee

Although few farmers invest in education for their children with an eye to government employment, their attitude to schooling is not the result of their unfamiliarity with the power of the written word. In the 1975 census almost half of the men of the community stated that they were literate.[49] Many farmers have studied the Koran, can read aloud from it, and pen simple notes such as those required for the sale of irrigation water, but only a few have more command of writing than is necessary for such tasks. Nevertheless, as we have seen, all basic transactions in land and water are the object of written documentation. The rudimentary literacy of many farmers is important here, but it is specialists, not farmers, who pen most formal legal documents. The men with greater literate skills either come from families with a tradition of literacy or are local men who have worked outside the area, in one case as assistant to a tax-collector. The shaikh of the upper wards was exceptional in his command of written Arabic. Men from the community who entered government administration in the early 1970s, and who in three cases were also pursuing higher education, belonged to families with a tradition of literacy established long before the revolution of 1962.

There are six literate specialists employed within the community, as teachers, Koran readers and document writers. Three of these men combine such services with a little farming. The other three have moved in from outside the community; in their mobility such schoolteachers resemble agricultural labourers, with whom they share the absence of fixed capital and the eminently transportable character of their skills. The man who in the mid-1970s was carrying out the duties of *amīn*, and whom we have met in this role in legal disputes, came into the community as a schoolteacher. He performed the duties of this post for almost twenty years, from the death of the community's *amīn* in the late 1960s to the assumption of the post by the former *amīn*'s educated second son in the late 1980s. Since this figure provides a central service in the community, let us consider the man a little more closely.

He hailed from a minor family of *quḍāh* and when young had studied for some years with scholars in his native town of al-Rauḍah, a centre of Islamic learning. Possessing the essentials of scriptural literacy, he had worked in other rural communities as teacher and scribe before settling in the community in the late 1960s. In the mid-

1970s he purchased a house in the community and was closely associated with the shaikh of the lower wards. He not only taught classes in school, being absorbed into the state school when this was opened in 1974, but also acted as ritual and legal specialist. He washed and prepared the dead, sang the religious chants for the groom at marriage, and read the Koran in fulfilment of vows undertaken by members of the community. He drew up documents for all the central contracts of daily life (marriage, divorce, gift, rental, exchange of property, wills, etc.). He attended the homes of the area, where he was as much in the service of women as of men, to read their documents aloud or to prepare new transactions.

The schoolteacher did not have the learning to carry out the complex calculations required, for instance, in the division of a large estate between several heirs. In such cases a more learned scholar resident in a neighbouring community would be approached either by the family itself or sometimes by the *wakīl* representing several of the heirs, to draw up the documents. But this local *amīn* did not simply possess a few "scraps of literacy".[50] By his social identification and his function, he formed the lowest rung in the ladder of an Islamic reading of social life. When people of the area were embroiled in a dispute wherein recourse might be had by one party or another to an Islamic court, they would seek enlightenment on their case from him. Whenever the *amīn* was uncertain of the response, he would pen a note concerning the question to a more learned authority of his acquaintance, or even to the *ḥākim* of the area. In turn, this chain of reference, which simultaneously guaranteed both the islamicity of the documentation he produced and the *amīn*'s very status, conditioned his freedom to manipulate. Documents he wrote would come before more learned authorities in the course of disputes. Both his precarious position in the community, where he had to be careful not to be party to false documents, and his humble position on the ladder of Islamic learning, encouraged the scribe to a literalist caution.

The two sons of this man came to enter government employment in Ṣan'ā'; to them their father appeared at times a slightly risible figure of the past, with his traditional dress and rigid ideas. But there was little sign that the Yemeni state was about to assume, through a cadaster or central property registry, the role of certifier of property relations, and so the services of this document writer, and eventually those of the son of the preceding *amīn* who was to succeed him, continued to be central to the legal processes of everyday life.

Men of the community entering literate occupations outside the community, especially in government service, have done so through two channels. The first is officer training. We have met the two men who achieved most prominence through this route in the 1960s and 1970s: the orphan son of a grain measurer of the community who as one of the Free Officers moved into civilian government[51] and the son of a farming family who distinguished himself as a paratrooper and very briefly as a local leader.[52] In politics both these men were strongly republican and progressive in their own terms. There is also a third man who entered government employment, again first through army training. Although his cousins' households appear little different from those of other modest farmers, this man hailed from a family with a tradition of literacy (the man's great-grandfather had come into the area as a scholar and married a shaikh's daughter). His subsequent career and politics were to lead in a different direction: through university study of law and *sharī'ah* towards the Ministry of Education and islamicist politics. Lastly, there were another two men of *qāḍī* families from the lower quarters, originally from outside the area but residing year-round in al-Wādī, who had entered government service; the younger of the two men was likewise studying law and *sharī'ah* in the university.

That formal education could lead to government employment was thus clear, although in the 1970s few men from the community had followed such a path. The rest of those counted as government employees in the community are much lesser folk: two old guards on the former summer palace of the Imam, two soldiers (one residing only temporarily in the community) and a *sādin* of the mosque who receives a tiny salary from the *waqf* – occupations that never excited much envy among local men.

In economic terms we have observed both unity and diversity in the local population. Overall we have found great stability in residence, a widespread distribution of landholding and a complementary division of labour among households. This division in turn entailed diversity: between agriculturalists and specialists and, among agriculturalists, between those with large landholdings and those with little or none. In the next chapter we shall analyse the basic forms of social association, house, household and family, against the background of these patterns of unity and diversity.

5

House, household and family

The kin group is not as "natural" a group as the household or the neighborhood.

Max Weber, *Economy and Society*, Vol. 1, p. 365.

Introduction

This chapter examines the forms of the primary social groups of the community. The approach to morphology is statistical; for all its abstraction, this will allow us to capture internal difference as well as cumulative contours and to think more in terms of pattern than of rule. The three forms of social association to be considered are houses (or what we shall call patronymic groups), households and conjugal units.

To the student of Chinese or European kinship who might read this text, the procedures of this chapter will appear commonplace, as well they should.[1] But to many a student of Arab society they are likely to appear unnecessary and therefore all the more tedious, since the nature of Arab family and kinship, structured about the male principle – from the marital bed through the patriarchal household to the agnatic lineage – is well known. A structuralist can describe the basic forms of Arab kinship with enviable economy: conceptual dichotomy of the genders, pre-eminence of agnation and filiation, construction of the feminine as the object of masculine honour, and preference for kin endogamy achieved through the classificatory extension of patrilineal parallel first-cousin marriage (FBD marriage) to wider groups of patrilineal relatives.[2] Domestic groups appear to be constructed from the bonds of kinship and alliance, the distinction between household (actual domestic arrangments) and family (understandings governing the right relations between kin) proving singularly infertile for the analysis of Arab societies.[3]

But the present study will persist with its drier and more laborious methods. It is only by documenting the forms of domestic and kin organization with sufficient completeness and precision that we can see not only the overall cultural pattern but internal variety. It is this diversity that will allow us to place the domestic domain in economic and political history. The exploration of diversity has not been a central concern of Western academic studies on Arab kinship and domestic structures. And while historians have begun to do sporadic work on women, they have hardly filled the gaps left by anthropology on the subject of family history and kinship.[4] It is not that anthropologists have been insensitive to diversity, quite the contrary.[5] Nor is it simply the legacy of orientalism's textual blinkers, colonialism's interest in stereotyping or the two together.[6] Rather it reflects structural blockages. On the one hand, the rarity of Western ethnography in Arab societies and its consequently exotic status in the Western academic market means that in any generation the volume of production and exchange is limited, and the market presses the specialist of one corner into service as generalist concerning "Arab society" at large. On the other hand, dialogue between Western ethnographers and Arab intellectuals remains thin on the ground. The reasons for this are both linguistic and intellectual. Ethnographers working in Western universities do not feel obliged to publish in Arabic, nor does the Arabic book market translate their production.[7] And, for reasons we shall explore below, the place accorded by Arab intellectuals[8] to the study of the family remains highly circumscribed.[9]

For Arab intellectuals, family and tribe are topics of perennial interest but only within the context of well-entrenched ideological battle lines. To wage such battles, the intellectual must by definition know the character of the Arab family and the place of the tribe throughout Arab history; painstaking documentation of these institutions in particular instances is irrelevant. There are two central debates, sharing similar discursive terms, which require of the participant a knowledge of the nature of family, past and present. Both emerged in the literary culture of the late nineteenth century as this took form outside the discourse of legal specialists and religious preachers.

The first concerns the nature of womankind and its consequences for family and society. From the late nineteenth century, contributions to this debate adopted a form that was to prove extraordinarily stable. In article after article authors compare female and male physical or mental characteristics and deduce from this comparison the proper role of woman in family and society; in article after article authors interpret the rights of women in Islam.[10] Subtending this indefatigable interest in the mind and body of woman in general and of "woman in Islam" in particular is one essential comparison: between, on the one hand, "the Western woman" and, on the other, a woman known from the 1880s as "the Arab woman", for a time in the early twentieth century as "the Eastern woman", and from the 1920s also as "the Muslim woman". Those in favour of change write treatises on the evolution of woman, in which Arab society appears in three versions, pre-Islamic, Islamic and Modern. Even Marxists or those influenced by the same tradition tend to adopt this basic division of history when writing about women.[11] At issue in this discursive tradition is the right ordering of society not mere documentation of what is already at hand; differentiation within Arab societies is flattened by the comparison with an "ideal-type" of the West and by the ordering of history about interpretation of Islamic doctrine. Even Arab feminists have found it difficult to sidestep this debate and impose their own terms for discussion. True, feminism has contributed other elements for social comparison than "West" versus "East": notions of patriarchy[12] and a critical eye to the discourse of gender, for example.[13] But whether because Arab feminists are forever drawn into argument with those who cast themselves as the defenders of Islam or for other quite practical reasons, the contribution they have made to the careful documentation of kinship and domestic organization remains surprisingly limited.

The second great debate of intellectuals for which a knowledge of the Arab family is required concerns the very nature of the social order; this pits religion in society versus the secular state (*dīn* versus *daulat al-'aqlanah*). In this exchange, both islamicist, in the name of faith, and secularist, in the name of reason, agree on the location of family and tribe. Both agree that out of the desert came the Arabs, steeped in tribalism and agnatic patriarchy.[14] For the islamicist the message of Islam permitted society to transcend tribalism and created a timeless, divinely regulated nucleus, the Muslim family, lying at the heart of Islamic society. For the secularist the starting point is the same; the Islamic reforms represent if not the final ideal, a step in the right direction appropriate to the historical moment, to be completed by the state legislating improvement in the status of women. For both camps (and their many mixtures) Arabs have a proclivity to regress: for the islamicist, towards ignorance of the message (*jāhilīyah*) and for the secularist towards stagnation and under-development (*takhalluf*). For both, backwardness is equated with tribalism, and tribalism needs to be cut back by the state: the State of Islam for the first, of Reason for the second. Thus the islamicists write tomes on the Muslim family, an object that stands splendidly outside the weathering of time.[15] And the secularists compose chapters and books on the history of the Arab family and Arab patriarchy.[16] The first does not purport to be a history at all; the distinguishing characteristic of the second is that this history draws not on anything that in the field of family history would be recognized as a source but rather on common knowledge.

Even on contemporary urban family patterns the production of knowledge in Arabic is minimal. There is the rare paper or book by a sociologist, stuffed with statistics and thin on analysis.[17] Perhaps the documentation of pattern and change in kin relations not only lacks a problematic to give it any meaning – even the old war-horse of evolutionary history, from tribe to extended patriarchal family to nuclear family, gallops unchallenged[18] – but also remains a subject faintly risible or even in bad taste. Why else should a sociologist with an official position in a secular state, al-Akhras at the University of Damascus, virtually apologize for even addressing the topic – by reference to the number of children not cared for properly at home but out on the streets of Damascus?[19] One would expect the topic to be one of the stock-in-trade of most sociologists. Why this silence? Is it because the family remains such a pivotal institution for the reproduction of inequality in Arab societies, where, after all, industry has not shaken the foundations of the domestic? Or is the greatest political taboo not religion *per se* but the vertiginous fertility of women? Or, in the contemporary scramble for identity of societies dropped into the blast-furnace of the world economy, has the family become ever more an icon, even to Arab secularists? Perhaps the condition for the worshipful preservation of this icon, this ideal, is indeed to represent nothing akin to it found in the here and now. However we explain it, the relative indifference among Arab intellectuals to documenting family past and present is striking.

So let us go back to our study with its quite ordinary procedures of family history, aware that the present effort remains somewhat of a lonely one in the crowd of writing on Arab society.[20]

Patronymic groups

The notion of a patronymic group, a group identified by a common surname, is bound up with idioms of naming. In the community people known well to each are often referred to simply by personal name and father's first name, "Fāṭimah 'Izzīyah" ("Fāṭimah of al-'Izzī")[21] or by personal name and surname (in adjectival form), "Fāṭimah Ḥumaidīya". The term surname seems apposite here; although some names, in the manner common among Northern Arabs, derive from a man's personal name, others derive from locality of origin, profession, nickname (e.g. "the rat" or "the lame"), or a wider stock of surnames that serve as family names. In the local idiom, a house (*bait*, pl. *buyūt*) has a name if its members are of any consequence. In a manner not so dissimilar to the polysemic uses of the English term "family", the *bait* may denote anything from a single household to a major religious lineage.[22] It is noteworthy, however, that the term so extensible is that for "house"; the first meaning of *bait* is a physical house or cluster of houses. Other Arabic terms for family, such as *ahl* (a kin group) or *'ā'ilah* (family, often conjugal family), are intelligible, but the standard term of reference is *bait*. If a man seeks to emphasize the political strength or cohesion of a rural house, terms such as *ḥabl* or *'aṣabah*, literally "rope" or "sinew"/ "closely bound group", may be invoked, but as epithets. The standard term of reference to such larger groups is again simply *bait*.

Turning to the distribution of surnames in the community, we find 127 names among the 316 households of the community identifiable by surname. In short, for some people a *bait* is just a house. But not for all: if we lay out the patronymic groups of the community according to total landholding, patterns emerge (Table 5.1). All the five top houses present some complexity; the largest contains thirteen households, the smallest six – numbers that suggest genealogical depth, if that is what is at issue, greater than a set of first cousins. Of these the first is almost entirely concentrated in one ward, to which it gives its name; it does present the appearance of a local descent group although I cannot detail the links between all the elements.[23] The second house in rank order is not so nucleated but extends over four of the lower wards. It is composed of three stems (Figure 7.2), the genealogical relationship of which was uncertain to those outside the *bait* and to its members.[24] Beyond second cousins, patrilineal links, if such there were, had faded in memory. By contrast, marriage links, property

Table 5.1 Size and landholding of patronymic groups

Number of patronymic group		Total land[1]	No. of households	No. of people	Mean land per hhld
1. 'Ākish		2,453	13	105	190
2. al-Abyaḍ		1,647	10	60	165
		1,348	12	90	112
		1,331	9	80	148
5.		1,139	6	48	190
6. Murghim		970	2	23	485
7. Ruqaiḥī		869	9	62	97
		740	2	28	370[2]
		668	9	50	74
10.		553	3	25	184
		528	3	25	176
12. Zawwāk		448	1	11	448[2]
		445	5	55	89
		415	5	25	83
15. Khabash		412	7	35	59
		410	4	19	102
		386	6	30	64
		349	4	29	87
		340	3	33	113
20.		333	6	52	55
		300	1	29	300
		300	3	14	100
		264	2	27	132
		261	6	25	43
25.		255	2	7	127
		228	3	19	76
		226	4	21	56
28. al-Ḥumaidī		225	4	21	56
		200	1	7	200
30.		200	2	10	100
Sub-total	(30)	18,243	147	1,065	124
Other landed	(48)	3,298	105	579	31
Total Landed	(78)	21,541	252	1,644	85[3]
Landless	(49)	–	64	293	–
Grand total	(127)	21,541	316	1,933	68
Unknown		55	8	21	7

Notes: The average number of households in a patronymic group is thus 4.9 (147/30) for the top 30 landed groups, 3.2 for all 78 landed groups and 1.3 for landless groups. 1. Land is measured in *makīls*, i.e. water measures. 2. These groups contain shaikhs. 3. A landed patronymic group is defined as any patronymic group of which one or more household owns some land.

history and alliances with other families immediately came to the fore in any discussion of the relations between the three stems.

Such complexity is less common below the top five *baits*. If we take *baits* 6–30 together, we find that the median size of the patronymic group is three households and the mean just under four; for the most part these are groups of brothers, or of first, maximally second, cousins. Furthermore, a number of households possess larger landholdings than groups of some size; compare *baits* 6, 8 or 12 with *baits* 20 or 24. It is noteworthy that the two shaikhs of the community come from such wealthy and large households but neither belongs to a large patronymic group.

The physical house, the large household, is a pivotal unit in local society; one does not need to belong to one of the large patronymic groups to attain political position. This said, at times in this century, two men of the top *baits*, 'Ākish and al-Abyaḍ, have been shaikh, the latter for much the longer period. The first man was murdered by his brother's sons, or so it is believed, and there were several men of prominence who were said not to be averse to his elimination from a dominating position.[25] The second man, shaikh just before the revolution, moved into Ṣan'ā' following thinly veiled threats; his half-brother cultivates the family lands. In this community the combination of a large patronymic house and political leadership may well be threatening to the balances of the local polity; certainly the shaikhdom has not descended smoothly in any one *bait*.[26]

Further down the scale the convergence between *bait* and physical house becomes yet more pronounced: among the rest of the *baits* with any land, the average number of households with a common surname is only just above two; among the landless it falls below two.[27] In short, localized extended groups of agnates are not found distributed equally across economic groups as an ubiquitous outgrowth of the kinship system; and even where they appear – towards the top of local society – they do not present a classical segmentary form, that is to say, their own members do not present them in such a form. And while it is true that the great religious houses – outside the scope of this book but eminently deserving of study[28] – retain a name across diverse regions of Yemen, we should not hope romantically that among the poor it is simply their mobility which hides their cousins from our tabular representation. With the partial exception of some market specialists, the links of the poor with distant kin are often anything but intense.[29]

The coincidence of land and numbers of men is echoed in the terms wherein inequality is discussed by local women: *al-kibārāt*, the big *baits* rich in both men and land, overweening in their pride (*kibriyā*); or *al-mashāyikh*, those men (and houses) able to compete for leadership (*mashyakhah*) in the community. There is nothing that disqualifies from inclusion in their midst the shaikhs of the community, with their large households but small *baits*.[30] The unit in terms of which we have been discussing the patronymic group, the household, has limits as a unit of measurement; for example, the average size of households of patronymic group 8 is fourteen persons, whereas that of group 25 is less than four. We shall return to analysis of the patronymic group (*bait*) in Chapter 7, but first we need to understand something of the forms of what we have termed the household.

Households

In designating units as households, I have followed the delimitation of domestic groups in the 1975 census.[31] The census enumerators listed as "households" all those who lived and ate together at the time. Simple physical co-residence was clearly distinguished from commensal units (a household); there were 324 households in 237 houses ("housefuls"). The enumerators identified one person as head of the household and then listed all others according to relationship to the head. Identification of headship was quite unproblematical in the many households where the head was a senior man with control over productive property (and hence the taxpayer), was recognised as the major political figure, and was responsible for women and children of the group before the local polity.[32] But in households where the oldest person was a woman, usually a widow, or in the cases of *frérèches* (households of two or more married brothers) the requirement of unitary headship was not always so apt. The identification of a single "head" of household is standard procedure in a household census; in many societies it is highly problematic.[33] In this community, however, the problems raised by the methodological reification of otherwise fluid units appear comparatively small.[34] This is not an economy where movement is so great and membership so fluid that it is difficult to designate a cluster of persons as a household, i.e. as *the* core domestic group. Among landed agriculturalists households had quite stable membership over important periods of time; it is only in the case of agricultural labourers that the composition and headship of the unit designated as household often appear more *ad hoc*.

A proverb of which local women are fond, precisely for its ambiguity, declares: *al-buyūt qubūr al-nās*, "houses are people's tombs". In this society domestic institutions should carry weight and possess their own secrets. It is the object of this chapter, however, to make such institutions intelligible in more humdrum terms, by describing their shapes in numbers, noting the differences between the forms and cycles of domestic groups in the economic strata of the community, and explaining these shapes in terms of the formation, dissolution and fertility of conjugal units and in terms of the shared activities and capital of households.

Household forms

The material analysed here consists of a census of household composition at one point in time. Yet we need to extract from such dry lists an understanding of the developmental cycles of domestic groups and of how these mesh with the activities households embrace – co-residence, commensality, child-care, care of aged dependents, pooling of income, production, and ownership of capital – the content of which necessarily differs across the economic strata even of this small society.[35] The lists capture these processes frozen, as it were, at one point of time. A historical understanding of the developmental cycle of households truly requires several registrations over time. But we do not have such registers. In their absence the best we can do to untangle the effects of the developmental cycle from those of wider socio-economic difference is to analyse the data on the basis of a methodological assumption of fundamental continuity in household forms over time.[36]

We may begin with two different distributions of the population of the community, each of which indicates something of household form (Figures 5.1 and 5.2). The first indicates that headship is almost always attributed to men but that households headed by older women are not unknown, even in the census.[37] And while few women are ever recognized as heads, there are also reasonable numbers of men in their thirties and even in their forties who are not designated as heads of the households in which they live. With regard to size of households, we find that although there is a clustering about the mean of 6 (40 per cent of the total population lives in households of

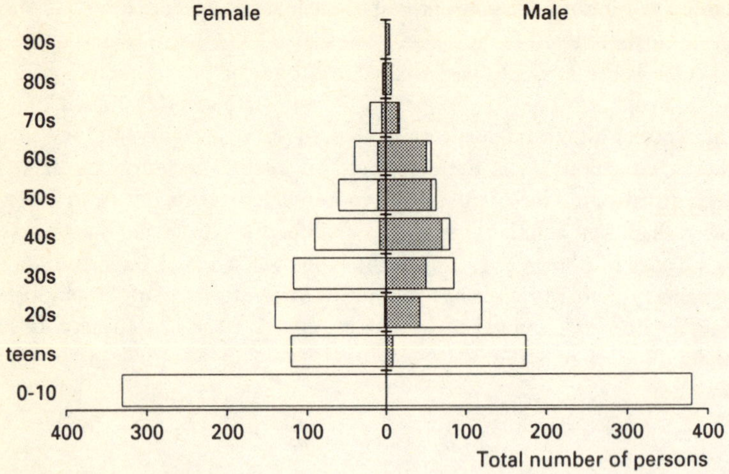

Figure 5.1 Household headship and age structure of population (hatching shows the number of household heads in each age bracket)

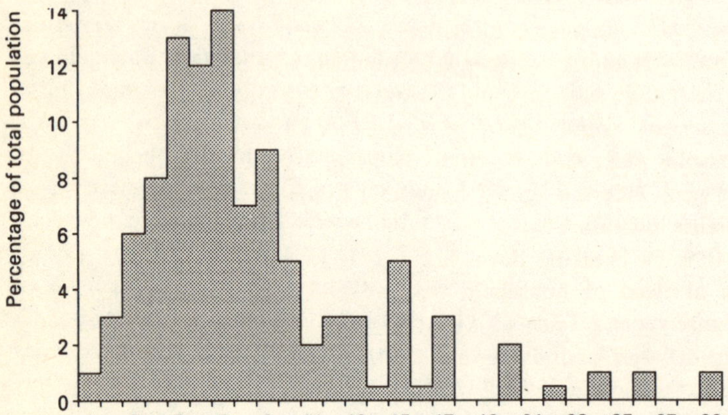

Figure 5.2 Distribution of population by size of household

Table 5.2 Typology of households by household wealth (per cent)

Type of household	Wealth category of household: Agric1 & Spec1	Agric2 & Spec2	Agric3 & Agric4	Total
Solitaries	14	3	2	6 n=20
Co-resident no union	5	2	1	3 n=8
Simple family	62	47	32	46 n=150
Extended family	12	26	17	18 n=58
Multiple families	7	21	49	27 n=88
Total	100 n=108	100 n=93	100 n=123	100 n=324

five to seven persons) it is the range in size, from a lone individual to twenty-nine persons, that is most striking. The divergences in household size appear too large to be solely the result of capturing households at different stages of a unitary type of development cycle. Indeed, if we set household type against age of head of household we encounter contrary patterns simultaneously (see Figure B.3). For example, while multiple family households increase gradually in importance with the age of household head, so too do households of solitary individuals.

It is by breaking down households by economic group[38] *and* by age of head of household that we find a clear pattern emerging (Figure 5.3 and Table 5.2). On the one hand there is a strong relationship between landholding and complexity of households, but on the other, the developmental cycle among specialists differs from that of any of the agriculturalists. Overall, three main patterns appear: that of landed agriculturalists where household size remains stable or increases with the ageing of the head of household, as married son(s) stay in the father's household; that of specialists where household size tends to fall as married sons establish themselves apart from their parents; and that of landless agricultural workers where house-

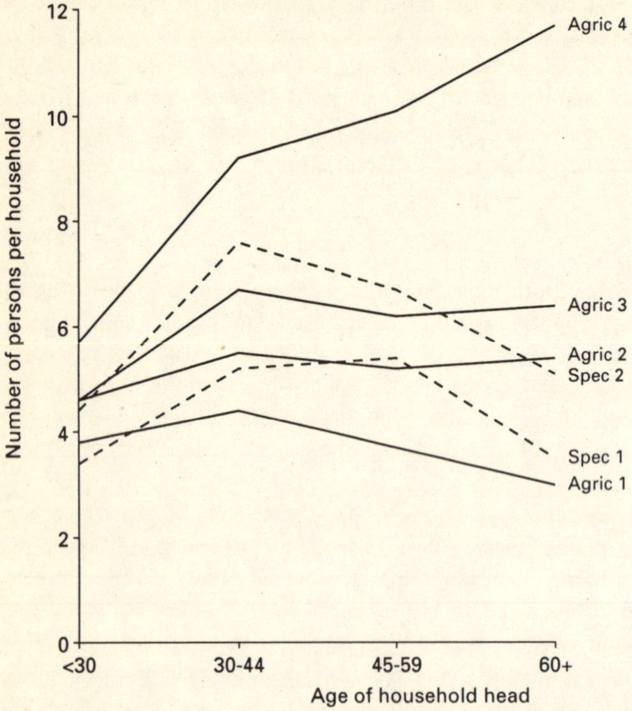

Figure 5.3 Mean size of household by age of head and economic grouping of household

holds are built about a single conjugal unit or its remnants, with virtually no complexity of structure.

An explanation of such differences requires an understanding of two processes: first, the cycles of conjugal units and child-raising that form the dynamic nuclei of such household units, singly or in combination, and second, the structure of activities that lead kin to remain together or to part in the manner reflected in our statistics. In this community households rarely comprise those not bound by kinship or marriage. Only one household included an unrelated agricultural labourer; another included an agricultural labourer and his wife who were related to the wife of the head of the household; in only two households of migrant labourers were members not bound by any tie of kinship or alliance. It is clear that we cannot understand the differences in household structure simply in terms of kinship, but must also consider the differing activities assured by groups of kin. But given that households are constructed out of conjugal units, that the major mode of recruitment is indeed marriage and child-bearing, we shall begin with these patterns of recruitment and reproduction, before turning to the logic of their combination according to the domestic economy of different strata.

Family and household

First marriage Both men and women marry young: 90 per cent of women marry by the time they reach twenty and 90 per cent of men by the time they reach twenty-five. The median age of first marriage for women, as given in the census, is only 15.9 years of age; that for men 19 years of age.[39] As this suggests, where both man and woman are marrying for the first time, the difference in age is not great; the groom is on average only about two years older than his bride among landed farmers and four among landless labourers. As this difference suggests, a poor man may have to work for several years before he possesses a home or means to marry, whereas among landed families a man's first marriage is his parents' gift.[40] Looked at from the vantage point of women, however, some women, married polygynously or to a previously married man, will find themselves much younger than their husbands on first marriage.

Almost everyone in the community marries. Even the "spinsters" of the community were at some time betrothed. We shall meet such a "spinster" in the figure of Fāṭimah, cousin of Karāmah, put aside by Karāmah's brother, Ḥamūd (Fāṭimah's FBS), in favour of his mother's brother's daughter.[41] Although the marriage was never consummated, Fāṭimah is given in the census as divorced. And so, legally, she was. Only some 3 per cent of women remain unmarried or divorced during the bulk of their reproductive years. Such spinsters occur among families with land; these fall into two types. In three cases a woman who had rights to land preferred not to marry; in two of these the woman farmed with her widowed mother, aided by a share-cropper. In two other cases the woman was due to marry a cousin, but the marriage was never consummated following the refusal of one party or the other. Thereafter the family did not permit the woman (and the property on which she had a claim) to be married to an outsider. But even life-long spinsters may suddenly turn to marriage should life at home become unbearable. One unmarried woman had for years headed the home of her brother (who had married his father's brother's daughter), but after her brother's death she came to face animosity from his widow and son. Her nephew beat her and refused to partition her share of the land. She took the matter to the shaikhs and to the central authorities but no one intervened effectively.[42] Determined to find another ally, she married a widower in Bait Na'am, an area which she knew well, as she had long specialized in buying trousseaux in Ṣan'ā' for brides there.

Childbearing Most women marry young, just after puberty or even before. And, as we shall see, women often remarry following divorce or death. There is thus a potential for women to bear many children. For the women of the older generation this did not mean, however, that they saw many children survive them. Although the data are not sufficient to produce hard demographic statistics, information from the survey of women is nevertheless suggestive of the structures governing reproduction.

The picture appears stark, but we should bear in mind that the survey included a high number of poorer women and all indications suggest that mortality is higher and marriage more unstable among the poor.[43] Among women over forty years of age the mean number of births was just under six. Given the low age of first marriage the average number of births does not seem very high. Many women reported miscarriages; women would breast-feed for a year or two and, given their nutritional status, would rarely conceive before they weaned the child; and, finally, in the old days, household recipes for contraception were not unknown. But equally important was the termination of marriage by divorce or death. Of women in their thirties, 28 per cent had been widowed, of those in their forties, 57 per cent, and of women above fifty years of age, 71 per cent (see Table A.4). Divorce was also an important factor and interrupted childbearing for many women at least for some time. High mortality and divorce meant that many women (and men) remarried: more than half of the women over forty years of age had been married two or more times (see Table A.5).

Of the children born to women over forty just over one in three was living at the time of interview. Thus, older women had on average just over two surviving children (see Table A.6). Death was most common following weaning, but stillbirth and perinatal death were also important (see Table A.7). Older women believe that child mortality is lower today than it was when they were young.[44] In their youth it was common for a girl to see her first two children die. One older woman remarked that in the early years of marriage she herself had been a child (*kunt jāhilah*, *ghāwīyah*); it was only after some years of marriage that she grew more reasonable (*'aqilt*). The death of little children is God's doing. A mother's sadness is enough and she is not blamed for her loss. So, too, when today more children survive, older women certainly do not attribute this to the qualities of their daughters or daughters-in-law but simply to medicine and powdered milk. The decline in child mortality promises to transform society, from the family to the locality to the nation.

Divorce There is an ambient assumption in studies of the Muslim family that the legal power granted men to divorce at will and to have ultimate custody of children – a power not softened in North Yemen by any modernist legal reform – must be directly reflected in practice.[45] Here as elsewhere the relationship between law and practice is complex: there are important differences in divorce rates (and practices of marital payment and inheritance) across the ages and spaces of Arab Muslims, all governed by roughly similar laws on divorce and custody.[46] In short, the explanation of such differences must inevitably be made in terms other than the law. So too, in the community under study, the logic governing the divorce patterns that we are about to examine derives from not only the wider legal order but also the local structure of relations, material and moral, of those allied in marriage.

This is not to say that the law is irrelevant. Three elements are relevant to an understanding of the legal context of the practices discussed here: the man's power of unilateral divorce, the woman's legal capacity to buy herself out of marriage (*bāb al-khul'*) by return of payments made to her at the time of marriage,[47] and the husband's ultimate right to child custody on expiration of the mother's writ of nurturing, itself conditioned on her not remarrying.[48] Thus there are two basic questions: first, how common is divorce, and second, how often does it lead to dividing a mother from her children?

Divorce rates are substantial: about one quarter of all marriages end in divorce. Divorce is more common in first marriages, 22 of 73 marriages (30 per cent), as against subsequent marriages, 7 of 38 of second marriages (18 per cent). Whether in a first or subsequent marriage, divorce occurs principally in the first years.[49] Half of the women divorced from their first husbands had been married less than three years. In line with this we find that in almost four-fifths of the cases the woman has no surviving children at the time of the divorce (see Table A.8).

These divorces in early marriage certainly do not merely reflect men sending home women declared "barren" after a few months or years of marriage. They reflect more complex patterns of negotiation. The high rates of infant mortality, especially in the early years of marriage, mean that many of these women had borne a child within the marriage. Although young persons, and particularly young girls, have little say in the choice of spouse before marriage, parents recognize that marriage is a matter also of man and wife, and that where they fail to agree, it is best to allow them to part. Marriage should not be war by other means: *ḥarb ṭūl al-zamān ʿaib* (endless war is shameful) is a proverb often adduced in this context. Older women counsel a younger woman unhappy in marriage to seek a divorce before children come to be involved. In short, grave sexual or emotional incompatibility between partners is negotiated in the early years of marriage; it cannot, after all, be broached before marriage.

The aspect of "love" that was negotiated before the marriage night, that between the two families so allied, can also lead marriages to dissolution. Behind the scenes it is usually a mother who arranges her son's marriage, although this is not always so. On occasion the mother's candidate may refuse or request postponement in the case of a very young girl. At his son's behest, the father may then arrange a marriage with a family with whom his wife has no links. And over time if this does not please the mother-in-law, she may well find means to undo the marriage.[50] But the continuity of "love" between spouses or between allied families clearly has its material components: divorce appears higher among the poor (eighteen of fifty-four first marriages of women over twenty at the time of the survey, i.e. 31 per cent) than among the more prosperous (ten of forty-one marriages, or twenty-four per cent). As we shall see, remarriage of widows is also more common among the poor than among the wealthy.

Remarriage In considering the patterns of remarriage we need to distinguish between remarriage following divorce and remarriage following widowhood. After a divorce most women remarry quite quickly; the median period before remarriage was one year, with a range of three months to six years. A single divorce does not stigmatize either a man or a woman; only in the case of repeated divorces do questions begin to be raised. Thus a man marrying for a first time may take a young divorced woman, who as a *thayyib* or non-virgin will receive a lower marriage payment, but may be regarded as a good match. For men, who must find the means to finance a second marriage after widowhood or divorce, the ease of remarriage appears linked to economic fortune. Of men over forty-five years of age the proportion without a wife (i.e. men either divorced or widowed) was respectively 17 per cent in Agric 1, 13 per cent in Agric 2, 10 per cent in Agric 3 and 9 per cent in Agric 4.[51] Wealth also appears to allow men to take younger second wives (see Table A.9). Although the numbers are small, the broad association of household means and the ability to recruit and retain women through marriage appears congruent with patterns of widow remarriage and polygyny explored below.

The patterns of widow remarriage reflect both the strength of the bond between mother and children and the widow's place in property relations in the household at large. As we shall discuss in the next chapter, a widow is entitled to a portion of her husband's estate and in turn her children will inherit from her; these are not negligible considerations among the more prosperous families of farmers. Whether or not a widow will remarry depends not so much on the age of the widow as on whether she bore surviving children to the deceased and whether her husband left productive property. In cases where a woman is widowed young and has no surviving children she is almost certain to remarry within a short period of time. Such a widow generally chooses to return to her natal home following the period of mourning. If she was married in a household with large landholdings she may receive a cash sum or an annual rent for her share in her husband's estate. Among more modest families she will probably receive little or nothing.

The widow of a landless man is likely to remarry whether or not she has children.[52] Her children may, moreover, remain with her. Among the poor, custody is as much a burden as an asset. If a widow has young children and her deceased husband's kin can offer no support, a new husband may agree to assume responsibility for her young children by an earlier marriage. In such cases he generally offers the woman the choice between a marriage payment while giving up her children and no marriage payment while keeping them. I

Table 5.3 Polygyny and economic status among married women: proportion of married women with or without a co-wife according to economic group of husband's household (per cent)

Type of Marriage	Economic group				
	Agriculturalists		Specialists		Total
	Landless	Landed	Lower	Upper	
Only wife	95	86	90	85	87
Co-wife	5	14	10	15	13
Total	100	100	100	100	100
	n=42	n=292	n=39	n=39	n=412

never heard of a case where a woman accepted the former. Nevertheless, among the poor, it does happen that a widow is separated from her children on remarriage. This may occur where she remarries into another community and one or another of her deceased husband's kin takes in her child. It is very rare among the landed.

Even among landed families some widows do remarry.[53] Not infrequently, a brother or other close male relative of the deceased marries the widow. In the survey, two out of forty-four widows (5 per cent) married a husband's brother. The levirate obviates separating a widow from her children; it also reunites property. Likewise in small households where the widow is the oldest person and the children still minors, she may remarry a man who can tend the land, as often as not her share-cropper.[54] In eight of the fourteen cases where widows with children remarried, either the husband moved into the widow's household, or with poorer women the new husband assumed responsibility for the woman's children by her first husband (see Table A.10). Among the top third of landowners (Agric 4) where households are often larger, a widow is unlikely to direct a household alone. In such households where the net of claims surrounding a widow with children is weighty, widows with children either remarry a male relative of the deceased or they do not remarry at all.

Polygyny Serial monogamy is more common than polygyny. Of men over fifteen years of age only 6 per cent had two wives and 1 per cent three wives; no man had four wives. In terms of women's experience, however, polygyny appears more significant: 13 per cent of married women have a co-wife; if we add widows, then 14 per cent of women are living with a co-wife.[55] But the distribution of such plural marriage is not uniform between economic strata, as it is associated with wealth (see Tables 5.3 and A.11). Of the women married in the top quintile of agricultural households (by landholding per married man) 29 per cent have a co-wife; in the top 10 per cent of agricultural households (again according to landholding per married man) 40 per cent of women have a co-wife.

Polygynous unions belong to two main types: the political and pleasurable unions of wealthy men, and unions where, a man's first wife having failed to bear him a son, he marries again in hope of an heir. An example of the second is al-ḥājj Qāsim Muqbil, who married three women in his search for a son. Although both of his first two wives bore him daughters, neither had a surviving son. Late in life he took, and eventually divorced, a third wife. She alone bore him sons.[56] Other examples are found among the political leaders: the two shaikhs and the "broker" leader of Ward 5. Each has two wives. One has no surviving children from his first wife, his cousin (FBD), but the other two took second wives as much for pleasure as for politics and certainly not for heirship.

ḤASAN AND LAṬĪFAH

But in matters of the bed there are exceptions. One woman, Laṭīfah, was married twice, both times as second wife, yet the two marriages could not have been less alike. Her first marriage was as a young second wife to an old man. Muṣṭafā had married twice before and his first wife had borne him a daughter, who predeceased him, but his second wife and life companion, Ḥamīdah, saw none of the twelve infants she bore him survive. As an old man, and with Ḥamīdah's blessing, Muṣṭafā married Laṭīfah. Ḥamīdah chose the girl, who was distantly related to her; she had suckled Laṭīfah's brother when one of her own children had died.[57] Laṭīfah bore her husband two sons and a daughter before he died. In his old age Muṣṭafā came increasingly to rely on a young man of the quarter, Ḥasan. Ḥasan had worked when young as assistant to Muṣṭafā, who was then a tax collector for the Imamic government in various regions. This experience had led Ḥasan to consolidate his command of literacy more than most men of the community. After the old man's death Ḥasan took over cultivation of the family's lands as share-cropper. Laṭīfah and Ḥasan had grown up together and were very fond of one another; Ḥasan often ate with the two women and both went unveiled before him.

Ḥasan had himself married several times. He was one of three sons of a man who had left only a small amount of land. He first married a widow many years his senior, moving into her house. His wife had inherited land in her own right and, although quite old by the time of their marriage, was said to have been quite pretty; the two lived happily together. Ḥasan's two brothers made quite different marriages though they too eventually settled with their wives. The elder brother emigrated to Aden, where he later married. He sold his share in the family house and plot to Ḥasan and returned only after the British left Aden. But his wife did not fare well in al-Wādī; she could not cook the food of the place. After some time the two moved to Ta'izz, where her brothers then lived. Ḥasan's younger brother married a *sharīfah* from a poor area in the East (the *mashriq*) who had come to al-Wādī as a nanny to a wealthy Ṣan'ānī family. He later returned home with her and was said to farm for someone in the East. He too sold his rights in his father's estate to Ḥasan. Thereafter Ḥasan and others of al-Wādī saw him only rarely in Ṣan'ā', as he tended to avoid them. It was said that he felt unhappy about having sold his land. Ḥasan had been able to buy up his brothers' shares thanks to his first wife, from whom he also inherited a small plot of land.

After the death of his first wife Ḥasan married a divorced woman from Bait Na'am, Khamīsah, a nice woman but a slovenly housekeeper. Ḥasan was patient with her and she bore him a son and a daughter. As the years went by, however, and she persisted in her ways, Ḥasan decided to take a second wife, Fāṭimah, a young girl of a family of labourers of al-Wādī. Fāṭimah proved a splendid housekeeper but the household witnessed a succession of disputes. Once when Khamīsah returned home, she complained to her brother, who then went to Ḥasan and obtained her divorce. Ḥasan remained with Fāṭimah, who bore him three sons and a daughter.

In 1972 Fāṭimah heard rumours that her husband was on the point of marrying Laṭīfah. Leaving her children behind she returned (*ḥāniqah*, "angry") to her parents' home. Ḥasan eventually calmed her feelings and Fāṭimah and Laṭīfah were soon in and out of each other's house once again. A year later Ḥasan's daughter by Khamīsah was married, and the women's celebrations took place in Ḥamīdah's and Laṭīfah's house while the men's gatherings were held in Ḥasan's home. Five years later a widower with a young daughter proposed a joint marriage to Laṭīfah and her elder son. Laṭīfah refused, arguing that her son was not yet ready for marriage and that the man's home was up on the cliffs and far away from water. But three years later, soon after her elder son married, Laṭīfah married Ḥasan. She remained with her children in the house of Ḥamīdah and her first husband, although relations grew increasingly sour between Ḥasan and her elder son, who maintained that he was now old enough to manage his father's lands. After the marriage of her second son, disputes escalated. The two co-wives moved into the tiny house which Ḥasan built for Laṭīfah, just by the side of his first house, that of Fāṭimah and her children. And so it was there, and not in the house that she owned, that Ḥamīdah came to die.

Conjugal cycles and household forms Among rich and poor, conjugal cycles exhibit common traits: both men and women marry young; the age difference between spouses is not great at a man's first marriage; divorce is not uncommon especially in early marriage; infant mortality rates are falling but mature women have usually seen more than half the infants they delivered die young; adult mortality is also considerable; high rates of divorce and widowhood are matched by common remarriage; and marriage is the normal state for both men and women. Yet within these broad patterns there are differences in the conjugal cycles, depending on the wealth of the household. Men of landed households marry rather earlier than labourers, and remarry younger second wives. Although clearly of several types, overall polygyny is strongly associated with wealth. Widow remarriage is generally avoided if this entails separating a widow from her children, but it is more common among the poor than among the wealthy. Put simply, a woman married into a prosperous household is more likely to remain in her marital home than a woman marrying a poor man: rates of divorce and widow remarriage are lower among established landowning families than among labourers and landless specialists. Overall, then, one part of the differences in size and structure[58] of households derives from differences in conjugal cycles, but only one part: the other derives from the nature of activities that the household embraces in different economic strata.

The working of households

Households are sites of co-residence, commensality, care of children and the aged, pooling of income, production, and ownership of capital. Their structures reflect differences in these activities between economic groups of the community. We can grasp the interplay of activity and structure by examining in turn the households of the landless and those of landed farmers.

The households of the landless: labourers and specialists The households of agricultural workers and of landless specialists are built around a single conjugal unit. Two unions are rarely found in a single household. Some time after marriage, or in a few cases before, a man sets up his own household with a budget independent from that of his parents. A father does not have the means to provide employment nor even sufficient housing once a son's wife has begun to bear children. Often the son will move some distance away from his parents, but this depends on where he can find employment. Thus, half of the landless men in their twenties head their own households, and roughly four out of five men in their thirties (see Table A.12).

The houses of labourers are small, most comprising only a single room and kitchen. Forty per cent of agricultural labourers rent their accommodation. The proportion is lower among market specialists: 13 per cent are in rented housing and 7 per cent in housing that comes with their work, e.g., innkeeper or guard. Rents are low and the owner often acts as employer, or at least as patron, of the family renting the rooms. Later in life a widowed parent may move to live with a son (or occasionally with a daughter), but so long as both older parents are alive and one or the other continues to earn a living, the two households are unlikely to reunite once they have divided. A substantial proportion of widows and widowers live on their own: 21 per cent of all widows and 33 per cent of those fifty years or more were living alone (see Table A.13). A widower, too, may live alone after the death of a wife, and in the case that he lives with a younger married son it is as likely as not the wage-earning son, rather than his father, who is designated as head of the household.

A number of poor women of labouring families used to support themselves by working for other houses. This is less common today, as mills and pumps have reduced the hours of domestic tasks. The wages that male labourers earn have also risen slightly and so women are in general less desperate to find work outside the household. But it was certainly never easy for a woman to support herself and her family by grinding grain, carrying water, and harvesting and guarding crops; and as we have seen, a woman with children in her charge would usually remarry after divorce or widowhood.

THE LIFE OF A LABOURING WOMAN

One such woman in the community was Fā'iqah. When still a child Fā'iqah was married to a man who lived west of where she had grown up near Khamr. On her marriage she travelled three days by donkey to reach the place. A labourer, her husband had nothing. She bore him two children, Sa'īd and Amīnah, and after nine years of marriage he died. She often went hungry during that time. She returned to marry her cousin (FBS), a labourer in a village adjoining al-Wādī. He did not provide for her at all and so she moved to al-Wādī, renting a tumbledown mud tower. Her husband gave her almost nothing and visited her only when he felt like it. She bore him one son but supported herself and the children by grinding grain for different houses.

Eventually she obtained a divorce from her husband. "What use is a man if all he does is to come and eat and gives nothing? I would only have had more children from him," she said bitterly. When Fā'iqah reached this point in her story she wept in rage. Even now her first son, Sa'īd, who lives in al-Ḥudaydah, has a good life, but doesn't look after her at all. Her second son has moved to Ṣan'ā'. As Sa'īd's wife (a woman from al-Ḥudaydah) does not welcome her, she lives with her daughter, Amīnah, and her daughter's husband, a landless *qāt*-runner. Fā'iqah continues to work, minding her daughter's four children, doing occasional day labour in the harvest season, and tending four or five sheep and goats, housed in a tiny compound in front of the one-storey house.

Other poor women have known lives as hard as that of Fā'iqah. When a woman marries miles from home, her family cannot negotiate on her behalf. The labourer lives the words of the proverb: Born in one place, you live in another, and you die in a third (*balad tukhlaq fī-h, wa-balad ta'īsh fī-h, wa-balad tamūt fī-h*).

Fā'iqah assumed responsibility for her children. Besides work at harvest in the fields, Fā'iqah laboured in the houses of more wealthy women at the most menial of tasks. For her, family scarcely extended beyond her links with husband and children; when her husband could not or would not provide for her and her children, Fā'iqah divorced him. Lastly, in spite of all that she had done for her sons, in the absence of property to employ them, they moved away to seek their fortune. Although the younger son returns sometimes to stay with his mother and sister, the two sons contribute little to the keep of their mother. The enduring work team is that of mother and daughter.

Although broadly similar, the household structures of the specialists differ at points from those of agricultural labourers. They include slightly more households with multiple conjugal units – 11 per cent as against 6 per cent. Training in a craft occurs within the household, and some market specialists, such as the more prosperous of the butchers, can usefully exploit a division of labour between father and adult son in procurement of animals, in slaughtering and in marketing. They may also have the means to provide housing under one roof for more than one marital unit. There was also the exceptional household of a carpenter who lived in the quarter of the wealthy surname group 'Ākish, in which quarter there were no other craftsmen. The carpenter had three wives, the eldest 47 and the youngest 25, each of whom had borne him children. The women, who were the subject of some gossip, were said to provide services to the wealthier households about them.

Some women of the specialist families themselves have a trade, as marriage-dresser, singer, bath-keeper, children's barber, or petty trader. The proportion of households headed by women, often women living alone, is comparatively high: 15 per cent of the households of landless specialists are headed by women, as against 8 per cent of the households of agricultural labourers. Or, to put it another way, some 12 per cent of the households of all specialists (Spec 1 and Spec 2) are headed by women, as against 6 per cent of all agriculturalists (Agric 1–4).

MIRIAM'S SAVINGS

Even where on the surface women appear economically invisible, some may play a central role. The wife of the most successful shopkeeper in al-Wādī was a prominent person in local women's society and the first person to whom most women in the community turned when they needed to borrow money. Miriam was married to her first cousin,

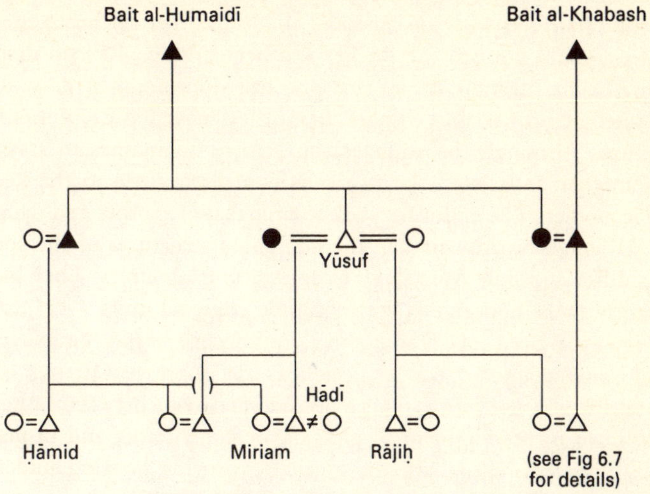

Figure 5.4 *Bait* al-Ḥumaidī

Hādī (Figure 5.4). She had one brother and an elder sister who was married to Hādī's full brother. Her own father had predeceased his brother and the family business was in the hands of her father-in-law Yūsuf.

Miriam's brother, Ḥamīd, left to seek his fortune in the Gulf before this was common, in early 1962. He was said to be studying and indeed, when he returned from the Gulf in the middle of the civil war he had nothing in his pocket. On his return he wanted to marry and so demanded a division of their estate. This was then divided between Miriam's father-in-law, the heirs of their paternal aunt (*bait* al-Khabash), and Miriam, her sister, her brother, and her mother. Ḥamīd then sold his share in the shops and in the main house to Miriam, who had made quite a lot of money by sewing.

Hādī, who had taken a second wife, was caught about this time in a scandalous position with a young girl. He had to flee the community and it was only some five years later that he was able to return. When her husband left, Miriam went to live with her brother in the small house he had built with the proceeds of the sale of his share in the inheritance. Miriam continued to earn her keep as a seamstress. Her father-in-law had driven out his third son, to whom Miriam's sister was married, and so only her husband's brother, Rājiḥ, who was not well, remained with her father-in-law and his wife in the big house. Hādī's father did all he could to persuade his son to return. Only when his father was on his deathbed did Hādī finally come. In his absence Hādī's father had granted Hādī's second wife a divorce at her request; she had borne only one child, a girl, born after Hādī had left. Just before Hādī's return home, his side of the family slaughtered a sheep in appeasement at Miriam's door to repair the damage done by their neglect of her; after all, she had been at home (*ḥāniqah*) for years. When her husband returned he failed to bring the gifts expected, appearing with only a few scarves for the girls, several dresses, and a small piece of gold for his wife.

Miriam accepted him back only on condition that he not take a second wife nor indulge in drink. She set him up in business again by lending him a lump sum to which Hādī added what he had brought back with him. Through managing her part in the inheritance he was able to purchase a diesel-powered mill. Since Miriam set him up in business, he has done well.

There were special circumstances in Miriam's case, notably her brother's indifference to holding property in the area and his interest in investing his capital elsewhere (he was the only man of the community to speculate on building in the capital well before the building boom of the middle 1970s). But, typical of women's economic individuality among specialists, Miriam's husband never controlled her earnings from sewing, even before his disgrace and departure. As a member of the same family she was trusted by her father-in-law. In her case, the moral code – or rather her husband's infringement of it – eventually left her on the inside and her husband on the outside, at the moment of his return. Thus she acquired control over capital before he did. By floating his business she could set the terms for the renewal of their marriage and retain ultimate control over her capital. She bore her only surviving children after her husband's return.

In general, the two features of the households of specialists which stand out when compared to those of agricultural labourers are their greater generational depth and the economic individuality of their women. These features reflect the different character of the work of craft and market specialists. Specialists such as butchers, tanners, *muzayyins* and builders, who have a craft which is taught by father to son, or in some cases by mother to daughter, possess a certain capital of knowledge and a place, albeit subordinate, within a community and market system. Others, however, such as tea-sellers, innkeepers and drivers, are often peripatetic, moving from one rented house to another and from one community to another in search of better prospects. But even among the more established specialists it is rare that brothers with adult children continue to work together, except in the case of traders where one brother may tend the land and the shop and the other arrange provisioning of the trade. After all, even the landowning specialists in al-Wādī are by and large modest folk. The only household of considerable complexity among the specialists, which comprised the head, his widowed mother, his two wives, their children, and his brother's young widow and children, belonged to a man from a learned landed family with long ties to the area; their *bait*, with a base some miles away, traditionally enjoyed the status of a *hijrah* of Hamdān.[59] He was a government employee, who decided to live year round in al-Wādī so as to profit from renting out his house in Ṣan'ā' to an employee of a foreign company.

The households of landed farmers Among landed farmers a son's family gradually succeeds that of his father without a sharp break in residence. The possibility of such complexity is etched in the lines of the tower houses of the community.[60] Only one in ten household heads aged forty-five or more has a son who had moved out to live in another house in the community. Three of the young men moved to a wife's home; each married an heiress (epiklerate daughter) and farmed the land of in-laws. Aside from these three, only eight other men lived locally in houses apart from their fathers. Most of these young men had simply moved next door – often from a crowded home to another house on which they had a claim by inheritance, sometimes through the mother – and continued to farm with their fathers. Just over half of the households headed by men fifty years old or more contained a married son, as did two-thirds of those headed by men sixty years old or more. Among landed farmers the number of married men per household tends to increase with the age of the household head, rather than to decline as it does among the landless (see Table A.14).

Where landholdings permit, a son works his father's land and remains by his side to succeed to the management of that land. In households with sizeable landholdings, a considerable division of labour is required to ensure planting, pruning, dusting, irrigation, guarding and harvesting of crops in both rain-fed and irrigated fields. Only recently have sons begun to adopt other occupations, such as driver or *qāt*-runner, and yet continue to live at home and to help in farming from time to time. And sons of prominent fathers, of men with exceptional landholdings, likewise succeed to a political capital which can only be reduced by their internal division. The organization of production, the strategies of heirship and the political weight of large households all contribute to a son's family remaining in the parental home.

This complexity is not, however, only an affair of men. When discussing conjugal cycles we observed that households with large landholdings collect and retain women. Although among the landed, few households are headed by women (5 per cent in the census listing),[61] the proportion in which the most senior person is a widow rises from 7 per cent of households in Agric 1, to 18 per cent in Agric 2, 20 per cent in Agric 3, and 21 per cent in Agric 4 (see Table A.15).[62] Women do work in agriculture, but equally their work in the home admits of a division of labour.

The domestic division of labour is structured by constraint as well as choice. Traditionally, one senior woman held the keys to the storerooms of the house; it was she who kept the grain stores, took out the measures for grinding, and, as stories concerning the hungry daughter-in-law testify, oversaw the nourishment of all in the house. Grandchildren are not immune to the charms of this figure; by preference they sit by her knees at mealtimes. The woman who manages the stores can also trade small amounts of produce with other women, in a domain where men do not enter.

The stores are in the first floor of the house, just above the stables on the ground floor. In the lower floors of a big house a room could also be given to nursing mothers and small children (*ghurfat al-bizā'*). Higher in the house each married man has his room, where his wife keeps her trunk of clothes, the key for which she wears around her neck; the senior woman of the house may have a room apart – again a commmonplace of women's story-telling is the daughter-in-law who manages to expel her mother-in-law from the upper rooms to the lower and the eventual retribution visited on the son or daughter-in-law by the senior woman – or may sleep in a reception room or *dīwān*; but in a large household younger married women often sleep in the "nursery" among the children, save for those evenings or parts of evenings when a woman joins her husband. A larger household allows some division of labour in childcare. Whereas a woman alone eagerly awaits the day that her daughter is old enough to tend younger siblings, women in larger households can take turns in guarding infants. So, too, in households with more than one adult woman the daily labours of cleaning, baking bread, fetching water, washing clothes and so forth are divided up and taken in turn.[63] This allows for some variety and even the occasional moment of freedom not available to a woman keeping a household on her own.

Although households are for the most part constructed about patrilineal succession, their complexity is not without the participation of women and even at times their solidarity, as we saw in the story of Ḥamīdah and Laṭīfah. The working of a complex household rests on a division of labour, not the natural love between male siblings nor, for that matter, between female siblings: one household distinguished by the quarrels of its two married women was a household where two sisters had married two brothers. The brothers finally appealed to the shaikh to calm the storms.[64] A minority of households are built about links through women, not through men. Among landed agriculturalists ten complex households (6 per cent of all households of landed agriculturalists) are structured around links through women: married daughter, married son from a wife's first marriage, and wife's married sister (see Table A.16) .[65] As the histories of Ḥasan and of Miriam suggest, women's individual property rights and women's own initiatives can inform the structures of households.

The development of complexity in the division of labour in a household depends on the character of the estate worked by the household. The household, the physical house, forms a central unit in the organization of production, reproduction and politics, but in the imagination of local men and women property does not belong ultimately to the house. We cannot speak of house-property, however important the social institution of the house and household. Local people conceive of property rights as vested in individuals: but these individuals and their properties are necessarily engaged in the status and continuity of a house. Domestic economy rests on the government of individual rights in the interest of the house, and thereby also on managing the consequences of the vagaries of demographic reproduction. It is a matter of government: a play of choice, persuasion, bargaining, law and compulsion. These are themes to which we shall return in the next chapter.

Patrimony descends; brothers can delay division but ultimately they work to divide patrimony; siblings – brothers and sisters – invite fission of what was once united. It is only alliance – women as wives, men as husbands – that can fuse properties. Thus a household almost never embraces two separate landholdings belonging to men living together in the household. The two households which contained such holdings were aberrant. In the first, one landholding was listed in the name of the head and a second in the name of his brother-in-law (more exactly, a joint holding of his brother-in-law and this man's brother who lived in another house). The household comprised the head, his widowed mother, his married sister, her husband and their children. The sister's husband had moved into the household and not only retained a claim on his father's estate but also cultivated it with his brother who lived nearby in the same ward. Moreover, unlike uxorilocal marriages to an heiress, where a son-in-law effectively plays the role in production that a son would have done, here the husband came in when his wife's brother proved unable to be a father. The head of the household had married but his wife had soon left him; he was said to be "part-woman", and was certain not to remarry.[66]

The second household was yet more tragically aberrant. The two holdings of the household were in the name of the father and in the name of the elder of his two sons. This son had married and produced children, whereas the second son was still unmarried. Some years earlier he had taken to threatening his father, demanding his own part in the family land. Eventually the father, in fright, partitioned his land. But this did not assuage the son. He wandered at night and disappeared for days, returning occasionally to terrorize his wife; he took his wife's jewellery and sold it – an act regarded as despicable. Eventually he left, never to return. His parents took over cultivation of his land and cared for his wife and children.

As this unhappy tale reveals, legal partition of an estate during the father's lifetime is close to the unthinkable.[67] On the contrary, legal partition is postponed, often well beyond the father's death. Thus, whereas *frérèches* represent 11 per cent of farming households headed by men, another 20 per cent of households cultivate land listed as belonging to brothers jointly or simply listed in the name of the deceased father. Nine per cent of all land is listed in the name of dead persons. Joint holdings among brothers are virtually the rule among younger household heads (of household heads aged between thirty and forty-five, 53 per cent hold land jointly, that is, 23 per cent with brother(s) inside the household and 30 per cent with brothers outside the household) but even among heads over forty-five years of age 20 per cent of heads have land owned jointly with a brother (or brother's son). The list reveals that over two-fifths (44 per cent) of the landholding households have a claim on a property jointly with persons in another household.

It is through alliance that land divided can be united. The postponement of division is intimately bound up with strategies for its reunion through marriage alliance. Thus households given in the irrigation records as comprising two holdings contain estates of man and wife, with, in all cases, the wife's land coming from her parents. Some 7 per cent of landholding households have two such separately listed holdings of irrigated land. The land listed in this manner under the names of women (or more often under the names of their deceased fathers) is by no means all the land on which women have a claim, from which they receive revenue, and which someday may be legally transferred to their sons. Rather the tiny proportion of land so listed results in part from the type of record and in part from the fact that cultivation rights to a sister's land usually remain with her brother for many years. The irrigation supervisor was concerned to record water rights, not the full breakdown of ownership; so in general he listed land cultivated by a woman's brother under the latter's name or under the name of their deceased father.[68] As we shall see in the next chapter, where sisters have a claim, brothers have a special interest in delaying the partition of land.

The morphology of houses and households reflects differences in both family cycles (reproduction) and economic activity (production and capital) between groups in the community. In the next chapter we will go beyond morphology to consider the symbolic and material exchanges that create and recreate the forms examined here.

6

Material exchange and moral order

An exceptional life: by way of introduction

Hā'ilah was a striking figure. One of two sisters who had no surviving brothers, she had stayed at home to care for her parents. Her father's patronymic group was small but wealthy. Her only cousin (FBS), Aḥmad Manṣūr, had married her older sister, but she was married to a man of a less wealthy family, who moved into her parents' house (Figure 6.1). Although Hā'ilah inherited only one-third of her father's estate (her third was nevertheless four times larger than her husband's landholdings), before he died, her father had also given her his cache of silver coin. This subsequently allowed her to buy rights to cultivate other good lands, to purchase the lands of her husband's brother[1] and to build a very large house. She grew up to manage all aspects of farming, and although her husband, and later her son, did most of the marketing of produce, there was never any doubt that she directed all that went on in the house, fields and market.[2]

Hā'ilah was a very good farmer. She dealt directly with any hired hands, often shouting down to them from her kitchen when, always much later than other women, she got round to making lunch. She had exceptionally strong hands and a broad back; on the rare afternoon when she attended a women's gathering, she arrived late and someone would invariably rise to give her a seat.[3] She chewed large quantities of *qāt*, while her husband, although he was said to have chewed much in the past, had given up *qāt* by the time he was middle-aged. Nor did he go regularly to the afternoon gatherings of men. He was thought by many men not to have a very strong character. Hā'ilah was an irascible woman quick to assert her status. On several occasions she quarrelled with women. In one altercation

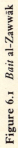

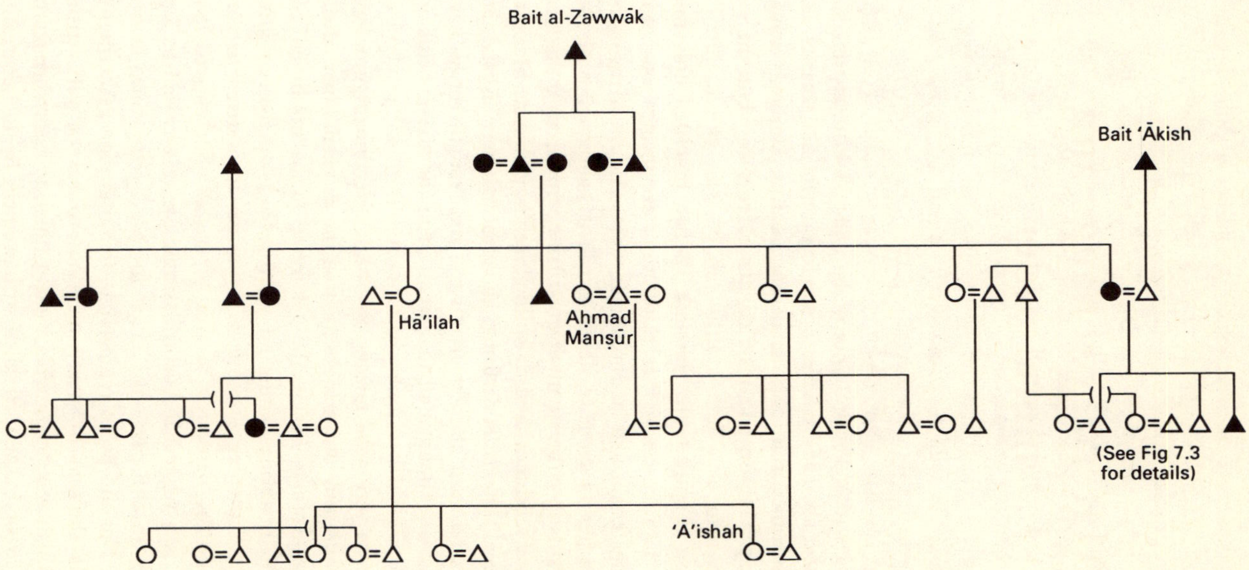

Figure 6.1 *Bait* al-Zawwāk

over access to water for washing clothes, both she and the girl with whom she clashed had to pay fines.[4] In another argument with a woman over a *nargileh* (water pipe) at a marriage gathering, both parties had to provide a sheep as *hajar al-bait*.[5]

Hā'ilah fought more than one lawsuit. She defended her cases herself, though usually with her husband by her side, against wealthy men of the quarter – even against her own cousin, the shaikh of the lower wards. But her opponents were not above using their status as men to undo her. On one occasion Aḥmad Manṣūr tried to stop her from building a yard around her new house; and the two went to court. As shaikh he suddenly banned all women unaccompanied by men from travelling into the capital by car. The drivers respected this ruling for two days only; no one took very seriously the shaikh's sudden concern with female honour; the ruling was interpreted as aimed at restraining Hā'ilah from pursuing her court case.[6] But Hā'ilah had her own allies. She won the case by appealing through her first daughter's husband to the shaikh of Hamdān, the shaikh of the wider area.

Hā'ilah had arranged the marriage of her first daughter to a prominent man, a local shaikh from the same community as that of the regional shaikh, and he had influence where Aḥmad Manṣūr was out of favour. On the other hand, she had married her second daughter, 'Ā'ishah, in line with her cousin's wishes, to the son of Aḥmad Manṣūr's sister, who was also the brother of Aḥmad Manṣūr's daughter-in-law. But Hā'ilah's daughter refused to put up with her mother-in-law, who was also her great aunt, and brought her husband down to live in her mother's old house. Likewise in line with her cousin's wishes, Hā'ilah married her son and third daughter in an exchange marriage to the house into which her elder sister had married; in short she wed her children to the grandchildren of her sister (who, along with her brother, had predeceased their father). But this double marriage did not work, probably for political reasons but in part at least because the daughter-in-law found life with Hā'ilah unbearable.[7]

Hā'ilah then arranged a second exchange marriage for the two with a neighbouring household of Bait al-Abyaḍ, the wealthy patronymic group of the lower wards long cool towards, although not opposed to, Aḥmad Manṣūr.[8] Her youngest daughter was still a child, and marriage not yet relevant. All of Hā'ilah's daughters were forthright women, who spent much of their time in the fields; her second daughter, 'Ā'ishah, quite unlike the first, was an indifferent housekeeper who never took well to the role of subservient daughter-in-law and whose myriad beloved children ran about dusty and unkempt. She spoke with passion of men's disdain for women, of the problems her mother faced, and of the way her own husband treated her (although, compared to many men, he appeared quite fond of his wife). Yet whatever women might say of 'Ā'ishah's poor housekeeping, the honour and warmth of all Hā'ilah's daughters was never questioned.

As one woman put it, Hā'ilah was both man and woman. She had to fight hard with men to hold her own and no doubt some men resented her; presumably her irascibility was not unrelated to her exceptional position. But she had many other qualities: even men spoke with respect of Hā'ilah as political actor, farmer and parent. And to women she was a figure of power.

Property systems and peasant society

It may strike the reader as strange that we start here by considering the reproduction of a household managed by a decidedly exceptional woman. But it is important to pause to ask why, beyond her strength of character, Hā'ilah came to combine roles often more sharply divided between the two genders. After all, there is nothing incongruous about Hā'ilah's household: her household and the marriages she made for her children follow logically from the property systems and politics of the landed farmers of this community. It was just that the estate she inherited and the demographic structure over three generations (her father's, her own and that of her children) allowed Hā'ilah to take centre stage and to set a model for her daughters in a manner not found in many households of the community. To understand such a household we need to comprehend, first, the broad rules of alliance, for example, that a man may marry his paternal cousin but not his niece (since, as 'Ā'ishah noted, had the law permitted it, Aḥmad Manṣūr would have liked to have taken her, too, as wife), second, the property system of the community and, third, the conjunctural history of this particular household. The property and inheritance system is structured by, but in no sense reducible to, Islamic law;[9] and the history of the household lies at the conjuncture of demography, property, politics and persons.

In studies of European farming populations, it is well near

axiomatic to start from demography and property. There has developed a tradition of the comparative sociology of peasant household structures and marriage systems that rests on typologies of domestic property and inheritance systems, considered in turn within the context of demographic schedules.[10] Even when enjoined to be structuralist in their reading of kinship, Europeanists still conceive of structures in such terms and not in those of structuralist anthropology proper (that is, in an abstracted vocabulary of kinship terminology and marital exchange).[11] Why should this be so? Scholarship on European rural and family history is vast, and evidence of the diversity of patterns of domestic organization and marriage across time, place and class is so sustained that the explanation of internal diversity, rather than internal unity, appears primary. Equally this focus reflects the position of Europeanists on the inside, so to speak; they may at times lose sight of wider communalities, which may distinguish European systems of kinship. An anthropologist with a comparative bent may on occasion attempt to capture the specificity of such systems, but even the study of the common in European systems of kinship starts from institutional history,[12] not simply from the abstracted text of canon law (in contrast to the topoi on the Muslim family among the Orientalists) or the atemporal analysis of kinship terminologies (as in a well-worn tradition of anthropology).[13] But this concern with internal differentiation and with property systems is not confined to the study of European kinship. As studies on Chinese kinship have grown more numerous and sophisticated, they too have taken a distinctly more historical turn, with the problem of differentiation displacing the earlier supposition of unity.[14]

By contrast, writing on Arab kinship and domestic organization has developed no similar comparative framework. In general, when property appears, it does so as an adjunct to structuralist models that enjoin marriage within the patriline. Thus, some authors advance retention of property within the patriline as an explanation of the custom of patrilateral cousin marriage;[15] but other authors, and clearly for sound reasons, reject such explanations in the interpretation of their own material.[16] But there is little attempt to consider why such an explanation for this custom appears convincing in some cases and not in others.[17] For reasons explored in the last chapter, the problem of differentiation in time, space and class has not been at the core of studies of Arab kinship. And yet, when one pauses to reflect, although there may have been continuity in Islamic legal provisions governing urban property,[18] there is every evidence that, among the Arabs, systems of production and agricultural property have been quite as mutable as those in Europe or China.[19] If in China or Europe systems of kinship and household in rural areas cannot be analysed in isolation from such historical contexts, how can such isolation be maintained in the analysis of kinship in Arab lands?

Let us return to Hā'ilah's household. There is a further lesson to be drawn if we look at the marriages of *bait* al-Zawwāk. All were with landed families of prominence, but it is not that which should retain our interest; after all Aḥmad Manṣūr is both wealthy and a local shaikh. Rather, the eye should follow the repetition of alliances in the ascendant generation in the marriages of the children of Aḥmad Manṣūr and Hā'ilah, noting that the marriages of Hā'ilah's children belong to the alliances of her *bait* rather than to those of the father of her children. Demographic history plays its part: Aḥmad Manṣūr was an only son with three sisters; from his two wives he had only one son and no daughters, whereas Hā'ilah was one of only two daughters to survive their father and herself bore four daughters and one son. By this accident of demography, and its corollary (the early passage of paternal property and house to an inheriting daughter) the social ties of Hā'ilah's house eclipse those of her husband's house for her children. Just as Hā'ilah's household is bound up with, yet divided from, and hence in contest with, that of Aḥmad Manṣūr (her cousin and the man who holds two-thirds of her father's land) so the marriages of her children do not simply flow smoothly in the paths chosen by Aḥmad Manṣūr. 'Ā'ishah moved her husband away from his father's household to her natal home; the first exchange marriage arranged for Hā'ilah's son and third daughter ended in failure. This exchange had linked them to a house pivotal in local politics, in which the wives of the two senior men (the sons of Hā'ilah's older sister) belonged to *bait* 'Ākish and the wives of their sons were both daughters of the shaikh of the upper wards. But this exchange marriage did not last long.

In other words, these marriages belong to a history, and a history structured by understandings about property. Marriage is far from a merely secondary alliance, a shuffling exchange of women between men who make society; marriage is itself structuring, or so at least it is among those with property. Often, where property and alliance flow more smoothly along patrilineal courses, we may not see that houses are constructed from property and marriage, because these structuring elements appear to be but incidental expressions of the patriline. But in Hā'ilah's household the inversions of the logic of the system allow us to see these elements for themselves. It is time to examine the logic of the systems of moral alliance and material transfer. We shall begin with marriage, aware, however, that in reality this point in the cycle never comes all by itself but rather within the context of everything in the way of property and persons that has gone before.

On marriage

Ritual

Marriage is the most elaborate of social ceremonies; it is also the most costly. The wedding is the ritual eye of the needle through which a man, but most particularly a woman, must pass to become a sexual partner and a parent. The ritual orders the opening of sexual relations between man and wife in explicit gestures performed under the direction of the female marriage-dresser (the *muzayyinah*), gestures known to everyone but which are left unmentioned in the songs performed by the *muzayyinah* during the wedding.[20] The songs are chaste in language, unlike the occasional ribald exchange between guests. The almost dour verses of the male cantor place the proceedings under the sign of religion; the *daushān* or *muzayyin* may shout out praises of the groom's house, but among men there is little formal commentary on the proceedings in the manner performed for women by the female singer. The songs for women are more fulsome, providing a generic panegyric on all the themes of a wedding save the sexual: the qualities of a bride and groom, the social status of the houses to which they belong, and the nature of marital alliance.[21]

There are two rhythms to a wedding: the *rites de passage* for the groom and the bride, and the wider exchanges woven about these two figures. The rituals of passage, of transformation of status, take a classic form for bride and groom: seclusion, physical preparation and purification, vulnerable, even magical, liminality, symbolically violent entry, and ceremonial integration into the new status. That said, the ritual and symbolic elaboration of such themes is much greater in the case of the bride than in that of the groom. His social adulthood is structured as a more gradual affair; the bride traditionally adopts a woman's head-dress at marriage, whereas her groom would have put on a man's headgear and dagger as soon as he began to show the first signs of puberty, if not before. The unequal symbolic weight given to the transformation wrought by marriage in the bride as against the groom is socially and symbolically overdetermined. The girl is younger than the groom; marriage may occur before a girl's first menses. Patrilocality means that the bride usually moves to the groom's house, rather than the groom to the bride's; in a society where women veil before all persons outside domestic space, this transition, where the woman comes to belong to a second domestic space, can be acted out in repeated veiling and unveiling. And the symbolic repertoire of this society employs an idiom of shedding blood for the marking of fundamental limits, or places in the idiom of J.Z. Smith.[22] In many neighbouring communities, the blood of the virgin bride is displayed; even in this community, which exhibits modesty in the treatment of the virginity cloth, the idea of a virgin's blood shines as a little dark heart behind the public ritual. And last but not least, the transitions of a life-cycle can be played out by women in a manner that is difficult for men: after all a man's gradual accession to domestic management necessarily entails a diminution of his father's authority. This process, with its unspeakable dark tones of patricide, is not ritually accented, neither at marriage nor, as we shall see, at childbirth, when a husband should aid in the dressing of the special room for his wife after childbirth, but he will play no part in the ceremonies marking the birth of his children.

The ritual for the bride excels in its refinement of liminal gesture: as the bride crosses a threshold of ritual importance, for example on the evening when she returns from the bath, an egg is broken at the door; the ululation of women (termed in local dialect *muḥjirah* or *taḥjīr* from the root denoting ritual marking off)[23] accompanies the bride crossing the threshold, the first line of painting (*naqsh*) on her arm, and her unveiling. The structure of veiling and unveiling is itself elaborate. During the days before the wedding night, the bride remains fully veiled when, led in by her mother or the *muzayyinah*, she enters the ceremonial gatherings of women. She is *muḥajjabah*, or in ritual seclusion;[24] and spends most of her time apart from the main gatherings of women in a separate room with a few close companions. It is only on the evening of the day (*lailat al-ḥilfah*),[25] when she is to go to the groom's house, that she is ritually unveiled. The bride, dressed and decorated by the *muzayyinah*, is first unveiled before the women and female guests of her natal house, to their *muḥjirah*. The *muzayyinah* is given a small sum. The bride is then taken in to see her father; a father who loves his daughter may weep. Then, after arrival at the groom's house, to which she will have been accompanied by senior men of the groom's house and the *muzayyinah*,[26] she is unveiled by the *muzayyinah* before the women of the groom's house, again to *muḥjirah*. Only after such formal presentation before women does she go with the *muzayyinah* into a room apart where she will receive her husband. She must give her assent before she is unveiled before him; and for this privilege the groom must pay not only the *muzayyinah* but above all his bride.[27] The groom will be under instructions to assert his control over the bride in ritual terms, by stepping on her foot (she is to withdraw the foot should he try) or other gesture, but whatever may come of such gestures, once she has been unveiled he is to grasp her temples with the fingers of his right hand and recite the *fātiḥah* and *sūrah al-ikhlāṣ* from the Koran. As on the two previous occasions when she was unveiled that night, the bride looks down.[28] This accomplished, the *muzayyinah* leaves the pair alone.

The bride is presented to the women gathered at her home and to the women of the household where she will live and work as a married woman. However difficult the first nights with her husband may be, if the marriage is to survive, it will depend on the girl's relations not only with him but also with the women of the marital house. The husband is, in the words of one older woman, but *ḍaif al-dīwān* – a guest in the living room; women live with women. The rhythm of the little drama of bride and groom seems at times quite drowned out by that of the wider exchanges within which the drama is embedded. The bride appears, not least in the early stages when veiled, quite peripheral to the sociability about her. The structure of these exchanges expresses not the tale of the lonely girl married off but the ideal of balanced exchange in marriage alliance.

The cycle of the full marriage ceremony extends over three weeks. Some time before the ceremonies begin, the basic payments, out of which the wedding itself is funded, will have been made. The marriage cycle opens on a Monday with a women's gathering in the groom's house, a celebration in his honour but in which he plays no role (Figure 6.2). It continues on the Tuesday with a gathering at the bride's house in her honour. On the Wednesday, after the bride's bath and ritual procession, there is a supper and an evening gathering, at which she receives gifts, and the clothing and jewellery offered by her family are shown to the women invited. On this day the clothing

Bride's home	*Exchanges*	*Groom's home*
Engagement lunch	← basic payments	
Monday (*dhibāl al-ḥarīw*)		Women's gathering in honour of bridegroom
Tuesday (*dhibāl al-ḥarīwah*) Women's gathering in honour of bride		
Wednesday (*yaum al-naqsh*) Bride's bath, procession in house, supper for *muta‘arrisīn* *ṭarḥ*, showing of bride's clothing from family	← *kiswah*	
Thursday (*lailat al-ḥilfah*) Dressing of bride, supper, evening gathering, bride unveiled before all women and her father	→ bride and *kiswah*	Groom's bath, men's gathering in afternoon, prayers, procession in streets, evening gathering Bride unveiled before women of groom's house and later before groom, bride receives *ḥaqq al-fitshah*
Friday (*yaum al-ḥilfah ṣabāḥ*)	→ bride's male relatives visit	*Jabr*, men's dancing, Friday prayer, lunch, men's gathering in afternoon
Monday (*thālith*) Lunch for groom	← groom with gifts to bride's mother and mother's brother	Women's afternoon gathering in honour of the bride
Friday (*sābi‘*)	→ women of bride's family with clothes from her family	Lunch, afternoon gathering of women
Friday (*shikmah*) Lunch, women's afternoon gathering	← bride returns home with women of groom's house	
Saturday Women's gathering in afternoon		
Sunday Women's gathering in afternoon		

Figure 6.2 Sequence of marriage ceremonies

(*kiswah*) provided by the groom's house is sent to the bride. On the Thursday the larger celebrations following the groom's bath belong to the men. At the bride's house supper is offered to the invited guests; this is followed by an evening gathering and the unveiling of the bride. Later she is taken to the groom's house, where she is presented to women and groom in the manner described above. On the Friday morning the bride's male kin visit the bride and groom, and in the afternoon after lunch men gather in the groom's house. On the Monday (*yaum al-thālith*) the *muzayyinah* quietly takes the virginity cloth to the mother of the bride, and later the groom goes with gifts to visit the bride's mother and mother's brother(s). A gathering is held for women in honour of the bride, at the groom's house. On the Friday (*yaum al-sābi'*) the women of the bride's family take with them the clothes and gifts which they had given the bride on the evening of her return from her bath; they have lunch in the groom's house and attend the gathering in honour of their bride. The following Friday the visit is returned and the cycle is closed; accompanied by the women of the groom's family the bride goes home, where she spends three nights before returning to her marital home.

The exchanges express alliance. The cycle begins and ends with the girl in her natal home: a woman does not shed her natal identity at marriage. She does not, so to speak, pray before her husband's ancestors as does a Chinese bride; nor is her marriage construed as the gift of a virgin as in North Indian tradition; nor does she assume her husband's name as does the European bride. The married woman remains her father's daughter. As expressed in the clothing sent by the marital home, her husband gives her cover (*sutrah*) socially and sexually, but she remains identified with her natal home.[29] This continuity of social identification is reflected in the structure of material transactions surrounding a married woman.

The cycle outlined above is the full form of marriage ceremony for the first marriage of both parties. Not everyone has the means to host all the gatherings outlined above; and some of the going to-and-fro is curtailed should the bride come from another community than that of her husband. Although the basic structure of the ritual is invariant, the degree and details of its performance vary according to the means and desires of families.[30] So too the payments made for the bride differ markedly, according to the status of the bride, the prior relations between the two families, and their wealth.

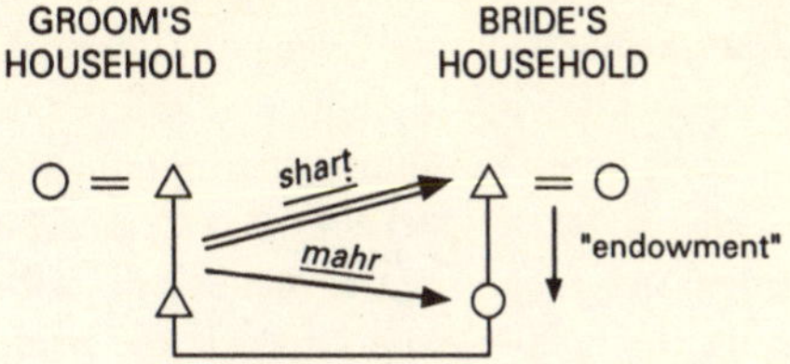

Figure 6.3 Major transfers at marriage

Payments

The payments made at marriage are of three main kinds: the costs of the festivities; a transfer from the groom (or his family) to the bride's guardian (the *sharṭ*); and an endowment of the bride at marriage (the *mahr*, *ḥaqq al-fitshah* and gifts from her family) (Figure 6.3). The costs of the celebrations are considerable. The feasting at the marriage of a labourer may cost him the equivalent of six months' wages. The groom's side usually covers all the expenses of men's feasting and entertainment; the groom's side also usually pays some of the costs of the women's entertainment and feasting, as well as those of the bride's bath and her marriage attendant (*muzayyinah*). The costs of celebrations in the bride's home are covered by the payment known as *ḥaqq al-nār* in Ṣan'ā', but which in the community simply forms part of the *sharṭ* payment. The dresses for the bride's sisters may also be purchased out of the *sharṭ*. The groom and his family receive some help with these expenses in the form of the *rifd*, the gifts of food brought by the inner circle of guests at the marriage (*al-muta'arrisīn*) and of the *jabr*, the sums given the groom by a wider circle of people on the Friday morning (Figure 6.4). These gifts to the groom and his family form part of long-term exchanges between relatives, friends and neighbours.

The major transfer, that from the groom's side to the bride's guardian, serves to mediate the relationship between the two houses whose children are wedded. Thus it varies markedly both in size and in the uses to which it is put. The payment will be higher the more the bride is felt to be alienated from her natal family at marriage and the greater the unknowns and the risks entailed in establishing a new relation between parties not previously bound. There will be virtually no *sharṭ* payment for a girl married within the household to her first cousin, but payments may be substantial for a girl of modest family

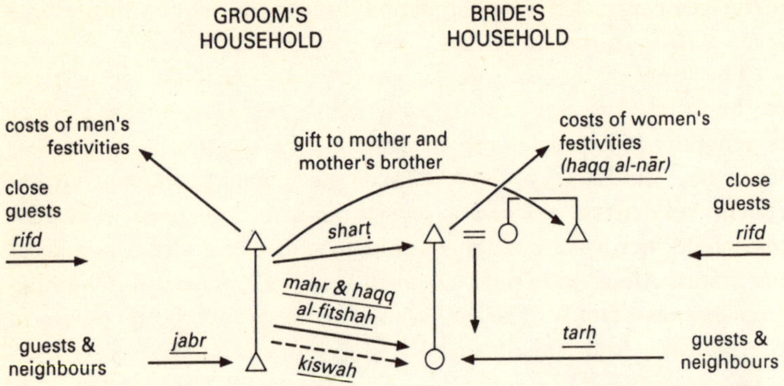

Figure 6.4 Full range of payments traditional at marriage

married into another community to a man whose family was barely known to that of the bride before the marriage proposal. The size of the *shart̤* payment for a bride also varies with her personal qualities (beauty, skills, and whether a virgin or previously married) and status of her family; as a member of her natal family, she possesses a reputation, a claim on property and a set of social links. But it is not only the total size of the *shart̤* that matters; equally important is the use to which it is put, notably whether the woman's guardian spends it on festivities, redirects a large portion of it to the bride, or retains it for his own use. We shall return to this question below. A gift eloquent of the links with the bride's family is that given by the groom to the bride's mother and mother's brother, often agreed upon in advance but taken only on the third day after the consummation of the marriage when the groom goes to have lunch with his bride's family.

The endowment of the bride comprises two parts: the *mahr*, the dowry payment from the groom's side, usually in the form of jewellery (often actually chosen by the bride's family) and those gifts which she receives, either directly from her own relatives (gifts from her mother and other relatives) or indirectly from the groom's side (gifts which her father or guardian purchases with part of the *shart̤* payment). There is also a small payment to the bride on the marriage night for her unveiling (*fitshah*).[31] The *mahr* must be paid, or formally promised, for a marriage to be valid according to the *sharīʿah*.[32] There is great variation in the relative value of the two payments, *shart̤* and *mahr*, but the average order of magnitude of the two payments in marriages contracted over the period 1915–75 is about two or three to one, *sharṭ* to *mahr* (see Table A.17).

The value of the *mahr* depends on the personal and social status of the bride. Although, as a rule of thumb, the payment for a virgin is generally twice that for a woman who has already been married, when one handsome young widow of good family, who was an excellent seamstress, married a second time to a man of a wealthy household, her *mahr* was almost as high as that of a virgin woman of her status. Along with *mahr* a woman receives jewellery and clothing from her own family. The importance of these gifts, both relative to the transfer from the husband's side and absolutely, varies considerably between the different economic strata. The poor tend to endow their daughters little or not at all at marriage, while the rich seek to equal the gifts coming from the husband.

Lastly, there is a gift that is not a gift: the trousseau of clothing which the groom's side purchases for the girl, the *kiswah*. This clothing remains legally the property of the husband (or his family). It is sent to the bride's family for inspection on the day of the bride's bath and returns with the bride on her wedding night. This is distinct from any clothing which the bride brings as her own property from her home.[33] Thus the clothing and jewellery which the bride receives from her own family is shown to the assembled women by the marriage attendant (*shāri'ah*) in the evening following the bridal party's visit to the bathhouse. The *shāri'ah* presents each item individually, from gold ring and velvet dress to hairbrush and slippers for the bath, lifting it from the trunk with a witty or sarcastic remark. She then identifies the donor, in demonstration of the girl's place in the hearts of her own family. By contrast, the *kiswah* is not shown to anyone but is inspected privately by the girl's family. If a girl runs home from the trials of married life (*ḥānikah* in the local expression, compare *munāshizah* in *fiqh*), she should leave behind all the clothing which belongs to her husband's family. In a souring marriage the treatment and location of the *kiswah* readily become a symbol of the state of marital relations.[34]

How can we characterize the transactions made at marriage? First, the payments are in moveable goods. Among labourers or modest farmers without much capital a mother may have to sell rights to a bit of land or even her own *mahr*, or a man may have to mortgage a plot of land to help to finance a son's marriage. Yet the payments are always paid (or promised) in jewellery and cash. The transfers can always be returned, with the exception of that part "burned" in the feasting and in the entertainment. The reversibility of payments is compatible with the importance of divorce, particularly divorce sought by women.

Second, the payments go to the bride's guardian and to the bride. None goes to endow a household or a conjugal economic unit; such payments do not include bedding, pots and pans, rugs, houses or land. Although *mahr* does not represent endowment of a conjugal fund, later in marriage – particularly after the birth of children – women's moveables may serve as a fund in times of need; this appears clearly from the uses to which women put their *mahr* in later life (Table 6.1). A woman's *mahr* is her endowment, however paltry. The women of the poor display all their wit in describing the trinkets with which their entry into a harsh life was strung. A husband has no right to alienate his wife's jewellery.[35]

Third, the endowment of the bride in moveables is consonant with the long-term cycles of property transfer among kin. Both husband and wife retain a claim on their parents' estates; neither claim is dissolved to endow the conjugal unit with real property. Since the girl's claim on real property is generally only half that of a boy, she receives an endowment in moveables when she moves to the marital home. This marks the girl's status in her marital home. So in families with real property the girl's side will seek to match the gifts sent from the groom's house. Among those without property, however, the girl tends to receive little from her father upon marriage; her *mahr* is the essence of her property. In such strata she retains, at best, a claim to maintenance and a roof should her marriage dissolve.

There is thus a different logic to marital transfers between houses with property and houses without. According to the wealth of the families, payments vary in total size (holding constant variations resulting from the relationship between the contracting parties) and in structure. Over the period 1915–75, total marital payments varied by an average factor of one to five, between the poorest strata and the most prosperous in the community; the value of *mahr* payments varied in the order of one to four (see Table A.18). The variation in marriage payments, while important, appears somewhat less great than the degree of inequality in the holdings of property within the community as a whole. In this sense, it may be that marriage is relatively more "costly" for the poor than for those at the top of the community. This impression is confirmed when we consider the direction and use of the payments made at marriage.

Table 6.1 The fate of a woman's *mahr*

6	A debt: husband has yet to pay all or part
	1 widow given *mahr* from deceased husband's estate
4	Stolen by outsiders
5	Taken by husband
	1 accidentally, likely to repay
	4 intentionally
4	Taken by father
	1 mother saved and replaced it
	2 father went bankrupt
1	Given to mother
2	Given to son to finance his marriage
18	Used in various ways
	6 sold to buy food
	4 sold in years of famine (*sanat al-thumānī*)
	2 sold to feed children
	3 used for medical expenses
	2 own medical treatment
	1 husband's medical treatment
	2 used for travel
	1 travel to join husband in Saudi Arabia
	1 travel to *ḥajj*
	7 invested *mahr*
	2 bought a cow
	5 pledged it to help finance house-building
60	Retained *mahr*
100	Total number

In the case of prosperous landed families, the father or senior male relative of the groom finances the marriage; the bride is the gift of a father and a mother to a son; the groom is consulted but the choice of the bride usually rests with his mother. The guardian of the bride is unlikely to retain very much of what he receives from the groom's family as *sharṭ* but will spend it on feasting, to the order expected of families of their status, and on jewellery, cash and clothing for the girl, sometimes of equal value to that which she receives as *mahr* and *kiswah*. By contrast, among groups without capital, the groom's family is less likely to be able to provide all the payments and the groom will probably need to save for a number of years before he can contemplate marriage. Furthermore, the bride's father

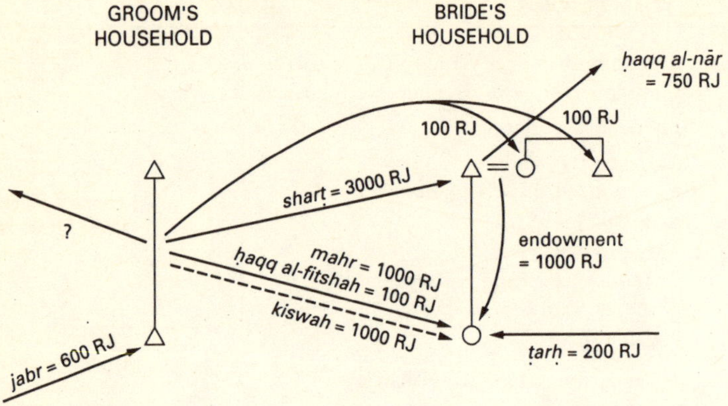

Figure 6.5 Marriage payments for a girl of a landed family

is more likely to retain a good portion of the sum he receives as *sharṭ* (Figures 6.5 and 6.6).[36]

In the landed family the bride's guardian gives a good part of the *sharṭ* payment to the bride at marriage, but in the poorer family the guardian retains most of the payment. These two tendencies should be understood not as fixed rules (i.e. bridewealth versus indirect dowry) but as broad trends corresponding to the nature of domestic relations in the two economic groups. Raising children spells sacrifice for labouring men and women; their dependence in old age on a son or daughter will also be more acute than the dependence of a man or woman with property. But poverty invites migration and, whatever the desires of the parties, often separates parents from adult children. When a labouring man and wife arrange the marriage of a daughter, they may have debts; in any case they need to accumulate the means not only to provide small gifts to their daughter throughout her married life but also to put something aside for a son's marriage and their own old age. In families where the cycle of youthful dependence, adult labour and aged dependence is not cushioned by possession of the means of employment, the senior generation's dependence upon the younger takes the form that when a daughter, in the prime of life, leaves her natal house, her father receives some compensation for the labour he invested in her.

By contrast, among families with considerable landholdings, the bride's guardian faces no such insecurity and his future "dependence"

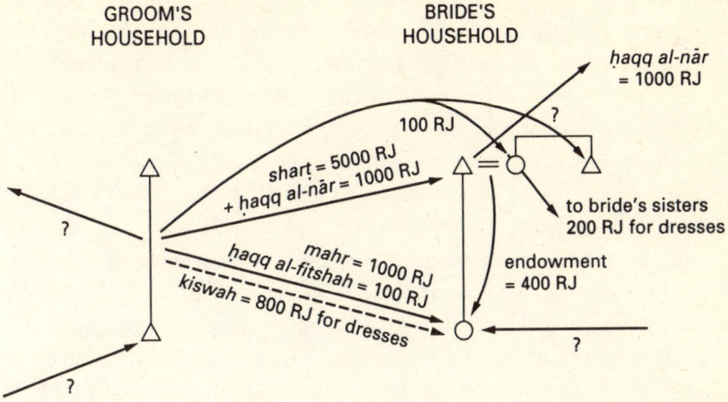

Figure 6.6 Payments at the second marriage of a woman from another village with a labourer

on what his daughter brings him is of quite another nature. For although he too may be concerned to demand very high conditions (the literal meaning of *sharṭ*) as a sign of his daughter's value, he would not like to appear in need of what he receives. His dependence on his daughter resides in the relations which her marriage generates or confirms. She will represent her father's house in her marital home. And among the landed the woman's identification with her father's house is also understood in terms of the land on which she has a claim. Such a conception of marriage invites more intense economic relations between intermarrying households, and so great care is taken over the marriages of girls from such families.

At one point the *muzayyinah*'s marriage songs have the bride accuse her father of selling her.

> Shame on you father, how could you have done it?
> Shame on you, what pushed you to do it?
> Did the red wheat beguile you
> Or was it the offer of gold?
> Did the willowy youth entice you
> Or was it the Dragoman?
> Shame on the seller for the sale he made.
> Good luck to you, buyer.[37]

Marriage, as another verse informs us, is properly alliance by mutual agreement; such is the noble model. Equating marriage to sale is a distinctly ignoble interpretation. In this society, as in many others, it can prove difficult for the poor to live by the noble model. Payments are in specie to the marriage guardian, usually the father and by law a man and so never formally to the mother whatever the practical relations in the household. As such, they can be transformed into any commodity. Hence the ignoble side of the noble model. The more a man retains of the payment given by the groom's side, the less authority he implicitly retains in the treatment of his daughter. In the case that a man marries his daughter to a family much richer than his own, his own power to intervene will be limited, although the payment given for his daughter may serve to buy her out of the marriage in the event of grave abuse. Equally, since such a marriage marks social ascension, a woman's mother may come to work closely with her daughter to ensure the success of the marriage and even spend large parts of the year in the son-in-law's household as an obliging nursemaid for her daughter's children. Marriage is, after all, a long-term matter. Even a poor man should not cut his links with his daughter on marriage. A father may retain a good part of the *sharṭ* but he too is expected to provide gifts to his daughter on ceremonial occasions throughout her married years. The tie of a married woman to her natal family and her continuous claim on their means is formally expressed at the major religious festivals and above all at the points when the relationship between the two families is gradually renegotiated: as a woman bears children.

On childbirth and the conjugal family

Childbirth

In the gatherings held in her honour during the forty-day period after childbirth, the woman who has given birth wears her black head-cloth turned forward over her decorated headband in the manner of a woman in mourning. Yet, aside from her head-dress, she is dressed in ceremonial jewellery and observes none of the other habits of dress of a woman in mourning. During the forty days after birth she is a liminal figure; in giving birth she passed through the doors of death but has given life. The mother tells us in the words of the *muzayyinah*'s songs:

> Oh my sisters, if you knew
> what I have seen at the moment of childbirth:

my grave began to open
and the cry of mourning sounded.
But today my tomb has closed
and the cry of joy rings out.[38]

"The cry of joy" is the *muhjirah*, the liminal character of which we noted in the marriage ritual, but which according to older women belongs rightly not so much to the bride as to the mother-after-birth, to a person who has recovered from a mortal illness, or to a person returned safely from the pilgrimage (*ḥajj*). As a man or woman who has been to the *ḥajj* approaches home, a sheep is slaughtered just before the threshold. In entering the person returning steps over the blood flowing from the animal. For a mother-after-birth no sheep are slaughtered; her natal family is to give her chickens, as well as grain, ghee, honey and spices, to be consumed during the period after birth. Rather, through a series of symbolic inversions, the mother is herself constructed, in women's oral tradition, as *ʿaqīrat rasūl allāh*, the lamb of the Prophet. The blood of childbirth has a ritual status. The mother's special foods are to strengthen the blood; she uses particular incenses to dry its flow. And in the songs of the *muzayyinah* the mother is addressed as *yā nifās*, with indirect reference to her condition.[39]

It is only on her visit to the bath marking the end of the forty days after birth that the ritual status of the *wālidah*, marked by the paraphernalia of protective symbols (*ḥijābs*) with which her ceremonial room is dressed, comes to an end. Sexual relations are proscribed during the forty days after birth, as they are during a woman's times of menstruation. But whereas women never speak of men seeking sexual relations during the latter, they do, on occasion, of the former. In religious tradition sexual penetration and semen is ritually polluting to both parties (both must wash before prayer); so too is women's blood. But in popular tradition two inversions may be observed: the blood of virginity, made to flow by male penetration, is granted almost magical status and the blood after childbirth is treated as a kind of purification, with male sexual penetration as abhorrent defilement. As one woman remarked, should a husband try to force himself on his wife during the forty-day period, she may licitly kill him in self-defence. She is the keeper of the house's culture and it is the husband's duty to assist in the preparation of her special room. Otherwise he stands outside.

The verses of the *muzayyinah*'s song speak of this relation in almost mystical terms:

> A child has come[40] to your husband
> from a precious tree whose roots lie in the seas
> and whose branches hang low.[41]

The *wilād* ceremonies where women gather every afternoon are in honour of the mother. The child is placed behind a white cloth embroidered with Koranic verses but is not feted in his own right. In the case of a first childbirth they are held even if the child has died. For the first childbirth a proper *wilād* is a woman's due. Ḥasan, whom we met in the last chapter, married his eldest daughter (the daughter of Mughītha) into a more wealthy household of his quarter; he felt that for her first childbirth his daughter was not given a reasonable celebration by her husband's family. The girl's husband was very much a junior in the household, which comprised his grandfather and grandmother and the large family of his father's brother. His own father had moved to a separate home near the shop he kept. The grandparents neglected to give the girl a proper childbirth ceremony after she bore her first child, saying that they already had enough trouble with their resident son's six children. After the forty days were over and the girl had been to the bath, her father took her away and gave her a full *wilād* ceremony at home for forty days. Since Ḥasan here protested against the treatment of his daughter, one woman who did not know the family asked whether her husband might not divorce her. In fact relations appeared good thereafter between the husband of the girl and his father-in-law. It appears that Ḥasan was negotiating not only his daughter's position in her new home but also that of her spouse. Although the celebration of the *wilād* for forty days after the forty-day post-partum purification period was most exceptional, not infrequently a young woman returns home to give birth, or is attended by her mother at childbirth.

Lasting for many days and attended exclusively by women, the gatherings in honour of the mother-after-birth are often experienced as a burden by the husband's relatives. A proverb – more popular among men than women – remarks acidly: rather two weddings than one birth (*'ursain wa-lā wilād*). On their "visit" to a married daughter who has given birth, a woman's natal family gives gifts of strengthening food (ghee and grain for *ma'ṣūbah*), chickens, spices and *qishr* (for the special fortifying drink, *qahwat al-wālidah*), incense and, in the case of the child being a boy, a little dress and the costs of circumcision.[42] In principle a woman's natal family provides her special foods for half of the forty-day period after birth. Childbirth is a time when a woman's natal family, engaged in the welfare of their daughter, seek to negotiate on her behalf. Unlike marriage, childbirth is often attended by strife between a woman's natal kin and her husband's family, as her relatives take up arms on her behalf.

Household and conjugal family

The ceremonial emphasis given the mother is not without ambiguity. The celebration of the mother who has given birth is matched by an absence of symbolic statement concerning the social maturity of her husband or the development of common interest between husband and wife. The involvement of the wife's kin at her childbirths reflects not only their concern with her good treatment. The children that the woman bears are the embodiment of *nasab*, the relationship between the two households, and in the case of political marriages, between two wider groups. In their visit, her family also makes a statement concerning the development of the relationship with their in-laws (*ansāb*).[43]

Childbirth is also ambiguous with regard to the married woman's ability to negotiate her position in the marital home. A young married woman is not bereft of means to protest conditions in her marital home; she can always return home *ḥāniqah* and very often does. But the birth of children not only establishes her in her husband's eyes; it also ties her to the marital home, whence the virulence of her own kin's intervention should they feel that honour is not being done their daughter. When older women look back on their lives, they often describe the first years of marriage as a time of insouciant childishness, brought gradually to an end by the responsibility of childcare. The early years of childbearing and childcare are the most onerous of all for women. The subordinate position of the younger woman leaves her with routine work in the household (sorting grain, cleaning the house, washing clothes) while at the same time the care of infants (*bizā'*) prevents her from full participation in women's social gatherings (*tafriṭah*). With the birth of every child she invests more of her life in her husband's household. Although in the case of a quarrel her mere departure from the household leaves chaos raging among her children, her husband's power of divorce is now another kind of threat, the sanction of cutting her off from her children. As women say, it is now an illusion (*kidhb*) to think that one can leave. A woman should stay for the sake of her children, particularly her daughters, who, if she leaves, will grow up under the feet of other women (*bain arjul al-nisā'*).

A woman's relations with her marital kin change over time; so, too, do those with her natal kin. A father, and after his death a brother, has a duty to visit and to give a small gift (*'asb*) to a married woman on the major festivals.[44] Traditionally such gifts are said to have consisted of part of the family's meat (*shirkah*) and some sweets (*ja'ālah*) but today the gifts are usually of money. Among families of modest means few women receive gifts from more than two male relatives, and many do so from only one – from the father, after his death from the brother, and after the death of a brother or if the woman has received her share of inheritance, only from her daughter's husband or her son, should he be living apart from his mother. By contrast, among wealthier families a woman is more likely to receive several visits, not all from men who are so closely related, and the sums she will receive may after a few years be sufficient to buy herself a piece of jewellery. Thus among poorer women surveyed the mean number of men who gave *'asb* was 1.8, and among women of somewhat more prosperous families, 2.5. It should be noted that the survey did not include many women of the richest families (Table 6.2).

It is men who are cast as the gift-givers. Children too receive gifts on the festivals and it is only when a boy begins to reach puberty that he ceases to receive gifts and accompanies men of the family on their visits to married women. Occasionally, however, if women have the means they may give gifts to their daughters. Taqīyah, the wife of a wealthy butcher of Ṣan'ā', herself born in the community, where her four brothers live, took pride in the gifts she offered her daughters on the occasion of the *'īd*. She had already given some of her own gold jewellery to her daughters, explaining that she gave to her married daughters, who were still young at the time, so that they would not have to depend on other people. Her words on this occasion had an edge to them since she uttered them in front of her brother's wife, her first cousin and also her husband's sister, who was known for stinginess. But Taqīyah had married the wealthy town butcher, whereas her husband's sister had married less well in the country and had to manage her household strictly if it were to prosper.

Table 6.2 Relatives who gave *'asb* to women

Women whose fathers were alive		Women whose fathers had died	
Relative through		Relative through	
36	Father		
28	father		
6	father's brother		
1	father's brother's son		
1	father's sister's son		
16	Brother	43	Brother
15	brother	36	brother
1	brother's son	6	brother's son
		1	brother's wife's father
6	Mother	9	Mother
3	mother's brother	5	mother's brother's son
2	mother's brother's son	1	mother's cousin (FBS)
1	mother's cousin (FBS)	2	mother's sister's son
		1	mother's father
2	Sister	4	Sister
1	sister's son	2	sister's son
1	sister's husband	1	sister's son's son
		1	sister's husband
1	Daughter	14	Daughter
1	daughter's husband	13	daughter's husband
		1	daughter
		9	Son[1]
		1	Share-cropper[2]
33	women responding[3]	66	women responding[3]

Notes: 1. Usually only sons living away from their mother give *'asb* in this fashion. 2. This man later married the widow. 3. This is the total number of women responding, some of whom receive gifts from more than one relative.

It is as a mature and experienced matron that a woman may be able to consolidate her gains. Inside the house she manages the stores, the kitchen, and the work of younger women and children. Watched only at a distance by her husband, with whom she now shares a common interest in the prosperity of the household and the future of their children, the woman who "keeps the key" has considerable authority over junior members of the household, children and younger women. Control of the stores provides the means for ceremonial exchange with other women, and also for small trade with other women in exchange for services or cash.

Keeper of the house's culture, the senior woman is able to undertake these exchanges and small investments not only because younger women, whose labour and consumption she supervises, assume the burden of onerous chores such as fetching water, making dung-cakes, doing the washing and tending infants, but also because she is able to capitalize on such sums as she has saved from gifts over the years and perhaps from payments on her share of her parents' inheritance. If women come to control part of their inheritance from their parents' estates, most do so late in life. The senior woman builds on her relations with her children, both practically and morally. The intensity of the mother's relations with her children is heightened by the clear division between female and male social spheres, and by the often tense and authoritarian relations between father and son. Indulgent and protective, the mother is the son's natural ally.[45]

Among families with property the pre-eminence of senior matrons rests not only on cycles of labour and management but also on cycles of the transmission of property. In general a brother takes over cultivation of his sister's land after the death of their father: this is in his interest but it may also be in her interest during her childbearing years. If a woman were to claim her land during this time, the cultivation of that land would surely pass to her husband and this might well avail her little. By leaving her share with her brother, she retains her claim on her family house and receives small payments which she can use to enhance her position in her marital home. This affords her some power of negotiation in her marital home and a refuge in the case of marital breakdown or early widowhood. The strategies of sister and brother coincide with those of the widowed mother, who may survive her husband for many years. The widow is loath to see her children partition, especially if this heralds a break between her son, with whom she usually lives, and her married daughter(s). The relationship between mother and daughter becomes, if anything, stronger after a daughter is married. In general, women of landed families marry near home and much of their social life builds on links through their mothers: a married woman often attends women's gatherings not with her mother-in-law but with her mother. It is usually only after her mother's death that a married daughter considers claiming her share and thereby cutting, in part at least, her ties to her natal home. By this time her son, seeking a margin of independence from his father, may also press her to claim her share in her parents' inheritance. Among more modest families she may sell out her share and invest the proceeds in marrying her son, in building a house, or in buying valuables or livestock.

But in most households there comes a day when a senior woman begins to lose her strength, and a younger second wife or daughter-in-law begins to take over her place in management of the kitchen. As the older woman grows weaker, she may withdraw more into herself, assuming tasks peripheral to the central management of the house. If widowed, she may be persuaded to gift her land to the son with whom she lives, something virtually never done by a father. Thus while some older women, by the conjuncture of relations in their household, remain cathedral in presence, others supplanted in the management of their own homes become but shadows of themselves. An old woman, no longer mistress of the house nor perhaps of her own property, turns to prayer, may observe extra fasts, and begins to prepare herself for death, the ultimate *ḥijāb*. In old age, men also withdraw from the rough and tumble of life, acquiring a gentleness rarely felt in younger men, but they, unlike their wives, never see fit to gift their property before the deathbed.

This sketch suggests certain broad patterns in family life. In spite of symbolic elaboration and material cost, marriages are frequently dissolved, particularly in the early years; common interests shared by the two spouses develop only slowly; the wife's ties to her natal family remain very important, especially in the early years; and the wife's position in her marital home changes markedly from subordination in the early years to considerable authority towards the end of her reproductive period, a progression reversed only when, in old age, she is divested of her role as senior manager of the household. Such marital structures correspond to the patterns of succession to control over productive property which privilege men over women and seniors over juniors. That is to say, the model of family development sketched above corresponds to the lack of joint conjugal endowment in real property at the outset of marriage, the recognition of a daughter's continuing claim on her parents' estate, and the merging of the spouses' estates only late in life, in the form of mutual rights of inheritance and above all in the passage of their estates to their children. Such is the noble model, but by its imbrication with property relations, it promises many variants not only among those without property, where labour and management condition family relations yet more directly, but, given the roulette of demography, property and politics, also among those with property. It is to death and the process of inheritance that we now turn.

On death and property

Mourning the dead

A specialist prepares the body for burial, the *amīn* among men and the *muzayyinah*, there being no locally resident female religious specialist, among women. First the specialist ties the dead man's jaw so that the mouth remains closed. He thus masks the mouth, or as it is put, *yulaththim al-mayyit*, the root *lathama* also providing the term for a woman's headcloth (*lithmah*) which a woman draws up to cover the lower part of the face before an outsider. The *amīn* washes the body four times, first in water, then with a local clay, then with soap and lastly with *sidr* (spina Christi).[46] The *sidr* both softens the skin and ensures that the deceased falls deaf.[47] Lastly the specialist purifies the body with incense. He straightens the toes and fingers; the body and features of a deceased person should be soft, not contorted; the features of a man, who at the moment of death has been asked of his faith by the angels, express whether he is destined for paradise. The specialist dresses the deceased completely. In the case of a man, the shoulder wrap (*liḥfah*) is draped round his head and shoulders in the manner that a woman wears her outer cloak, or that, among men, the shawl of the bridegroom is draped over his head and shoulders as he returns home from the bath on his wedding night. And lastly, the specialist wraps the body in the shroud (*madraj*) and ties it round.

Only men bury the dead. Lowered from the bier, as prayers are recited,[48] the deceased is lain on his right side, head in the direction of Mecca. The shroud ties are loosened. Every man casts three handfuls of earth into the open grave.

In the case of women the *muzayyinah* announces the details of mourning ceremonies to be observed by the family and whether the family accepts *mujābarah*, the gifts of food from neighbours and relatives during the first days after the death.[49] By tradition, families receive mourners for ten days but many do so only for seven. Men gather to mourn for fewer days than do women, often in the evenings when a specialist may recite *sūrahs* from the Koran. Women remember the deceased in the afternoons. On the third, seventh (and tenth day, should the mourning continue for the full ten days) a family with means will pay a specialist *nashshādah* to recite religious verses. The *nashshādah* is provided with incense; sweet basil is given to women, not to wear as an ornament[50] but simply to be held; the fragrance of basil is said to be of paradise, as is that of quince. Women dress in black and wear their headcloths pulled forward over the decorated headband. A woman of the house passes with rose-water. The chants of the *nashshādah* are punctuated by the sobbing of the relatives, as the bereaved evoke the deceased. The bereaved should express their grief; madness stalks them and they need to mourn. And other women will weep as they recall the ones they too have lost. The expression of grief is invited and yet controlled, checked by senior women who call for prayer and silence when they sense that due limits may be exceeded. Men do not bewail together in this fashion, and women, when they seek to restrain the open expression of grief, invoke the sterner mode of men, that of prayer, as the model of decorum.

The days of mourning are intense but contained. Women of the deceased wear black for at least three months beyond the period of mourning; and celebrations of marriage or childbirth are postponed or curtailed for some time after a death. Death has a sanctity (*al-maut la-hu ḥurmah*). But, by contrast with marriage and childbirth, the ritual gatherings for mourning are not drawn out for many days. They are in honour of the deceased so there is no ritual expression of the consequences of the loss to the house, save in the extent of the ceremonies and numbers of persons received. And there is no ritual allusion to the property of the deceased nor to its division. Matters of property are quite distinct from the rituals of mourning.

Transmission: prae morte, post mortem

An older woman may have parted with her property some years before death, giving her daughter(s) some of her jewellery and her son(s) title to her lands. But women do not always do this, and indeed some women never come to control the land on which they have a claim so as to be able to dispose of it before death.[51] Among men it is rare that a man will have made detailed provisions for his succession. He may do so if he leaves minor children or only daughters, or if he seeks to privilege one heir over others.[52] Thus Hā'ilah's father, who left only daughters, quietly gave his silver coin to Hā'ilah before his death.[53]

In the case that a man is to leave minor children he may appoint an executor (*waṣīy*) to administer the estate until such time as all children have grown to majority. One man of the wealthiest of the patronymic groups, Aḥmad Ismā'īl 'Ākish, appointed the former *amīn* as executor. This was to protect the interests of his children, who were still minors, against the men of his family. The *amīn* did his duty by the children and only when the last had grown up did he give them their documents of inheritance (*fuṣūl*) and supervise a full and fair appointment and partition of the lands. Aḥmad Ismā'īl had designated one plot in the lower lands of the community as *waqf*, with the proceeds going to the *amīn* and to his sister, out of which the *amīn* was to read the Koran in his memory.

But in 1976, years later and after the death of both men, Aḥmad Ismā'īl's son, Ḥusain, would no longer allow the son of the former *amīn* to enter the plot. Ḥusain said that his father had made two mistakes in his life: the first when he took a wife from *bait* Murghim (the largest and individually richest household in the community, see Figure B.2) and the second when he was buried in al-Ḥajab (the cemetery in the lower quarters) rather than the cemetery of the ward of *bait* 'Ākish. Aḥmad Ismā'īl was the only man of *bait* 'Ākish ever to be buried in al-Ḥajab. He had chosen al-Ḥajab so that his friend, the *amīn*, would wash, dress, and bury him and receive the due recompense, as he did for all those he buried in the lower cemetery.

As for Ḥusain's remark concerning his mother, one older woman explained it in these terms: "His mother's brothers are troublesome, although if things had been as they should have been, Ḥusain would have been pleased that his father had married from such a good family, since something would have gone to the children after her death. But his mother was married in an exchange marriage, with her husband's sister marrying her brother. As for the inheritance, each brother simply held on to his sister's share and no land ever changed hands."

Law and documentation

The rules governing the inheritance of property belong to the realm of *sharī'ah*, not common law. This explains the appointment of the *amīn*, the local Islamic legal specialist, as executor of Aḥmad Ismā'īl's estate. The principles according to which an estate is divided are those obligatory (*al-farā'iḍ*) in Islamic legal tradition.[54] In other words, the provisions of Islamic law provide the conceptual framework within which all negotiation over the division of an estate occurs. This is not to say that the process of division is a mechanical application of the law;[55] the law determines the rules of the game, not the outcome in every instance.[56]

The distribution of shares can prove complex, necessitating documentary specialists, but the general principles are simple enough. Property moves downwards to children of both sexes; female heirs receive one-half the share of competing male heirs, that is to say, a daughter receives half the share of a son. The downward movement of property does not exclude the passage of a limited share to spouse[57] and, if alive, to parent.[58] In the absence of a son, a portion of the estate may pass to the deceased's siblings and to paternal cousins.[59]

These principles of division apply to two-thirds of the estate, regardless of the wishes of the dying person. A person may legate one-third of his estate but not to an heir. A legation to an heir is valid only if all other heirs give their legal assent to the legacy. The only way round the provisions of inheritance is to gift property (before death-sickness)[60] or to endow it as a *waqf*, but aside from individual plots endowed in *waqf darīs*,[61] in the manner of the plot designated by Aḥmad Ismā'īl, farmers do not tie up their property in *waqf*. Family *waqf* requires considerable documentation, provisions for administration, and the freezing of land in perpetuity – forms of management more appropriate to urbanites than farmers.[62] The properties of farmers do not justify such expenses.

Among farmers the relative size of the share inherited plays a central role in determining which of the heirs will accede to management of part or all of the estate. Whereas it is easy for urbanites to subdivide revenue from landed estates (and among farmers the produce of land can be distributed according to quota-shares), the management and the working of land cannot always be so easily partitioned.

There are several stages in the full division of an estate. The first is the identification of heirs and the evaluation of their relative shares. This is often referred to as *qismah*, but *qismah* is also used for the whole process of division. The second step is the *ḥaṣr*, or survey of the contents of the estate. The first two steps should be carried out shortly after the death of a person. The third stage is the allocation (*ta'yīn*) of particular properties to different heirs, and the fourth is the transfer of usufructuary control over such properties. These last two steps are often postponed for many years.

If a man dies leaving only minor heirs and without appointing an executor, as occurred in the case of the carpenter killed as he was stealing *qāt*, the local shaikh and *amīn* carry out the survey of belongings immediately after the death. Local political authority will likewise intervene when a man dies without male heir and without appointing an executor for his estate. Families try to keep political figures at arm's length from their successions, but it is common that the local shaikh and ward leader play the role of attestor (*'ādil*) to the survey and division of property into shares or that a female heir, to protect her interest, request a local political notable with knowledge of the law to represent her interests (as *wakīl*). For their services these men receive some recompense; families both require the certification of such figures and yet seek to limit their access to the affairs and silver of the house.

It is meritorious to arrange for complete documentation before one's death, but it is rare for a man to do so unless he knows himself to be leaving minor heirs. Such documentation as a family may have, moreover, is in general not equally distributed among all family members. Women who are married out of the family often leave with their brothers such documents as there are concerning their property. Even if women have documentation of their relative share and of the composition of the estate (*fuṣūl*) they rarely possess all the older documents (bills of sale, past inheritance documents, and so forth) which may be necessary to establish the validity of those that they do hold, should they have to go to court to obtain control of their part in an estate. Thus the manager of an estate usually stands in a strong position, not only because of the extra part in the estate which may be granted him for his work on the land (termed *sa'y*) but also because he may hold the bulk of family documents. It is only the rare inheriting daughter, on the model of Hā'ilah, who finds herself the manager of a house on her parents' death.

One man who provided for full documentation of his property before his death and proceeded to appoint an executor (*waṣīy*) for his estate was al-ḥājj Qāsim Muqbil; he did this since he was leaving minor heirs and a situation of potential conflict behind him. He also bequeathed a plot of land to his *waṣīy*, the only son of a sister who had predeceased him. The first marriage of his sister had been to a farmer who took up shopkeeping but failed; her husband then began to sell his land to support his two wives and children. Eventually, he sold all and went bankrupt. Al-ḥājj Qāsim's father obtained a divorce for his daughter who returned home with her only child, a son, then aged seven. After some years she remarried. Her son, Sa'd al-Ghaithī, grew up without land, supporting himself by whitewashing houses and by carpentry. Only when al-ḥājj Qāsim fell ill and entrusted the young man with a few fields in a *maḥmā* share-cropping agreement did people speak of a sudden change for the better in Sa'd's fortunes. And so it was that, before his death, al-ḥājj Qāsim arranged for the documents of his estate to be prepared and had the specialist pen a bequest (*waṣīyah*) designating a plot of land for his nephew and appointing him executor (*waṣīy*) of the estate.

Al-ḥājj Qāsim Muqbil chose to do this because he was leaving two wives, three adult daughters from his first two wives, and three minor sons from a recently divorced younger third wife, and he anticipated conflict after his death.[63] His first two wives having borne him only daughters, al-ḥājj Qāsim had taken a third wife when he was about fifty years of age. Shortly before his final illness he divorced this younger wife, who, by local standards, had been pampered. Al-ḥājj Qāsim had built her a little house among the vineyards and for years had doted on her. She had an operation for goitre and a *maulid* celebration upon her recovery, for which the most expensive *nashshādah* of Ṣan'ā' was hired.[64] But after her divorce it was said that, far from having been grateful, she and her mother had abused her husband's generosity; rumours circulated concerning her trips into the capital. Women described al-ḥājj Qāsim's illness following the divorce as unnatural, the work of black magic (*siḥr*) by his divorced third wife. During the mourning period after his death, she returned to his house as "mother of his children" (*umm al-aulād*)[65] and had to be evicted by order of the shaikh.

Women might have been more sympathetic to the divorced third wife in the case of a man other than al-ḥājj Qāsim. But as older women remarked, he was the only man they knew who had freely and fully divided his father's property between himself and his sister and who had even built her a house near his own. But then, on reflection they also remembered hearing of a man in a neighbouring village, who was said to have summoned his sister on the tenth day after the death of their father and to have taken out the *faransī* (Maria Theresa thalers, the old silver coin of Yemen) in front of his sister and her husband. These he had wisely kept hidden lest they be noted by the *qassāmīn*, those responsible for assessing the estate and appointing shares, who between them would have had to be given no mean part of the silver. He gave his sister every third *faransī* and went on to divide the land. And as if that were not enough, he told her not to worry: he would do his duty by her, would bring her the customary gifts at the festivals and would visit her whenever she bore a child.

Such fairness was remarkable enough to merit comment. "Not so usually!" exclaimed an older woman. "No, only after lawsuits, quarrels and problems is land ever divided. For them the only thing off-bounds (*ḥarām*) is what they cannot get their hands on. The real basis of division is power: the strong man (*al-muqwīy*) takes all."

On practice

It is worth pausing to consider why al-ḥājj Qāsim Muqbil, like the legendary man of the neighbouring village, was such an exception when he divided his father's lands according to the letter of the law. Al-ḥājj Qāsim belonged to a small patronymic group of the lower wards that intermarried with other like houses of the ward. As an only son he had already come to manage his father's plots of land by the time of his father's death. His mother having predeceased his father,[66] the only other heir to the estate was his sister, who had returned home with her young son after her first husband had failed entirely to provide for her. In giving his sister her share in the estate, al-ḥājj Qāsim was nevertheless to manage the cultivation of all the land for some time.

The succession was distinguished by its simplicity. There was documentation for the estate; the estate was not subject to outstanding legal conflict nor had it been bound reciprocally to other estates through exchange marriages; the number of heirs, only two, was small for the reasonable size of the estate; and honouring a sister's right did not promise the immediate dismantling of an existing farming unit.

Such simplicity is exemplary and not found in all neighbouring houses. Al-ḥājj Qāsim's first wife was from a neighbouring house whose history of succession, to which we turn below, could not have been more different. In any succession the individual character of property right stands in tension with the household management of farming. Unless the estate is a substantial one, the dominant manager, often the holder of the largest share, will seek to tranform the absolute rights of the holders of small shares into purely usufructuary claims. At the level of a single household, demography is like the game of roulette. And the historical character of right, both in terms of the marriage alliances forged and of unresolved anterior contests over right, weighs heavily on the decisions of heirs in many successions.

A tangled succession, where the estate was small, the heirs many, the skeins of marriages commensurate, and the history of litigation correspondingly complex, was that of *bait* Khabash, whose family house, occupied by the dominant heir, stood just across the way from that of al-ḥājj Qāsim. The inheritance dispute was generally regarded as excessive. "Oh, that has made it into the newspaper," remarked one older woman. The dominant heir, Ḥamūd Khabash, who resisted partition, had not only said that he would let his father's lands go to dust rather than divide, but he was doing just that. Farmers did not approve of such spiteful neglect. Once when Ḥamūd had refused to irrigate a plot in al-Qariyah, still under his management but from which he was to pay off a debt to his cousins, farmers considered his neglect so shameful to the community that they themselves went down to irrigate the plot.

THE HISTORY OF A HOUSE

The background to the conflict was described to me by one of the heirs, Karāmah (Figure 6.7). When her father, Sa'd, died, leaving three daughters and a young son, her father's younger brother, Ḥusain, took over responsibility for the care of Sa'd's widow, his young children and his land. Before his death Sa'd had given his elder daughter Maimūnah (AY) in marriage to Ḥusain's first son Aḥmad (BB) and had also bethrothed Karāmah (AX) to his brother's second son 'Alī (BA), and his own son Ḥamūd (AA) to Ḥusain's only daughter, Fāṭimah (BZ). The third daughter, Ḥalīmah (AZ), was married to Sa'd's sister's son, al-ḥājj Qāsim Muqbil. Karāmah waited seven years between her betrothal and the consummation of her marriage, since her cousin was five years her junior. Her brother, Ḥamūd, never consummated his marriage with Fāṭimah and married instead the daughter of their maternal uncle. After the death of her father, when the cousins began to quarrel over the estate, Fāṭimah was eventually divorced; she was never to remarry. By arranging an

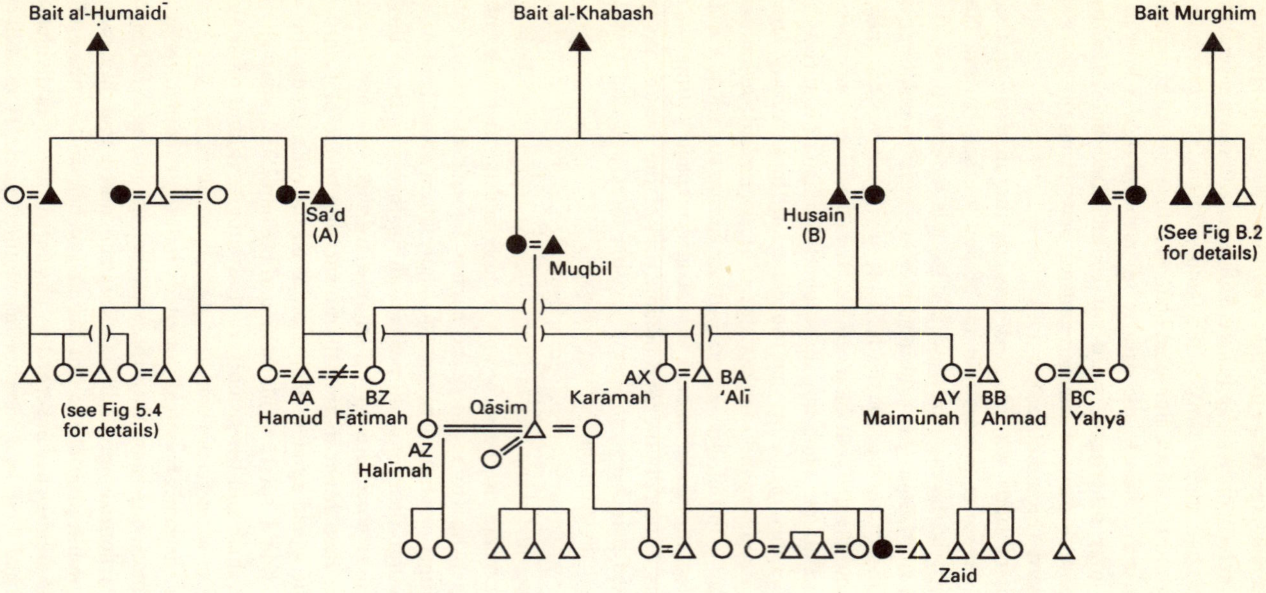

Figure 6.7 *Bait* al-Khabash

exchange marriage between their children, Sa'd and Ḥusain, who had respectively one son and three daughters and three sons and one daughters, had sought to keep the family united and to let virtually no land go to outsiders. But after Ḥamūd refused to consummate the marriage with Fāṭimah, the balance of in-marriage was broken and tensions over inheritance were not counteracted but exacerbated. From Ḥamūd's point of view his cousins were taking the lion's share of the estate (Figure 6.8, B).

The joint lands were divided between the children of the two brothers only after the death of the second brother, Ḥusain. Ḥusain had, moreover, taken a third of Sa'd's lands as recompense for his expenses and labour (*sa'y*) during the years when the children were young. On Ḥusain's death the lands of his children were fully appointed and divided, but Sa'd's estate, as well as that of his wife, was not divided at the same time between Ḥamūd and his three sisters. Of these lands the father had appointed a third as *waqf darīs* for which his son was the administrator. The sisters had at first simply gone along with this, but when they learned that such a *waqf* was not valid unless they gave full and formal agreement in writing (*ijāzah*), they refused. Legally the land became part of the joint estate again. The sisters then began to seek a division in earnest and eventually challenged their brother in the courts.

In the suit they won recognition of their rights to their father's house, in which Ḥamūd had simply denied that his sisters had any part. The judge also began to appoint the lands of each heir, but the sisters then had to abandon the lawsuit for lack of finance. When their brother continued to refuse to give them their lands, people began to urge them to grant permission for the proceeds of the land appointed as *waqf darīs* to be enjoyed by their brother (*ijāzah fī 'l-ghillah*) though not to grant him ownership of the plot until such time as he would agree to a division of all the other lands. But such an offer would surely avail them nothing now, and after all these years Karāmah and her sister were ready to give their brother almost anything so as to secure something for themselves.

As for the lands they had inherited from their mother, these were actually more important than those of their father, especially as they were in a flourishing condition. Karāmah noted that her own experience would probably be just like that of her mother: the estate in which her mother had inherited a substantial share was divided only after she had died. In the case of her mother's lands, Ḥamūd likewise

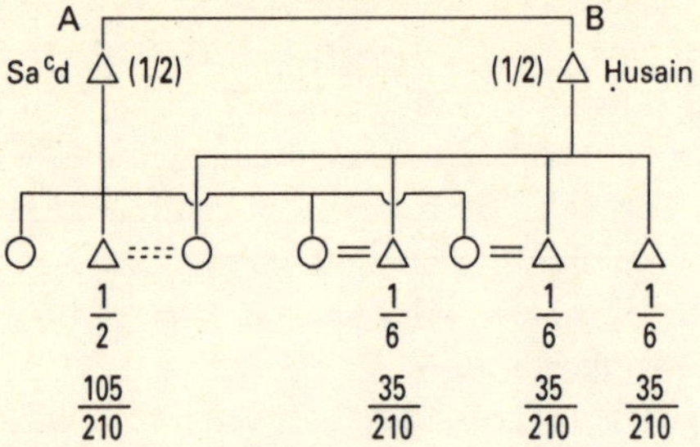

A - The patrilineal ideal, ignoring shares of women.

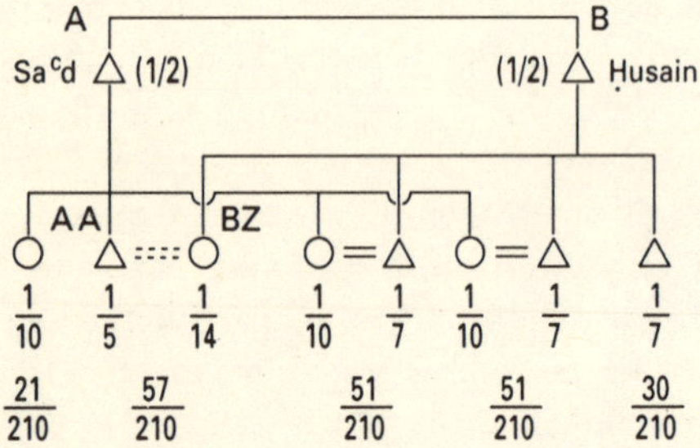

B - Stage 1, jural division with intended marriage of Ḥamūd (AA).

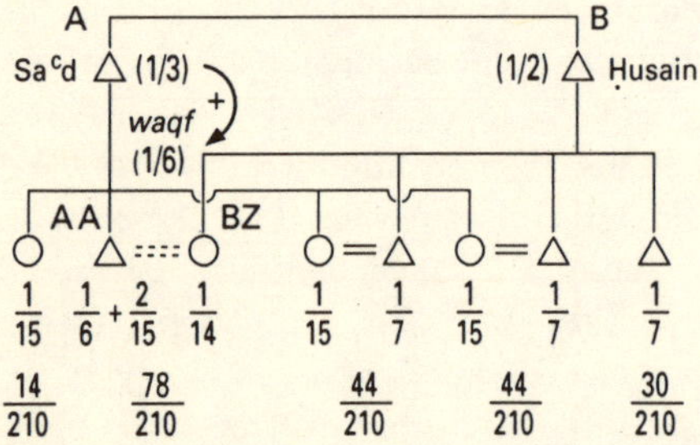

C - Stage 2, with *waqf darīs* and intended marriage of Ḥamūd.

Figure 6.8 Stages in the division of the estate of *Bait* al-Khabash

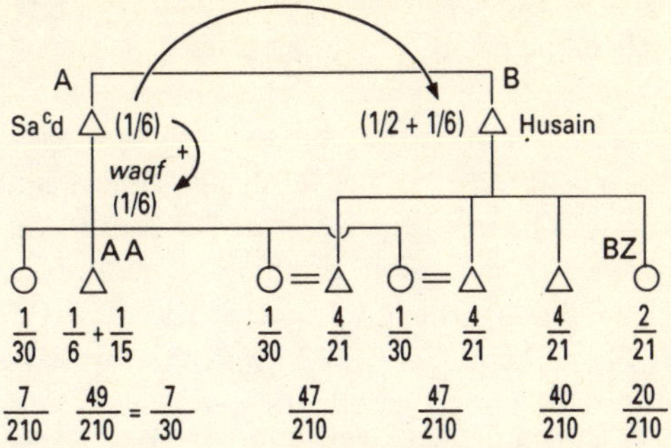

D - Stage 3, with Ḥusain's appropriation, and with Ḥamūd's intended marriage broken.

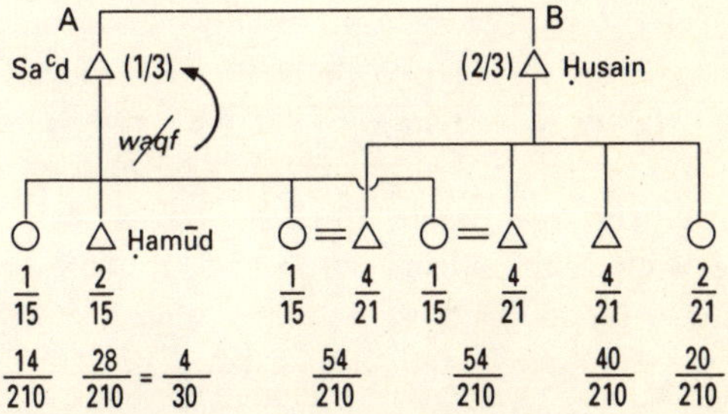

E - Stage 4, with *waqf* annulled, with Ḥusain's appropriation and with Ḥamūd's marriage broken.

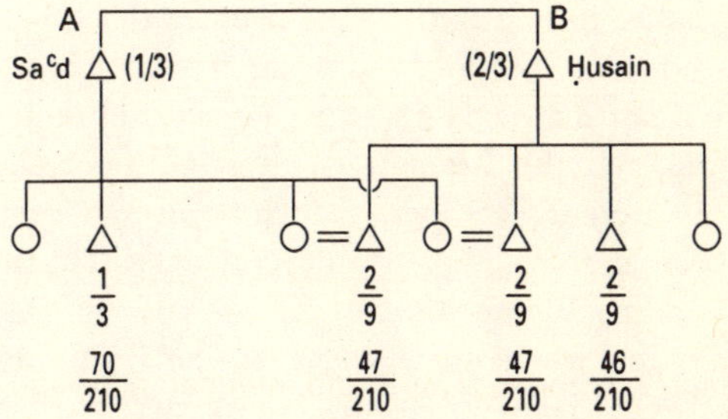

F - The resolution, in which women's shares are virtually ignored.

impeded any division. Karāmah had gained possession of two rooms in her mother's house, to which her sisters of course also had rights, simply by going to stay there. Karāmah's son already lived in one room, and she, her husband and two unmarried daughters had to move into the other after her husband's house was destroyed by floods in 1975. The one time Karāmah's son had gone out to irrigate one of the plots (appointed in principle to the women but still under Ḥamūd's cultivation) which her brother had deliberately left without irrigation, Ḥamūd had threatened his nephew with a gun. Since then the major part of her father's lands were simply neglected; in a few years they would be completely bare. Ḥamūd had declared that he did not care: when old he would rely on his son, now a student, who would some day become a government employee.

The case was exceptionally bitter, not only because, by the nature of the marriages, the sister's claims were transformed into patrilateral cousin rivalry, but because time multiplied this initial complexity. With the partial exception of the gentle husband of Karāmah, the men in the family were renowned for their stinginess, which, if not laudable, was perhaps not surprising. There were four male heirs and four female heirs to an estate which was not of the scale for them all to live as comfortably as had their fathers, children of a legal scholar who had had good relations with the central authorities and had married the daughter of the local shaikh. Even during their lifetime the fathers had considered how to favour their own children. The elder brother, Sa'd, had attempted to reserve a certain portion for his son through a *waqf darīs*, because if the *farā'iḍ* had been followed to the letter, his son would have been entitled to only two-fifths of his estate, while the two daughters married to their cousins would have taken an equal proportion, and altogether the three women would have taken the major part of the estate. The younger brother, Ḥusain, had taken a portion of Sa'd's estate (as *sa'y*) in return for caring for his children; and this he may have thought only fair when Ḥamūd wedded his mother's brother's daughter after refusing to marry his father's brother's daughter. Moreover Ḥusain had three sons, while Ḥamūd was Sa'd's only son.

Full division would inevitably entail an important loss of status and property for Ḥamūd. He was determined to avoid this. As years went by, the second generation had begun to recast marriage alignments. Karāmah's only son married the daughter of the co-wife of Ḥalīmah, the sister who had married al-ḥājj Qāsim; Ḥamūd found an

ally in Maimūnah's son Zaid, a self-righteous man with a certain degree of success first in the military and then, after studying law, in the Ministry of Education.[67] Thus, although Karāmah and Ḥalīmah had won the first round of their case, they were unable to see it to completion because by now Zaid, Ḥamūd's friend, threatened to use his influence in the government to slow up and to raise the costs of the legal battle beyond what any of them could afford. Time was not on the side of the sisters. Karāmah's husband and Ḥamūd went to court over an irrigation channel in grain lands they held back-country, and her husband and his brothers were also involved in litigation with their maternal kin over their mother's inheritance. Karāmah began to be worn down by troubles: her daughter died in childbirth at the age of fourteen and Karāmah blamed herself for having agreed to the early marriage of her daughter; her husband's house, tumble-down as it had been, was destroyed by floods of 1975 and now she faced the animosity of her maternal relatives as both she and her son shared her mother's family house with two other households. Her brother was prepared to let the women's share of the land shrivel and die; and if ever they were to obtain their land, it would be years before it could be profitable again. So Karāmah could at best laugh at the "stinginess" of *bait* al-Khabash; she spoke of her own house as though she no longer belonged to it.

In the case of *bait* al-Khabash two brothers had married women from wealthy families and had sought, through a trio of marriages between their children, to preserve all that they had, both their own land and the land that came in with their wives. However, one brother had three sons and the other only one. Considering only their own lands, and ignoring for the moment claims through the mothers, and assuming that all the in-marriages went through according to plan, the only son of the elder brother stood to inherit, even without the *waqf*, a large share of the once joint estate (Figure 6.8, B), but with the *waqf* he stood to gain more than twice as much as his cousins (Figure 6.8, C). The younger brother, Ḥusain, therefore grabbed one-third of his deceased brother's lands, a move that would have more or less equalized the share of the four cousins.[68]

At this point Ḥamūd married his mother's brother's daughter in order to consolidate his claim on his mother's estate, which had not yet been divided.[69] Ḥamūd was now cultivating all of his father's lands and was resisting their partition, while the lands of his uncle had been partitioned immediately after the uncle's death. At this

point the court threw a spanner into the works by declaring that *waqf darīs* was no longer valid without the agreement of all eligible heirs:[70] Ḥamūd saw his nominal share of seven-thirtieths drop to four-thirtieths, considerably less than the share of his three cousins (Figure 6.8, D and E). From Ḥamūd's point of view, his cousins were bitter rivals, made more so by his sisters' gradual espousal of their cause, and he resisted his sisters' efforts to effect a partition of their joint inheritance. Indeed he went further and made an alliance with one of his sister's (and cousin's) sons, in an attempt to break his sisters' resolve, something which Karāmah was clearly feeling at the time I knew her.

Figure 6.8, A through F, shows the relative shares that Ḥamūd and his three cousins in principle stood to control at the various stages of the evolving dispute. The account is idealized because it does not take account of the mothers' lands, and it gives a false clarity to the timing of the various manoeuvres. But if one considers the timing of partition on its own, as a factor that influences succession to management and so to land, a certain idealized clarity is no bad thing, in view of the complexity of actual practice. In this one story we have examples of three ways in which the timing of partition can affect succession to land. First, Ḥusain's lands were partitioned immediately after his death, in order to make sure of an unprincipled acquisition from his brother Sa'd, an act that was against Ḥamūd. Second, the postponement of the partition of Ḥamūd's mother's family estate enabled Ḥamūd to increase his claim by reactivating the alliance between the two families through marrying his mother's brother's daughter. This postponement also exemplifies the often piecemeal character of partition, whereby Karāmah was able to gain possession of two rooms in her mother's family house though she was unable to get any of the land. And third, the partition of the lands of both Ḥamūd's parents was resisted by him, not just postponed, to the extent of alienating many in the community.

House and polity Karāmah and her sisters fought their court cases against their brother before judges of Islamic law. During the latter years of the Imamate, they could go to the *ḥākim* of al-Wādī and al-Qariyah, who lived locally, but since the Republic, they have had appeal to judges in Ṣan'ā'. Local political authority, in the person of the shaikhs, appears absent from this contest. This is not because such figures uphold another tradition of law. There is no other law

for succession to property than the Islamic. Indeed, as we noted above, if a man dies without male heir, or without executor and leaving only minor heirs, the local shaikh and the *amīn* take in hand the succession. They do this, however, in the absence of, and hence in lieu of, an adult male successor and householder. In the course of a normal succession the shaikh or *amīn* may likewise represent the legal interests of a female heir when so delegated by her. But the task of the *amīn* is to provide houses of the community with the documents of Islamic legality and to advise the shaikh and local powers on points of Islamic law; it is not to act as judge.

When Ḥamūd threatened his cousin's son with a gun and when he spitefully refused to irrigate a plot in al-Qariyah, his actions became of concern to local political authority. By the first he endangered the internal peace of the community and by the second he brought dishonour on the men of al-Wādī. As we have seen, in protecting the peace the shaikh may appeal to central authority. But it is not within his authority, drawn as this is from that of the heads of households, to proceed to their undoing within their homes and properties. Only the figure of Islamic justice, as representative of a law of just patriarchy that transcends the daily examples of only too human abuse in the name of masculine preeminence, can restore right inside a house in this manner. The power of this law to restore justice even to those jural minors under the protection of a man, derives from its religious character and transcendent exteriority to the ordinary run of daily domestic negotiation.

This seeming exteriority has two rude practical concomitants. It is a justice bound up with class: in practice, the justice of the Islamic judge is costly. Judgement will almost always come down on the side of the minor heir, but the financial power to pursue this justice is rarely on the same side. Appeal to the Islamic court of the city is a way of ruining an opponent; the threat of intervention by Zaid (BBA), who had studied law and now belonged to channels of power in the city, worked to dissuade the minor heirs from further attempts to secure their rights, enforcement of a first judgement itself requiring further appeals to the court. The conceptual exteriority of the court also means that the court stands on the outside when it comes to enforcement. In the face of outright refusal by the dominant heir to honour a decision of partition, enforcement of a court decision is anything but automatic. Enforcement may prove possible only when all levels of political agency come together: the Islamic court backed

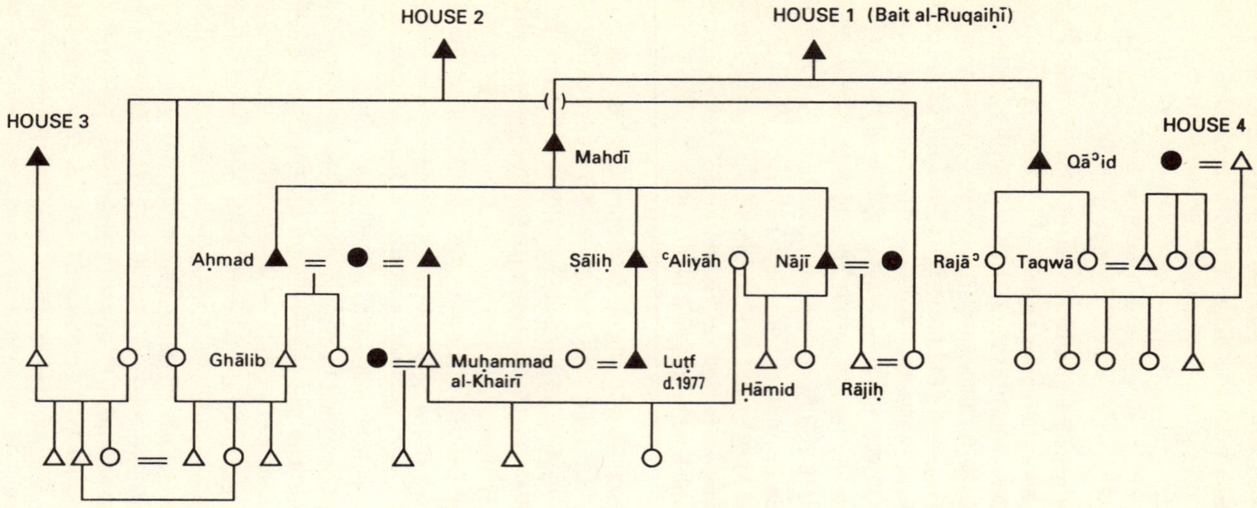

Figure 6.9 *Bait* al-Ruqaiḥī

by figures of the state, local political agency, and all the minor heirs against the dominant householder. A case where such forces began to converge was that of *bait* al-Ruqaiḥī.

SUCCESSION AND A COURT ORDER

The dominant manager of a family estate, Ghālib Aḥmad Mahdī al-Ruqaiḥī, and his first cousins (FBSs) were resisting implementation of a court order (*ḥukm*) that awarded a half-brother, Muḥammad al-Khairī, one quarter of their lands. At the time Ghālib Aḥmad (Figure 6.9) held effective control of his father's lands and of the lands of his father's brothers' sons. The background was as follows. Aḥmad Mahdī, Ghālib's father, had married a widow who brought with her a young son by her first marriage. The boy, Muḥammad al-Khairī, inherited from his father a considerable amount of land in other areas but when his mother remarried, he stayed with her. His step-father, Aḥmad Mahdī, sold most of the land when the boy was still young but many years later on his death bed he wrote a testament (*waṣīyah*) in which he bequeathed land to his wife's son in settlement of the debt.

At his death Aḥmad Mahdī left one son from Muḥammad's mother and a daughter. Nājī Mahdī, the brother of Aḥmad, died a few years later leaving a young widow, 'Alīyah. Muḥammad al-Khairī then married 'Alīyah and brought up Nājī's daughter and two sons, the elder, Rājiḥ, from Nājī's first wife, and the younger, Ḥāmid, from 'Alīyah. There was also a third brother, Ṣāliḥ Mahdī. His son Luṭf never seems to have had any control over land: in early manhood he went mad for some years, fell into debt, and sold – or, according to his wife, gave away – his land to his cousins.

All the land remained undivided and largely under the control of Ghālib Aḥmad, who had received from his father, the eldest of the brothers, the bulk of the family documents. When Muḥammad finally brought suit against Ghālib Aḥmad, Rājiḥ and Ḥāmid joined forces with Ghālib in spite of their differences. At the time Ghālib Aḥmad and his family shared the big family house with the households of Muḥammad al-Khairī and of Ḥāmid Nājī. Rājiḥ Nājī lived apart in the house of prominent Ṣan'ānīs whose land he share-cropped. Muḥammad al-Khairī's case was clear and the court eventually awarded him a quarter of the land managed as a unit by Ghālib Aḥmad. The sons of Nājī paid lip-service to the ruling, but they refrained from carrying it out; Ghālib Aḥmad and his son flatly refused to recognize the claim.

After the decision the three households continued to share the family home and to farm roughly as before, with Ghālib Aḥmad supervising the irrigation and marketing of produce. Ghālib Aḥmad refused to divide the land and feelings ran high. One day when out picking *qāt* for market, Ghālib Aḥmad and Muḥammad al-Khairī and their sons fell to shouting and hurling stones at one another. Ḥāmid called the ward head (*'āqil*), fearing lest they draw their daggers; the *'āqil* notified the shaikh, who in turn appealed to the regional shaikh to send out soldiers and lock them all up lest they kill each other. By holding them quietly in fetters for a time the shaikh hoped to have them calm down and to realize that if they did resort to violence, the aggressor would be known and could not expect to go unpunished. The political community had the sanction of banishment, and Ghālib Aḥmad al-Ruqaiḥī, wealthy, aggressive and overweening, had his enemies – among them the head of the ward ("*ḥāfat al-Ruqaiḥī*") where they lived. This man had taken in the dispossessed cousin, Luṭf Ṣāliḥ, as a labourer and continued to care for his young widow after his death. To date, however, Ghālib Aḥmad's constant threats to resort to violence allowed him to retain control of all that he held.

A second linked court case promised to increase the pressure for a division. In this the husbands of the two daughters, Rajā' and Taqwā, of Qā'id al-Ruqaiḥī opposed their cousin (FBSS), Ghālib Aḥmad, and his half-brother. The two women contended that their inheritance had passed to their father's brother and thence to his son. Ghālib Aḥmad maintained that the women's father had died in debt and that his remaining land had been sold to cover his debts. The women's husbands did not deny that their wives' father had left some debts, but noted that he had paid some of them and that land had remained after the debts had been paid off.

Both the judge (*ḥākim*) and the governor (*'āmil*) had been involved in the case. This had lasted two years before the day was fixed to survey (*ḥaṣr*) the lands mentioned in the family documents and to appoint (*ta'yīn*) the women's share on the ground. As the judge and the governor stood by the first plot, reading from the documents, the contending parties began to disagree. Each side claimed that the plot was theirs. "One word led to another and the club cracked," a witness exclaimed. "The *ḥākim*, who was slow-moving, was caught in the midst and received a harsh blow before he extricated himself. Sensing what was coming, the governor, rather more shrewdly, stepped out of the way. The disputants fell to it and were about to draw their daggers when the onlookers intervened, rushing up to pull the embattled men apart. The bystanders only stopped the brawl by pounding the disputants with clubs."

Some went to jail and others to the hospital. Muḥammad al-Khairī was badly beaten, but the others had only slight wounds. The two parties had their injuries cumulatively evaluated, and one party paid the other the difference. As for the judge and the governor, one side was to give 2,000 riyāls and a bull (as an *'aqīrah*) to the judge and the other to present the same to the governor. The fine imposed was certain to hurt the weaker party, the house into which the women were married, more than the stronger. The costs of two years of litigation already weighed heavily upon the women's in-laws. A friend lamented that they had become involved in the suit at all, to which he said they had been encouraged by the shaikhs; it would all bring them no good.

The snowballing of claims sketched above appeared likely to lead to a partial settlement between the parties; the financial cost of pursuing the conflict was beginning to mount even for the dominant figure, Ghālib Aḥmad. At the moment when Ghālib Aḥmad and his allies came to blows with his cousins' husbands, all the political figures, the Islamic and the shaikhly, the state and the local, were standing present. The networks of authority converged, and it became more difficult for Ghālib Aḥmad not to make some concession. But in a world of practical politics where the house is also a government, justice could at best take the form of only partial concessions wrested from the manager of the house by the coalescence of minor shareholders, local political leadership and state judgement.

Conclusions: juridical model, social model

If we step back from the detail, these accounts of long-term strategies and battles over property may serve to give a sense of the historicity of family among the landed of the community, of how the past is written into present relations through the skeins of claims and marriages. As the local proverb notes, houses are the tombs of people. Among those with property the cycle of exchange rests on recognition of a son's primary and a daughter's secondary rights to property in the natal home, and on the mutual claims on property established for spouses. This cycle entails a woman's endowment at marriage from both her marital home and her natal home, her continuing claim on her natal home, and the long postponement of partition until marriages of the third generation have been settled. The broad structural characteristics of family among the propertied invite such a juridical model of relations.[71]

But there are problems in such an abstraction from context. If we are to speak of a system of family built in the model of an ideal family of property, then two truths, also much emphasized in these pages, vanish from sight. The first is the irreducibility of the family structures of those without property to this model: among the poor the cycle of advancement and restitution concern the products of immediate labour. Such cycles are far shorter and built rather more harshly on direct exchanges. The second point concerns the limits of a juridical model for understanding the cycles of family, even among the propertied. Our case histories have revealed the variety of individual experience. A social analysis cannot, for that, be a catalogue of all the possible variations that the meeting of demography, production, property, and personality produce. It must rest on a representation of patterns as a whole, their statistical panoply so to speak. We have attempted this for household forms. Were such data available it would be possible to analyse statistically all the sets of heirs and the model types of succession within the population of households as a whole. In the absence of central registration of all civil and property transactions, such reconstruction remains an elusive prospect and we are reduced to the typologies suggested by our case histories. As we have seen, moreover, a statistical morphological analysis of the systems of devolution would make little sense without its simultaneous incorporation of the recombination of right effected through marriage. For, as every case history has revealed, it is in the nature of partible inheritance that what is divided through descent is reassembled through marriage, in conservative but different combinations. In closing, then, let us consider the patterns of marital alliance at the level of local society as a whole.

7

Alliance: house, community and polity

When a man marries, a bond is tied between two groups, because a man inherits from his wife and a woman inherits from her husband and the family relations become entwined. This is laid down in the book of God, praise be to Him.[1]

Anonymous, *Kitāb al-man'ah*, fo. 54a.

Introduction

Studies of domestic organization, kinship and alliance among European peasants have long been conducted according to a "native theory" that has its roots in comparative law.[2] This theory explains differences in systems of domestic organization and alliance by reference to the local legal norms governing the devolution of peasant property rights. One recent comparative study based on this literature proposes a typology of alliance systems according to the form of succession (to management) and of inheritance (of property) in the parental estate. It argues that in those systems where rights of both succession and inheritance are partible, alliance is characterized by a number of "marriages between cousins at the centre of large groups of kin".[3] It is within this larger group that the principal recombination of properties occurs from generation to generation. Were the community we are studying a village in Europe, its legal traditions would no doubt be classed under this rubric.

Historical scholarship on Europe has gone beyond such juridical models[4] and general typologies to document patterns of alliance over many generations[5] and to demonstrate change in domestic and alliance systems in a single village according to movements in production, demography, legal construction of property, and state administration of the village and domestic domain.[6] But the fundamental terms of analysis have not changed dramatically.

This European tradition for the study of peasant kinship and domestic systems has remained largely impervious to what anthropology has proposed as universal theory for kinship, notably comparative study of kinship terminology and structuralist analysis of kinship. For example, in a recent encounter between what we may call a "Europeanist" and structuralist theory, Lamaison queries the utility, for an understanding of European family systems, of the typology of alliance proposed by structuralist theorists, notably the unitary character of "complex systems" of kinship. This term, deriving from the work of Lévi-Strauss,[7] groups together marital systems defined not by positive preference or prescription but by prohibition of marriage with certain categories of kin.[8] In other words, the tradition analyses marriage, even in "complex systems", in terms of a typology of exchange and "loops" defined in genealogical space.[9] By contrast, Lamaison gives priority to economic and political criteria for identification of the social units of alliance and of the relevant sets of marital partners. This leads him to stress historical change in marriage systems which he finds obscured by the notion of a unified field of "complex" systems of alliance.[10] Far from "universalist" anthropological theories taking over the Europeanists, the latter's "native theory" focusing on "property complexes" has won adherents who have attempted, in turn, to analyse kinship systems elsewhere in terms of systems of property and devolution.[11] And, likewise, as a tradition with common roots in Europe's "native theory" of comparative law, Marxism too has often been hostile to the formalism (and biologism) of terminological kinship analysis.[12]

The situation appears a little different in studies of kinship and domestic organization in Arab societies. Here the "universalist" anthropological theories have had a better reception. And the "native theory" in question has been of another kind. During the years when comparative analysis of kinship terminologies dominated anthropological study of kinship, ethnographers seemed to hear the subjects of their investigation, nomads and villagers, single out one genealogical figure in their accounts of marriage, that of patrilineal parallel cousin marriage.[13] Certain Arab rural groups clearly valued the practice, presenting it as a preference or even, at times, as a duty.[14] Anthropologists analysed Arab marriage as constructed around a core of "father's brother's daughter" marriage, classificatory or actual.[15] The focus upon FBD marriage was eventually brought into question, in part under the pressure of structuralism, by the simple observation that interpretation of the alliance system could not be confined to one figure in genealogical space but had to embrace the totality of alliance patterns.[16]

A subsequent important attempt at interpretation grew out of a dialogue between structuralist theory and the local political discourse of kinship. There were three chords in local (that of the Algerian Kabyle) discourse which found an echo: first, a sense of categorical compulsion governing kinship and alliance, a theme where the structuralists rejoined the literature on honour;[17] second, the fundamental cognitive and structural divide represented in gender, with the discourse of kinship and alliance differing between men and women; and third, status, not property, as the proper idiom for interpretation of alliance.[18] Thus for Bourdieu, the "native theory" with which the Western ethnographer should open a conversation was local oral tradition. But as the recent work of Bonte and Conte demonstrates, an ethnographer so disposed can also expand the "dialogue" to take in the written tradition of Arab genealogists.[19]

In recent years the internal coherence and the boundaries of the construct "Arab kinship" have appeared increasingly problematical. At issue is not the evident fact that Arabic imparts a common expression to kinship relationships: there is a shared core set of kin terms[20] and a general idiom designating relationship – "*qarābah*" – which implies "closeness" rather than "flesh and blood". But, just as in historical Europe, so across the time and breadth of Arab societies, both the social units engaged in making marital alliances and the patterns in genealogical space of those alliances have differed markedly.[21] Once such variation among Arab populations is taken into account, their traditions often appear less clearly differentiated from those of their neighbours. Anthropologists and historians have explored the common aspects of family systems about the Mediterranean. But how are these defined? Broadly indeed: for Tillion the Mediterranean was the cradle of ancient class society and for Peristiany of the ethos of honour.[22] Others have stressed the common traditions of "Middle Eastern" peoples. D. Eickelman, for example, has argued that ethnography of Arab groups does not reveal the uniform presence of the anthropologist's structures of "Arab kinship", notably patrilineal lineages and a preference for, if not a rule of, classificatory FBD marriage.[23] All that is common, he argues, is far more general: a tendency to "close" marriage, the capacity to transform, by marital alliance, purely social bonds into "kinship", and the resulting ambiguous "practical" kinship which confounds descent, alliance and intense social links in a single idiom of "closeness". Once stated at this level of generality – as a way of speaking not a structure – "Arab" kinship disappears into the wider category of "Middle Eastern".

Not all anthropologists who have taken the Middle East as their framework for generalization appear as confident as Eickelman of the coherence of patterns of kinship and alliance within this geographical compass. R. and N. Tapper, writing from an anthropological tradition which gives more place to the notion of structure than does Eickelman's Geertzian cultural transactionalism, suggest the following caveats.[24] First, there are principles of inheritance and marital prohibitions common to all Muslims which can hardly be considered as specifically Arab or Middle Eastern, unless we confuse origin with contemporary jural norm. Second, "lineage endogamy" and parallel cousin marriage are not confined to the Middle East. And, lastly, within the region, there are major differences between marital regimes, in terms of the stability of unions, the responsibility for a married women assumed by her husband or vested in her kin, and the importance of patrilineal parallel cousin marriage as against marriage to other cousins. If the Arabs, in general, tend more than their northern neighbours to identify a married woman with her natal kin, to permit divorce, and to prefer FBD over other cousin marriage, there is also evidence of great variation among Arab populations.[25]

Finally we may consider the recent reading by P. Bonte, the most rigorously analytical and, perhaps for that, the most internally contradictory.[26] Writing in the vocabulary of Lévi-Strauss, Bonte juxtaposes a series of studies defined as Mediterranean and yet doubts the coherence of this geographical frame.[27] The theme of his collection is "close marriage",[28] but Bonte comes to ask whether the study of genealogically close marriage raises questions any different from those encountered in the analysis of any "complex" system of kinship.[29] Here affinity represents not so much "exchange" between two distinct groups as the very mode of constructing identity within an affinal group. Bonte treats "Arab kinship" as a sub-type of systems of "close marriage", but in recognition of the formal, as opposed to the descriptive, character of his model, he rightly places it within quotation marks. In his analysis of "Arab kinship" he draws not only upon the oral tradition of the groups with which he is familiar but also on the high written "native theory" of Islamic *fiqh*. *Fiqh*, unlike the European tradition of comparative law, is a radically nomothetic tradition. Thus, all that Bonte can extract of a sociological nature from this tradition is its legal prescription of marriage equality, *kafā'ah*.[30] Women should be married to their equals. The question implicit in this formulation – equals in *what* domain? – is a topic much discussed by the legal scholars and one that inevitably invites consideration of the concrete factors structuring alliance (and the social units intermarrying) in historical cases. But faithful to his quest for a formal model, Bonte does not follow this lead.

In the rest of this chapter we shall do just the opposite, treating affinity not as an abstract sign nor as an idiom defined within a closed sphere of "kinship" but as alliance in a world that is material and political as well as cultural. We shall take seriously the criteria which Yemeni legal scholars consider to establish "equality" – "identity" in some sense – at marriage: status, reputation and wealth. Geographical proximity is also discussed by the jurists, not under the rubric of *kafā'ah* but as a condition admissible in a marriage contract. Of all the components of "equality" the scholars give most attention to wealth, since the duties a husband may ask of his wife and the standard of maintenance he owes her vary according to his wealth. In this limited sense, the jurists' terms coincide with the attention given to property in European discourse of comparative law. By giving a central place to property in our discussion of alliance, we certainly cannot be said to be unfaithful to the "native" written tradition.

The question to be explored is how affinity creates and recreates the social and material structures in the community under study. The men and women making these choices share much with others: with other Yemenis, a concern with status rank; with other Arabs, a common language; with other Muslims, a legal tradition;[31] with other peasant societies, strategies to ensure the cultivation and devolution of land within families; and with men and women in other class societies, an understanding that the status of families passes through both daughters and sons. Our object will be to analyse the structures of marital alliance of a community which belongs to all of these worlds at once; it is not to argue, in the kind of exercise of boundary definition reviewed above, for a definition of the particular pattern according to its "affinity" with only one of these categories of "kindred".

Alliance: politics and economy

Marital alliances, the links between houses, are drawn in a space both political and economic. In order to explore how alliance is structured by, and in turn structures, this space, we shall need first to identify the patterns of affinity according to single principles. In fact, spouses are never so singly defined, but possess at one and the same time a status, a site of residence, an occupation, a certain property, and a place in a family. But in analysis we need first to trace the patterns of alliance according to single vectors, and to restricted combinations of the same, if we are to sense how, at the level of a population, alliance creates systematic form. Then we can proceed to consider the complex bundle of criteria which define social status for any one person, and the manner that making a match may sometimes require pairing not identical rank on all scales but a high rank on one scale with a low one on another. Finally, then, we shall be able to relate these patterns in political and economic space to the figures of alliance recognizable in terms of genealogy.

Status and alliance

As we have seen,[32] status categories were not simply reducible to occupation, but represented the political institutionalization and idealization of a division of labour.[33] In the Imamic state, status categories enjoyed an ideological legitimacy which masked the often imperfect correspondence of status distinctions and the division of labour at the level of local communities. Zaidī jurists considered status as an important factor in marital equality, although they did not go so far as to judge a difference in status between spouses a legal bar to marriage.[34] The revolution of 1962 undertook to erase such distinctions from law and the state, although not, as subsequently in the People's Democratic Republic of Yemen, forcibly also from local society.

In Ḍahr, as in most of the Yemeni countryside, the majority of men and women consider themselves *qabā'il* (or, as it is sometimes put, *'arab*). Other status groups are thus much smaller in size. The statuses also differ in the degree to which they are thought to be a matter purely of descent. One category, that of "*qāḍī*", always had more of an acquired character than the others. Under the Imamic regime, the *qāḍī* house was one distinguished by learning and exempted from the common contributions paid by local agriculturalists (*qabā'il*); the structures of learning and the *hijrahs* of the major *qāḍī* families were akin to those of the great *sayyid* houses. But, unlike the status of the *sayyid* which can be conceived purely as a matter of

Table 7.1 Status of wife by status of husband

Wife's status	Husband's status *sayyid*	*qabīlī*	*muzayyin*	*qāḍī*	Total	
sayyid	7	1	–	–	8	(2%)
qabīlī	1	287	1	3	292	(89%)
muzayyin	–	–	19	–	19	(6%)
qāḍī	–	6	–	5	11	(3%)
Total	3%	89%	6%	2%		100%
	8	294	20	8		n=330

descent – women tell tales of how almsgiving to an indigent *sharīfah* brings magical benefit to the benefactor – the *quḍāh* remained learned commoners at heart.

If we examine marriage patterns according to status categories, we find that in no group are marriages completely closed (Table 7.1). But whereas the marriages of *qāḍī* families appear quite open, marriages linking persons of *sayyid* or *muzayyin* status to those of different categories remain exceptional. In general the marriages between two *qāḍī* families match those of literate tradition and occupation, whereas those joining local *qāḍī* and *qabīlī* families are alliances of farmers, whatever the name or learned ancestors of the former. The acquired character of the distinction means that little is lost if women of these families marry men of good farming families.

The *sādah* claim descent from the Prophet: this absolute distinction invites preservation by marriage. But marriages are made by families that also have their place in economic space. In economic terms local *sayyid* households differ: the two established families of the community are farmers with a tradition of literacy, the others are landless market folk. Any departure from status in-marriage among the first group has a political as well an economic character; among the second it is more likely to reflect the economic context of the marriage market. The marriages of the two local landed *sayyid* houses stand out from those of other farmers primarily in that they have married women from al-Qariyah, a centre of *sayyid* families (Table 7.3). In the older generation, Amat al-Laṭīf, a woman of the more prominent of the two local families, had first been married to a man of the Imamic family itself. Although she bore her first husband a son, the marriage lasted only a few years and she subsequently remarried her deceased sister's widower, a relatively poor man of the second landowning *sayyid* house of the community. Amat al-Laṭīf's daughter married her mother's brother's son, but the marriage ended in divorce.

In recent years, both *sayyid* families have arranged marriages more in line with their respective economic status in the community. Amat al-Laṭīf's stepson, her sister's son, married the handsome sister of an agricultural worker from al-Maḥwīt. Amiable but unambitious, this only son never learned to read, unlike his father, and worked as a guard on Dār al-Ḥajar. In the early 1970s, Amat al-Laṭīf's brother, the most prominent *sayyid* of the community and head of the market ward, gave his daughter to a *qabīlī* landowning family.[35] From the start the girl refused her husband's advances and the marriage was quickly dissolved, but some years later she was married a second time, and more happily, to a man of another prominent *qabīlī* farming family. These marriages have the stamp of a positive strategy on the part of her father, the senior man of the family, who has made his life in farming, legal services and local politics.

At the time of the national census in 1975, the daughter of this man was living at home, divorced from her first husband. The marriage between a *sayyidah* and a *qabīlī* that appears in Table 7.1 belonged to a *sharīfah* of more humble economic status.[36] A poor woman, orphaned as a child, Kādhiyah had moved to Ḍahr with her husband, a soldier posted for a while to Dār al-Ḥajar. A *qabīlī* from a poor north-eastern area, he was Kādhiyah's fifth husband and more than ten years younger than his wife. After he was transferred out of al-Wādī, he came to see Kādhiyah only on leave. She described him as kind but lamented that on his departure she found herself out of pocket. Kādhiyah supported herself by exchanging small amounts of produce and herbs, obtained from women of the community for clothing given her in Ṣan'ā' by the secluded women of trading families from her natal area of al-Bayḍā'. It was only a matter of time before her husband saved enough to marry a younger wife. Kādhiyah cultivated her ties with the wives of merchants in the hope that they might ensure her livelihood in the years to come. For Kādhiyah, the utter absence of family meant that her status had never opened out a network for marriage. Time and again she had married as best she could, according to the harsh rule of the economy. Backed by her wit, her elevated birthright might at best serve to open the doors of genteel trade and service in the homes of wealthy women.

Whereas after the revolution of 1962 a *sayyid* family might magnanimously deign to disregard former tradition, the *muzayyin* inherited a far more difficult legacy. The only marriage linking a boy of *muzayyin* origin to a girl of a "higher" status joined a labourer, son of a local butcher, to the sister of a friend from Lower Yemen with whom he worked in a laundry in Saudi Arabia. The pair did not reside in the community but had stayed there for a few weeks following their marriage in 1975, before leaving for Saudi Arabia. In an obvious sense, then, this alliance belongs to the new economy of oil revenue. Most *mazāyinah* of the community, however, still worked in crafts and market occupations. Their small numbers required marriage networks outside the community, with families of similar status in al-Qariyah, Ṣan'ā' and villages of Hamdān; in spatial terms these networks reflect their place in the market systems of the pre-oil economy. Thus, whereas 95 per cent of the men in *muzayyin* households were born in the community, 85 per cent of their wives came from elsewhere.

The political basis of status-rank came to an end with the Imamate; its economic basis was likewise being transformed by the flow of oil revenue throughout the peninsula. Marriage alliance is a conservative domain. But even here fissures reveal the underlying politico-economic context of alliance. Thus, if we examine the spatial distribution of marriage not by status but by occupation and landholding, we find that the out-marriages of the *sādah* and the *mazāyinah* belong also to more general patterns of an economic and political nature.

Spatial patterns

As Skinner and others have observed, spatial patterns of marriage are in themselves eloquent of fundamental economic and political structures.[37] It has been suggested that the social radius within which 80 per cent of marriages are contracted may represent a primary political and economic unit. Thus, in Skinner's studies of early modern China, it was the series of satellite villages about a market town which were the critical zone of connubium. In the case at hand, given the political importance of the local community and its construction from the households of landowning agriculturalists, we will perhaps not be surprised by two observations: first, among landed farming families

Table 7.2 Birthplace of married women whose husbands were born inside Wadi Ḍahr according to economic group of husband (per cent)

	Born inside area	Born outside area	Total	
Landless workers	52	48	100 6	(n=23)
Landed farmers	81	19	100 76	(n=290)
Lower specialists	24	76	100 8	(n=29)
Upper specialists	49	51	100 10	(n=39)
Total	72 n=273	28 n=108	100 n=381	

almost 80 per cent of all marriages were made with other families of Ḍahr, and second, whereas landed agriculturalists favour such spatial proximity, families of other occupations have adopted a much more open orientation in the marriage of their children.

Underlying the spatial patterns of alliance are two factors: land and occupation. We have already noted the importance of these factors for the mobility of men (see Table A.19). They appear equally central in determining the mobility of women at marriage (Table A.20). At issue is not simply difference in the husband's history, since if we consider the unions only of men born in the community, the different patterns of alliance appear even more contrasted (Table 7.2).[38] The landowning farmers stand at one pole and the "lower" specialists at the other. Both the landless agricultural workers, based in farming but without land, and the "upper" specialists, many of whom own a little land but all of whom make their living from dealings in wider networks, fall closer to the centre.[39]

The small group of specialists, here divided only into upper and lower, are not as uniform as it might appear. The marital patterns of men long established in market services, shopkeeping, trading, crafts, or the service of the central government differ from those of men more closely integrated with local farming, for example, drivers who run cars in and out of the capital, with close relatives all in farming (see Table A.21). The first group tend to marry women from outside, regardless of whether or not they own land. Of these, the marriage patterns of those in government employment and in market services differ from all others: among them, men of families with land are more likely to marry women from outside than men without any land. If in the case of the *mazāyinah* working in market and service occupations, a humble status also obliges them to search for wives outside, this is not so for specialists of other statuses. Economic and occupational networks are at stake here.

For agriculturalists the community is the stage on which men act. Their marriage patterns reflect the political centrality of the local community, whereas affinal relations outside do not appear to reflect wider political structures but simply the social links of particular families.[40] Among landowning farming households, backbone of the political community, only two-fifths of the wives from outside come from Bait Naʻam or other villages of Hamdān. The others come from Ṣanʻā' (12 per cent), the villages of Banī 'l-Maṭar (22 per cent), Banī 'l-Ḥārith (12 per cent), or areas further afield (14 per cent).[41] In short, unlike marriage within the local community, marriage within the "tribe" Hamdān does not exhibit a clear political logic. Thus, Banī 'l-Maṭar and Banī 'l-Ḥārith belong to Bakīl, the "opposing" alliance system, and Ṣanʻā' does not belong to the "tribes" at all. This structure of connubium appears congruent with the "administrative" character of the "tribe" and the primacy of the local community in daily political life.

It also corresponds to an interest in land rights. Among agriculturalists, not only do those who own land tend to marry within the community, the more land they hold, the more they do so (Table 7.3).[42] The spatial pattern of alliance within is eloquent of such strategies. Poorer agricultural households often take wives from outside (and generally from villages less wealthy than the community). When they make marriages within the community, they tend to do so with families nearby in the same ward or with relatives in the same house. More prosperous farming families marry far less with communities outside, but at home their alliances extend across the length and breadth of the community. In terms of the local polity, the alliances of the poorer agriculturalist families are forged primarily with relatives or neighbours close by them, or else outside the community altogether, encysted, or excluded, respectively. By contrast the marriage networks of the wealthy families criss-cross the local polity, as it were, encircling it (see Tables 7.3 and A.22).

Table 7.3 Place of wife's home according to landholding of husband's household among all agriculturalists (per cent)

Wife's home	Quintile rank of household landholding					
	First	Second	Third	Fourth	Fifth	Total
In home	2	11	9	3	6	6 n=20
In same ward	18	30	19	24	24	23 n=80
In next ward	2	13	17	24	25	19 n=64
al-Wādī	9	11	24	26	34	23 n=80
(Subtotal)	(31)	(65)	(69)	(77)	(89)	(71) (n=244)
Bait Na'am	4	7	2	3	1	3 n=10
al-Qariyah	0	0	8	1	0	2 n=6
Elsewhere	65	28	21	19	10	24 n=82
Total	100 13 n=45	100 16 n=54	100 17 n=58	100 23 n=78	100 31 n=107	100 100 n=342

Land and marriage

On hearing of an exchange marriage proposed between the children of two wealthy brothers (in which one of the sons was still a child and much smaller than the buxom cousin chosen as his wife) an outsider, the wife of the *amīn*, exclaimed: "They don't marry girls, they marry fields." The principle which she deplored holds true only in a general, statistical sense. Families do, of course, marry girls: in the case of the proposed exchange, the plans eventually had to be abandoned. A strong character with a raucous voice, the older sister of the younger brother declared that she did not want the cousin proposed; and doubtless her female cousin was little enchanted at the prospect of taking a child as a husband. Only some years later were the older sister and younger brother betrothed, again to a pair of siblings, from a neighbouring and suitably wealthy, but unrelated, house.[43]

As we have seen, land in the community is scarce and valuable; it passes to (and through) women by inheritance. Thus we will not be surprised to find that marriage strategies respect "equality" – and thereby work to perpetuate "inequality" – in rights to land. In general the landholdings of spouses and families intermarrying are strongly correlated statistically.[44] Such correlations concern only land in the community. It is difficult to judge the economic importance of claims on land elsewhere enjoyed by women married in from elsewhere. Certainly, if we consider all women married in from outside as having no claim on land in the community,[45] the correlation between the respective landholdings of spouses' families is stronger than if we consider only the land of women born in the community.[46] This reflects the simple fact that the proportion of wives from outside is much higher among small farmers.

Such general correlation is not incompatible with large differences in the wealth of intermarrying families in some cases (see Figures B.4 and B.5). In any marriage the parties concerned consider not only land but also labour needs, proximity, personal qualities and prior family relationship. But overall, the distribution of land through men or through their wives proves statistically much alike (see Tables A.23 and A.24). As we saw earlier in spatial terms, the landowning households of agriculturalists form a semi-closed set for marriage. From the point of view of both men – where a local woman can transmit valuable land and extend a man's local network of relations – and women – where proximity to natal family is regarded as protection against abuse and insurance of a place in women's society – the first choice is to marry a spouse from the community. Marriage of equals is the norm, but as we noted in Chapter 5, there is also some hypergamy as women collect through marriage in the households of the wealthy (see Figures B.4 and B.5 and Table 7.5).[47]

In terms of land rights the broad contours of alliance are clear. But the relations of kinship in which these are woven remain to be examined.

Kinship and the circles of marriage

Local terms of alliance

Marriage with a cousin, particularly a patrilateral parallel cousin, is a common enough occurrence in the community under study (see Table A.25). It is not, however, a practice lauded or pronounced in the form of a rule by people of the area.[48] Nor is the term for patrilateral parallel cousin (*ibn/bint al-'amm*) extended in a classificatory sense to a wider set of preferred prospective spouses. In the women's wedding songs, the marriage celebrated is one to an outsider; the bride reproaches her father and male agnates for having accepted the suitor and letting her leave home; only in this indirect manner do the songs allude to agnatic right (and duty) with regard to a girl's marriage.

With similar irony, at the end of a long talk about her life and land, Karāmah (whose inheritance dispute was described in the last chapter) bade me to convey the following advice to women abroad: never marry a father's brother's son. Karāmah regarded me as a potential publicist of her case; her family, although too numerous for their modest landholding, had a tradition of literacy, and in a rather idealistic way she saw a place for the written word. She was making a structural point, not complaining about her husband, of whom she was quite fond. But, with a gleam in her eye, Karāmah recalled that many years ago, before her father died, he had summoned her to say that her future was secure: he had betrothed her to his brother's son. They would care for her, he had said. Now, after a lifetime bound into relentless conflicts over the same few fields, Karāmah smiled wryly at the men of her family.

'Ā'ishah, whose landowning mother, Hā'ilah, we also met in the last chapter, similarly deplored the tangle of family relations within which her own marriage was embedded – *zawāj al-ṣudaqā'*, "marrying close friends of the family". Her marriage was not with a cousin: rather 'Ā'ishah's mother-in-law was her mother's cousin; her husband's sister was married to her mother-in-law's brother's son, himself the son of the co-wife of her mother's sister (see Figure 6.1). 'Ā'ishah had quarrelled with her mother-in-law and, after many battles, secured the move of her husband and family to one of her mother's two houses. She had cause for jealousy: her sister-in-law had married the only son of 'Ā'ishah's mother's cousin, Shaikh Manṣūr, whereas 'Ā'ishah herself had married one of four brothers. In spite of her mother-in-law's pretensions, her husband's family's land did not allow for the standard of living she had been used to at home. The two marriages formed an exchange of sorts, but one in which her sister-in-law had fared far better than she had.

The *ṣudaqā'* embrace all close relations of the family, such as the men who give a gift at the *'īd* to one or another of the women of the household. As 'Ā'ishah's words indicate, repeated cross-cutting ties combining affinity and descent are not restricted to those related patrilineally. Whereas for Karāmah the burden of past relations corresponded to the weight of a joint patrimony and contested succession, for 'Ā'ishah the mesh of marriages joined those with claims on what were still quite separate estates. In both cases the repetition of marriage promised the subsequent reunion, so-to-speak, of lands divided earlier. By contrast, marriage with an outsider, *zawāj al-mukhrijī*, leads out of the net of close ties, of claims and counterclaims to – in 'Ā'ishah's imagination at least – a place without encumbrance, where marriage should prove smooth. 'Ā'ishah had as models her elder sister's successful marriage to a prosperous shaikh of the neighbouring community and her parents' marriage, where her father had moved in to help farm the land. When she spoke of her own marriage, the contrast between insider and outsider was thus more a matter of redoubled affinity than of common descent.

The two are not always sharply distinguished. For example, during a wedding gathering I asked my hostess about one of the other guests. The woman was known as *bint* al-Shaqīf; I enquired as to whether her husband was of *bait* al-Shaqīf or of *bait* al-Dau'ānī, the two houses being close by one another. "*Min-hum, fī-hum*" ("from among them") came the answer. "Of which house?" I repeated. My hostess noted that she was not certain just who the woman's husband was, but that it was all the same since the two houses were one, just with different names. I subsequently asked the *amīn* about the two. No, he said firmly, they were two houses: it was just that they intermarry (*yatanāsabūn*).

These anecdotes tell of the tendency to repeated links by marriage, both within a patronymic group and between those with different patronyms. As the response concerning the marriage of *bint* al-Shaqīf reveals, affinity marks identity, although in a more open manner in women's speech than in that of men.[49] If one asks a woman whether she is related to her husband, she may point to a common point in an ascendant generation, to a double relationship of affinity in the present, or simply to a common home settlement. Such categories may overlap, but all (and not simply descent) are considered relevant in judging the degree of "closeness" (*qarābah*) between spouses.[50] For example, marriage to a mother's brother's son may also be seen as inter-generational exchange or return marriage: the mother was married into the girl's father's house and the girl returns to her mother's natal house. Or descent and spatial location may be stressed:

a woman married to a father's brother's son may describe the marriage as "*fī 'l-bait*" – "at home". Women stress active links, and rarely detail relations beyond second cousins; indeed when the relation with a spouse is any more distant than a first cousin, they often simply mention a relationship as being through the father (or through the mother) with little effort to trace the details of the genealogical connections. This vocabulary, which stresses affinity and proximity and tends to forget distant relations in past generations, corresponds, after all, to the fundamental units of alliance in the community: houses rather than lineages.

The frequency of "close marriage"

Local men and women distinguish three forms of alliance where a kin link is redoubled by alliance: marriages of related women to related men (which we shall call "crony" marriage), exchange marriage, and marriage to consanguineous relatives.[51] All of these forms of alliance appear with considerable frequency in two surveys, the first compiled from the 1975 census and the second, my own smaller survey of 1977. Over one in ten women has a close female relative also married into her husband's household. Many households (about 40 per cent) contain only one married woman. If we consider only households with two or more married or widowed women, we find that almost one in five women has a female relative married in the household. Marriages of closely related women into a house may well entail considerable restructuring of identity and property. The household of the most prosperous shopkeeper of the community took this principle quite far. The shopkeeper had settled in the community but found a wife for his eldest son from his home town. After his first wife died, he himself married his daughter-in-law's mother, by then herself a widow, and took the rest of her three children under his wing. And, later, he married the second daughter of his wife to his second son. The marriages flourished and the trader built a large house where all lived together. In this case, the repeated marriages of related women marked the merging of two households into one.

Over one in ten women married in an exchange marriage. This figure includes brother/sister exchange marriages and roughly contemporaneous exchanges involving widowed parents (or step-parents) and their children, but not long-term intergenerational cycles of exchange such as when a girl marries a cross-cousin. And in about half of these exchange marriages the spouses were in fact also related through consanguineous links in an ascendant generation.

These two forms of redoubled link are striking and often dovetail with the frequent marriages between relatives with a common ascendant. About one woman in five was married to a first cousin and about one in ten to a more distantly related man. Relationship through the father generally has precedence in speech over relationship through the mother, but even allowing for the ties through women hidden by a patrilineal idiom, it is also more frequent: thus in about one out of four marriages, spouses reported relationship through the father and in about one in eight, through the mother (see Table A.25).

Taken together, in almost half of all marriages a woman has a double link to her spouse: through recognized consanguineous relation, "exchange" marriage, or marriage of a close female relative in the same household. And in about a fifth of these, or a tenth of all marriages, spouses can be said to be triply linked, as when four cousins were married in exchange or "crony" marriages.

Economy and "close" marriage

Marriage along established paths of kinship and prior affinity plays a part in constructing identity at all levels of society. As we have seen, marriage to those deemed "close" customarily entails lower payments than does marriage to an outsider, where the payment may serve as an ostentatious pledge toward the value of the new relation, or a hedge against risk in the case of divorce, or, in hypergamous marriages, the price that an outsider must pay to take a girl away from her home and from her parents. Marriage reuniting what was once joined is thus, among the poor, the most economical form of marriage and, among the rich, a reaffirmation of identity and of common property. For both it is a conservative strategy, but one rather more central to the rich than to the poor.

There is some evidence that this is so statistically. Although the samples of the two surveys are of limited size, their results, when viewed together, suggest certain regularities. Both reveal higher rates of kin marriage among landed farmers than landless agriculturalists or specialists. The census survey indicates that landed farmers marry kin more frequently than the other occupational groups taken together: 37 per cent of all marriages among the former linked kin, as against 27 per cent among the latter (see Table A.26).[52] And a similar

Table 7.4 Proportion of women married to a relative grouped according to occupation of husband (smaller sample: first marriages only) (per cent)

Relationship of husband	Landed farmers	Landless labourers	Lower specialists	Upper specialists	Total
No relation	57	82	65	71	66 n=67
Some kin relation	43	18	35	29	34 n=34
Total	100 n=42	100 n=22	100 n=23	100 n=14	100 n=101

Note: The difference in the percentages in this table and those in the second column of Table A.25 in Appendix 4 results from the latter being based on a weighting of the same data.

result appears from the smaller survey (Table 7.4). In both the surveys, however, the "lower specialists" appear to have higher rates of kin marriage than do more wealthy specialists: the closed marriage circle of the *mazāyinah* presumably plays its part here.

The data on exchange marriage derived from the census suffer from similar limitations, but if taken as indicative of half of the population rather than predictive for the whole, they reveal two trends. Here again landed farmers appear to make exchange marriages more often than other occupational groups. Of the other groups, we find that the "upper" specialists appear to favour exchange marriage over kin marriage as they move to forge contemporary bonds with other households rather than continue in established paths of kinship (see Table A.27).

Landed farmers form a semi-closed set for marriage and, as we have seen, they tend to make marriages with families of like wealth. Given the desire of more wealthy families to conserve what they already possess, we will not be surprised to find that the families with the most land also have the highest rates of consanguineous marriage (compare Table A.28 and A.29).[53] The alliances of prosperous agriculturalists appear to be built about a choice of "in-marriage" or marriage from similarly wealthy houses anywhere in the community. It is striking, moreover, that both exchange and "crony" marriage also peak among the wealthy farmers (see Tables A.30, A.31 and A.32).

It follows from the semi-closed nature of marriage networks among landowning farmers that there be a second, smaller peak of close marriage among the poorer households of the set. In spatial terms these households either take wives from other communities or tend to marry very close to home, since the men of such households rarely succeed in marrying women from more wealthy landed households of the community. And so, indeed, we find evidence of a smaller second peak, in consanguineous kin marriage,[54] in exchange marriage, and in "crony" marriage, among the lowest-ranking landowning farmers.

There are two central characteristics to the marriages with kin. First, marriages to patrilateral relatives are more frequent than marriages to matrilateral relatives. Second, first-cousin marriages outnumber marriages described as being to more distant kin.[55] In the community as a whole, although wider networks of kin, notably the patronymic house, can be relevant, the children of siblings represent the most important circle of kin in marriage. Both of these characteristics are logically consonant with the systems of transmission of land in the community: their male dominant character, the recognition of individual rights to divisible property, and the common practice of postponing division of land for a generation but rarely much further.

Marriages between consanguineous kin also appear to be associated with strategies within the kin group itself. This can be seen if we relate types of kin marriage to the relative size of the landholdings of spouses' families (see Tables 7.5 and A.33). Marriage to patrilateral kin clearly contributes to creating marriage between "equals" among landowning farmers. Patrilateral marriage is also common in cases where the woman has a substantial claim upon property (by comparison with that of her patrilineally related spouse) as opposed to cases where her claim on land or property is relatively less significant. In the latter, links through female kin, which are infrequent in cases where her family's land is larger or equal to that of her spouse, rival or even outweigh links within the patriline.

From one vantage, the practice of retaining women in marriage where they have a substantial claim on land (and other property) is eloquent of men's power over women. But even here the making of marriages is not an affair in which men alone play a part. Women who, unlike Karāmah, belong to a powerful group in local society and see the land on which they have a claim worked by their own household have less reason to mock the consequences of marriage to

Table 7.5 Type of marriage according to relative size of husband's and wife's family land measured by total household landholding, agriculturalists only (per cent)

Type of Marriage	Relative size of landholding: Wife's > husband's	About equal	Husband's > wife's	Total
No relation	21	41	38	100
	62	54	59	58
Father's brother's son	28	55	17	100
	19	18	6	14
Mother's brother's son	–	–	100	100
			8	3
Father's sister's son	–	33	67	100
		3	8	4
Mother's sister's son	33	–	67	100
	4		4	2
Distant through father	17	54	29	100
	15	23	15	18
Distant through mother	–	100	–	100
		2		1
Total	20	43	37	100
	100	100	100	100
	n=26	n=57	n=49	n=132

Note: The criteria for inclusion in the category of "wife's family land greater" was where the wife's family's land was more than 30 per cent larger than the absolute difference between the husband's and wife's land divided by the sum of the two families' landholding; in category "equal" where the difference between the two was less than 30 per cent of the combined sum; and in the category of "husband's land greater" where the difference between the husband's and the wife's was more than 30 per cent greater than the sum of the two holdings. Compare Figures B.4 and B.5.

patrilateral kin. They are quite as eager as their menfolk to maintain the wealth and identity of the larger "house". If a handful of senior men control most of the major decisions about land, the women of such houses too find it in their interest to have women of the house at the core in each generation.

As we have seen, patronymic groups larger than five or six households occur only among the more prosperous landowning farmers.[56] Such a group forms – indeed is formed by – an affinal network.[57] Unlike many Arab rural groups, especially among pastoralists, where an ideology of patriliny overlays practices of alliance that result in the group forming, in genealogical terms, a cognatically related set,[58] in the community under study we find little such ideology.[59] Here, the reaffirmation of identity and common interest through marriage within the group is quite transparent both to actor and observer. In conclusion, let us look closely at marital alliance in one such prominent group of the community.

Marriages of a patronymic group

Bait al-Abyaḍ is the second richest patronymic group (see Table 5.1). Its ten resident households are not nucleated but are found in four different wards of the lower part of the community. Figure 7.1 depicts the structure of the households of *bait* al-Abyaḍ and their total water rights at the time of the census. The households include ten resident households, plus an eleventh headed by Aḥmad 'Abdullāh. As we shall see, this man, son of an eminent pre-1962 shaikh, moved into the capital after conflict and to ensure the education of his sons.[60] The household does not appear in the census, although in fact Aḥmad 'Abdullāh's half-brother, his divorced sister, and the married son of his second wife, Taqwā, all spend much of their time in al-Wādī.

Figure 7.2 depicts the recent history of marriage in the three main sections of *bait* al-Abyaḍ (house A on the diagram). Houses A1 and A3 on the diagram are said to be descended from two brothers; house A2 was believed to be more distantly related, but no one felt the need to trace the exact connection. A brief comparison of the two figures suggests several observations. In few households do we find very many sons surviving in the upper generations, and in households 7 of A2A and 9 of A3D there are only daughters to succeed. This is true in spite of the multiple (although not always polygynous) marriages of men of some wealth. The low rates of survival of children together with the patterns of plural marriage engender a certain complexity in household structure. This is true not only of households 5 and 9, which we shall consider below, but also of households 1 and 2. The former head of household 2, whose first wife (an FBD) bore him only daughters, late in life took a

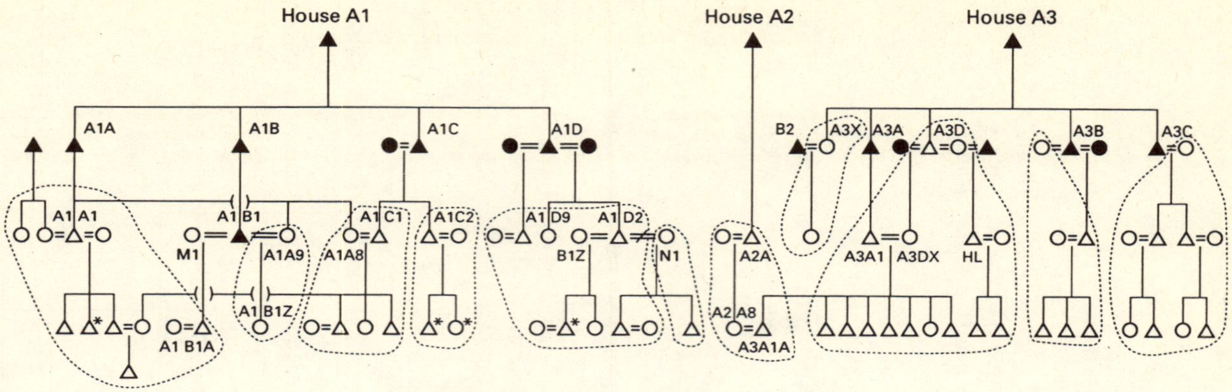

Household	1	2	3	4	5	6	7	8	9	10	11
Land in water measures	368	190	180	150	380	123	125	80	290	68	73

Notes: 1. Those marked with an asterisk were married or divorced between the time of the census (Figure 7.1) and the time of Figure 7.2.
2. Children in households 1, 9, 10 and 11 have been omitted from Figure 7.2 since they were not of marriageable age.
3. Household 5 resides largely in Ṣan'ā', so its members were not included in the census. The number of children of the younger couples is thus not known and they have been omitted from this diagram.

Figure 7.1 Household structure and land at the time of the census: *Bait* al Ab yaḍ

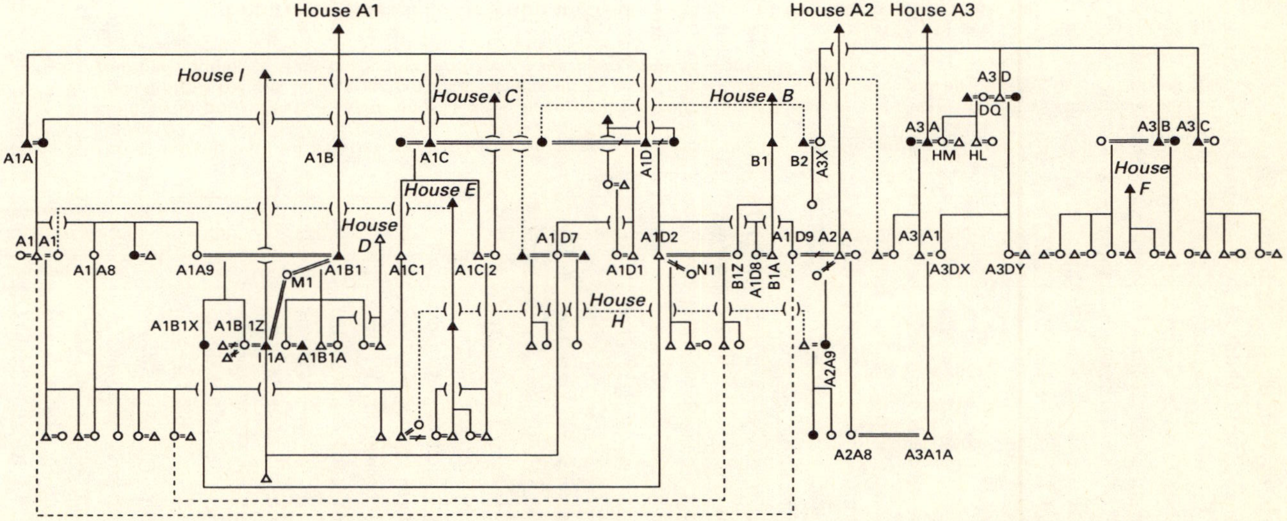

Key: House A1, A2, A3 – Bait al-Abyaḍ; House I – Bait ʻĀkish. Spouses who are not linked on the diagram to houses A to I belong to other patronymic houses.

lines of immediate descent

lines of more distant descent within a patronymic house

= or marriage continuing or terminated by death

≠ or marriage terminated by divorce

Figure 7.2 Marriages of a patronymic house: *Bait* al-Abyaḍ

second wife, a young widow.[61] Before he died this wife bore him a son and a daughter. These children grew up under the care of his first wife, but at the time of the census, the pair having just married, the son and his new bride were living in their uncle's house. In terms of cultivation the relations between household 1 and 2 were close. A1A1 held all his father's and mother's land – the latter was substantial as was the land owned by his first wife and her sister – and the portion of his sisters had not yet been appointed. He and his sons also cultivated, together with A1A9, A1B12 and A1B1A, the lands left by A1B1. As this case suggests, the households with exceptional landholdings are also those where land remains undivided and where land from more than one stem is recombined. At the same time the diagram also suggests that there is nothing in the property system which requires that land be farmed in such large units since extra-family share-cropping contracts are possible, as we shall see in the case of household 8.

Bearing these remarks in mind, let us return to consider the marriages of this house. The figure is dense with the lines of alliance.[62] There are a series of exchange marriages (with houses B1, D, E, F and G); of repeated bonds where first marriages proved successful (with houses C, I and G); of patrilateral parallel cousin marriages (A1A1/A1D9, A1A9/A1B1, A1A8/A1C1, A3A1/A3DX); and slightly more distant patrilateral marriages (A1C1's daughter/A1D2's son, A1B1X/A1D2, A3A1's son/A2A8, A2A/A1D9). As the marital history of this last woman (A1D9) reveals, divorce is not uncommon, even between patrilateral relatives; indeed, to preserve legibility, not all the marriages which ended in divorce have been included on the diagram. And, lastly, men of wealth in the house (A2A, A1D2, A1A1) or related to the house (I1A) marry polygynously. Let us consider the background of some of these marital alliances, focusing on unions where rights to land or political considerations played an important part in the passions of households. This is, after all, one of the most wealthy groups of the community.

In the easily legible right-hand side of the figure where the marriages of house A3 are depicted, marriages are less involuted and with the exception of household 9 of A3D the households are rather less wealthy than those of house A1. Such patrilineal marriages as there are join men of *bait* al-Abyaḍ to women (without surviving brothers) who stand to inherit: Mabkhūt (A3A1) to Luṭfīyah (A3DX) and Mabkhūt's son to Ḥamūdah (A2A8), the daughter of al-ḥājj

Yaḥyā (A2A). For many years before and after Luṭfīyah's wedding, the stepson of Luṭfīyah's father helped in cultivation. The background was as follows. After the death of his first wife, Luṭfīyah's father (A3D) had married a widow who came with children from an earlier marriage, an older daughter and a adolescent son. The widow did not bear any children to Luṭfīyah's father, but her son 'Alī (HL) from her first marriage, who later married a girl of a labouring family in the community, helped in the farming and in running the pump which Luṭfīyah's father owned. The household also regularly employed and sometimes housed a labourer. But as time passed and Luṭfīyah's husband established himself in the household, tension grew between Mabkhūt and 'Alī, an "outsider" to the patronymic group. One evening when 'Alī was returning from prayers at the mosque, a shot rang out as he entered the door of the big house. Hearing his cry, 'Alī's wife ran from the house and, taking her cloak from her head, waved it above her shouting for help. Her cry and her gesture – a woman's tearing off her cover, thereby calling on men to reestablish moral order – brought the men sitting nearby in the marketplace to her aid. In the days that followed there was general agreement: Mabkhūt had fired the shot. Yet, as the men who clashed belonged to one household, the shaikh did not attempt to intervene and formally the assailant was treated as unknown (see case 10 in Appendix 2). Within two months and with the aid of his stepfather 'Alī began to build a small house apart; within a year he and his family moved out of the big house into which his mother had married.

Houses A2 and A3 had more than their share of inheriting daughters. The two marriages of Mabkhūt and his son (the latter to Ḥamūdah, the daughter of al-ḥājj Yaḥyā), promised to make them prominent men. Although al-ḥājj Yaḥyā had married three wives, neither of his sons had survived to take over his lands. His second daughter, Taqīyah (A2A9), who had married a man of another patronymic group with which *bait* al-Abyaḍ later came to blows over irrigation water, died when floods destroyed her husband's home (see case 44). Her younger daughter, her husband's brother and husband's uncle all died with Taqīyah in the house. Ḥamūdah (A2A8) and Mabkhūt's son would inherit all. Women remarked caustically that *bait* al-Abyaḍ was doubtless relieved to find that none of its land would now pass to the house with which it had fought. Alliance with house H into which Taqīyah (A2A9) had married was not in fact to end, but in the next round a woman was married into, not out of, *bait* al-Abyaḍ. A young man of another household (the son of A1C1 on the left of the diagram who had divorced his FBD) married the handsome young widowed sister of Taqīyah's widower.

In contrast to Luṭfīyah and Ḥamūdah, 'Alīyah, the only child of the sole surviving sister in the upper generation of house A3 (A3X) and of a man of house B, had refused to marry her father's brother's son (see household 8 on Figure 7.1). House B, 'Alīyah's father's family, was rather less wealthy than her mother's. 'Alīyah and her mother held both her mother's lands and those of her father, B2. She and her mother supervised cultivation and the work was done by a man of a neighbouring family on a share-cropping basis. The two women had taken in the share-cropper's first surviving son; his wife had seen a succession of infants die and was counselled to "give the boy away" to protect him; when about five the boy returned to live with his parents but remained very attached to the women for whom his father farmed. 'Alīyah was a central figure in women's society. She arranged many gatherings, comforted women in difficult times, and had an exceptionally wide circle of friends outside the community. But women feared for what might happen after her mother's death. They worried lest 'Alīyah later find herself in the unenviable position of her cousin Ḥamīdah, (A1D9): neglected, dependent, and with no say in the cultivation of her lands that remained in the hand of her brother. 'Alīyah should marry, but it was quite unclear to whom. Although women admired her, men spoke with unease of this tall and somewhat plain woman who had never been wed.

'Alīyah's mother's marriage was but one of several linking houses A and B. 'Alīyah's cousin, B1Z, was the first wife of Aḥmad 'Abdullāh (A1D2). Aḥmad's father, 'Abdullāh (A1D), had been a respected shaikh for many years before 1962. Aḥmad 'Abdullāh later came to be shaikh for a short time, but his detractors subsequently described him as ruthless and grasping. He was alleged to have forced his father to divorce both his wives so that they would not inherit. After his first marriage with B1Z, Aḥmad 'Abdullāh had married two other women, both of whom stood to inherit land (Figure 7.3). The first was Taqwā (N1), a woman without brothers, who did come to inherit a fair portion of land. And the other was a young second cousin (A1B1X). At the time of this girl's marriage, her father (A1B1) had only the two daughters; it was later that he took a second wife (M1), who bore him a son. But the girl (A1B1X) died within a year of marriage. Aḥmad 'Abdullāh built a political alliance with Ḥasan

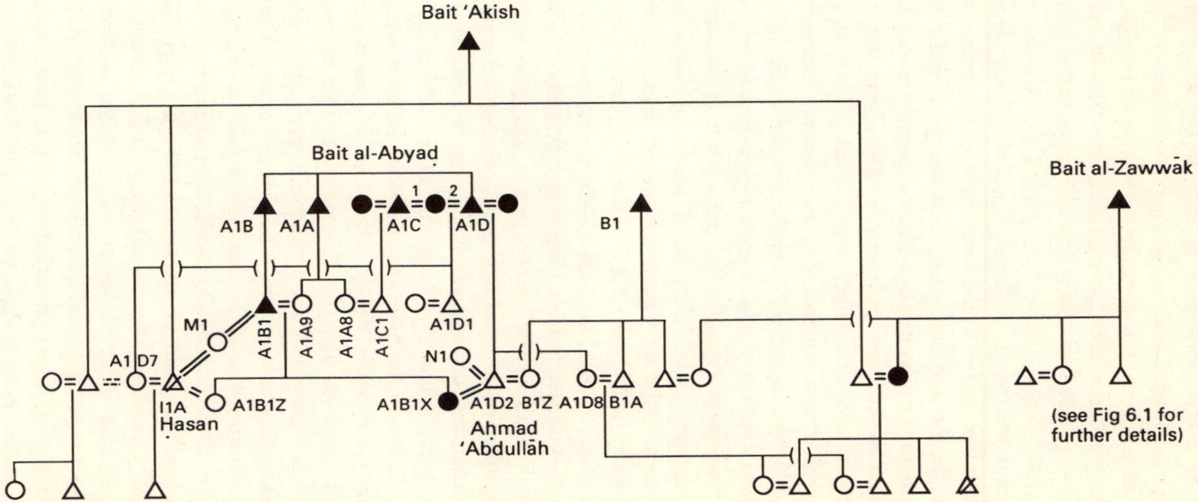

Figure 7.3 Details of the marriages of Aḥmad 'Abdullāh and *Bait* 'Ākish

Muḥsin, the leader of the richest patronymic house in Ḍahr, *bait* 'Ākish (House I). This promised to secure the hegemony of houses A and I (or at least of the dominant section of house I). Ḥasan Muḥsin, to whom Aḥmad's half-sister Khamīsah (A1D7) was married, and to whom at the time of his death two other women from *bait* al-Abyaḍ[63] were also married, was the most powerful man in the community.

But Ḥasan was murdered, allegedly by his brother's sons, in the course of a dispute over land in the family (see case 13). His brother's wife was the sister of the man who succeeded Aḥmad 'Abdullāh as shaikh: her two sons, although openly recognized as "murderers", were never exiled from the area (see case 12b). By contrast, in the case of two other men who killed their cousin in the course of a dispute over land, the murderers had to leave the community for seven years until blood-money was finally paid and accepted (see case 15). In the case of Ḥasan's murder, the death was treated as accidental or unresolved manslaughter and blood-money was contributed by all the men of the community. After the death of Ḥasan, Khamīsah, Aḥmad 'Abdullāh's half-sister, remarried another man of *bait* 'Ākish by whom she later had a son and a daughter. Ḥasan's two other wives, who had not borne him any children, returned to *bait* al-Abyaḍ. The two political figures who were to succeed Ḥasan and Aḥmad 'Abdullāh as leaders had marriage ties with other sections of *bait* 'Ākish. In spite of its wealth, *bait* 'Ākish has been politically divided since that time. Although the political undoing of the alliance of Ḥasan Muḥsin and Aḥmad 'Abdullāh came from within *bait* 'Ākish, the manner of the resolution of the *diyah* payments suggests that other prominent families also felt threatened by this alliance between leaders of the two richest patronymic groups of the community.

Some years later Aḥmad 'Abdullāh himself received threats to his life. He decided to leave the area and moved to the capital. Cultivation of the land he controlled passed to his married son from his second wife, his brother-in-law, Muḥammad (B1A) and his younger half-brother, a man without political ambitions. The lands of 'Abdullāh (A1D) had never been partitioned; Aḥmad 'Abdullāh was said to refuse a division of his father's land. After he left the area, his second wife, Taqwā (N1), sued for divorce and eventually secured it, but only at the price of further alienating her sons from their father. Taqwā was an only daughter who had inherited land, and from the time of the divorce, Aḥmad 'Abdullāh treated her sons as though their mother's land was all they were to receive.[64] But negotiations for partition of the estate of 'Abdullāh were just beginning. Aḥmad 'Abdullāh's sister (A1D8) who had been married in an exchange marriage with B1Z, began to request division of the lands on which she had a claim; the lands which she stood to inherit were more important than those coming to Aḥmad 'Abdullāh's wife (B1Z) from her family's estate. In 1976 the community was rife with rumours about two threatening letters found by Muḥammad on the door to a garden which he had been cultivating for Aḥmad 'Abdullāh (see case 30). Whoever had written the letters sought to divide Aḥmad 'Abdullāh from his brother-in-law Muḥammad. Opinion differed as to whether Muḥammad himself or the murderers of Ḥasan had planted the letters. Several years earlier, Muḥammad had agreed to marry his daughters to the very two men of *bait* 'Ākish who had murdered Ḥasan Muḥsin many years before. A strange alliance this appeared at the time; the least that could be said, as women remarked, was that Muḥammad did not dare to refuse the suitors.

In the histories of Aḥmad 'Abdullāh and Ḥasan Muḥsin, we see two strategies of powerful and wealthy men almost in caricature: marriage to women who stand to inherit land and the deepening of political bonds through marital alliance. The violence that stalked the alliance of these two men is evident, but, then, the wealth of the two men and the play for power which their alliance embodied were equally exceptional. It was Ḥasan's nephews who killed him; later they went on to kill their own brother, after he had asked their father to set him aside some land. The order of domestic government, between those with a claim on a common estate, is truly a political matter among the wealthy. Along the fault lines where land should be divided, violence can threaten this order. A murder within can reduce a patronymic association to its component parts: the tower houses of the wealthy. A household, a house must be governed internally before it can lead in the political community of other houses. The murders destroyed not only the alliance with *bait* al-Abyaḍ but also any wider political role for the rest of *bait* 'Ākish for many years thereafter.

Marital alliance: form and economy

The case study of *bait* al-Abyaḍ exhibits clearly the three possible forms of "loop" or closure of marital alliance that may be traced on a genealogy – marriage to consanguineous kin, repeated "crony" marriage and exchange marriage. Those who live in such marriages can, and often do, describe such alliances in precise genealogical terms. This should not surprise us. An exact genealogical model exists both in written law and in the minds of actors, prescribing those whom one may not marry and those from whom one should inherit. This noble model of kinship, bound up with the devolution of individual property right, lies behind both the precision (in terms of "biological connections") with which individual alliances can be described and the disinterest in tracing distant (and practically unimportant) links.[65]

Yet this case history also underscores the limits of such formal analysis. In practical terms one patrilineal parallel cousin marriage is simply not the same as another.[66] For example, the marriage of Luṭfīyah (A3DX) will surely not end in divorce like that of Ḥamīdah (A1D9) or that of the daughter of A1C2, nor was it ever a question of Luṭfīyah moving into her husband's house. And it was certainly not simply personality that allowed 'Alīyah to refuse to marry her father's brother's son, but something – rather as in the history of 'Ā'ishah, the daughter of Hā'ilah – to do with the property and social weight of her mother's side of the family. It is worth reflecting on what this means. At another level from formal genealogical parallelism, property (and the division of labour) creates irreducible differences in the social units "exchanging women" or "allied" by marriage.

If this is true even between the households of a single landowning patronymic group, it is all the more evident at the level of the community as a whole. The nature of the social units entering into marital alliance differs between the rich and the poor in this one community: from the imposing tower houses of the wealthy with their accumulated property and labour to the mobile little clusters of labourers in their rented rooms. Among the landowners, the social units known as houses are sufficiently lasting for us to speak of marital exchange and alliance between them; and they may form wider patronymic associations of varying size and coherence. But among the poor, if two pairs of siblings marry one other, the exchange of labour is immediate and promises little of the tangle of such marriages among the rich that continues to haunt their children through the claims of property. And, not being bound (or blessed) by the weight of property, the poor appear to elaborate less frequently those forms of alliance which replicate other links.

Although the people of the community share common idioms when speaking of marital alliance, in spatial and in genealogical terms the actual marriage networks of the community's economic groups have been seen to differ. This observation may serve to remind us of the impressive rates of spatial and genealogical "close" marriage among landowning farmers. For the latter the political community is a special boundary for marriage, in a manner surely related to the possession of irrigated land of exceptional value.

Thus, although the building of identity through redoubling marital alliance may well characterize marriage networks throughout Yemen as a whole, there is little reason to expect the intensity of systems of "close" marriage to be as great among urbanites or even in areas of more extensive agricultural production as in this rich irrigated valley. In other contexts, the spatial and genealogical networks of marriage may be considerably more open.[67] There, too, spatial analysis of marital networks should reveal fundamental economic and political configurations: attention to the "closures" of marital exchange could well throw light on certain of the social processes grouped under the label "segmentation".

In this chapter I have examined alliance in statistical terms, so that general patterns and divergences can emerge from the sum of individual cases. The individual instance occupies a particular site in the relations of production, property, politics and sodality. The attention I have given to such particular cases corresponds to an uneasiness over anthropology's fascination with categorical compulsion, with the explanation of general patterns as rules. In this society "kinship" is simultaneously a matter of intense tangible exchange between persons in a particular historical setting and an abstract idiom of genealogical reference, historically and practically bound up with a powerful and uniform legal ideology of devolution and marital prohibition. The emphasis in this study has been on the former aspect, on the daily practical exchanges of kinship. In the case study of *bait* al-Abyaḍ we noted that one cousin was not equal to another in the terms that actors care about when making a match: labour, reproductive capacity, property, political weight and prior sociability. It is the intense material and moral exchanges in these domains that render particular men and women "close" (*qarīb/aqribā'*) to one another. By approaching "kinship" from this vantage we can see legal discourse as such and not reduce the living exchanges of kinship to an abstract idiom of legality and rule. And on the topic of that old chestnut of Middle Eastern anthropology, "cousin marriage", the "problem" proves meaningless when posed generally, because the moment a social historian approaches kinship concretely, the abstract edifice of genealogical consanguinity (and its comparative problems) comes tumbling around his or her head.[68]

8

Conclusion

In conclusion I would like to consider, in terms such as a person familiar with the history of European communities might use, the character of the rural community we have studied. Here we return to two themes subtending this study: one from political economy – the nature of property – and the other from Weberian sociology – the simultaneously communal and contractual nature of social relations.[1]

Property enters into the construction of persons: *māl* (land, productive wealth) belongs to persons; *māl* is what parents should leave to children. Households are built from the conjuncture of properties and their persons devolving through time and uniting in licit and fruitful alliance. The female singer has the husband address his childbearing wife: *yā māl*, *yā 'aḥnaj māl* (land, dearest wealth). The metaphor escapes no one: the fertility of a woman is both the ground for affection and the object of contract. This does not mean, though, that the woman (as person) cannot herself own property (*māl*). In the very constitution of family, contract and affection meet.

Persons work together in households, contributing or establishing a claim on property. In households men hold the means and symbol of that property's defence: weapons. Men's weapons may be hung behind the mother-after-birth, alongside pictures of the Ka'bah, vases of rue, photographs of men, and Korans in decorated pouches: the mother is protected. Men of different houses combine; a political community has so many men, so many rifles, but the weapons are not held in common. What does belong to the community as such? The community does not own *māl*; it has common right (*ḥaqq*) to the uncultivated pasture land (*maḥjar*) and to the total entitlement of irrigation water from the stream. The community does not allocate usufructuary rights to a common resource; the irrigation supervisors merely administer the distribution of private right. Aside from domestic use, water rights belong to the holders of land (*māl*), to each according to the area he holds.

A Europeanist considering this community might well remark on the congruence between the egalitarian ethos of the local political community and its notional construction from the heads of land-owning households. The egalitarian but competitive ethos – which is not to say that local families are all equal – would not surprise an historian familiar with European communities of landowning peasants who practice egalitarian devolution of land rights between both male and female children. The local community is composed of land-holders, with specialists and landless agriculturalists having but a marginal political presence. The affective bonds which tie this community of competitive households together are expressed in dense village connubium – among landholders – and only secondary exchange with outside. Amidst the more wealthy landholders we find tight networks of affinal and consanguineous relations, some but not all built about a patronymic group of several households.[2] The overall structures of alliance would not appear surprising to a Europeanist, although certain of the mechanisms might strike him as distinctive: recruitment of members through women in marriage, not through adoption of children; hypergamy of women permitted by the association of wealth and polygyny; and the legal possibility of marriage closure in every other generation, between first cousins.

Far more than these minor differences in a generally familiar structure of alliance, what does appear remarkable is the avowedly contractual character of local political association. We have seen that a group may elect to change its political affiliation altogether, although, as we have also seen, the political interests at stake in the inherited and thereby institutionalized order may render true re-alignment difficult in practice. But notionally the only legitimate basis for association is the assent of householders, their contractual con-fraternization. To a Europeanist raised on Weber the link between household possession of weapons and property, and political association in the idiom of a contractual confraternity will, on reflection, appear unremarkable.[3] Such difference as there is lies in the ritual form, not an oath as in Weber's "sworn confraternity", but shedding the blood of animals, privileged image of liminality and sodality in this society.

The resulting local political association becomes more than the sum of its parts: it makes and enforces law. The status of this local law will also cause little surprise an historian of Europe: like the law of Weber's urban "commune" it represents "illegitimate domination" in the eyes of the state/church, which casts itself as unique source of legitimate law and dominion.[4] The other face of such contractual confraternity is the ability of the community so engendered to exile or to exclude a man;[5] the other side of local law-making is the duty of community authority to police relations between households under its jurisdiction.

The contractual basis of political association entails explicit fiscal undertakings. It is not only the state that conceives of the local community in terms of taxation. Members think their co-responsibility in fiscal terms. Common cause is not so much the categorical compulsion of a tribal name as rallying-cry[6] as an institutional procedure for the reckoning of common dues on bases such as head-count or landholding. A man is a member where he contributes to the common fund.[7] As the practice of payment of legal amends to the common fund reveals, this fund provides institutional form for the co-responsibility of community members.

The village community stands within two hierarchies of power: the shaikhly and the state. Morphological idioms of tribal structure obscure the evident fact that the social forms distinguishing the village community are not replicated at other levels of "segmentation". To elicit social form this essay has sought to employ statistical methods, by combining a series of distinct observations. For all its coolness, statistical representation has allowed us, in our description of social groups, to minimize employment of both substantivist idioms (e.g. lineage and tribe) and morphological abstractions (e.g. segmentation, opposition, corporation).

The contexts within which local, regional and national shaikhs act have not proved to be nested versions of one in the next. It is the local community that is the site of common right in pasture and irrigation water, the place of inherited residence and intense connubium; this is where men meet face-to-face to legislate, to reassert their political allegiance, to police, and to select a shaikh, and this is where men's co-responsibility takes the everyday form of a standing common fund. The higher-level rural political unit, the *qabīlah* (Hamdān in this case), is a different kind of social framework, one that has long been the unit of administration for the government. The regional shaikh keeps the tax records. Government administrators are appointed at this level and the regional shaikh is the figure through whom they deal. As we have seen, enforcement of a decision from a state court requires the collaboration of state and shaikhly authorities at this administrative level. The drawing of the boundaries of such regions (the tribes) has been wrought slowly at the conjuncture of the economic geography of the region (including the location of trade routes), historical patterns of economic stratification (underlying regional leaderships) and the interest of state authorities in the collection of taxes. While fixed for long periods of time, the assemblage of local communities into the "fourths" or "fifths" of "tribal" organization is a process where, time and again, regional leadership encountered the interests of nascent state formations.[8]

Lastly it is almost meaningless to speak of shaikhs who have power on the national stage as somehow growing out of "tribal" morphology. The exceptional position of the paramount shaikh of Ḥāshid, 'Abdullāh Ḥusain al-Aḥmar, speaker of the parliament in 1993 and leader of the major islamicist party of Yemen, is the product of familial, political and personal history, within (as his present position suggests) the framework of developments on the national stage.[9] By contrast, in the league or "confederacy" of Bakīl, the morphological counterpart of Ḥāshid, there is no single figure of remotely similar power; indeed for many years there was no universally recognized paramount shaikh.

The second hierarchy of power to which the local community has always belonged is that of the state and its officials. In the past, as we have argued, this did not always entail administrative organs so much as networks of family and dynasty and quasi-domestic institutions of learning and rule. Government was not only imposed but also invited, in the figure of the judge. The households of local communities belonged to a legal order not in the modern sense of a regulatory state but in the sense that the law defining person, property and licit alliance was the written and learned law of God, itself the law of the state. The most intimate of conflicts belonged to the religious judge and so ultimately, although not always immediately or necessarily, to the state.

Over the last twenty years, and since the beginning of the research for this study, North Yemen has seen vast growth in government employment, declines in local grain production, and booming consumer imports fuelled by oil-rent. Against this background, and at the top, the two hierarchies of power, the shaikhly and the state, have merged into one. The very stability in the figures frequenting the corridors of power during those two decades reveals how well the two have combined to form a ruling coalition, if not a ruling class.

The images of political order to which we gave much attention in this study – domestic government, male violence and honour, local identity and local law – appear today quite transformed. The household has become dependent on the market for the needs of its residents; the independence of its internal economy has shrunk apace, and with it the value to society of women's "domestic" production. The tower house never had an external precinct wall; its door faced the street. But the tower villa of today's capital, with tinted plate-glass versions of the Ṣan'ānī window, stands locked behind high walls. The multiplication of such palaces and their closeted women is not only a testimony to the art of domestic architecture in Yemen and to the continuity of personal patronage in government, it is also a very modern siphoning of public wealth into private accumulation. After all, wealth today comes quite literally from the state, site of control over the various flows of oil-rent and international "aid". Anthropologists have often described a man's dagger and his rifle as the material expression of his honour; weapons were manipulated with symbolic effect in dancing, dispute resolution and marriage ritual;[10] only rarely were they drawn with deadly intent. But today the tradition of arms-bearing is invoked as moral licence for a free market in heavy arms and the highway system taken as an invitation to make the avenues of the capital a venue for settling scores. The powerful local identities of rural men and women are recast into regional identities, as a "tribalism" to be traded through the major shaikhs (and their political parties) against patronage or employment in the state. There have been other mechanisms whereby the agencies of the state worked together with the very local solidarities of rural communities – the history of the Local Development Boards in Yemen provides examples[11] – and by-passed the regional brokerage of leaders installed in the capital, but in the 1990s these mechanisms appear less central to political process. And lastly, political discourse seems to have stood on its head the old social logic of law. As the economic foundations of domestic government are eroded, the courts of Islamic justice, increasingly subject to a bureaucratic not a personal quasi-domestic order, come to represent less a place of refuge, than of discipline, for women. And, more generally, those who only some years back drew their legitimacy from presiding over traditions of local justice (and law-making) do themselves today declare the very notion of popular law-making illegitimate: the paramount shaikh of Ḥāshid proclaims that the sole legitimate source of law is God's *sharī'ah* and that the idea of popular sovereignty in law is nothing more than a weapon in the arsenal of foreign secularism.[12]

This is not the only possible nor the ultimate reworking of the legacy of rural political tradition. That tradition, always the object of contest, does not necessarily lead to the "tribalism" of today's shaikhly politicians. Even twenty years ago, a wider circle of men made law and chose leaders, kept order and controlled violence, and were contested by their women in the courts of the state. Such a legacy, in its Weberian illegitimacy, has elements that can yet be recast in more popular and more egalitarian modes.

Notes

1 Introduction

1. On Yemeni architecture see Varanda (1981).

2. By North Yemen I refer to that part of Yemen which from the time of the withdrawal of the Ottomans was ruled by the Ḥamīd al-Dīn Imams. The Mutawakkilite Kingdom of Yemen came to an end in 1962 with the declaration of the Yemen Arab Republic. In South Yemen, the British had occupied Aden in the nineteenth century and the area remained under British Protectorate rule until 1967 when, at independence, the People's Democratic Republic of Yemen was established. In 1990 the two states united as the Republic of Yemen. Cf. Burrowes (1991) and Tuchscherer (1994).

3. For the former see Burrowes (1987) and for the latter see Messick (1993).

4. On *daulah* cf. Meissner (1987: 111 and 415).

5. Cf. al-Mu'allimī (1981). See also Messick (1993).

6. Such institutions are, by contrast, found in the Tihāmah.

7. al-Wāsi'ī (1927: 198); al-Jāwī (1975: 19).

8. Cf. al-Ḥibshī (n.d.); al-Sayāghī (1978).

9. For an early twentieth-century example, see the conflict between Banī 'l-Ḥārith and the blacksmiths and carpenters of Ṣan'ā' in al-Wāsi'ī (1927: 245–6).

10. Cf. Dresch (1989).

11. Cf. Asad (1986) for a critique of Gellner's dramatic sociology in which tribe is an actor.

12. The term "segmentation" derives from Durkheim and is used in anthropology to refer to stateless societies, or societies with weak central government, in which local communities are relatively autonomous and divided, by mutual opposition, as if into "segments". See the discussion below for the adoption of this concept in the anthropology of Yemen and Chapter 3 for its importance in the anthropology of Arab rural societies more widely.

13. Cf. Gingrich (1993) who makes economic autarchy a defining condition of tribal society and thus the tribal a model for an original state of society from which "de-tribalized" urban forms have grown.

14. Cf. Aristotle, *The Politics*.

15. Grosrichard (1979).

16. Abu-Lughod (1990). Serious discussion of the relations between domestic and political institutions remains confined to "women's studies": compare Tucker (1985) and essays in Keddie and Baron (1991).

17. Cf. Messick (1993: 75–98).

18. Albergoni and Bédoucha (1991).

19. Cf. al-Akwa' (1980).

20. Cf. Gellner (1981). Abu-Lughod notes a further division between studies on 'Islam' and those on 'segmentary society'. On the problems of such a division see Colonna (1987).

21. Goody (1977a).

22. Foucault (1976: 51–67), Donzelot (1977: 49).

23. Cf. Berque (1978) for an earlier study with an historicist lens on a comparable society in North Africa.

24. Cf. Adra (1982), Caton (1990: 25–35) on tribalism as ideology, and Dresch (1989) whose analysis is avowedly idealist.

25. As we shall see, these are communities of free agriculturalists who own their own land and possess considerable political authority for self-government. In this sense they are not classic peasantry. But they are communities in which the basic unit of managing and working in agriculture is a household and where family demography and strategies of transmission and alliance are intimately bound up with agricultural success or failure. In this sense they belong to the world of "peasantry" and the term is used to force comparison with the important literature on rural organization in other complex agrarian regimes.

26. Anderson (1983), Foucault (1979).

27. Cf. the discussion of status rank in Chapter 2.

28. The world-view of the literate tradition was faithful to its classical sources until the very end. For a study of continuity and change in this late tradition see Messick (1993). For a reading of the classical tradition, in which justice is order, compare al-Azmeh (1986: 2–13 and 31–41).

29. Glaser (1885: 202–4), Rathjens (1951: 175–7), Chelhod (1970: 63), Bornstein (1974: 11), Dostal (1974: 3), Serjeant (1977) and Gerholm (1977).

30. The work of Serjeant expresses an intense commitment to the distinction of the *sayyids*: see for example his panegyric of Imam Aḥmad in Serjeant (1982). Compare Bujra (1971) for a remarkable anthropological study of status in the town of Ḥuraiḍah in the Hadramaut at the end of the British period.

31. This is in contrast to authors of the late Imamic period who, consciously modernizing, had eschewed mention of such internal distinctions, focusing on the geography, administrative divisions, origin of the Yemeni people (lists of names of groups) and hoary pre-Islamic antiquity. Compare al-Akwa' (1971), al-Shamāḥī (1972) and al-Waisī (1962).

32. Cf. 'Umar (1970: 101–4) and Shalan (1993) who reviews the debate.

33. Cf. al-Attar (1964: 103–6) and Ghālib (1962) who writes of the "aristocracy" and al-Sharjabī (1986).

34. *Sha'b*, in its modern meaning of "the people", has been a common term in Yemeni political discourse since the late Imamic period: cf. Messick (1993: 52).

35. See Dresch (1990b: 280) and 'Abd al-Salām (1988: 80) on President 'Alī 'Abdullāh Ṣāliḥ's statement.

36. Cf. also Caton (1990: 216–48) on relations between ideologies of tribalism and state.

37. Abū Ghānim (1985: 332–3).

38. Abū Ghānim (1985) and Dresch (1989). Other relevant works on Yemeni tribal organization are Adra (1982 and 1985), Dresch (1984, 1986 and 1988), al-'Alīmī (n.d.), Stevenson (1985: 63–89), Gingrich and Heiss (1986: 16–20), Weir

(1986), Meissner (1987), Tutwiler (1987), Bédoucha (1987), 'Abd al-Salām (1988), Swagman (1988a), Caton (1990: 20–35), Albergoni and Bédoucha (1991) and Gingrich (1989 and 1993).

39. Niebuhr (1792, ii: 50–52) provides an account of Ḥāshid and Bakīl in the eighteenth century. Cf. Dresch (1989: 24–5) for the location of these groups.

40. Cf. Dresch (1989: xii and xiv) on method and the epistemological virtues of association with shaikhs of national prominence and Abū Ghānim (1985: 17) on the knowledge afforded by his being a native tribesman and p. 60 on his disdain for the detailed description common in the anthropology of "primitive societies".

41. For example, Abū Ghānim (1985: 50–51).

42. For the irrelevance of economy and ecology see Dresch (1989: 336–8) and (1990b: 263–4). Weir (1991: 88) has taken issue with Dresch's dismissal of the economy. Compare also Lancaster and Lancaster (1992) for whom the ethos of Arabian tribalism is not only portable but so distant from earthly economy as to induce that state of grace which Marx believed would come only with the glowing funeral pyre of the division of labour: a tribal man works only as his fancy takes him.

43. Dresch (1989: 117).

44. Populations following the Zaidī school of law live mostly in the mountainous regions of the area of Dhamār north. People of Tihāmah and Lower Yemen (south of Yarīm), together with those further east and south, are primarily Shāfi'ī in legal tradition. There are also communities of Ṭayyibī Fāṭimīs (Ismā'īlīs) in the area of Manākhah, Najrān and the ward of Ṭaibah in Wadi Ḍahr.

45. Gellner (1981) or for a succinct restatement (1990). Nor do we find, as in Gingrich (1993), a quasi-evolutionary continuum whereby local communities can be characterized as lying between the truly tribal (self-governing, egalitarian, arms-bearing, economically autarchic) and the "de-tribalized" urban (governed, inegalitarian, disarmed and market-oriented).

46. al-Maqramī (1991).

47. Durkheim (1933: 174–81) for ethnographic citations.

48. Lewcock, Costa et al (1983: 137–42) and Varanda (1981: 264–5).

49. Cf. Swanson (1979), al-Qaṣīr (1986) and Tutwiler (1987).

50. See Tutwiler (1987) for an attempt to analyse political change in terms of economic history.

51. The union of the two Yemens entails, on the one hand, the numerical preponderance of Shāfi'ī population (Tihāmah and areas south and east of Dhamār) in the nation as a whole and minority status for the Northern Zaidī populations whose leaders have enjoyed a privileged political role in the government and particularly the agencies of security of the former Yemen Arab Republic and, on the other hand, the presence of the Socialist party which, whatever its practice, has as ideological bases the Yemeni population as citizens and the state as regulating agency of the *res publica*. Thus, from the early 1990s, and building on the Islamic education institutes which had been introduced during the 1980s parallel to the state school system in the North, the great shaikhs of Ḥāshid worked to support the more combative and structured ideologies of islamicist party politics.

52. Cf. 'Abd al-Salām (1988) who argues that this union has always been a

central feature of Republican ideology in such figures as al-Zubairī and Zaid al-Wazīr.

53. Cf. the articles by Adra, Dresch and Lambert in Tuchscherer (1994). Messick (1993) had, for much longer, been concerned with developments in national political culture.

54. Serjeant (1979: 192) estimates that the Yemen was self-sufficient in grain production until the early 1930s. Lambert (1991: 141) states that by 1986 the Yemen Arab Republic was importing 70 per cent of its food.

55. *Qanāts* are underground aqueducts built to carry water from its source, usually at the foot of a hill or an escarpment, to points often considerable distances away.

56. For studies on such small-scale irrigation systems see Varisco (1982 and 1983) and Betzler (1987).

57. Al-Wāsi'ī (1927: 121 and 198).

58. Compare Yemen Arab Republic, UNDP (1971: 20–38).

59. Cf. Botta (1880: 82).

60. This statement remains a hypothesis, suggested by observations made during work in wadis Maur and Rimā' (in 1973–4 and 1980 respectively) and during a month's stay in the villages south-east of Ibb in 1973. Aspects of the impact of Ottoman rule on local government in the Ibb area are discussed in Messick (1978).

61. For this period see al-Sālim (1971).

62. 'Ubayd Allāh (1972).

63. Compare *Kitāb al-siyar* in Ibn al-Murtaḍā (1947–9).

64. For this period see Serjeant (1983: 71–101), al-'Amrī (1985) and Meissner (1987: 106–19).

65. On the development of administration under Imam Yaḥyā see Messick (1993).

66. Cf. Dresch (1989: 142).

67. Compare Mundy (1983).

68. Cf. Montagne (1930: 325).

69. Compare al-Wāsi'ī (1927: 203), who speaks of the shaikhs asking for fiefs after aiding Imam Yaḥyā to victory against the Turks in 1905: 'When the tribesmen saw that the Imam had conquered and taken control of the Yemen, they began to act in arrogance, revolt, unruliness and discord. They claimed that it was only because of their strength and courage that the Turks had left. Each tribe then wanted control over one of the areas (*makhālīf*) of Yemen, which are called fiefs (*qita'*), that is to say that the Imam would bestow it as a fief, giving it to them so that they could enjoy its taxes (*wājibāt*) themselves' (my translation).

70. Compare story of al-Qu'darī in Mundy (1983).

71. Cf. Serjeant (1983: 101).

72. Goitein (1955: 10).

73. The reign of Imam Yaḥyā is given here with the final withdrawal of the Ottomans, but his effective reign began in 1904 when he entered Ṣan'ā'. Al-Wāsi'ī (1927: 182–203 on 1321AH and 197–8 on the famine of that year).

74. For late nineteenth- and early twentieth-century Yemeni Jewish emigration to Palestine, see Klorman-Eraqi (1981).

75. Cf. al-Abdin (1979) and Douglas (1987).

76. See al-Jāwī (1975) and Burrowes (1987: 30–31).

77. Cf. Lackner (1985: 26–50).

78. See Wilson (1989) for a discussion of Ḥāshid and Bakīl in older texts.

79. Compare Dresch (1989: 102–4) and Burrowes (1987: 49–51) for the background of Shaikh ʻAbdullāh b. Ḥusain al-Aḥmar.

80. Lackner (1978: 137–71) gives a summary of economic development during the period.

81. Compare Burrowes (1987: 44–5 and 80).

82. The older routes of emigration had been to E. Africa and the United States, but Yemeni men had also found work as far afield as Great Britain, West Africa and Vietnam.

83. See World Bank (1979) on the Yemeni economy of the period.

84. *Catha edulis*, a shrub of which the leaves are chewed for their stimulant and mild hallucinogenic qualities.

85. The Yemen Arab Republic alone is much more populous than its richer (in oil) and larger neighbour, Saudi Arabia. The unification of the two Yemens was achieved in 1990 only after the production of oil in commercial quantities in North Yemen and the retreat of the Soviet Union from world politics. In the long run a unified Yemen could represent a formidable political rival to the Saudis. Saudi investment in Yemeni "decentralization" will certainly continue.

86. The region to which the community belongs has long had close relations with the capital and with central power. Niebuhr (1792, ii: 103) wrote: 'The prince of Hamdan is distinguished for his power, and the antiquity of his family; he being descended from the tribe of Hamdan, which was known long before the days of Mahomet. Yet, with these advantages, he has been reduced to a state of vassalage, probably because his country was too plain and too narrow for defense against an enemy.' Niebuhr (1792, ii: 89) explains that the armies of the Imam of Ṣanʻāʼ were drawn from Ḥāshid and Bakīl and that the principal commanding officers of this army were four tribal shaikhs, those of "Hamdan, Wada, Sefian and Khaulan".

87. The rise in the price of *qāt* outstripped price inflation of most imported goods over the period: see Weir (1985) and Kennedy (1987).

88. This theme is found not only in journalism, but also in anthropology: compare Stevenson (1985: xi–xii) and Adra (1982: 18).

2 The locality: images of place and political order

1. Eight wards according to the national census of 1975, but in this the census appears to have combined the two upper wards into one.

2. Ward 8 and Ward 2 on Map 3.

3. The theme of the giants of pre-history recurs in Yemeni tradition. Compare Lambert (1991: 145–6).

4. In al-Hamdānī's *Iklīl VIII*, (1931: 74) Ḍahr is described as a place with a "wadi and a fortress, all attributed to [*mansūb kull dhālik ilā*] Ḍahr ibn Saʻd".

5. The same traditions occur in al-Hamdānī (1931: 77). Needless to say, contemporary oral tradition is unlikely to be innocent of this famous text.

6. Compare al-Hamdānī (1931: 77–8) on the fortress Dauram.

7. Such tales are reminiscent of the history Dresch (1989: 177) describes as being "in the tribal mode", the paradigm of such dateless tales of conflict between groups being the texts of al-Hamdānī's *Iklīl X*. Dresch's treatment of the genre as a form of history is sensitive but somewhat vitiated by its isolation from other historical modes. Thus he makes no mention of al-Hamdānī's *Iklīl VIII*, for which parallels also exist today in oral tradition among tribesmen. And by restricting the "tribal mode" of history to such heroic tales (which do indeed present a schema of the manner of relations between groups in the manner sketched by Dresch) and neglecting the everyday "modern" history of rural communities, Dresch elegantly primitivizes the "tribes" of contemporary Yemen, whereas in fact these communities have several traditions of history, including modern history as portrayed in school texts and on the mass media.

8. Al-Wāsi'ī (1927: 67).

9. Cf. Kelley (1984).

10. Islamic legal theory privileges oral testimony, but the practice of litigation requires written documents. Compare Wakin (1972) and Messick (1990). So too, customary law is, in theory, primarily an oral law. But in practice documentation of decisions is critical. Compare Mundy (1989).

11. Cf. Mundy (1989) for a detailed discussion. The most important of the ruling dynasties were the Sharaf al-Dīn Imams of Kawkabān in the seventeenth and eighteenth centuries, the Ottomans in the late nineteenth century, the Ḥamīd al-Dīn Imams from the early twentieth century; and the religious sects are the Ṭayyibī Fāṭimīs, so-called Makārimah, largely in Ward 4 of Wadi Ḍahr, and the Zaidī Imams, notably the Ḥamīd al-Dīn, with a base in Qariyat al-Qābil.

12. Some of this water allotment may have been used to irrigate state lands but most was presumably sold back to the communities and so did represent "a payment" to the state by the communities.

13. Much of the common catchment area, shown on Map 2, is loosely linked, even today, in a subsection of Hamdān. In al-Hamdānī's day the areas (of Ḍahr, Ḍula' and Rai'ān) shown on Map 2 formed a *mikhlāf* called *mikhlāf* Ma'dhin, al-Hamdānī (1968: 106).

14. al-Hamdānī (1931).

15. al-Hamdānī (1948).

16. Dresch (1989: 387).

17. Literally, the phrase means "those who put the turban (*'imāmah*) on your head". There is also perhaps a play of words on the word imām.

18. Rural leaders can both give to and withdraw their political allegiance from the Imam. Compare al-Wāsi'ī (1927: 196) for an account of the *mubāya'at al-'ulamā' li-'l-imām Yaḥyā* (the recognition of Imam Yaḥyā by the scholars) which is followed by pledges of support by shaikhs and leaders ("*wa-wafadat ilay-hi al-ru'asā' wa-'l-mashāyikh wa-'l-ajnād min al-aghwār wa-'l-anjād.*").

19. The justification in Islamic law of such an action would be under the category of *qasāmah*.

20. For discussions of the concept of *hijrah*, see Serjeant (1962), Dresch (1989: 149–50) and Albergoni and Bédoucha (1991).

21. Compare also cases 46 and 47 in Appendix 2.

22. Compare the category of *ajīr* in the manuscripts: Anonymous, *Talqīḥ al-ḥukkām*, 43r. and *Kitāb al-man'ah*, 49a–51a. The hired hand and servant are under the protection of their employer according to these texts. There were other categories of person who could be taken under protection by an individual or group in tribal areas, such as guests.

23. Compare Mundy (1983: 530 and 532 note 20).

24. The butchers refused to lower their prices. They slaughtered far fewer animals than butchers in Ṣan'ā' and primarily bought locally produced animals. Hence their margin of profit was much less than that of the urban butchers.

25. At the time of this study there was no pressure to develop these lands and hence to gain private rights in them. That development was to begin only from the late 1980s leading to sustained legal contest over rights to land in the *maḥjar* adjoining cultivated fields.

26. The term for this collective pasture land, *maḥjar*, derives from a root denoting pasture-land marked off for exclusive use (cf. Piamenta (1990, i: 84) and Serjeant (1976: 113). Only pasture-land is thought of in this way as a commons.

27. This is the vocalization of the term *makhuwwah* current locally; cf. Piamenta (1990, i: 4).

28. This is the rule of thumb for the full *diyah*. Compare the case discussed below, where a quarter of the *shar'ī* blood-money is dropped for the sake of brotherhood (*mukhuwwah*).

29. Or *bait wa-'arḍ*. In 1974 the total number of adult men in the community was 545, but only 400 were liable for the *gharāmah* based on the *ḥāl* count. Excluded from payment were figures such as soldiers (*'askarī*) or government employees, mosque-keepers (*sādin al-jāmi'*), learned scholars (*fuqahā'*) or men of religious status granted protection by the community. Poorer village servants were also exempted, as was anyone with a physical disability. Cf. the discussion of payments in Meissner (1987: 248–60).

30. Men of the community said that during their lifetime the basis of assessment on *māl* had changed from area of land owned to *zakāt* tax paid. The principle was now "payment according to the harvest" (*al-ghurm bi-qadar al-ghillah*).

31. Cf. case 38 in Appendix 2, where the brother and his son are accused of theft from a neighbouring house.

32. For the full text see document 1 in Appendix 3. This text is that of a draft of the final version, not the final document itself.

33. The eight notables were the ward heads of the community and other powerful figures, notably the son of a man who had been shaikh just before the revolution (cf. p. 192 on Aḥmad 'Abdullāh).

34. The full or "tribal" *diyah* was twice this sum, about 15,000 riyals in those days.

35. The *amīn* noted that the widow had of course moved all valuables, particularly those stolen from others, to her parents' home.

36. Although the ruling that no blood-money whatsoever be due appears exceptional, there is historical evidence of traditions where blood-money was reduced

for a thief killed while stealing. Summarizing Glaser's description from the years 1882–8, Rossi (1948: 5) notes that theft was punishable by a fine, an offer of sacrificial animals and the return of the object stolen. And if the thief killed, his relatives could not seek vengeance but were to receive only an indemnization of 40 talers, far less than the standard blood-money of the time.

37. Cf. Meissner (1987: 246–7) on contract in politics.

38. Cf. the redrawing of "tribal" boundaries in Meissner (1987: 252 and 268) and Tutwiler (1987: 245–53 and 367–9).

39. Movements of youths (*shabāb*) were a feature of political action in other areas during these years, cf. Stevenson (1985: 83–6) and Tutwiler (1987: 294–300).

40. The kind of negotiation attempted by the lower section, where it chose to ally itself with the "opposing" confederacy or political association, was certainly nothing novel. Al-Hamdānī, in *Ṣifat jazīrat al-'arab*, describes tribal groups changing allegiance by a specific verb form (*yatahammadūn, yatabakkalūn*).

41. Compare the discussion of social status couched in two fetwas in al-'Ulufī (n.d.: fos. 245–6). The manuscript is dated 8 Rajab 1162 AH (1750 AD) and the British Museum catalogue states that al-'Ulufī lived in the twelfth century AH, but E. Rossi (1948: 10) states that al-'Ulufī died 19 Sha'ban 1056 AH. The first discusses whether a man of religion may avoid the marketplace on the grounds that entering it diminishes his stature:

> *dukhūl al-sūq li-'l-fuḍalā': mā yuqāl fī ba'ḍ ahl al-zamān mimman la-hu faḍl wa-diyānah ṣārū yataḥashshamūn wa-yataraffa'ūn 'an dukhūl al-aswāq wa-qaḍā' al-ḥawā'ij ma'a 'l-ḥājah ilā dhālik fī ba'ḍ al-aḥwāl wa-yad'ūn tawahhuman anna-hu yaḥṣul bi-dhālik inḥiṭāṭ min al-martabah wa-qad kān dhālik min akhlāq al-nabīy ṣallā 'llāh 'alay-hi wa-āli-hi wa-sallam wa-'l-khulafā' ba'di-hi wa-kadhā kathīr min al-a'immah wa-kān min akhlāqi-hi ṣallā 'llāh 'alay-hi wa-sallam al-rukūb ma'a 'irdāf al-ghair wa-bi-ghair ikāfin wa-ṣārū yataraffa'ūn 'an dhālik.*

Al-'Ulufī rejects the arguments of some men of religious distinction of his day that avoidance of the marketplace had been a custom of the Imams and even of the Prophet Muḥammad. On the contrary, al-'Ulufī argues simplicity of life was always a prophetic virtue. The discussion goes on to the more difficult question of whether a man of religion may refrain from praying the common Friday prayer. Here the judgement is much harsher, and in almost no circumstances is such avoidance justifiable.

The following question (ibid., fos. 246–7) equally concerns social status. Building on a long literature it debates the question of which of two brothers is the superior: a learned scholar who because of his poverty has to live from the tithe or a farmer who supports himself from his own land and pays all the dues God imposed on him. A question concerns two brothers, one of whom is learned and excellent and the other a common man. The learned man, however, is so poor that he eats from the public treasury (*bait al-māl*) and lives off taxes (*zakāt*), whereas the other is a farmer, working his own land, living off it, and paying all the dues that God imposed upon him. Which is the better man? The answer is that if the learned man shares his gracious qualities with his brother, in short teaches and guides him, then he is much the superior. If he does not carry out his duty of admonition, the working man is superior to the man who lives off the surplus of the other's labour.

42. Compare the tradition of al-Qu'darī in Mundy (1983: 529).

43. On *sayyid* genealogy cf. Meissner (1987: 160–64) and Vom Bruck (1991: 208–15).

44. There is a saying: "*ishtaqq sayyid, ruq'-hu bi-qāḍin*": a *sayyid* was ripped, patch him up with a *qāḍī*. How a family became recognized as *qāḍīs* has been little documented, although Serjeant (1977: 237) and Dresch (1989: 136–40) have contributed pertinent observations. Families of Islamic learning often had this status within a particular rural area for generations. But that the central government did not fully control all rural areas nor possess a developed bureaucracy did not mean that the position of such learned families depended only upon the relations of the family with the rural community. Ties with those at the centre were likewise a factor in their position in the local community. There is evidence that the Imams sought to regularize the variant statuses of men of learning and to associate their interests more closely with those of the Imamate. The account of how one family was recognized as free from customary dues and enjoying rights to tax revenue suggests the reciprocal determination of the political position enjoyed by a family in a local community and the formal recognition of such status granted by an Imam. Thus the late Qāḍī Aḥmad Zāhir noted that among the family documents he had inherited was a *raqm* from al-Imām al-Manṣūr 'Alī (presumably al-Imām al-Manṣūr 'Alī b. 'Abbās al-Ḥusain, 1189–1224 AH, 1775–1809 CE) stating that the men of his house (*bait* Zāhir) were *ajbār* (i.e. freed from paying dues at the entry to Ṣan'ā', all taxes even those in *sūqs*, and contributions, *ghurm*, to tribal funds), and were to enjoy rights to the government taxes (*zakāt* and *wājibāt*) of a particular area. The *qāḍī* noted that the Imams did this to make sure of the allegiance of certain families of religious distinction ("*ahl al-ḥall wa-'l-'aqd*"). This form of recognition was known until the time of his grandfather, he added. Qāḍī Zāhir noted that the *qabīlīs* (tribesmen) do not know this now, but then he paused and corrected himself: "Yes, they do know that we were *ajbār* but they simply do not take it into consideration any more. For example, during the recent *'anā'* (common labour) on repairing the main channel of the stream after the flash-flood, fines were levied on all those who did not go out to work, regardless of their status." The *qāḍī* added, however, that he did not go nor did his two sons, who went into Ṣan'ā' to repair his elder son's motorcycle. And they were not fined, presumably since no one missed them as they never work in the fields.

45. The science of genealogy (*'ilm al-ansāb*) is a written one. Compare the popular text of al-Suwaidī (n.d.) in which the ancestry of all mankind, but in most detail the Arabs, is traced back to Adam.

46. Among the most famous of this genre in the last two hundred years are al-Shaukānī (1929) and al-Zabārah (1929 and 1941/1958).

47. Zabārah (1957: 87) notes in his introduction that his list of the *sayyid* family names was also published in the Ṣan'ānī newspaper *Al-īmān*, vol. 93, Muḥarram 1353 AH/1934. He states that he did not include all families who believed themselves to be *sayyids*.

48. Abū Ghānim (1985: 105).

49. There is for example a local family, al-Ḍaḥḥāk, the name of a famous leader in the writings of al-Hamdānī. Cf. Dresch (1989: 167).

50. Men of service refers to those known as *mazāyinah*, *banī 'l-khums*, or "*khadam*", the former two names being the most common in the Ṣan'ā' area. *Khadam* in this sense is not to be confused with the *akhdām*. In practice such statuses are intimately associated with "dishonourable" occupations – bath-keeper, butcher, *qashshām*, blood-letter. In the area of Ṣan'ā' *banī 'l-khums* is used as a synonym of *mazāyinah*. The name *banī 'l-khums* is something of a puzzle, used in historical texts to indicate those who accompanied warriors and received a portion of the booty though they did not themselves fight. Compare Landberg (1920, i: 645–7).

51. One version of this tale was told me by a learned *'ālim'*, another by a woman of a family of dyers, and the third by a woman bath-keeper. A similar origin myth is reported in Glaser (1885: 205). Several European writers have reported hearing the origin of people of this class explained in terms of individual failure, as tribesmen who violated the code of honour in their own community were driven from home and offered no choice but to enter another community as "servants lacking in honour" (*khadam nāqiṣ al-muruwwah*) performing demeaning occupations. Such an explanation was never offered me.

52. Compare the work of Mermier (1985 and 1989) on the society of Ṣan'ā'.

53. The cluster of urbanites and market specialists in the lower wards accentuates differences between the upper and lower wards of the community.

54. Unfortunately the list I acquired from the *waqf* does not distinguish irrigated from rainfed land. The estimate given here is not satisfactory, based as it is on casual remarks. The total value of the proceeds per annum of these lands was over 80,000 riyāls in 1974, at a time when the tax paid on *qāt* by the entire community was some 12,569 riyāls, suggesting a total revenue from *qāt* of well over 800,000 riyāls. This figure would suggest that the *waqf* must have been larger than the estimate given above but would certainly set a maximum size of some 10 per cent of the land of the area, even if all were in the irrigated belt, which is not the case. The *waqf* lands are subject to the same share-cropping agreements as other lands. Thus, in the irrigated belt the share-cropper owns (either by developing the land or by buying the value of the "labour" – *shaqīyah* as it is called) the plantings, walls and guard-house, and the *waqf* owns only the soil. This makes it difficult for the *waqf* to oust a cultivator suddenly and grants the share-cropper the value of his investment. By the same token, the very poor were not able to acquire rights to share-crop such land, not having the initial capital; established families cultivated the land.

55. Compare case 27 in Appendix 2; her husband is BC on Figure 6.7.

56. *Man takhaṭṭā min al-bāb ta'ammal qad buddil al-qāḍī bi-qummāl.* The nickname of the husband's family was "flea".

57. Cf. the incident described above where this butcher served as spokesman of the butchers.

58. *Duwal*, plural of *daulah*: ruling dynasty or house.

59. The remark is also expressive of divisions among those who appeared as equals in status. In this case there were two elements. Rivalry existed between the

two patronymic groups to which the women belonged as they were the largest of their status category in the community and the two from which the community's butchers came. The singer's house had several men and women who remained in the traditional occupations of *muzayyin* (public announcing, marriage attending, slaughtering at marriage, measuring of grain at the payment of *zakāt*, and circumcising) whereas the other family were all butchers and far more prosperous than the singer's family. The wealthy butchers often sought to set some distance between themselves and the common village *muzayyin*. The speaker's son, who married the daughter of a poor *muzayyin* from another village, would tease his sons when they could just speak, "Are you the son of a butcher or the son of a *muzayyin*?" There was little doubt in his mind as to which was superior.

60. For Zabārah's handbook of *sayyid* houses, see p. 40.

3 Law in the locality

1. Cf. Messick (1993) for a discussion of the institutions of *fiqh* in Yemen and their transformation over the twentieth century.

2. For law in general as educative project see Cain (1983).

3. This service legitimated their social distinction: cf. note 41, p. 212.

4. The phrase is that of Moore (1978).

5. Cf. the documents published by Abū Ghānim (1985), al-'Alīmī (n.d.), Dresch (1989) and Weir (1991).

6. Smith (1987: 46).

7. Cf. Rossi (1948) on the term. The literal meaning of *man'ah* is prevention and protection.

8. The animal offered in reparation of the first is termed *ghilāq* or *riḍā'*. The animal offered in reparation of trespass or fracas is termed *hajar*, the act of killing the animal being *tahjīr*.

9. *Arsh* in Islamic tradition. Cf. cases 20 and 29 in Appendix 2 where the *amīn* evaluated the injury.

10. By contrast, in the late Imamic period there was a locally based official, see Mundy (1989: 112). On these two figures see Messick (1993: 171–2). For the administrative structure of this period, see Yemen Arab Republic (1978: 42–51).

11. Aḥmad al-Ghashmī was to succeed assassinated President Ibrāhīm al-Ḥamdī as head of state in 1977. In 1978 he also died by assassination.

12. Cf. Rossi (1948), Rathjens (1951) and Mundy (1979).

13. Gellner (1969, 1981 and 1990). For critiques of Gellner's North African sociology and segmentary models more generally see Hammoudi (1974), Berque (1978: 480–82), Lucas and Vatin (1982: 47–8), al-Taufīq (1983: 107–8), Asad (1986), Caton (1987), Colonna (1987 and 1990), Mahé (1993) and Munson (1993).

14. It draws explicitly on the French colonial sociology of Montagne (1930), Ibn Khaldūn's *Muqaddimah*, and British social anthropology, which adopted the term segmentary for the analysis of African, primarily stateless societies, notably Evans-Pritchard (1940 and 1949), Fortes and Evans-Pritchard (1940) and Fortes (1953).

15. Cf. Colonna (1990).

16. Messick (1990 and 1993: 221) argues that documentation is more common between close kin than between traders in the market place.

17. Albergoni and Bédoucha (1991: 28).

18. On the relationship of women to Islamic legal authority, see Mundy (1978).

19. For example, one older acquaintance of mine from a family of dyers in Ṣan'ā', following an introduction by the wife of a Minister of the Imam, was able to pursue her (and her sister's) court case before the Imam himself. In this the sisters challenged their brother over division of the family house. The woman stayed in the household of the Imam in Ta'izz for a month. The sisters won their case. Likewise, women whose guardians want to force them into a marriage may seek refuge in the house of the Islamic judge, signalling their appeal for redress by the removal or burning of their outer head-coverings at the door of the house.

20. According to Zaidī *fiqh* a woman need not veil before the Imam or an Islamic judge (*ḥākim*). Thus the woman of the family of dyers was told by the Imam that she need not veil before him; he addressed this married woman as *yā bintī*, "my daughter".

21. By contrast the girl from another village (of a family of weavers) married to the son of a local butcher did appeal to the shaikh; see the notes on document 3 in Appendix 3.

22. To remark on this is not to imply that familial litigiousness is peculiar to Yemeni society. On the one hand, relations of gender and age are everywhere political and not without conflict. On the other, familial litigiousness appears to be common in class societies where family corporations manage the bulk of productive capital. A great deal is at stake in such disputes. For an exemplary study of family litigiousness, see Claverie and Lamaison (1982), and also Sabean (1990); for a general statement on the litigiousness of families under the *ancien régime*, see Donzelot (1977: 49–51).

23. Cf. the discussion of patricide in Mahé (1993).

24. The family has long been an object of ideological polemic on the part of legal authority with universal pretension. Compare Mundy (1979). The only campaigns under the Imamate for the application of Islamic law concerned the family. In 1931–32, Imam Yaḥyā (1904–48) launched a campaign to enforce "Islamic" marriage law in rural areas. *Qāḍīs* were sent out, backed by soldiers, to oblige farmers to marry their daughters at a suitably young, respectable age. It was alleged that rural families, holding out for high brideprices, preferred to keep their girls for work at home. In what village people term *sanat al-ṣamīl*, "the year of the big stick", the Imam dispatched preachers (*khuṭabā'*) and men trained in *fiqh* to the centres of the rural areas to arrange marriages. According to the late al-Qāḍī Aḥmad Zāhir, who was sent in this manner while still a student at *al-madrasah al-'ilmīyah* in Ṣan'ā', the campaign took place in 1350 or 1352 AH (1931 or 1933). Qāḍī Zāhir explained that the campaign was occasioned by many of the rural tribesmen (*qabā'il*) failing to marry their daughters. They preferred to keep the girls at home for their labour and feared that by giving their daughters in marriage, the girls could alienate land which they eventually stood to inherit. He added that some girls had become pregnant and so, to combat this decay of morals, the Imam initiated the campaign. He recalled with amusement how in one night in the town of Marmar, the centre of Hamdān, he had married forty couples. He

went on to say that for each marriage he had received a riyal, half from the bride's family and half from the groom's, but he added that other envoys accepted nothing less than five riyals. Ḥusain al-'Amrī informs me that there were two such marriage campaigns, the first in 1931–32 and the second in 1949–50.

25. This section is indebted to discussions with Alain Mahé.

26. Heads of the quarters are also chosen but they tend to play a secondary role in legal settlements. Compare cases 11b and 33; the head (*'āqil*) in case 33 later became shaikh.

27. For example, men have explained to me that the practice of irrigating from downstream to upstream is a recent innovation, while al-Hamdānī (1931: 76) states that irrigation was practised in this manner in the tenth century. And it is hardly problematic that the ruling suspending blood-money for a thief killed in the act, discussed in the case concerning the murder of the carpenter in Chapter 2, may well have historical precedents.

28. Cf. Mundy (1989).

29. Cf. Berque's observations concerning "public law" at the village level in Berque (1978: 374–84).

30. On the definition of *man'*, compare Rossi (1948: 29).

31. Compare Albergoni and Bédoucha (1991) on *hijrah/tahjīr*.

32. Cf. Chapter 2 and Mundy (1989: 121–2).

33. al-Attar (1964: 103).

34. Cf. Dresch (1989) for whom such groups are "estates in the tribal peace".

35. al-Attar (1964).

36. Abū Ghānim (1985), Dresch (1989), Albergoni and Bédoucha (1991).

37. This is usually an Islamic court of the state (cf. cases 5, 11a, 16), but consider case 12a where the arbiter consulted is the distinguished army officer and Republican politician from the community, a man of *muzayyin* origin.

38. Compare cases 6 and 10 where, had the violence concerned two separate households, the shaikh would presumably have tried to intervene.

39. On guarantors see al-'Alīmī (n.d.: 102) and Dresch (1989: 93–6).

40. In case 34 men are fined following a fight between their wives. Among men, fines are imposed primarily as deterrents to further conflict as in case 43. In the case of the irrigation system, however, there is a fixed schedule of fines in water for water theft or inadvertent loss.

41. In case 51, following a quarrel in the bathhouse between women of al-Wādī and al-Qariyah, the shaikhs of the two communities fixed a separate day for women from each place. With the female bath-keeper to enforce the ruling, it has generally been respected.

42. Compare also case 36 where the shaikh both protects and in return extorts payment from a butcher.

43. In these cases the shaikh judges according to the terms of Islamic law. This point has also been made by al-Alīmī (n.d.: 47–8).

44. Compare the cases discussed in Chapters 2 and 4.

45. Compare Mahé (1993) on the legal institutions of the Kabyle. Revealing of the marriage of the two traditions are the texts of tribal law held by the late Professor R.B. Serjeant (see Anonymous or uncertain authorship). These embody the fusion of traditions which can be observed at the level of practice. For example,

the *Kitāb al-Man'ah*, which probably dates from the eighteenth century, comprises three parts: the first covers the major contractual relationships of *man'ah*, including the sections *kitāb al-jiwār*, *rafīq*, *ḥalīf*, *dhimmah*, *ḍiyāfah*, *ṣihrah* and *ṣulḥ*; the second deals with particular questions (*masā'il*); and the third with the major contracts of *shar'* on marriage and inheritance. Concerning marital relations, we find in the first section a "chapter on in-lawship" (*kitāb al-ṣihrah*) and in the third, a digest of the standard categories of the Islamic law of marriage (*nikāḥ*, *ṣadāq*, *ṭalāq*, *nafaqah* and *riḍā'*). These are preceded by sections on the transmission of family property: *ḥajr*, *waṣīyah*, *mawārīth*. Whereas the section on *nikāḥ* contains only a summary of the terms of the marriage contract, the book on in-lawship not only treats of the penalties due in cases of a failure to observe the rules for escort of a woman between her two homes, or in cases of violence or verbal abuse between in-laws, but it also contains statements about the ideal character of relations between spouses and between those bound by in-lawship. The former derive from *man'*, the latter from the wider moral literature of Islamic tradition. On these texts see Rossi (1948) and Obermeyer (1981).

46. Compare document 3 in Appendix 3.

47. Dresch (1990: 83–4) remarks that the conflict between Imamic and tribal justice (*sharī'ah* and *'urf*) is more a matter of jurisdiction than of content.

48. It was only in 1980 that this *de facto* recognition was given force of law in the *qānūn al-taḥkīm*; see al-'Alīmī (n.d.: 68).

49. In the words of Rousseau (1755: 337): "Economie ou Oeconomie, (Morale et Politique). Ce mot vient de οικοσ, maison, et de νομοσ, loi, et ne signifie originairement que le sage et légitime gouvernement de la maison, pour le bien commun de toute la famille. Le sens de ce terme a été dans la suite étendu au gouvernement de la grande famille, qui est l'état." [The word Economy or Oeconomy, is derived from οικοσ, a house, and νομοσ, law, and originally meant only the wise and legitimate government of the house, for the common good of the whole family. The meaning of this term was later extended to the government of the great family: the state.]

4 The village economy

1. Far-fetched in space but, before oil, India was no further in Yemeni popular imagination than North Arabia. Beyond the Hijaz the zones where Yemen had long historical relations were Greater Syria, India and East Africa.

2. Bujra (1971: 190–91).

3. For an analysis of these terms in the Muqaddimah, see al-Azmeh (1982: 53–7 and 69–71).

4. Cf. Bédoucha (1987), Meissner (1987: 234) and Dresch (1989: 78).

5. A comparison of Table 2.1, where status is set against landholding, Table 2.2, where occupation is set against status, and Table 4.1, where occupation is set against landholding, reveals the limits of such correspondence.

6. In this calculation all landless labourers have been treated as agriculturalists, although on occasion many also work in building.

7. The proportions here of landless persons who have moved into the com-

munity from outside doubtless reflect the relative wealth of the local agricultural community. But accounts of poorer brothers who sold (or otherwise lost) their rights to land and left the community suggest that – albeit in smaller numbers – landless men moved out of, as well as in to, the community.

8. In *fiqh* the water of the stream is subject to right (*ḥaqq*) but not full ownership (*mulk*), the latter applying only to the water of wells or *qanāts*, i.e. where a built structure is seen to be at the origin of the water supply. Cf. Caponera (1973), Varisco (n.d.) and Mundy (1989).

9. In 1976 water diverted deliberately or through negligence was repaid in kind along with a one riyāl fine per *ṭāsah* diverted when the stream was irrigating in the community, but at the higher rate of four riyāls plus the water in kind (or, alternatively, four *ṭāsahs* for one taken) if the misappropriation took place when the stream was irrigating in al-Qariyah. In the latter case the irrigation supervisor of al-Qariyah would join the supervisor from al-Wādī in evaluating the theft. Their judgement was law and could not be contested by a farmer.

10. The Ottoman categories of land tenure were never applied in the mountains of Yemen.

11. There are a few plots in *waqf darīs*, land put in *mortmain* the proceeds of which are to go to reading Koran for the soul of the deceased, but many of these endowments are of questionable legality (when the manager appointed is also an heir) or in practice revert to private ownership with time. Compare the two small *waqf darīs* discussed in Chapter 6, pp. 148 and 155.

12. Lease and share-cropping agreements are the most likely to be orally contracted, the terms of such agreements being closely determined by local conditions of production.

13. It is this principle that appears to have come to the fore in the late 1980s (after the time of this study) when developments such as road building, construction, and quarrying increased pressure to grant private rights in the outlying areas. In 1991 court cases for acquisition of title were based on extension of right from the cultivated plots into the adjoining areas. This process of "privatization" can be justified by the lack of recognition in Islamic *fiqh* of community "commons", as opposed to state domain.

14. Compare Documents 2 a, b and c in Appendix 3.

15. Cf. Appendix 3, document 2a.

16. See Appendix 3, document 2b.

17. The shaikh of the lower wards did not read or write; the shaikh of the upper wards was a man of some education.

18. It represents one and three-quarters *dhirāʿ ḥadīdī* square.

19. There are also minor rights and duties governing irrigation channels adjoining a plot. It is the responsibility of a landholder to maintain the principal off-take channel in the vicinity of his field as well as to repair the subsidiary channels feeding into his land; in return he may plant *sayyāl* trees (used for poles in grape arbours or ceilings) along the main channel should this adjoin the wall of his plot.

20. The *ṭāsah* is a local time-measure of water. See Rossi (1953: 354).

21. Indeed by 1980 irrigation from the stream was to cease entirely and by 1991 the fall in the ground water-table was to prove so dramatic that farmers of the area began to sense that their way of life was doomed.

22. Although I do not have figures on land sales, these did appear more common in the rain-fed lands. Compared to irrigated land the relative value of rain-fed land has fallen dramatically following the flooding of the Yemeni market, from the late 1960s, by grain imports. Swanson (1979) discusses the impact on producers of the fall in the relative value of grain.

23. Cf. Mundy (1979 and 1988).

24. Such arguments have been advanced with regard to the application of Islamic *farā'iḍ*, cf. Mundy (1988: 49 and 114).

25. Within Yemen such systems existed in the wadis of Tihāmah, cf. Mundy (1985 and 1988: 56–60).

26. Cf. case 37 in Appendix 2.

27. This figure derives from the records for the distribution of stream water.

28. The Pearson correlation coefficient of size of household and total land-holding is 0.6196, significance 0.00000 (n=246).

29. In the past labourers from poorer agricultural areas in the west and north came as short-term migrants, returning annually to their villages in late spring for the season of rain-fed cultivation in their home villages. Such seasonal migration, where women and not only men moved for work, is now much less common.

30. For a discussion of this term, see Adra (1982 and 1985).

31. Cf. Swanson (1979) and Tutwiler (1987).

32. On the history and spread of *qāt* see Schopen (1978), Weir (1985), al-Maqramī (1987) and Kennedy (1987).

33. This mixed strategy was later to make new sense when in the 1980s imports of fruit were curtailed to support the local production and fruit prices climbed to levels fetched by *qāt*.

34. An agriculturalist, R. Revri, studying *qāt* farming, surveyed the division of land use in 1975 in the three riparian communities sharing the stream. The figures he gives in his draft report are, however, for all cultivated land in the three communities, both rain-fed and irrigated land. Taking all cultivated fields together, he estimates the division of land use as follows: 57 per cent grain, 23 per cent mixed fruit and *qāt*, 15 per cent *qāt* and 5 per cent grapes. Since such figures conflate irrigated and rain-fed fields, they are of limited value. My estimates given here are best considered as informed guesswork. I am most grateful to R. Revri for allowing me to consult his draft paper.

35. This was not because farmers were hidebound and resistant to change. The more prosperous farmers were experimenting with what was available. Some tried a chemical insecticide on *qāt*. This would have been adopted faster, had it not proved toxic to anyone consuming the *qāt* within a fortnight after spraying. In 1977 a wealthy pump-owner purchased a mini-tractor, presumably for use in the small irrigated fields, but he had yet to do anything more than drive up and down the main road by the time I left.

36. Cf. pages 44 and 192.

37. Cf. Bourdieu (1970).

38. The first motorized mill is said to have been introduced to Ṣan'ā' in the 1940s. The first mill appears to have been brought into the community in the late 1950s.

39. Cf. case 8 in appendix 2 where a female landowner accuses her son of having done so.

40. Gerholm (1977: 55) describes *qāt* as a "democratic" crop compared to coffee, the older cash crop of the region of Manākhah.

41. It was only from the late 1970s that the municipal government of Ṣan'ā' began to establish large outlying *qāt* markets.

42. Prices for a good bundle (*rubṭah*) rose from between three to five riyāls in 1973 to eighteen to twenty riyāls in 1977 and have risen far higher thereafter.

43. Cf. *bait* al-Ḥumaidī, p. 113.

44. See p. 112 for the history of this woman.

45. Compare case 36 in Appendix 2.

46. Consider the confrontation between the local butchers and the Ministry of Supply, p. 30.

47. Compare cases 3, 52 and 53 in Appendix 2.

48. Cf. p. 48.

49. 46 per cent of the men indicated that they could read and write; a further 13 per cent reported that they had had some schooling but were not fully literate. Among women only 2 per cent reported having any education at all.

50. The phrase is used by Dresch (1989: 139).

51. Cf. p. 48.

52. Cf. p. 37.

5 House, household and family

1. The situation appears a little more complex in the field of Indian kinship studies, despite path-breaking studies, such as that of Fox (1971); the emphasis on family in its relation to systems of religion and caste has tended to leave in the shade more prosaic political and economic aspects of household and family that invite comparison with other stratified societies. On the last point compare the remarks of Béteille (1992). For a review of studies of family in India, see Uberoi (1993).

2. Bonte (1991).

3. Cf. Netting et al. (1984) for this distinction.

4. Although scholarship in "women's history" necessarily entails some documenting of family patterns as, for example, in Tucker (1985), it rarely explicitly engages with anthropological schema. When historians have addressed the ethnographic literature – compare Guichard (1977) – it has been as backdrop to other historical problems. The only major piece of scholarship on Arab family patterns in the pre-modern period remains that of Goitein (1978) on the Jews of medieval Cairo. A promising departure, in keeping with the development of social history by Maghrebi historians, is the series of studies based on the family *waqf* dossiers of Tunisia edited by Ferchiou (1992).

5. See Granqvist (1931 and 1935), Rosenfeld (1957 and 1976), Cresswell (1970), Aswad (1971), Maher (1974), Khury (1976), Seddon (1976), Geertz (1979), Peters (1980a and 1980b), Abu Zahra (1982) and others.

6. For an example of the first see Lecerf (1956), of the second, Patai (1969

and 1973) and of the third, the chapter on the Muslim family in Gautier (1937: 36–47).

7. Thus of the works cited in note 5, only Cresswell has been translated into Arabic. Ethnographers themselves of Arab background working in Western universities generally publish very little or not at all in Arabic.

8. Cf. Ziyādah (1991) for the social identification of the term intellectual (*muthaqqaf*). The definition of an Arab intellectual here is those who write in Arabic and contribute to intellectual debates conducted in Arabic; at issue is not social origin.

9. By contrast the linguistic and intellectual divide appears far more happily porous in the case of studies of the domestic domain in Turkey, cf. Erder (1985) and the exemplary work of Duben and Behar (1991).

10. This account is based on a survey of all articles touching on family or tribe in the journals *al-Muqtaṭaf* (from the 1880s onwards) and *al-Hilāl* (from the 1890s) as well as of modern intellectual and cultural revues (e.g. *al-Fikr al-'arabī*, *al-Mustaqbal al-'arabī*, *al-Bāḥith*, *Dirāsāt 'arabīyah*, etc.). The survey was supported by the Department of Anthropology, Yarmouk University, Jordan.

11. For an example see Saadawi (1982).

12. Cf. Mernissi (1982a); for an example of her use of the term patriarchal see Mernissi (1982b).

13. Cf. on this topic the exceptional work on Arabic literature of Ṭarābīshī (1977).

14. For the problems in such notions, compare Mundy (1988: 24–48). For a concise recapitulation of this history by a sociologist compare al-Akhras (1980: 20–27). Such accounts smack of "orientalism in reverse", to borrow the phrase of al-'Azm (1981).

15. The literature is enormous. For brief bibliographies see Haddad (1982: 219) and Abdel Kader (1984: 162–5).

16. Ḥaṭab (1976), Sharābī (1977: 27–47 and 1992), and Barakāt (1984).

17. Compare al-Akhras (1980: 18 and 23), who himself complains that family is not a domain of much interest to Arab sociology.

18. Cf. Ḥaṭab (1976).

19. al-Akhras (1980: 64–5). It may be noted that Damascus is not Rio de Janeiro in this or any other regard; but nevertheless the unspoken terms here must be class, gender and fertility. Among certain labouring and artisanal strata children are working and not at school; what their mothers are doing, short of simply failing to care for their children, remains unexplored in the text.

20. Lonely at times but not really alone: the wider project of a social history of everyday life in Arab societies is one to which many are today contributing. On the themes of concern to this essay see, in particular, Valensi (1977), Sharārah (1981), al-Taufīq (1982), Hammoudi (1988) and Ferchiou (1992).

21. Al-'Izzī is an epithet for Muḥammad.

22. It is a commonplace that such basic domestic/kin terms are polysemic and require further definition for the unit in question to be clear. See Goody (1972: 103).

23. The two other wards named after families present no such uniformity; in one of these, Ward 2, a number of houses are said to be related in some way or

another to the "name" of the ward, but I never heard any interest expressed in the nature of their relations.

24. Quite exceptionally to my usual methods of research (compare Appendix 1) where I conversed almost exclusively with women, I also collected the full version of this genealogy from a man of the family. He was a younger man and it is possible that older men might have had more details on anterior generations. But the absence of detailed genealogical links between the houses, in this case at least, is not simply the result of a female vision of kinship as opposed to the male.

25. Compare cases 12 and 13 in Appendix 2. For this history see p. 194.

26. In many parts of North Yemen there are hereditary shaikhly families. Careful local history is required to unveil the political and economic conditions that coincide with the presence of this phenomenon in some areas and its absence in others.

27. Given the very restricted size of such groups, I saw fit to employ the term "patronymic group", not "patronymic association" employed by Cohen (1965) to describe the Palestinian "*ḥamūlah*". The latter, which I have myself studied in North Jordan, is a more associative type of organization than the "houses" examined here.

28. Cf. Vom Bruck (1991) on *sayyid* houses.

29. Compare the history of the labouring woman, p. 111.

30. Such households can be of considerable complexity: consider the composition of the household with the largest landholding in Figure B.2 in Appendix 4. This is one of two households in patronymic group 6, *bait* Murghim.

31. The typology of household forms adopted in this chapter is that of Laslett (1972: 23–40); on the 1975 census see Appendix 1.

32. As discussed in Appendix 1, the analysis for this chapter combines data from a list of taxpayers and water/landholders together with the household census lists.

33. Yanagisako (1979).

34. Cf. the discussion in Appendix 1.

35. Cf. Goody (1958) and Netting et al. (1984).

36. Rigorous demographic analysis would require cohort data for such analysis, that is, data on household composition at different ages of the heads of households in question. Because historical data is not available, if any meaningful analysis is to be made of the data at hand, some very strong assumptions have to be made about the comparability, say, of household structures of those in their twenties or thirties and the household structures that their parents, now say in their forties, fifties or sixties, knew when they were young. This may be an unwise assumption especially where demography, even more than household structure, is concerned. For example, many older women believe, and, by and large, data on their child-bearing histories appears to bear out their opinion, that infant mortality was higher in their youth than it is among their daughters today. Thus the bulges in household size on Figure 5.3, Agric 2 and Agric 3, where heads are aged 30–<45, may reflect the combination of some complex *frérèche* households with nuclear households having a large number of children, following a jump in the number of surviving children among women in their late twenties and thirties.

37. The number of women in the teens age bracket is low. I do not have an

explanation for this; perhaps the ages of some married women are overestimated. I could not find evidence of underreporting of young women in any of the households which I knew.

38. The economic breakdown employed here and throughout this chapter under the same rubrics (Agric 1–4 and Spec 1–2) is as follows. Agric 1 and Spec 1 includes landless agricultural workers and landless specialists respectively. Agric 2 and Spec 2 represent the lowest third of landowning farmers and the upper half of specialists. And Agric 3 and Agric 4 comprise the upper two-thirds of landowning farming households. The ranking of farming households is on the basis of total landholding per household and hence corresponds roughly to the quartiles in Figure 4.1A. Specialists are divided into two groups on overall economic criteria; those grouped in Spec 1 are all landless whereas all but two of the households in Spec 2 own a little land.

39. This statistic is based upon the age of first marriage as reported for men and women under forty-five years of age. All statistics concerning age provide only rough guides. In my survey of women (see Appendix 1) I tried to estimate age by asking women whether they were married before or after their first menses and by trying to fix the date of their first marriage in relation to contemporary political events. The census-takers also sought to estimate ages in relation to well-known political events.

40. Among men aged forty-five or less, the mean age at first marriage of labouring men in Agric 1 is 22.1, of farmers in Agric 2 and Agric 3 it is 19.3, and in Agric 4 18.5. The age at first marriage of men aged 45 or less is 20.3 in the lower specialists Spec 1 and in the upper specialists Spec 2 it is 18.9.

41. The family history is described in Chapter 6.

42. See case 5 in Appendix 2.

43. The survey of 101 women is too small to provide any indication of differential child mortality or fertility by wealth. The proportion of poorer women in the survey was about twice as large as in the population of the community as a whole.

44. Mortality has dropped but still remains important. Compare Table A.6 in Appendix 4. In the census returns the mean number of children living with married women in different age groups was as follows: among married women under 20 (n=98) the mean was .049, married women 20–<25 (n=130) mean 2.03, married women 25–30 (n=121) mean 2.88, and married women 30–<35 (n=138) mean 3.07.

45. Such assumptions are found in scholarship. For example, Gerber (1980) presents very interesting data concerning transactions by women in Bursa. But he closes the paper by noting that the position of women could never have been as good as it seems from the documents studied, given men's legal power of divorce. Surely, even in the case of divorce, the practical consequences of abstract legal powers must be documented and cannot simply be deduced from the letter of the law.

46. There are important differences in divorce rates within Arab Muslim societies, not only, as has been remarked by Cuisenier (1975) and Tapper (1991), between Turkic/Iranian and Arab societies.

47. The jurists limit the amount a woman can be made to pay to the total sum

offered by the man on marriage. Compare Ibn al-Murtaḍā (1972: 123–4) and commentaries. Here again practice exhibits other logics.

48. The *bāb al-ḥaḍānah* (literally chapter on nurturing) in the commentary on *al-azhār* of al-'Ansī (1938) is somewhat ambiguous. It grants a mother the right to care for her children so long as they are not able to care for themselves (to feed and dress themselves). In the case of a girl the period may extend until she is married – the minimum age of marriage in the *sharḥ* is nine years – but with the boy the shorter period is relevant. The child is seen to have a right to such maternal care. Yet although the mother has the right to care for children when they are young and she may claim a small sum for childcare and maintenance of the children from the husband, the text also notes that if the father can prove that he can find a woman who will care as well for the children as the mother but who will not charge for the childcare the father may take the children young. In practice, payment for maintenance of the child does seem to establish rights of custody in the long term, especially in the case of the daughter. For example, in one case in Ṣan'ā', for many years the father contributed a small amount for the care of his daughter but when the girl was about eight or nine her mother and grandparents decided not to accept nor to claim – they had once taken the father to court to secure payment – any more from the father lest he thereby be able to reclaim the girl. Women lose the right to care for their children upon remarriage. For most young women, therefore, divorce means separation from their children. Compare al-'Ansī (1938, ii: 521–32). I have not been able to consult the Republican rulings in *Al-Qawānīn al-shar'īyah al-islāmīyah, qawānīn al-mawārīth wa-'l-waṣāyā* of 'Abd al-Karīm al-'Ansī to see what emendations may have been made on this point.

49. In the survey I inquired about the duration of marriage and the period before remarriage. I noted all cases where the woman had a clear idea of the length of time she was married, twenty-three cases for first marriages and ten for subsequent marriages. The duration of first marriages that ended in divorce ranged from three days to seventeen years, with a median of three years. Of subsequent marriages that ended in divorce the duration of marriage varied between four months and five years, with the median eighteen months.

50. For one such divorce see document 3 and notes in Appendix 3.

51. The figures are: in Agric 1, 5 of 30 men, in Agric 2, 4 of 31, in Agric 3, 4 of 39, and in Agric 4, 4 of 45.

52. Although the numbers are small, it is noteworthy that among the landless no widowed woman was living with a father, brother or sister.

53. Of widows who remarried, the median duration of first marriage among those without children was only eighteen months, of those with children, ten years. The median period before remarriage was, in both cases, about eighteen months.

54. Compare the account of Ḥasan, p. 107.

55. These figures derive from the census. In the community co-wives almost without exception formed part of a single household.

56. See p. 150 for al-ḥājj Qāsim Muqbil.

57. Laṭīfah's brother was a milk-son (*min al-riḍā'ah*) of Ḥamīdah.

58. The households of men with several wives are classified as multiple households.

59. See Betzler (1987: 81). The family are considered *qāḍīs*, not *sayyids* as Betzler states, cf. al-Zabārah (1957: 209).

60. See Varanda (1981: 291) for the plan of a middle-sized house in al-Wādī.

61. For the most part these households are small and their landholding modest: a spinster whose land is jealously farmed by her brother; an old divorced woman living alongside her brother who farms their land; and two older widows each of whom lives with a long-divorced daughter. But in a handful of cases a widowed woman is listed as head of household even though the household contains her married son(s); and in one case a woman with children by her first husband is named as head while her second husband, a labourer who tends the small plot of land left by the widow's first husband, is listed last of all in the household.

62. The reason for the discrepancy between this figure and that in Table A.16, in the row entitled "widow(s)=top generation" is that, here, solitary widows are included whereas in Table A.16, solitaries are listed separately.

63. Women speak of when it is their *daul* or turn. Before the introduction of power-driven mills, when all grain was ground at home, such a rota of routine labour was all the more precious.

64. Compare case 4, Appendix 2.

65. This includes rows "Daughter extension" through "Widow and widow's sister's family" for Agric 2–4 in Table A.16.

66. It was believed that he was a hermaphrodite.

67. Even more so, patricide is an unimaginable crime (cf. Mahé (1991)) whereas fratricide is probably the most common type of murder.

68. The manner in which land is listed in the records corresponds to the way in which it is farmed and also to the rights to land as known to the irrigation supervisor. The listing greatly simplifies rights to land and the supervisor occasionally adopted a short-hand method of referring to land under joint cultivation. It should be taken not as a complete record of ownership but as an indication of the major patterns of holding and working land.

6 Material exchange and moral order

1. Hā'ilah's brother-in-law, Yaḥyā, was an unlucky man. Plagued by ill health, he gradually built up debts. He sold the title of his share of land to Hā'ilah, while retaining the right to cultivate (*shaqīyah*); some years later he sold the title again to an outsider. When this became known he had to flee the community. Hā'ilah bought out the other purchaser, taking over both the cultivation of Yaḥyā's plot and his half of the family house. She later sold the house to the acting *amīn*. Yaḥyā fled to Ta'izz, where he worked for a time as a porter in the market. When it became known that he was a man of good family (*ibn nās*) he was put in contact with a shaikhly family, owners of the whole of an irrigated wadi, who hired him as a factotum on their lands east of Ta'izz. Eventually his wife, daughter, son named Mahdī, and Mahdī's wife and child joined him. But the son's wife found the life beneath her. She returned home, and after the death of her young daughter, her father obtained her divorce. Six months after the divorce Mahdī himself fell ill and died in a matter of days. Yaḥyā's wife, Fatḥīyah, then took her daughter and

returned to her home to mourn the death of her son. Her brother and family lived with her mother in an old two-room house. He worked as a *qāt*-runner and was without land of his own, but he refused to let his sister return south again. When Yaḥyā came to fetch his daughter, his brother-in-law insisted that he return to the community, pointing out how much his wife's illness had worsened during her time in the south. Fatḥīyah suffered from a degenerative circulatory ailment that made it impossible for her to do as much work as before in the kitchen. Yaḥyā agreed to return home. He rented a rough two-room house from a farmer and found work whitewashing houses. His daughter, a beautiful girl, did the heavy housework for her mother. Yaḥyā's history was known to all. The phrase, "he is selling his land", evokes tragedies such as that of Yaḥyā.

2. Compare case 8 in Appendix 2, where Hā'ilah confronts her son with the accusation of holding back a part of the proceeds of a sale of *qāt*.

3. Women gather almost every afternoon to socialize, either informally at a neighbour's house or more formally in the gatherings for marriage, childbirth or death.

4. See case 32 in Appendix 2. Six years later this girl was to be married to Hā'ilah's son in the second exchange marriage of her younger children.

5. See case 31 in Appendix 2. For the term see Chapter 3, note 8.

6. Compare case 17 in Appendix 2.

7. In Figure 6.1 only this first exchange marriage is represented. The second exchange with a household of Bait al-Abyaḍ is depicted on Figure 7.2.

8. On Bait al-Abyaḍ see pp. 184–95.

9. The property system in practice is never simply "the law applied". See the discussion of such questions in Berkner and Mendels (1978) and Cole and Wolf (1974: 175–205).

10. Cf. Augustins (1982), Berkner and Mendels (1978), Smith (1984) and Wrigley (1978).

11. Cf. Lamaison (1991) and the discussion in Chapter 7, pp. 167–8.

12. Cf. Goody (1983).

13. For Yemen compare Chelhod (1973: 52–3).

14. See Pasternak (1972), Cohen (1976), Wolf and Huang (1980) and Watson (1985).

15. Cf. Tillion (1966).

16. Compare the arguments advanced in Holy (1989) and the review of these debates in Davis (1977: 198–218) and Eickelman (1981: 128–32).

17. For the Middle East no one has attempted to propose a typology of household forms and marriage patterns according to productive and property regimes such as might provide a comparative vantage on the forms and meaning of "cousin" marriage in Arab societies. This said, the work of Emrys Peters points, at times, in such a comparative direction. Compare Peters (1980b) in which the issue of difference is central.

18. To say this is not to deny Ottoman innovations such as *waqf al-ijaratain*. But such change in urban property regimes is vastly overshadowed by the scale of diversity in productive and land tenure systems in rural areas from late antiquity through the twentieth century. And almost all of the social history on Arab lands has concerned the urban, not the rural, areas.

19. Cf. Mundy (1988).

20. In urban settings the *shāri'ah* or marriage-dresser may be a specialist separate from the singer. In the village the *muzayyinah* usually performs all the tasks: accompanying the bride, dressing and decorating her, singing the songs, managing the giving of gifts and the distribution of meat at meals, ceremonially unveiling the bride, and conveying the virginity cloths to the girl's mother.

21. The songs and tales of women are to form the object of a separate monograph. A fuller treatment of wedding and childbirth ceremonies will be given there.

22. Compare Smith (1987). On many ritual occasions this is done by shedding the blood of a sheep or bull. To say this is not to support the sometimes vulgar reduction of the blood of virginity to the image of the sacrificial lamb, in the manner proposed by Combs-Schilling (1989) for Morocco. True, the bleeding of virginity is symbolically privileged since it marks male penetration, the beginning of sexual congress, and the successful seclusion of a daughter by her natal family (and most particularly her mother). And in good patriarchal tradition, menstrual blood is, by contrast, treated as defiling. But in communities where public showing of the cloths is expected, the blood does not have to be let by the groom but may in case of need (the girl's refusal of the groom's approaches and/or the groom's inability to go through with the act at the required moment) be let by the *muzayyinah*. And lastly among women, it is not this blood, nor the idea of the virgin pierced, that is honoured in speech with the image of the sacrificial lamb, but rather the mother after childbirth, a figure often referred to by her magical bleeding (*al-nifās*) and one routinely described in women's oral tradition as *'aqīrat rasūli 'llāh*, the sacrificial lamb of the Prophet. Compare the remarks on the treatment of childbirth below.

23. This form comes from the root *ḥjr* but is related etymologically to the root *hjr* in Yemeni Arabic. I am grateful to Mounir Arbach of IREMAM, Aix-en-Provence, for clarification of this point. See also Albergoni and Bédoucha (1991: 29–30). Compare the term *tahjīr* used for the act of killing an animal (termed *hajar*) given in restitution of offence to a place ritually marked off (a place described in Arabic as "*al-maḥall al-ladhī la-hu ḥurmah*") and the term *maḥjar* for interdicted pasture, territory.

24. The root *ḥjb* possesses a resonant complex of meaning, extending far beyond the notion of everyday veiling. *Ḥijāb* is not only ritual protection or immunity, it is even used for the protection of death, as in the phrase where a woman calls for death, *allāh yudakhkhil-nā fī ḥijābi-hi 'l-'aẓīm*. The groom is also, if to lesser extent, *muḥajjab*.

25. The term appears to refer to the formal invitation for meals to the full guests of the wedding, *al-muta'arrisūn*, for that day.

26. Only in the case that she is from another village do men of her natal house accompany her; in such cases the ritual may include other elements, such as the bride swinging aloft her father's shawl as she enters the marital house and sleeping behind that shawl the first night in the marital home.

27. Not only the bride but also the *muzayyinah* may present her own demands. The *muzayyinah* of the community remained a Royalist for years past the revolution of 1962; she used to require that the groom say "long live the Imam" before

she would unveil the bride. Her tradition caused much merriment; the groom usually gave way.

28. *Musajjimah* is the phrase used to describe the pose, which is also maintained at the beginning of women's gatherings on day three, *yaum al-thālith*, and day seven, *yaum al-sābi'*. (The ceremony itself is referred to as "*al-thālith*", "the third".)

29. Thus in tribal legal tradition a husband may punish his wife physically but may not insult her or her family. He must pay amends for any verbal injury. Compare Anonymous, *Kitāb al-man'ah*, folio 59a: "*wa-idhā ḍarab al-rajul zaujata-hu fa-lā shay' 'alay-hi wa-idhā sabba-hā 'aw sabb ahla-hā wajab 'alay-hi 'l-naṣafah bi-miqdār al-shatam.*" (If a man beats his wife, there is nothing due; but if he curses her or curses her family, then he owes amends according to the gravity of the insult.)

30. And the personalities also play a role. For example, it is customary to paint the candles which are lit for the bride on *yaum al-dhibāl*, the day of the wicks; in the marriage songs she is likened to a white candle, and indeed, like the candle, her face, hands, and feet are decorated with small black designs of *naqsh*. In one wedding the candles had not been so decorated. Women judged this typical of the bride's mother, a woman who simply had never had an eye for the finer things in life.

31. This is the urban terminology; in many rural areas it is termed *ḥaqq al-ṣabāḥ*, "the morning payment" with indirect reference to sexual relations.

32. In most cases, the *mahr* appears to be paid at marriage and not left as a debt: compare Table 6.1, where only six out of 100 women reported that they had not received their *mahr* at marriage. Likewise, unlike the Levant, there is no tradition of *mahr muqaddam* and *mahr mu'akhkhar*, the first being paid at marriage and the latter at divorce by the husband or on his death. In cases where the *mahr* has not been paid by the death of the husband, the wife will be given her *mahr* out of her husband's estate.

33. See Figure 6.2, where the girl's clothing from her natal home is brought by her mother and other relatives a week after the consummation of the marriage, in contrast to the *kiswah*, which goes with the bride on the night she first goes to the groom.

34. Compare document 3 in Appendix 3.

35. This appears to differ markedly not only from dowry in more distant realms such as N. India or Europe – compare, for example, Sharma (1980) and Hughes (1978) – but also from the treatment of women's *mahr* in rural areas of Jordan today. The differences in the actual character of marriage payments and their fate in different areas of the Arab world needs to be documented more carefully and to be examined comparatively.

36. Figure 6.5 concerns the marriage of a girl of a landed family (given in an exchange marriage but for which a *sharṭ* payment was made). Figure 6.6 concerns a marriage consummated some two and a half years later, between a young divorcee from another community and an enterprising labourer of the community, known to his wife's family only through an intermediary.

37. My translation is from one of the four cycles of marriage songs which I recorded in 1976–77 and later transcribed. The Arabic colloquial verse runs:

'Aibata-k yā 'bā wa-mā 'skhā-k
'aibata-k mā 'llī dahā-k
aw dahā-k al-burr al-aḥmar
aw dahā-k ṣarf al-dhahab
aw dahā-k al-walad al-ahyaf
aw dahā-k al-dirkumān
'aibat al-bayyā' mā bā'
niyyata-k yā 'l-mustarī.

38. *Lau tibṣirain yā khawāt*
mā rait ḥāl al-wilād
'ad kān qabrī futiḥ
wa-ṣakkat al-mu'didah
wa-'l-yaum qabrī ghuliq
wa-ṣakkat al-muḥjirah.

39. Landberg (1942, iii: 2807) gives *nifās* as *accouchée*. Lane (1893, I/viii: 2829) gives *nifās*, childbirth, as derived from *nafs*, blood, and with secondary meaning as "the blood that comes forth immediately after the child".

40. Literally, "has fallen".

41. *Zauj-ish wuqu' lu-h walad*
min shajarah ghāliyah
'urūqu-hā fī 'l-biḥār
wa-aghṣānu-hā danniyah.

42. Both the visit and the gifts are referred to as *ziyārat al-bint*.

43. Compare the heading of Chapter 7 for the definition of the relationship created by marriage found in the introduction to the chapter on "in-lawship" (*kitāb al-ṣihrah*) of the *Kitāb al-man'ah*. In this interpretation marriage creates a bond (*sabab*, a rope, is another expression often used in the manuscripts) between two families. The identities of the two parties, like their property rights, merge only in their children. In a somewhat less islamicized version of tribal custom, *Kitāb al-tabyīn fī 'l-man'*, fo. 23r, the author notes concerning the jural relationship established by marriage: "*wa-kadhālik in al-zaujah mātat laisa la-hā 'aqīb wa-hum al-aulād lam tanqaṭi' al-ṣahārah abadan li-tawshīj al-nasab fī-mā baina-hum.*" (If the wife dies childless, then the marriage relation is cut, but if she leaves descendants, that is the children, the marriage relation is never cut because of the intermingling of descent between them.)

44. Such visits are always made at the *'īd al-aḍḥā* but usually also at *'īd al-fiṭr* and *'īd sha'bān*, the Zaidī holiday in memory of the coming of the first Zaidī Imam to Yemen.

45. Such a division of roles is often clearly etched. In one family, the senior woman, Ḥadīyah, was an intelligent and strong-willed character. After the evening meal, every young child in the house (Ḥadīyah's two younger children and one or two of her grandchildren) sought to fall asleep close by Ḥadīyah or on her lap if possible. Even her third son, aged by then about ten, would try to fall asleep with his head on her lap; she would sometimes playfully rebuke him, pushing him away and telling him he was no longer a baby, but he would ignore her, calling her

bluff. Indeed, one time when discussing her eldest son's indifference to his meek wife, Ḥadīyah noted proudly that he had slept by her side until the night of his marriage. (He had married at eighteen.) One evening her husband had gone upstairs as she and the children remained below; her husband called to her. She returned to say that he wanted his son to come rub his feet with oil. She pulled the boy up, took down the cup of oil from the ledge, and gave it to him. The boy shuddered at the thought of touching his father's feet, and as he went out the door, turned round with a look of anger and said: "filth".

46. This description derives from the *amīn*, not the *muzayyinah*.

47. Hearing is believed to be the only sense which can survive after a person's death.

48. The *yāsīn* and three *tahlīls*.

49. Women of neighbouring households work all night in the house of a death to prepare the meals for the families and neighbours on the first day after burial. Closely linked families may make gifts of food (*mujābarah*). But some families may prefer not to receive important *mujābarah*, since, however much they receive from others, they will still need to provide extra meat for the lunches offered the mourners. By declaring that it does not want *mujābarah*, a family thus reduces the exchange of food and numbers at meals, restricting non-family to the afternoon receptions.

50. That is the *mushqurī* worn in the head-dress.

51. Compare the history of *bait* Khabash, pp. 153–60.

52. This was usually done through a *waqf darīs*, see below in the discussion of Bait Khabash. When it privileged an heir to the succession, such an arrangement was always of dubious legality. Compare the case of Aḥmad Ismā'īl and the *amīn* discussed below.

53. See p. 120.

54. Zaidī *fiqh* is almost indistinguishable from Sunnī *fiqh* with regard to succession, notably in that the daughter can never take the entirety of an estate.

55. See Cole and Wolf (1974: 175–205) for an analysis of the force of inheritance law as cultural ideology in communities where the practice of the devolution of real property is in fact determined more by ecology and economy than by the letter of the law. The law does not mechanically determine practice, but large areas of social life prove unintelligible without reference to the law.

56. Or, as Berque (1944: 65–6) noted, what counts is not so much the system of quota-shares as the manner of their redistribution between heirs.

57. In competition with children the wife (or wives) take, at most, an eighth, the husband a quarter. In the case that a woman dies childless and without surviving parents, her spouse is entitled to half his wife's estate; maximally, in the same circumstances, the widow can claim only a quarter of the estate of her spouse. Compare the digest of Islamic inheritance law in Coulson (1971).

58. A mother is entitled to a maximum share of one-sixth and a father one-third in competition with children of the deceased.

59. All classes of sibling, germane, consanguine and uterine, have a claim to inherit although on different principles.

60. Gifts made in death-sickness are subject to the same limitations as bequests. See Coulson (1971: 59–73).

61. A *waqf darīs* is an endowment in perpetuity made to support recitation of the Koran, often for the soul of the benefactor. As in the case of the *waqf darīs* of Aḥmad Ismā'īl, such provisions tended in fact to be dissolved after a generation or two among farmers.

62. In family *waqf* the revenue of a *waqf* is allocated to descendants of the person making the endowment, its revenue reverting to charitable purposes only if all entitled relatives and their descendants die.

63. See Figure 6.7, where Ḥalīmah is one of the three wives of al-ḥājj Qāsim Muqbil.

64. *Maulid al-nabīy*: the ritual celebration of the birth of the Prophet. A woman specialist (*nashshādah*) chants the traditional account of the birth of the Prophet. *Maulids* are celebrated not only on the day of the birthday of the Prophet but towards the end of the forty-day post-partum celebrations and on any joyous occasion, particularly after recovery from a grave illness.

65. A woman with small children has rights of custody and of maintenance in return for her childcare. Cf. note 48, p. 225.

66. Al-ḥājj Qāsim does not appear to have attempted to secure his part of the inheritance from his mother, who, like his first wife (the niece of his mother), was from *bait* Khabash. As described below, the estate of his mother was massively oversubscribed and highly contested. Perhaps he simply received a cash settlement.

67. Cf. p. 88 on this man.

68. In such cases there is of course a tension in the "equality" of partible inheritance: the children of brothers who had equal landholdings, simply because of numbers, not to mention marriage, may come to have very unequal landholdings. This is clearly recognized by those concerned: brothers, as in the case of Sa'd and Ḥusain, often endeavour to reestablish "equality" on behalf of their sons.

69. Cf. p. 185 for evidence that matrilateral cousin marriages are more common in cases where the mother's family estate is larger than the father's.

70. Although people describe this as a Republican ruling, it is in fact not clear whether such arrangements were actually valid in Imamic times without the consent of all the other heirs. Compare the discussion in al-Shamāḥī (1939: 44–5). Imam Yaḥyā judged that most of such bequests, whether called *waqf* or *hibah* or *nidhr*, were properly *waṣāyā* in Islamic law. Since he also judged (p. 33) that a *waṣīyah* may concern only one-third of an estate and that a *waṣīyah* to a direct heir is only valid with the formal agreement of all the other heirs, it is not clear just how different the Republican ruling is. This also suggests the important question of how Islamic law was interpreted locally, and the degree to which document writers in the countryside followed the norms of the centre.

71. Cf. Goody (1989) for such a model.

7 Alliance: house, community and polity

1. *Fa-man ṣāhar ilā qaumin fa-qad in'aqad al-nasab baina-hum li'anna 'l-rajul yarith min al-mar'ah wa-'l-mar'ah tarith min al-rajul wa-tuwāsij al-arḥām wa-dhālik manṣūṣ fī kitābi 'llāh subḥāna-hu.*

2. Augustins (1982: 39).

3. Augustins (1982: 54).

4. Cf. Assier-Andrieu (1984) for a critique of the juridical tradition of Le Play.

5. Cf. Segalen (1991).

6. Cf. Sabean (1990).

7. Lévi-Strauss (1949).

8. For the notion of complex as opposed to elementary or semi-complex systems of marriage, see Héritier (1981).

9. See Héritier (1981: 137 and 149) and Héritier-Augé and Copet-Rougier (1991).

10. Lamaison (1991) objects that in modern industrial societies the social unit that engages in marital alliance comes close to being reduced to the person, bearer of his labour, and that the scale and demographic mobility of populations involved in marriage (with unions themselves becoming more unstable and increasingly resembling serial concubinage) means that the semi-closure of sets for marriage, a condition for redoubling genealogical links by alliance, becomes so eroded that we cannot speak of complex systems as a unified category. He then goes on to argue that in "traditional" peasant society, where such semi-closed sets are found, the social units of exchange are defined in a totally different manner by relations of property.

11. Cf. Goody (1977b) for such an attempt.

12. Cf. Gauffrey (1990).

13. This figure also had a special status in the "native theory" of European kinship: banned by the Western Catholic church, its prohibition was at times contested by Protestant reformers. Cf. Goody (1983). In European missionary writings close marriage was a custom roundly denounced: compare Thomson (1886: 292–4) for a Protestant judgement that manages to combine condemnation of Catholic widening of the list of prohibited degrees with opposition to close marriage on hygienic and social grounds.

14. Indeed, the attempt to revive the theme by Holy (1989) suggests the disquiet of at least one anthropologist that discussion of this Arab "native theory" has disappeared from the discipline.

15. Cf. Eickelman (1981: 129–30) and Bonte (1994c) on this literature. For Chelhod (1965) the custom derives from the bedouin origin of the Arabs!

16. See Peters (1963, 1980b), Geertz (1979), and Bourdieu (1972: 154–267).

17. See Bourdieu (1966) for a contribution to this literature.

18. See Bourdieu (1970 and 1972: 71–151). His "Outline of a theory of practice" (1972: 154–267) at the same time remains faithful to this legacy and yet goes beyond it: compare Verdon (1991: 141–56). See also Bonte (1991).

19. Cf. Bonte and Conte (1991).

20. But see Peters (1976: 27–8 and 61–5) who warns against assuming that a term has the same meaning everywhere.

21. Cf. Maher (1974) and Peters (1976 and 1980b).

22. Tillion (1966) and Peristiany (1976).

23. Cf. Eickelman (1981: 109–16).

24. Cf. Tapper and Tapper (1992–93).

25. Cf. Peters (1976: 29–37).

26. Cf. Bonte (1994a and 1994b).
27. Bonte (1994b: 10).
28. Bonte (1994a).
29. Ibid.: 21.
30. Bonte (1994c: 378–84).
31. This tradition defines personal status, including paternity, inheritance, and the prohibited degrees for marriage. Thus, Islamic law forbids one to marry a parent (and parent's spouse) or a grandparent, a child (and child's spouse) or grandchild, a sibling or sibling's child. One may marry a first cousin. A man is likewise forbidden to take as co-wives women related to one another within the degrees outlined above (i.e. a woman and her mother, father's wife, grandmother, daughter, son's wife, granddaughter, sister or niece). Lastly breast-feeding a child creates fictional kinship (milk-brotherhood) which acts as a bar to marriage. See Schacht (1964: 162–3).
32. See p. 39–42.
33. For a mechanical reduction of status hierarchy to occupation see Chelhod (1985, iii: 15–38). By contrast, see the lucid treatment of political institutionalization by Bujra (1971: 104–14). On idealization cf. Gerholm (1977: 157). For an exemplary analysis of rank versus power cf. Bloch (1977).
34. Compare al-Shamāḥī (1939: 45–8), for the judgement of Imam Yaḥyā: the legal criterion for a valid marriage is religious piety; a marriage is valid even if the spouses are not equal in all the worldly aspects of *kafā'ah*, such as wealth, descent and reputation, if the woman agrees to the marriage. The section is entitled *ightifār al-kafā'ah fī 'l-nikāḥ bi-riḍā' al-mar'ah*. Compare also the text on the subject edited by Nasir (1955). For the Hadramaut, where status descent was on occasion given legal status in readings of *kafā'ah*, see Bujra (1971: 93–4).
35. Compare Dorsky (1986: 45) for the marriage of a girl of *sayyid* descent from 'Amran to a man of *qabīlī* descent from a neighbouring village.
36. Cf. pp. 46–7.
37. See Skinner (1964) and articles on marriage in C.A. Smith (1976), particularly those by Adams and Kasakoff and Jackson.
38. As for the wives married to men born outside the community, 89 per cent of the wives of the landless agricultural workers born outside came from outside (n=27) as did 50 per cent (n=4) of the wives of the men in landed households born outside; the figures for lower specialists were 75 per cent (n=12) and for upper specialists 100 per cent (n=1) respectively.
39. Tables 7.2, A.20 and A.21 concern married and divorced women from the ages of twelve to ninety. In these, any historical change in marriage patterns, or differences in marriage patterns depending on whether the marriage is a first or a later marriage, remain invisible. If one groups marriages according to the age of women, the same major relationships appear with landholding and of occupational orientation. Yet one finds that a somewhat higher proportion of older than of younger women, in both landless and landed households, were born outside the community. The difference is sharper among the landless than the landed, although in both cases it does not appear to be of an order to suggest a radical change in marriage patterns over the period.

There are several possible factors at work here. First is the declining importance of grain-producing areas back-country. Many of the prominent farming families own grain-growing land back-country and have long-standing ties to such areas. The growing market supply of imported grains and the reliable cash income from increased cultivation of *qāt* have combined to reduce the importance of grain-lands to these households. Second, in the case of the landless, since the late-1960s internal migration for agricultural work has fallen, following the possibility of male migration to the oil-producing states. With the remittances from men working abroad, fewer women needed to seek work in agriculture outside their village. Third, among older women we also be seeing the statistical impact of the different character of second and third marriages as compared to first marriages, which tend to be arranged by parents with families close by them. The proportion of wives born outside the community among landless households rises from 56 per cent among women aged fifteen to thirty to 72 per cent among women aged thirty to forty-five to 73 per cent among women forty-five and over. The comparable figures in landed households are 22 per cent of married and divorced women fifteen to thirty, 27 per cent of women thirty to forty-five, and 30 per cent of women forty-five and over.

40. Such marriages are of different types: they range from the rare political marriage with a leading family in the wider region (compare the marriage of Hā'ilah's first daughter, discussed on p. 122), to marriages of the few Ṭayyibī Fāṭimī families of quarter 4 to families of the same sect in Ḥarāz, to the occasional marriage of a man of the community to an attractive sister of a migrant labourer (compare the marriage discussed above, p. 137), to marriages arranged by a male or female go-between on behalf of a modest family of the community which has met difficulty in finding a spouse for a son or daughter locally.

41. The total number of wives was sixty-five. The source was the 1975 census.

42. Table 7.3 concerns the place of birth of all married or widowed women in the households of agriculturalists, grouped according to the quintile rank of total household landholding. The breakdown is by total household landholding; since size of landholding is strongly associated both with household size and with polygamy, the fifth quintile contains almost as many women as the second and the third together. For the purpose of analyzing marriage, however, total landholding appears more suitable than landholding per married man as it reflects well the economic and political status of the older generation of men and women in such households, whose own marriages enter the table and who also make the decisions concerning marriages of the younger generation.

43. Compare p. 188, household 4. The pair married Hā'ilah's two younger children, in the latter's second exchange marriage.

44. The exact definition of the measures I have used is as follows. The land of the husband was calculated as land he himself owns or, if he is a junior man in a complex household, that of the household. The land of the woman is that of her natal home: that of her parents, if alive, or if not, that of the brother tending her parents' land, regardless of whether or not the woman has claimed her land. Although such measures are workable, they clearly have weaknesses. The alternative would be to divide the larger unit into what should some day be each claimant's share. But our study of inheritance suggests the difficulty of such an assumption.

Using total household landholding presumes, however, that strategies of marriage concern alliance with the household as a whole. Among wealthy and powerful families this is a fair enough assumption, but treating the individual as identifiable with the larger holding on which he has a claim does produce anomalies. For example, in one family with six daughters and only one son, the daughters had already agreed not to claim their shares in the inheritance, for they would thereby ruin their brother and obtain rather little themselves. And indeed although all of the daughters had married men of the community – a source of pride to their mother – their husbands had far more modest landholdings than their brother stood to inherit, with their assistance. In their marriages, not only the economic status of the house but the actual portions that would (or in this case would not) accrue to the daughters had escaped neither side.

The correlation of total household landholding is slightly stronger than that of landholding per married man, presumably reflecting the importance of the larger unit and of relations between household seniors in the arrangement of marriage. The correlations relate to currently married women only. Correlation coefficients for total household landholding of the two sides are Pearson product-moment 0.449, P=0.000 and Spearman rank-order 0.501, significance 0.001 (n=190 in both cases). The coefficients of correlation for husband's family land with wife's family land per married man are Pearson's R 0.415, P=0.000 (n=174) and Spearman rank-order correlation coefficient 0.445, significance 0.001 (n=174).

45. This is generally true but not in all cases. If there had been earlier marital exchanges with families outside the community, a woman married in from outside could have inherited rights to land in the community from her mother. Compare also the two Ṣan'ānī women, discussed in Chapter 2, who married their local share-croppers.

46. The Pearson correlation coefficient is 0.4757, P=0.000 (n=271).

47. Compare Figure B.4, which concerns only marriages where the wife was born in the community. In this the ratio of marriages where women marry "up" to those where they marry "down" is four to three (i.e. in both cases marriages falling beyond plus or minus 9 degrees of freedom). If we consider only those cases where the husband's landholding is significantly larger than that of the wife's family as against cases where the wife's family landholding is significantly larger (cases lying beyond plus or minus 46 degrees), the proportion of marriages "up" to marriages "down" is almost two to one.

48. In anthropological literature, preferential FBD marriage is assumed to be a rarely questioned tradition. It should be noted, however, that in the Zaidī legal tradition scholars have condemned *compulsory* cousin marriage. Compare the legal *responsa* published by Rossi (1948: 11–15).

49. Cf. Bonte and Conte (1991: 45–6).

50. In Arabic the term used for kinship is *qarābah*, literally closeness; if one asks a woman whether her husband is related to her, one asks *hal yaqrab la-ki zauju-ki?*, literally, is your husband "close", i.e. related, to you? Equally, the term *nasab* signifies both descent and affinal relation; only the context indicates which is at stake.

In Anonymous, *Kitāb al-tabyīn fī 'l-man'*, fo. 22r, defines in-lawship (*ṣihr*) as *nasab*, "kinship": "*A'lim anna al-ṣihr ḥukmu-hu aghlaẓ aḥkām al-man'ah li'anna-*

hu iltazam bi-'amr lā yaḍmaḥil abadan bi'anna 'l-ṣihr nasaban li-qauli-hi ta'ālā: wa-ja'alnā-hu nasaban wa-ṣihran." (Realize that the legal category of "in-lawship" is one of the most weighty categories in *man'ah*: it is binding by virtue of that which never dies as [appears from] the Almighty's words, "and we made it descent and in-lawship".)

51. These are the three forms of closure or "loop" possible in terms of "biological" genealogy, cf. Héritier (1981: 149).

52. This is not statistically significant by normal standards, but then we are dealing with half the population. The cross-tabulation here produces a raw chi square of 3.43 and significance of 0.064. The data from the census survey is not entirely satisfactory given uncertainty as to whether the marriage registered was a first or a subsequent one, the large differences in the size of the samples, and a high proportion of unknown values in certain categories. Thus, the small number of labourers contains such a high proportion of unknown values and so few valid values as to render the statistic of dubious value.

In the census survey, where subsequent and not only first marriages are at issue, 37 per cent of marriages are between consanguineous kin, whereas in the smaller survey of first marriages the proportion is 43 per cent. The 37 per cent breaks down as follows: 12 per cent to the father's brother's son, 3 per cent to the mother's brother's son, 4 per cent to the father's sister's son, 2 per cent to the mother's sister's son, 13 per cent within the wider patronymic group, and 3 per cent to more distant maternal kin. These figures are from a distribution weighted according to number of married women in each quintile, excluding Quarter 4. In fact the sampling is reasonably well distributed: the proportion of missing values is lowest among the top quarter of landholding households, but only by a margin of some 6 per cent. The unweighted distribution reveals only marginally higher rates of kin marriage.

53. This appears regardless of how one groups households, whether on the basis of total landholding or of landholding per married man, and whether on the basis of the landholding of the husband's household or on that of his wife's family.

54. This appears if one groups married women according to their natal family's wealth or according to total landholding of husband's household, but not if women are grouped according to landholding per married man in husband's household. Grouping households according to total landholding or landholding per married man heightens or flattens the lower peak. This is largely because a number of very large households with important landholdings have relatively modest figures of landholding per married man; such families are very prone to marry "in". But relatively high rates of "in-marriage" appear likewise among those with small total landholdings (and small landholding per married man).

55. Clearly, in purely formal genealogical terms, given the high rate of marriage within the community, most spouses probably have some common ascendant, but purely formal "biological" connection is not at issue. What is under discussion are the wider kin ties recalled by the persons themselves.

56. Size of patronymic group and size of landholding per household are positively correlated, if rather weakly. Here all households were considered, even those where there was only one of a given patronym. The Spearman rank correlation coefficients of mean total household landholding with that of the number of

married men in the patronymic house is 0.424, significance 0.001 (n=127) and with the total size of the patronymic house 0.569, significance 0.001. The correlation between the mean landholding per married man in the patronymic house and the number of married men was 0.342, significance 0.001 (n=127) and with the total size of the patronymic group 0.511, significance 0.001 (n=127).

57. It is noteworthy that the correlation of the mean landholding of all the women married into a patronymic group with the mean landholding of all men in the group proves considerably higher than that of the landholding of spouses taken pair by pair. (Compare the statistics in note 44.) Correlations based upon the mean total landholding of women married into patronymic groups containing two or more households gives a Pearson R correlation of 0.712 with significance level of 0.00000 (n=70) and a Spearman rank correlation coefficient of 0.732 with a significance level of 0.001 (n=70). The correlation coefficients based upon mean landholding per married man are Pearson 0.535, significance 0.00000 (n=65) and Spearman 0.593, significance 0.001 (n=65).

58. Cf. Bonte (1991).

59. Cf. Bédoucha (1994) for the absence of an idiom of "lineage" in another part of Yemen.

60. Because the exact size of this household was not known it was excluded from the calculation in Table 5.1. If its substantial landholding is also included, the total landholding of the patronymic group is 2027.

61. The first husband of this woman, a man from al-Rauḍah living in the community, was murdered by relatives. Some years after her second husband (A1B1) died, she married (as third wife) Ḥasan Muḥsin 'Ākish (I1A) who was murdered only a few weeks after the marriage. At the time of the census she lived between her brothers' house, that of her married sister in Ṣan'ā', and that of her children by A1B1.

62. In some cases, marriages that ended in divorce are noted as well as those that were not dissolved. See the key to the diagram.

63. Properly speaking one was of the house, a daughter (A1B1Z) of A1B1, and the other (M1) was an "outsider". But as the young widow of A1B1, by whom she had three children, M1 was intimately associated with *bait* al-Abyaḍ.

64. Compare case 6 in Appendix 2 where one of the two sons tries to force his mother to give him part of her land.

65. Meillassoux (1990: 40–43).

66. This is an observation developed by Bourdieu (1972: 100–101) in his analysis of cousin marriage among the Kabyle.

67. Compare the figures given by Dresch (1989: 288) and Chelhod (1985, iii: 76–90).

68. Cf. Meillassoux (1990) and Gauffrey (1990).

8 Conclusion

1. Communal or affectual, i.e. with an emotional sense of the common, may translate the Weberian concept *Vergemeinschaftung* and contractual or associative Weber's *Vergesellschaftung*.

2. Cf. Sabean (1990: 425) on the emergence of "cousin networks" and close networks of "affinal and consanguineal relations through marriage and ritual kinship" under economic conditions of competition for credit and land.

3. Cf. Weber (1978, ii: 1249).

4. Cf. Weber (1978, ii: 1250) and Oexle (1992: 757–9).

5. In the case of a landowning member of the community, usually only for murder or grave sexual offense; in the case of migrant workers for much lesser cause (compare cases 15, 46, 47, 48 in Appendix 2).

6. On the name as *dāʿī/daʿwah*, cf. Dresch (1989: 79–80 and 88).

7. Cf. Meissner (1987: 248–9).

8. See Meissner (1987: 377) for the western highlands and (1987: 399–409) for comparative discussion.

9. Cf. the praise of the shaikh's role as builder and defender of Republican Yemen in Dresch (1994: 79).

10. Cf. Adra (1982), Caton (1987) and Dresch (1989: 245).

11. Cf. Cohen et al. (1981) and Swagman (1988b: 63–7).

12. See interviews with Shaikh ʿAbdullāh al-Aḥmar in *al-Ḥayāt*, 10326: 14 May 1991, and *al-Wasaṭ*, 144: 31 October 1994, pp. 33–4.

APPENDIX I

Notes on field research and statistical sources

Field research

As noted in the preface, the field research for this study was carried out over three and a half years between October 1973 and April 1977. A few notes on this research may help the reader judge its context.

At the time when I began living in the community I spoke and read some Arabic, but it was several months before I came to speak the dialect. For the first eighteen months I lived with the family of the acting *amīn* in a house that belonged to prominent Ṣan'ānīs. After this house was sold to butchers of the area (the community preferring the house to be bought by local butchers rather than by the regional shaikh) I retained a separate room on the common courtyard and gradually began to prepare my own meals. By that time I was less of a stranger to the community.

During the first year of my stay I was also engaged in writing up other research work: a survey on the health of mothers and children for UNICEF carried out in the summer of 1973 and two months' work on an IBRD study in Wadi Maur in the Tihāmah in December 1973–January 1974. This allowed me to become a known figure in the community without having to throw myself hastily into research there before I knew the dialect or local conventions. It also meant that I did not stress my identity as one carrying out research on the community itself and always thereafter I felt unable to attend the social or political gatherings of men. I spent most of my time with women and conversed with men almost exclusively in familial contexts and in the presence of their womenfolk. The only exception to this were the two or three afternoons a week I spent studying Arabic grammar and the rudiments of Zaidī *fiqh* with the late Qāḍī Aḥmad Zāhir of Qariyat al-Qābil.

Appendix 1

During my first two years of residence I wrote up notes on events and exchanges observed each day, but I carried out few structured interviews (all with men concerning agriculture and irrigation history). It was only during the last year that I carried out a survey of women's marital, childbearing and property histories, and tape-recorded women's oral tradition (story-telling from a number of women and marriage and childbirth songs from four specialist marriage attendants from Banī Maimūm, al-Wādī, Ḍula' and Ṣan'ā'). At no time did I employ an assistant in my research, although an older female friend accompanied me as chaperone on several visits during the last months of my stay to conduct formal interviews with the shaikh of the upper wards. In 1974–75 I myself worked as research assistant for the study on *qāt* consumption headed by John Kennedy of UCLA and for the Ṣan'ā' part of the exhibition, "Nomad and City", held at the Museum of Mankind in London in 1976.

During the time of the research I was unmarried and in my late twenties; my father paid a visit after I had been living in the community for two years. Finally, I should say that my understanding of the material gathered in the mid-1970s is also framed by shorter visits over a longer period. I visited the community briefly in 1971 and 1972 (accompanied by my mother) and for longer periods in 1980, 1983, 1985 (accompanied by my husband), 1991 and 1994.

Statistical sources

Sources on household and population

a) Census data (1975) In 1975 the government of the Yemen Arab Republic carried out its first full population census; this was funded and in part overseen by the World Bank. The enumerators collected the following information: personal name, father's personal name, patronymic, mother's first name, relation to head of household, sex, age, birthplace, marital status, age at first marriage, literacy, years of residence, occupation, type of house, number of dwelling rooms in house, number of households in house, address and houseowner. The census enumerators were instructed to list as "households" all those who lived and ate together.

Although at the time many Yemenis dismissed the results of the census on the grounds that wary respondents had misled the enumerators, the results of the census in al-Wādī were good, perhaps because the chief enumerator was himself from the area. Furthermore, the area was relatively highly literate and free from major political conflict with the government or inside the area. There was also little fear of conscription at the time. This is not to say that all facts are "correct": certainly two old ladies, a few small households, and doubtless a few children were missed; ages are no more than estimates; people understated the number of rooms in the house; some families may have reported female children as male; but the general contours were very good indeed for the many houses I knew personally. Undercounting seems at most 5 per cent of the population. Unquestionably the results from some other areas, notably large parts of the Tihāmah, were far less accurate.

In establishing household composition in the area I have relied upon the household census returns gathered in the 1975 census, supplemented or corrected at a few points by my own data. I am most grateful to those who permitted me to copy by hand the original household sheets. I could never have gathered such information myself, nor could I have given better estimates of ages.

b) Women's survey (1977) In 1977 I carried out a small survey of 101 women resident in the community. This included questions on women's marital history (age at marriage, marital payments, relation of husband, duration of marriage, cause of dissolution of marriage), childbearing history (for each marriage, the succession of pregnancies, with deliveries, sex of child, and age at death for children who died), and property history (fate of marriage payments, gifts received on the *'īds*, and property claims). This survey has an overrepresentation of poorer women, who were less inhibited in answering questions concerning their property. I have had to weight the results in any comparison with the wider population.

Sources on the distribution of wealth and landholding

a) Records of irrigation rights (1973–74) These provide an indirect measure of landownership in the irrigated lands. I transcribed records of some seven "turns" of the irrigation system during 1973–74, the originals of which had been made by a man known for his probity who had been called in to act as supervisor following complaints about collusion between the previous supervisors and powerful individuals.[1]

Since water rights are tied to landownership in the irrigated belt, the records give an accurate idea of relative holdings in the most valuable land. However, such records do not provide any indication of the relative quality of land, nor of the state of the plantings, nor of ownership of rain-fed fields, which we have seen to be a secondary but important element in the wealth of many families. Nor of course do they give any indication of landholdings outside the community.[2] Furthermore, the irrigation records do not provide full details of claims on land and in the case of joint ownership often give only the major holder(s). In particular, the claims of women are frequently not mentioned. If this were not limitation enough, land held in full (*mushārakah*) agreement may be listed under the share-cropper and not the owner; only in the case where the share-cropper has land in *maḥmā* rather than *shirk* is the holding specifically listed as cultivated "for so-and-so", i.e. the owner. Nevertheless, given the relatively favourable status of the share-cropper (*sharīk*), one would be equally wrong not to take his share into account. And whatever its limitations, the listing has the great virtue of being a record acted upon and largely, if not entirely, respected on a day-to-day basis. In that sense the record may in fact give a more accurate picture of actual control over land and water than the complex private deeds of inheritance prepared by *fuqahā'* and than the other indirect measure of wealth I have studied, that of the tithe paid to the state on *qāt*.

b) List of tithe paid on *qāt* (1975) The tax list provides, I believe, a rather less reliable measure of relative wealth than does the irrigation record. The distribution of tax paid is far less unequal than that of rights to irrigation water. The reasons behind this are not, I suspect, that small holders cultivate *qāt* far more intensively but are, rather, of another order. The Republican government did not set great store by agricultural tax and it allowed local men to assess the tax due.[3]

The system is close to one of self-assessment and the local men who are responsible for collecting the tax are inevitably subject to all manner of pressure and have little special allegiance to the state. Although the Republican government continues to collect the tithe, which is formally a religious tax and tied in Zaidī law to the religious character of the state, clearly it does not attach much importance to the small and declining proportion of state revenue provided by such direct agricultural taxation. Rather, in order to tax some of the fortunes spent and made on *qāt*, the government tried for some time to tax produce as it passed through checkpoints into Ṣan'ā', in short through market taxes rather than direct agricultural taxes. Therefore, I doubt whether any farmer paid the 5 per cent proportion of the value of yields due on land irrigated by pumps. Those who came closest to paying such a percentage were the small rather than the large farmers.

In examining the distribution of wealth I have generally utilized the irrigation records rather than the tax lists since I feel that the latter give a falsely "flat" image of existing inequalities. In terms of the rank order of the two distributions there is in fact a high degree of correlation.[4]

Quality and relationship between the statistical sources

As for a quantified measure of the other major form of wealth described in these pages, ownership of wells and pumps, I do not have precise data on the return of various pumps nor, in three cases, on the exact division of shares between members of a patronymic group. I can therefore do little more than indicate the relative position of individuals and family groups who did own pumps. Without exception the pump owners were prosperous farmers before they acquired pumps.[5]

Because I cannot quantify the relative value and exact distribution of pump ownership, I have based my analysis of inequality solely on the data concerning landownership in the irrigated belt. It should be noted, however, that the overall distribution of wealth (landownership, income from cash crops, and ownership of pump wells) is surely even more unequally distributed than what is suggested by the data on ownership of irrigated land alone.

When compared to the record of those paying tax on *qāt*, which takes the form of a list of names, the irrigation records appear more complex. Because they record how a person uses his allotment, the listing notes the person's total allotment, where water is used, whether it is sold or received from another, whether any water has to be retained in repayment for accidental or deliberate theft, and lastly any water outstanding from the last turn or advanced on the next. Besides simple names of individual owners, many holdings are listed in other ways, such as "the sons of Rāshid", "house al-Rāshid", "Rāshid and his sister", "the heirs of Rāshid", or occasionally "in the name of Rāshid" where Rāshid is deceased, a form referring to property inherited from the deceased. All such forms of reference to holdings, whether simple names or complex forms, can only be interpreted in relation to household structure and to family history known from other sources.

In spite of the inevitable problems concerning the definition of a household, the three enumerators, acting under the supervision of a man born in the community, appear to have been reasonably consistent and to have recorded units that correspond quite closely to farming or to consuming units. Thus, if we consider the households cultivating land on which tax was paid, we find that 71 per cent of these households have as taxpayer the individual head of household as given in the census returns and another 4 per cent the name of a deceased man standing for his widow and children. But if we compare households as given in the census to the person holding land in the irrigation records, we find that in 56 per cent of households the person given as holding land corresponds to the head of the household, in 1 per cent to brothers living in the same household, and in 5 per cent to a widow and children. Thus, on the one hand, for a majority of households, the residential unit, as given in the census, coincides with the farming unit, as given in either the tax or the irrigation lists. On the other hand we should not expect the two kinds of units to correspond any more closely, since the domestic unit is in continuous development: its partition for some purposes occurs at a different stage from its division for other purposes.

In order to abstract a general idea of the distribution of landownership among the residents of the community, I linked the three lists (household, irrigation rights, and *qāt* tax) together. In this I assigned the sum of irrigation rights or *qāt* tax that would be listed, for example, under the name of the head of the household, to the entire household, and I noted the person or group under whose name it was recorded. In 22 per cent of the entries in the irrigation record, people in two or more households (e.g. brothers, sisters, father and son, etc.) had claims on the same holding. In some 7 per cent of households with irrigation rights and in some 5 per cent households paying tax, persons in the household had separate claims on two entries in the lists. In order to obtain household totals I had, in the former case, to assign shares to separate households, and in the latter case to add holdings together to obtain a "household total" of irrigation rights and *qāt* tax paid.

Notes

1. After this man demonstrated that there was not in fact any overall shortage in irrigation water but rather a slight excess if properly distributed, he quit the post as he found it very time consuming and little remunerated. He also expressed his fear of opposing "the big people" who were accustomed to getting rather more than their fair share. The discussion of land tenure in this chapter relies on his records. and presumably the actual amount of land men possess. Judging from his remarks it seems that the division of water is often, in practice, more unequal than the distribution he recorded.

2. As noted, a number of the major landowning families in the area do have considerable holdings of grain-growing land "up-country". Thus, in the absence of more systematic data I feel justified in assuming that households who own considerable land in the irrigated belt in general also own grain lands. There are, however, a few families for whom such a correspondence does not hold true.

3. Compare al-Abdin (1975) for a discussion of taxation. Although I did not systematically investigate the manner of collection, it was clear that the ward heads had a role in making sure that every landowner paid tax, however little, and the local shaikh had overall responsibility. The shaikh of the tribal area also had copies of the tax registers. Compare the system of *amānah* as described by al-Abdin and which, in Imamic times, was restricted entirely to the northern mountainous areas.

4. The Spearman rank correlation coefficient is 0.8424, significance 0.001.

5. Several of the families who installed pumps already owned part or all of the well on which the pump was subsequently mounted. Most were among the most prominent families. About half of the pumps (six) are owned by individuals or brothers. The two shaikhs of the community each own a pump. The other pumps are owned jointly by two or more persons. In the case of one very unsuccessful pump some seven persons had shares, including two women. Unfortunately I do not have a good idea of the net profits of pump owners.

APPENDIX 2

Descriptive table of dispute settlement[1]

1. Disputes are ordered by social group concerned. Unless otherwise noted, all cases occurred during the years 1973–77.

	Parties	Sex of Parties	Underlying issue	Precipitating Event	Legal Tradition	Arbiter/ Judge	Settlement	Action taken	Outcome
	Juveniles								
1	Young children	M–F	none	boys hit girls	local policing	local shaikh	boys warned	—	—
2	Adolescent boys	M–M	social status[1] of son of thief	thief's son beats boy with rock	local policing	local shaikh	aggressor in local jail for 2 days	—	dispute ends
3	Adolescent boy/local teacher in school	M—M	authority of teacher[2]	boy beats teacher at school; head closes school in protest	informal arbitration	local shaikhs; govt. official[3]	father to discipline son	—	—
	Inside household; immediate family								
4	Two sisters (married to two brothers)	F–F	sisters [-in-law] quarrelling; bad insults	husbands complain to shaikh	*man'ah*	local shaikh	women fined; *hajar*[4] given to house; if quarrel recurs double payments	fines paid	tension drops
5	Brother/ spinster sister	M–F	sister's rights to land and maintenance	brother beats sister; she has cousin write note to Governor[5]	govt. policing; Islamic	none: public pressure	none	soldiers go to brother's house; are given lunch & *qāt;* do not find brother	tension continues

6	Son/mother	M–F	son wants mother to give him some land	son threatens mother with a gun	none	none: public knowledge	none	—	underlying tension continues
7	Stepson/ stepmother	M–F	after marriage stepson wants widowed stepmother to move out	stepson strikes stepmother; wife leaves	informal arbitration	man of quarter	mediation; wife returns	—	dispute becomes public knowledge tension remains
8	Mother[6]/son	M–F	mother's control over income	mother accuses son of retaining money from *qāt* sale; son weeps in public	none	none: public knowledge	—	—	tension abates

1. The aggressor was a son of the man killed for stealing *qāt*, see case 41.
2. Cf. cases 52 & 53.
3. See case 12a: the man was then a Minister in the government.
4. *Hajar* is the term used for an animal offered to restore the inviolability of a place where conflict is especially offensive, e.g. a walled plot, house, market place or bathhouse.
5. The cousin is a government employee.
6. This figure is Hā'ilah, who is described in chapter 6. She also appears in cases 17, 31 & 32 where she is referred to as A.

	Parties	Sex of Parties	Underlying issue	Precipitating Event	Legal Tradition	Arbiter/ Judge	Settlement	Action taken	Outcome
9	Son/father	M–M	remarriage of widowed father; father's right to dispose of his property	son steals father's money	none	none: public knowledge	—	father sells some land to warn son	tension abates
10	Daughter's husband/ stepson[7]	M–M	rights of stepson to property	daughter's husband shoots at stepson	none	none: public knowledge	—	—	stepson moves out
11a	Half-brother[8]/ full brothers	M–M	claim of half-brother on stepfather's land since his own inheritance had been sold by stepfather	half-brother seeks division of land on basis of stepfather's will	Islamic	Islamic judge; *ḥākim* of district[9]	claim upheld	dominant heir refuses division of land	tension continues
11b	as in 11a	M–M	as in 11a	men of house quarrel in *qāt* field; violence feared	govt. policing	quarter head, local shaikh & shaikh of district	—	shaikh of district requests govt. soldiers to lock men up to calm them	tension latent, see case 28 below
12a	Brothers	M–M	son steals *qāt* & money from father	father complains	informal arbitration	govt. figure (army officer)[10]	father to designate plots for son	no plots designated	tension continues

12b	Brothers	M–M	brother seeks division of family land	murder[11] (brothers suspected)	*man'ah;* Islamic	shaikhs	*shar'ī diyah* to to son's heirs	father pays *diyah*	as in case 13 below
Cousins and nephews; separate households									
13	Brothers/ brother's sons	M–M	property willed by grandfather to murdered man; political alliances of murdered man	murder;[12] dying man accuses brother's sons	*man'ah*	local shaikhs	community to pay *diyah;*[13] murderer not formally identified	*diyah* paid	skeleton in closet of community; suspension of political group's pre-eminence

7. The father married twice. From his first wife he had two daughters and from his second, none. His second wife brought in her two children by a first marriage. Of his daughters, one married out and the other remained in her father's house married to a patrilateral cousin. At the time of the incident the household thus comprised two marital units, the daughter's and the stepson's. The daughter's husband was set to become a wealthy man and was keen to exclude the stepson from any claim on the estate. See the discussion of this household in chapter 7.

8. Half-brother through the mother.

9. The "district" is both the wider "tribal" area to which the community belongs and a government administrative unit, the *nāḥiyah.*

10. Man of the community of very modest background (grain measurers) who became prominent army officer and government figure in the early Republic.

11. Murder c. 1970; the murdered man was himself regarded as one of the murderers of case 13 below.

12. Murder c. 1967, see also cases 12a, 12b and 14 which are all related.

13. In cases of murder within the community the blood-money *(diyah) is* reduced by one-third for the sake of brotherhood and paid by the households of the community.

	Parties	Sex of Parties	Underlying issue	Precipitating Event	Legal Tradition	Arbiter/ Judge	Settlement	Action taken	Outcome
14	Cousins	M–M[14]	underlying grudge (see case 12)	cousin steals money from cousins/uncle	none	none	none	—	thief (boy) flees area; mother visits boy
15	Cousins	M–M	property dispute	cousin murdered	*man'ah*	local shaikh & shaikh of district	*diyah* to be paid	murderer banished until *diyah* paid	mother refuses to accept *diyah*
16	Cousins	M–F	inheritance from patri-estate; in-marriage	death of all older parents	Islamic	several judges	*shar'ī* rulings	land inherited from grand-mother divided up but not land from grandfather	tension continues but litigation ceases because of high cost
17	Cousins	M[15]–F	right of female cousin (A) to build wall for courtyard	female cousin threatens to take case to govt. official	local policing	shaikh of district	objection withdrawn	—	female cousin builds courtyard
	Husband/wife, in-laws from two houses of the community								
18	Husband/ wife[16]	M–F	couple live in wife's natal home;	marital quarrel at *'īd*; wife	informal arbitration	man of quarter	mediation	wife returns from sister's	tension abates

			his family refuses him any economic independence	goes to sister's house				house	
19	In-laws	M–M M–F	increase in marriage payments	father asks more for daughter; girl then refuses marriage	*man'ah*	local shaikh	*hajar* (bull) to groom	*hajar* given[17]	marriage cancelled
20	Married woman[18]/ husband's brother	M–F	relations of brother to family economy	brother-in-law strikes his sister-in-law when he finds her picking tomatoes from his family's land	Islamic	local shaikh	bruise on woman evaluated by the *amīn*[19]	none	tension continues

14. The adolescent cousin who stole the money was the son of the man murdered in case 13; he stole from those believed to be the murderers of his father.
15. The male cousin is the local shaikh, hence his sensitivity about appeals to higher authority. In an effort to stop his cousin he announced that no women could travel alone into the capital. The announcement remained in effect for one day but was then ignored by everyone. See chapter 6.
16. Daughter of A, living with husband in house owned by A. See case 31.
17. The bull was divided as follows: one-quarter to the disappointed groom, one-quarter to his father, one-quarter to the community, one-eighth to the shaikh; of the destination of the last one-eighth I am unaware.
18. Daughter of A, living with husband in house owned by A.
19. He evaluates the gravity of the injury according to schedule of recompense *(arsh)* as given in *fiqh*.

	Parties	Sex of Parties	Underlying issue	Precipitating Event	Legal Tradition	Arbiter/ Judge	Settlement	Action taken	Outcome
21a	Husband/ wife	M–F	marital quarrel in early marriage	wife remains at natal home, refuses to return	Islamic	Islamic judge	wife to return to husband	none	tension continues
21b	In-laws	M–M	as in case 21a	husband storms into wife's family house; demands wife	*man'ah*	local shaikh	*hajar* (bull) to in-laws	*hajar* given	tension abates; wife later returns to husband
22	Married man/his sister-in-law	M–F	tension in exchange marriage	man hits sister-in-law in wife's family home	*man'ah*	none	wife's family demands sheep in recompense[20]	sheep given	tension abates
23	Widow/ husband's relatives	M–F	rights of widow to part of husband's estate	widow takes husband's brothers to court	Islamic	Islamic court	none	widow gives up legal action for lack of funds	property stays with husband's kin
24	Divorcee/ husband's relatives	M–F	husband dies in woman's *'iddah*[21]	woman seeks to inherit from former husband	Islamic	*ḥākim* of district	triple divorce judged binding no inheritance for woman	—	—

Husband/wife, wife from outside the community

25	In-laws	M–M M–F	marriage to outsiders arranged by men; relations souring	wife repeatedly returns home; terms of divorce settlement	*man'ah;* Islamic	shaikhs, governor	girl's side to return half of marriage payments	half of payments returned to groom's family	divorce given by husband
26	In-laws	M–M	marriage to outsiders; man living in wife's community as labourer	wife's family steals all man's belongings	?	local shaikh	none	shaikh defends man when he enters wife's community	man divorces wife and returns home
27	Wife/ husband	M–F	childless marriage of woman with land to local farmer who marries 2nd wife	husband marries 2nd wife; 1st wife seeks divorce & to have husband give up her land	Islamic	*ḥākim* of district	none	settlement out of court: wife pays high price for divorce	husband gives divorce

20. The sheep due is termed *rīdā'*.
21. The *'iddah* is the three-month period after divorce in which a woman cannot remarry and is due maintenance from her former husband.

	Parties	Sex of Parties	Underlying issue	Precipitating Event	Legal Tradition	Arbiter/ Judge	Settlement	Action taken	Outcome
	Houses related by marriage, in present or preceding generation								
28	Two houses related by marriage	M–M M–F	tension over division of estate	governor & *ḥākim* come to divide land; fight breaks out & the *ḥākim* is injured	Islamic, *man'ah*	Islamic judge & governor	2000YR & bull to each govt. official; all wounds evaluated & the difference paid	fines paid	tension continues over inheritance
29	Two families living in one house	M–M F–F	crowded conditions after family moved into joint house[22]	children fight; parents argue	*man'ah*	local shaikh	injuries of children evaluated; father lays down dagger with shaikh	difference in injuries paid	problem in house made public knowledge
30	Brothers-in-law	M—M	one family living in Ṣan'ā' for political reasons[23]	a note is delivered that threatens the in-laws[24]	govt. policing	govt. soldiers; governor	soldiers collect note; claim made vs. community[25]	none, but notification of govt. checks violence	tension abates, underlying issues remain
	Different houses (patronymic groups) of the community, by type of case								

Priority of access

31	Women guests at wedding	F–F	access to water-pipe	quarrel between A & a younger woman	*man'ah*	local shaikh	1 sheep from each side to other; bull to wedding house,[26] other restrictions[27]	bull for house offered; both sides agree not to exchange sheep	women ignore shaikh's rulings about water-pipes
32	Women at washing place by stream	F–F	access to water	quarrel between A and a younger woman	*man'ah*	local shaikh	fines based on offence; more due if repeated[28]	fines paid	tension drops

22. The family had lost its house in floods which swept the area; they had a claim on the house in question by inheritance through women in the ascendant generation.

23. The man was shaikh in the period before 1962 but had to move out of the area after 1965. There was considerable tension building up concerning the women's rights to land since the two brothers-in-law had married two sisters and their sons were now demanding land from their mothers. Compare case 6 where the son of the sister of the former shaikh spent a night threatening his mother. See chapter 7.

24. The note was ostensibly from the exiled brother-in-law threatening his brother-in-law if he did not give up those plots owned by the former which the latter was cultivating.

25. By reporting the matter to the government, the man living in Ṣan'ā' accused people of the community (in fact the shaikhs) of seeking to stir up trouble between him and his brother-in-law so as to harm the two families.

26. This is called *hajar al-bait*.

27. The shaikh ruled that no tobacco water-pipes would be allowed in women's evening gatherings during wedding celebrations and that only those women guests specifically invited to such evening gatherings would be allowed to attend evening celebrations.

28. (A) was to pay YR300, the younger woman YR400. The common payment was due since each woman had struck the other; the additional 100 was due from the younger woman since she had also insulted (A) in speech. If the two quarrelled again each was to pay 1,000 riyals and a bull.

	Parties	Sex of Parties	Underlying issue	Precipitating Event	Legal Tradition	Arbiter/ Judge	Settlement	Action taken	Outcome
33a	Men of same quarter	M–M	priority in purchasing a tent from a local trader	quarrel; one man draws dagger in marketplace	*man'ah*	quarter head	sheep due to man offended for knife drawn	offended man forgives	quarrel ascribed to arrogance of man who drew dagger
33b	Men of same quarter	M–M	as in case 33a	man who bears witness is insulted by man who drew dagger	*man'ah*	quarter head	offended parties demand bull for market[29] & sheep for man insulted	?	?
	Insults to reputation								
34	Women of same quarter	F–F	rumours about a woman receiving men during Ramadan	woman reports gossip to woman in question; blows; 3 houses & men involved	*man'ah* local policing	local shaikh	bull to each house & YR200 each to community; husbands put in local jail and fined[30]	sheep given instead of bulls	tension subsides
35a	Butcher/ wealthy farmer	M–M	—	farmer, angry at slow service, slaps butcher	*man'ah;* local policing	local shaikh	shaikh promises to imprison man who slapped	shaikh does not in fact imprison man	butcher takes up case with other local shaikh

35b	As in 35a	M–M	—	as in 35a	?	other local shaikh	2nd shaikh notes failure of 1st shaikh to act; advises butchers to go on strike for one day	butchers do not sell meat for one day in protest at shaikh's action	protest noted; shaikh of district informed of local shaikh's failure to punish farmer
	Theft and accusations of theft								
36	Butcher/ farmer	M–M	theft of wine press	farmer finds the butcher trespassing on his garden	?	local shaikh	butcher sells land to farmer for YR1500[31]	butcher buys back his land from farmer	silence kept about winepress

29. This is called *hajar al-sūq.*

30. The conflict was complex. The woman (B) who was the object of the gossip and her labourer husband were from outside the community but protected by the son of the local shaikh, who was undoubtedly friendly with (B). The fight broke out between the two women when the female neighbour (D), a well-known gossip, reported to (B) that (C) had complained that her husband spent all his time with (B). (B) struck (D), the blow constituting an offence. The gossip-mongering in itself constituted an offence. The husbands of all three women became involved. Statements were taken from the women by the local shaikh. The settlement was as follows: a bull in reparation to each house and YR200 to the community chest from the women. It transpired that three men had chewed *qāt* in (B)'s house one evening in Ramadan and had had breakfast *(iftār)* there. Each of the three (husband of C, son of the local shaikh and his friend, a butcher) had to pay YR500 to the community chest. After threatening to fight each other, the husbands of (B) and (D) were put in the local jail for the night, fined YR200 each and told to come to some agreement or else they would have to pay more to the community chest.

31. The background was as follows. The butcher had the wine press in Ṣan'ā' but word got out and he moved the press to his garden in the area. Someone stole the press and the butcher went looking for it. He was found by the farmer in the garden. A deal was struck. The butcher was forced to 'sell' his land to the farrner, with six months' delay in payment. By borrowing from his brother, the butcher raised the money and 'bought' the land back The local shaikh received YR100 for facilitating the sale and the document-writer YR40 for writing the documents.

	Parties	Sex of Parties	Underlying issue	Precipitating Event	Legal Tradition	Arbiter/ Judge	Settlement	Action taken	Outcome
37	Men of same quarter	M–M	—	man found in plot stealing *qāt* during Friday prayer time	local policing	local shaikh & men at mosque	—	owner of plot goes to mosque; shaikh & men beat thief	man exposed as thief; his wife & children weep
38	Govt. official (from community)/ a carpenter, reputed thief[33]	M–M	—	belongings of official's family, just brought out for family's summer stay, are stolen, worth YR8,000	divining;[32] local policing	local shaikh; diviner in al-Ḥudaydah consulted by shaikh's son & men	carpenter & his son, are put in local jail for a week then freed[34]	none	case unsolved
39	Farmer/ young man of same quarter	M–M	young man suspected of stealing *qāt*	farmer finds young man in his plot, accuses him of trying to steal *qāt*	*man'ah*	none	accused enters house of farmer with weapon, demands a sheep *(riḍā')* for the false accusation	sheep given	tension subsides
40	Cultivator/ same young man as in case 39	M–M	suspicions about young man	young man found in plot in mid-afternoon	local policing	local shaikh	Ṣan'ānī landowner threatens to report thief to	document[35] drawn up by shaikh: next time young man	tension subsides

						governor; local shaikh intervenes	is caught, he is to be reported to Ṣan'ā'	
41	Farmer/ carpenter	M–M	—	carpenter found in *qāt* plot at night, fights back, is killed	community regulation; Islamic	local shaikh; shaikh of district; govt. official[36]	earlier community ruling: no *diyah* due for man killed while stealing *qāt*	*shar'ī diyah* collected from all households for the sake of mother, son & widow	—
42	Men of same quarter	M–M	—	man is accused of stealing *qāt;* admits offence to local shaikh	*man'ah*	local shaikh	one sheep for plot;[37] another for owner	first sheep given, 2nd forgiven	tension resolved

32. The shaikh's son and some men from the community visited a famous diviner in Ḥudaydah. The shaikh's son looked into a dark bowl of ink and saw the outlines of a man who looked like the carpenter, together with his son, waiting outside the house at the moment of the crime.
33. It was the brother of this man who was killed while attempting to steal *qāt* at night; cf. case 41.
34. It was alleged that the shaikhs had been bribed but no evidence was produced to support this allegation. The carpenter had a reputation as a thief. The government official also appears in case 12a.
35. The document is termed *raqm.*
36. See case 12a.
37. This is termed *hajar al-buq'ah* .

	Parties	Sex of Parties	Underlying issue	Precipitating Event	Legal Tradition	Arbiter/ Judge	Settlement	Action taken	Outcome
	Land: boundary markers								
43	Two farmers	M–M	—	farmer accuses neighbour of moving boundary marker	*man'ah*, Islamic	local shaikhs	boundary marker to be restored as per the documents[38]	boundary marker set right	tension subsides
	Irrigation from spate flood								
44	Farmers of two houses	M–M	—	fight over water diversion; one man stabs other	*man'ah*	local shaikh; govt. soldiers	2 bulls & YR4,000 to wounded man; YR2,000 to shaikh & soldiers	sums paid	tension drops
	Case involving a local man living outside the community								
	Rights to a house								
45	Butcher/ his brother resident outside the community	M–M	rights to father's house	brothers fight over house rebuilt by resident brother[39]	local policing	local shaikh	resident brother alone has rights to house	shaikh imprisons brothers who fought	shaikh prepares document stating settlement[40]
	Cases involving a party from outside the area living in the community								

	Priority of access								
46	*Muzayyinah*/ wife of labourer from outside community	F–F	—	quarrel over access to water; women tear head scarves off, scratch each other	*man'ah*, local policing	local shaikh	labourer & family to be asked to move out of community	labourer leaves with his family	—
	Theft or accusations of theft								
47	Farmer/ *daushān*[41]	M–M	—	farmer accuses a *daushān* of stealing *qāt*	local policing	local shaikh	local shaikh asks *daushān* to leave	*daushān*s leave	—
	Rights to build a house on common land of village								
48	Farmer/ labourer from Arḥab	M–M	labourer building house on common land	farmer complains to shaikh	*man'ah*/ local policing	local shaikh	labourer to abandon house & to leave area	judgement implemented	labourer leaves

38. The guarantors having been appointed for the two sides, the documents were read out before all. The two shaikhs of the area were present as well as other quarter heads. A measurer verified the fields. The judgement was that the border marker had indeed been moved. It was reestablished so that both fields shared the spate irrigation channel. Both sides were formally bound by the undertaking that if either moved the marker he would owe a bull and YR1,000 to the community as fine (*adab*).

39. The house had been a ruin and was completely rebuilt by the resident brother.

40. The document states that the resident brother holds all rights to the house he built on the site of his father's former house and excludes the two non resident brothers from any part in it.

41. The *daushān* is a specialist bard who singing the praises of men on occasions such as weddings. *Daushān*s tend to move from one area to another, dwelling in tents. They are socially marginal but honoured. This status meant that some disapproval was expressed of the shaikh's decision to ask the *daushān* his family to leave, in the absence of hard proof against the accused.

	Parties	Sex of Parties	Underlying issue	Precipitating Event	Legal Tradition	Arbiter/ Judge	Settlement	Action taken	Outcome
	Cases involving one party from the community and another party from the downstream community								
	Irrigation from spring[42]								
49	Farmer / irrigation supervisor of downstream community	M–M	long-term disputes over water between riparian communities	farmers found stealing water; blows exchanged; supervisor uproots tree on their land in next community	govt. policing; community irrigation rules	local shaikhs; govt. soldiers	men from two communities put in Ṣan'ā' jail as dispute escalates between both communities[43]	men released from jail	tension subsides
	Priority of access								
50	Man of community/ man from downstream community	M–M	—	man stepped in front of other while praying in bathhouse; they quarrelled	*man'ah*	local shaikhs	bull due to the bathhouse[44]	bull given	problem resolved
51	Women of community/ women from downstream community[45]	F–F M–M	existing tension between communities over water rights	fight between women of both communities in bathhouse; men escalate conflict	*man'ah*, community rules	local shaikhs; shaikhs of districts; *'āmil;* govt. soldiers	one bull due from each side to bathhouse; other bulls for injuries; separate days fixed for women of each area	system of separate bath days observed	tension drops

Cases involving one party from outside the area representing a government institution and another party from the area

The school

52	Head of school from Ṣan'ā'/ local woman	M–F	teacher disciplines boy with cane in school	mother comes to school, strikes school head 4x with stick	*man'ah*, local policing	local shaikh	shaikh calms head, prevents him from informing Ministry & promises that incident won't be repeated	—	—
53	Egyptian teacher/ farmers	M–M	teacher struck boy in school as punishment	father & brother of boy come at night & threaten teacher	none	teacher from area is present & restrains farmers	Egyptian teacher does not inform Ministry	local shaikhs informed	—

42. For ordinary theft of water from the spring flow, or for negligence, the irrigation supervisors handle minor infractions on a day to day basis. Such infractions are repaid in water and so do not constitute legal cases for the purposes of this table.
43. As the men had struck the supervisor and direct retaliation (uprooting the tree) occurred, the government had to step in to cool tempers. Men of the community had laid their daggers in the hands of the shaikhs and had begun to take up watch on the borders of the community lest general fighting break out. After about two days the men were let out of jail and the affair forgotten, presumably since direct retaliation had been taken so the parties were quits. Also, more men had been imprisoned from the community of those who had been caught stealing than of the downstream community. The men stealing were known trouble makers in their own community.
44. This is termed *hajar al-ḥammām* .
45. This case occurred c. 1969 when tensions were high between the two communities over rights to irrigation water from the stream.

	Parties	Sex of Parties	Underlying issue	Precipitating Event	Legal Tradition	Arbiter/ Judge	Settlement	Action taken	Outcome
	The Ministry of Supply								
54a	Butchers/ Ministry of Supply	M–M	surveillance of price of meat; inflation	employee of Ministry is cheated by local butcher when buying meat	market inspection; govt. policing	none	most butchers put in govt. jail for two days[46]	costs divided among all butchers	matter is taken up with local shaikhs
54b	Butchers/ Ministry of Supply	M–M	as above	Ministry sends order to shaikh that local butchers must use kilogram weights & charge Ṣan'ā' prices	?	local shaikhs	shaikhs tacitly ignore the order after appeals by the butchers for protection	—	—
	Cases involving the community as corporation								
	Government claim for blood-money from the community								
55	Govt. officials/ Community	—	territorial basis of liability for *diyah*	murdered man from outside locality found on community land	govt. policing;[47] *man'ah;* Islamic	governor; shaikhs	govt. demands blood-money from the community for dead man	local shaikhs refuse to pay *diyah*; shaikhs & quarter heads imprisoned; local men close roads	police investigate & find the murderer; claim against community dropped

	Conflicts with riparian communities over rights to water from the stream system								
56a	Two upstream communities/ downstream community[48]	—	anterior ruling of govt. in early 20th century over division of water	sinking of motorized pumps in upstream areas; decreased stream flow	Islamic; govt. arbitration	special govt. tribunals	pumps to be shut off on days when the stream is in downstream communities	ruling not carried out; more pumps sunk	downstream area feel wronged; they too finally sink pumps
	Conflict between upstream and downstream sections of the community								
56b	Upstream/ downstream areas of the community	—	division of interest between upstream pump-owners & downstream spring flow users	downstream section secedes from community, allies itself with another distant community	community rules	local & national shaikhs	none	a year later downstream sections rejoin home community once again	overt riparian tension subsides

46. It was reported that the man who actually had cheated and some of his relatives, the poorest of the butchers, were not imprisoned. See chapter 2.

47. Here the government, out of expediency, sought to hold the community responsible before it had completed investigations. This procedure has some basis in Islamic law in the category of *qasāmah*. As the leaders of the community argued, it later proved that the body had simply been driven out of Ṣan‘ā’ and dropped over the cliffs.

48. Concerning these legal contests see chapter 2 and Mundy (1989).

APPENDIX 3

Arabic documents[1]

1. Working paper for judgement on murder of carpenter

باسم الله الرحمن الرحيم
تصدت الدعوى من الشيخ أحمد منصور الزواك الثابتة و كالته على الحرة خيرية بنت ضفران الحجالي والدة القتيل الحاج محسن بن العزي يحيى حاتم وأيضا عن زوجة المذكور محسن بن العزي يحيى حاتم قائلا في دعواه انه في يوم الأحد الموافق ثمانية عشر في شهر المحرم ١٣٩٤ وجد محسن العزي يحيى حاتم قتيلا بطعنة في ظهره في الجانب الأيمن وطعنة في شقه الأيسر مما ادى الى ازهاف روحه ووجد منقولا من موضع سودة حق بيت ركيم وقد كان وصول الناظرة عامل همدان ومجموعة معه وثم وصل الشيخ حسن أحمد الغربي اخيرا وقص آثار الدم من الموضع المذكور ووجه السؤال الى بيت ركيم واعترفوا ان القتيل المذكور في اليوم المذكور وصل الى الموضع وسرق القات منه واعترفوا ان القاتل منهم حيث ان ولد حسين ركيم اراد ان يمسكه فهجم عليه وطرحه الى الأرض ومدافعة عن نفسه طعنه وبعد ان سمع الشيخ حسن أحمد الغربي كلام بيت ركيم اخذ حمود بن حسين ركيم الى حبس الرادع (فمضيقين) في حكم الله ولما سمع محسن محسن ركيم اجاب ان اولاد حسين ركيم هم من الوادي وعلى الشيخ واعيان الوادي الاجابة في ذلك وحضر من اعيان الوادي احمد بن سعد معيد والحاج عبد الله أحمد عاكش وصالح بن حمود القزلي والحاج محمد حمود عاكش والحاج احمد بن حسن صالح الضاعي والحاج احمد بن خالد عبد الله والشيخ أحمد عبد ألله الابيض والسيد عبد الرحمن بن عبد الكريم المنصور اجابوا اعيان الوادي المذكورين انه لم يلزم عليهم الاجابة وهذا غريم وغريمه وليس لهم دخل في ذلك اجاب محسن بن محسن ركيم على ان الجواب من اعيان

الوادي والشيخ تهرب من الواقع حيث ان به مراقيم سابقة فيمن وجد يسرق فدمه مباح وبه مراقيم مختصة على المذكور في نفسه ان اذا اعتدى على احد فدمه مباح اجاب شيخ الوادي الحاج أحمد منصور الزواك بانكار المراقيم اجاب الحاج محسن بن محسن ركيم انه ملتزم بايصال مراقيم عامة في الوادي وخاصة بالقتيل فابرز قاعدة حكمت تراضي جميع اهل الوادي عقال واعيان وافراد حسب توقيعهم جميعا ادنى القاعدة وقال فيها لما كثر السرق وغيارات القات واباحة الطرقات واستباحة الممتلكات ولم يوجد من يردع البطال ولا سلك لطريق الحق فارتضوا الناس على هذا على كل واحد من وجدوه يسرق قاتا او غيره بوادي ظهر فان دمه مباح وان لصاحب الملك الحق في قتل السارق الذي يوجده يسرق في أي موضع فان ذمة القاتل للسارق بريئة بتراضي جميع اهل الوادي الموقعين ادنى هذا كل واحد منهم اباح دم المعتدي للسرق اذا كان من الوادي او من طيبة واما اذا كان السارق مخرجي ووجدوه يسرق وقتله المسروق فلا يلزم المسروق الا غرمه من جملة أهل الوادي وكذلك في الاستطراق من استطرق قال غيره فأدبه خمسون ريالا وحبسه اسبوع وايضا تراضوا ان من وجدوه يلوي في الوادي بعد الساعة اربع بدون عذر فأدبه خمسون ريالا وحبس اسبوع وتاريخ هذه القاعدة شهر صفر ١٣٨٨ وكاتبها امين الوادي الحاج حسين بن أحمد الظفري المعروف لدينا وامضاءات كثيرة معظم اهل الوادي ولما امليت هذه القاعدة على الشيخ أحمد الزواك فاخوي القتيل الحاج مسعود حاتم ويحيى حاتم اعترفوا ان له سوابق في السرق وابرز الحاج محسن محسن ركيم بان للقتيل سوابق في السرق وقد سبق ان تحدثنا بعد الحادث الى وجه حسن أحمد الغربي بان السارق المذكور اعتدى على سرق القات في الموضع حق سودة فزحر به حمود بن ركيم فهد عليه السارق وضرب به الى الأرض واراد قتله ومسك حلقه ولما خاف حمود بن حسين ركيم على ازحاف روحه فدافع على نفسه ومسح الجنبية وطعنه طعنة واحدة ولولا هي ان السارق قتله والناس على قواعد ضوابط وبعد ما حرر كان منا الحكم بالدية الشرعية رحمة لوالدة القتيل وزوجته وولده القاصر وكان من الوكيل وأخوي القتيل طرح الربع من الدية مقابل المخوة مع ان القتيل كان له سوابق وشهرة التهجم الى بيوت المواطنين كما عرفنا من اقوال عيان الوادي ان المذكور سبق ان سرق بيت محمود الزواك وبيت محمد الشحمي ايضا له سوابق سرق في ضلع.

2. Working papers for settlement of boundary dispute

2a. *Statement concerning role of guarantor (two documents prepared, one for each guarantor)*

حضر الحاج حسين حسين ركيم وضمن على الحاج محمود عوض العزي برضاه واختياره وهذه الضمانة هي على ان الحاج أحمد منصور الزواك يطلع ينصب الوثن في الموضع المسماه الحمرا في المحجر بين محمود عوض العزي وحميد عيسى همدان على ما كان منصوبا سابقا هذا بعد ان رضى محمود عوض العزي وحميد همدان وقلد الشيخ أحمد الزواك قلاده مهمه بان لا يجامل مع احد وبعد نصب الوثن يجرا المساح في الموضع المذكور والخيار لمحمود عوض العزي اما املا ما في بصايره وما بقى لحميد همدان او يملي حميد همدان ما خصه من الفوائد وما بقى لمحمود عوض العزي وهذا في حضور الحاج محمد عبد الله المخلافي والحاج أحمد حسن الدحم والسيد عبد الرحمن المنصور والحاج عبده حسن الناظر وحرر بتاريخ السبت الموافق ٤١ ربيع ١٣٩٤ كتب أمين الوادي .

2b. *The* raqm *of the judgement itself*

باسم الله الرحمن الرحيم

بموقف شيخ وادي ظهر الحاج أحمد منصور الزواك والشيخ الحسام الحاج حمود العزي مسعود وقع حضور الحاج محمود عوض العزي جابر وغريمه حميد بن عيسى همدان من أجل الوثن الفاصل من قبل بينهما في الموضع المسما الحمرا من اوطان وادي ظهر همدان بوادي الجاكي فكان من المشايخ انتخاب اثنين ضمناء فالذي ضمن على الحاج محمود عوض العزي هو الحاج علي خالد عبد الله وهذا برضا الغرما جميعا والضمنا كذلك وحضورهما ثم وقع الوصول الى فوق موضع النزاع وامليت البصاير حق الطرفين واجرى المساح فقد صح ما تحت يد الحاج محمود عوض العزي في الموضع المذكور حسبما حكته بصايره في الجهة القبلية بشرق ست مأه لبنة وثلاثين لبنة ظهري ما أكتسبه عوض العزي من بيت همدان والذي صح بيد حميد بن عيسى همدان في الجهة العدنية بشرق والمحدودة

غربيا ملك محمود عوض العزي وذلك ثمان مأة لبنة ظهري والذي راوه المشايخ والعدول والضمنا حسما للمادة وقطعا للعلاقة هو ان يثبت كل أحد من الغرما المذكورين على ما تحرر بعد المساح حسبما قرره المساح ويبقا الوثن الفاصل على عادته ومن تعدا بعد هذا الى الوثن او الى الرهق والمسقاء فان أدبه رأس بقر وألف ريال حيث انه لم يكن لاحدا من المذكورين الاختصاص بالمسقا كون الموضع يشرب موج وحرر بتاريخ ١٨ ربيع الاول ١٣٩٤ كتب أمين الوادي حسن عبد الكريم العبيد .

2c. *Note not included in the final version of the* raqm

قد وقع الطياف لموضع الحمرا في وادي الجاكي ما بين الحاج محمود عوض العزي وحميد عيسى همدان بحضور مشايخ الوادي والأعيان والضمنا الواصفين اسماهم ادنى هذا وبعد المساح حسب ما حكته بصاير محمود عوض العزي صح ما أكتسبه الحاج عوض العزي من بيت همدان ست مأة لبنة وثلاثين لبنة في الجهة القبلية بشرق والذي صح ما تحت يد حميد همدان ثمان مأة لبنة ظهري في الجهة العدنية بشرق والذي أمروني المشايخ بتحريره ويثبت الطرفان على ما قرره ويبقا الوثن عادته ومن تعداه او قدم الى المسقا بعد هذا بتحويل او اخرار فان أدبه ألف ريال ورأس بقر لكون الموضع يشرب موج وهذا كان في حضور الغرما والضمنا والمشايخ والمساح والعدول بتاريخ ١٨ ربيع الاول ١٣٩٤.

3. Agreement between "in-laws"

رقم بيد الحاج أحمد حلاوة وبيد الغرش مثله

بسم الله الرحمن الرحيم

قد كان الاتمام بين الحاج أحمد سعيد حلاوة وبين نسبه محمد رفيق الغرش على ارجاع ابنته لدى زوجها راجع أحمد حلاوة في بيت والده بعد ان حلف الحاج أحمد وزوجته الحرة لطفية على عدم المضاررة منهم لزوجة ولده بشيء وقد كفل الحاج محسن عبد الله معيد على الحاج أحمد في كلما يلزم الزوج لزوجته وفي الرعاية منهم لها وعليها الامتثال لأمر زوجها وعمها وعمتها وان لا لها الخروج من البيت الا بأذنهم وقد ألزم محمد الغرش على ان يوصل ورقة كفالة الحاج علي العزي حرب عليه وذلك في سلوك ابنته لدى زوجها وامتثال أمره هو ووالده ووالدته وعلى المرأة أن تعمل في البيت مثل امثالها من الناس في المحل وقد ألزم نفسه الحاج حمود علي زالف أن لا يقبل الحرة وردة بنت محمد رفيق الغرش أن تصل الى بيته أيضا وصار التراضي بين الطرفين اذا حنقت ابنة الغرش فعلى زوجها مرافقتها الى بيت والدها فان ثبت ولها حجة فعلى حلاوة غلاق الغرش برأسين غنم وان حنقت وليس لها حجة فعلى الغرش ارجاع ابنته فورا مع زوجها وعلى الغرش غلاق حلاوة برأس غنم هذا ما كان الاتمام عليه وقد التزم الغرش بارجاع ابنته مع زوجها يوم الخميس الأقرب باذن الله كان هذا في حضور الشهود وهم أحمد الخولاني والحاح مقبل الحمامي من الوادي وحرر بتاريخ ٢٤ شهر القعدة من الحقير مهدي الهجالي.

The context of this document is as follows. The marriage here working its way to dissolution united two families that had not previously been linked and lived in separate communities three hours' walk apart. They were both of market status: the boy's family were prosperous butchers in the community while the girl's family were far less wealthy weavers, although some of the men of her family had emigrated to work in Saudi Arabia. The boy's mother had chosen a local girl but she was too young to marry at the time. So, the son being impatient to marry, the men of the family arranged the match through an intermediary at a market where they went to ply their trade once a week. Since there were no prior bonds between the families, the marital payments were comparatively high given the low social standing of the girl's family. The share of the payments that passed to the hand of the girl's father (10,000YR as *shart)* was large compared to that given the girl (1,500YR as *mahr)*. The father seemed in no hurry to settle much of this payment upon his daughter, who was marrying into an unknown house considerably wealthier than his own.

The girl did not take to her husband, the most dour of the sons of the family, nor the mother-in-law to the bride, who corresponded to none of the older woman's networks or ambitions. By the tenth month of marriage the girl had returned to her natal home eight times; and eight times her husband or father-in-law had gone to fetch her back. (In common law the groom or a male member of his family must accompany the bride to her natal home. Should they fail to do so they will owe amends to the family and the woman. This coming and going is thus of legal relevance.) Slowly the two sides had entered into a cycle of dispute where each side sought to prove that it was the other who did not want the marriage. By the eleventh month both parties seemed prepared to terminate the marriage: so why did the groom not just "send her paper", that is, give his wife a divorce, as was his prerogative? The sticking point was the high payment made at marriage, for if a husband divorces, the marital payment remains with the wife's family, whereas if the bride's relatives seek the girl's release they must return at least part of the sums received at marriage.

The first move to involve formal legal authority was made by the bride herself. Early one morning she went to the shaikh of her husband's community, whose house was nearby, to complain of her husband. The girl's allegations were later conveyed to the mother-in-law by the shaikh's son's wife. The girl was reported to have complained that her husband had twisted her arm when she had refused to have sexual relations since she was menstruating. In women's company the girl certainly complained of her husband's lack of sexual manners. Her father was also said to have brought the question up in later stages of the divorce negotiations. This is, however, a decidedly grey area on which to build a case. As the Yemeni proverb notes, "No one knows what is between a woman and her husband." The shaikh stood in a doubly paternal relation to the girl, since she was both a woman from outside the community and belonged to the status group of market people. At noon on the same day the shaikh spoke to the husband. In the afternoon the young husband took his wife home to her family.

Five days later, after her father-in-law had come together with a soldier dispatched from the Governor's office – the two communities belonged to the same administrative circumscription or "tribal" area – the girl's father took the girl back to her husband's house. During the days the girl spent in the marital home each side started to prepare a case against the other; each tried to provoke the other to utter a serious insult or to demand an end to the marriage unilaterally. The one common area of investment, the clothing which the groom's side had given the girl at marriage, was a subject of claims from both sides. Only ten days after she had returned to her husband's house, the girl decided to return to her natal home, her father-in-law refused to accompany her, and she left alone carrying her trunk of clothing on her head.

It was her father who initiated the next stage in the legal prosecution of the dispute. He took a local document writer to the house of his in-laws. The scribe proceeded to mediate by drawing up a written agreement between the two sides. Since the girl's father refused to enter the house, the document was drawn up in the courtyard, with the young goats, the half-deaf old grandmother, myself the foreign guest, the dung pit and the washing tub all as background. Others in the courtyard included the groom's mother (Luṭfīyah) and father (Aḥmad Sa'īd), the girl's father (Muḥammad Rafīq al-Gharash) and the document-writer (al-Hijālī). The mother-in-law summoned me, in the hope that I would testify that the girl did no work. All were shouting at once. After some time al-Hijālī silenced them, securing agreement about how and when the husband should escort his wife home.

The girl's father refused to admit the witnesses proposed by Luṭfīyah, arguing that the family simply did not want his daughter (*yubghadū-hā*). Unfortunately, this unsophisticated man then proposed to have his own daughter bear witness to the fact that they did not want her, although clearly as a party concerned she could not bear witness. He then demanded that the mother-in-law swear that she did not want the girl. The older woman refused, rejoining that they had not abused the girl, starved her, left her naked or beaten her. "Oh, so you would beat her now?" howled the father, beside himself with rage. At this, al-Hijālī, perhaps fearing violence, broke in: "*Tanāsabū:* act like those bound by marriage." The boy's father answered, "*Nasabnā:* we are in-laws."

The girl's father demanded new clothing, shouting that some of what had been given had dated from Luṭfīyah's wedding. Al-ḥājj

Aḥmad Sa'īd cut short the girl's father on the topic of the *kiswah* by noting that he should have returned it at the time of marriage had it not been acceptable. Al-Hijālī heard the various arguments, calming each heated speaker in turn. He disposed of the contentions of the girl's father with the statement: "If she has clothes, she can go outside the house; if she has no clothes, she can stay inside."

Al-Hijālī then proceeded to write down and read aloud the agreement he was drawing up between the two families:

> *Bismillāh al-rahmān al-rahīm.* An agreement was reached between al-ḥājj Aḥmad b. Sa'īd Ḥalāwah and his relative by marriage, Muḥammad Rafīq al-Gharash, to return his daughter to her husband Rājiḥ Aḥmad Ḥalāwah (living) in his father's house after al-ḥājj Aḥmad and his wife, the free woman Luṭfīyah, swore that they had not harmed their son's wife in any way. Al-ḥājj Muḥsin 'Abdallah Mu'īd [a third party] undertook to guarantee that al-ḥājj Aḥmad would provide all that a husband owes a wife and all the care that his parents too owe her. She in turn must obey her husband, father and mother-in-law and not leave the house without their permission. Muḥammad al-Gharash promised to deliver a document certifying that al-ḥājj 'Alī al-'Izzī Ḥarb [a third party] undertakes to guarantee this for him, that is, the behaviour of his daughter towards her husband and her obedience to him and his parents. As wife, she must also work in the home as do other women in the village. Al-ḥājj Ḥamūd 'Alī Zālif [the husband of the girl's maternal aunt, living near the husband's home] undertakes not to admit the free woman Wardah, the daughter of Muḥammad Rafīq, should she come to his house. The two sides agree that if the daughter of al-Gharash goes home, her husband must accompany her to her father's house. If she can produce proof against them, then Ḥalāwah must give two sheep to al-Gharash. But if she goes home without good cause, then al-Gharash must return his daughter immediately to her husband and make amends to Ḥalāwah with a sheep. This was agreed and al-Gharash promised to send his daughter back with her husband on the coming Thursday, God willing. This occurred in the presence of the witnesses, Aḥmad al-Khaulanī and al-ḥājj Muqbil al-Ḥammāmī, both of al-Wādī, and was written on the 24th day of al-Qa'dah 1396 by the humble Mahdī al-Hijālī.

The document changed little. Before it was ever written both parties knew the rules governing the escort of a wife to her family home. Both parties knew the local values that should govern the relations of families bound by marriage. It was the elements of Islamic tradition which, for the girl's side at least, seemed both less familiar and unlikely to restore the equality of respect that should underlie the relations of those bound by marriage. The document stressed the wife's duty to obey her husband and to labour in his house; it made no reference to the issue of the clothing, so central to statements about honour but of no issue in law. The father left unassuaged, disappointed with the document that had been drawn up.

On the appointed day the husband, again in the company of a soldier from the Governor, went to fetch his wife. But the Wardah's father was absent, a fact which the soldier duly noted. Two days later Muḥammad Rafīq returned his daughter to the husband's family. Not long afterwards the girl returned home for a last time, refusing ever to return to her husband.

Full legal negotiations began. The local shaikhs of the two communities met several times to negotiate a settlement on behalf of the two parties. On occasion the two fathers also met before the Governor. In the last session, all came together to hear the respective claims of both sides but by then agreement had in fact been reached: the wife's father was to return 5,000YR, half the payment received by him, and the husband was to write the legal divorce.

There was one last move. The boy's mother still sought to retrieve the clothing they had given the girl; unlike any other clothing which her father gives her, the *kiswah* remains the property of the marital family in local custom. But the girl's father proved willing to swear that he had never received it. This closed the matter legally.

Some three and a half months after he divorced Wardah, Rājiḥ Aḥmad married his mother's original candidate. The payments for that marriage were just over 5,000YR.

Although none of the negotiations for this divorce were conducted before Islamic authorities of the state, it conformed perfectly to the category of *khul*ʿ in *fiqh* and was sealed by a written *ṭalāq* (divorce) drawn up by a document writer in Ṣanʿā'.

Note

1. In all documents the text has been transcribed directly from the original without correction of grammar or spelling. The original personal names have been changed to pseudonyms throughout.

APPENDIX 4

Statistical tables and figures[1]

Table A.1 Distribution of landholding by ward

Ward	No. of people	No. of hhlds	No. of landed hhlds	% hhlds landed	Total land[2]	Mean landed holding
1	85	17	12	71	1,178	98
2	336	64	37	58	3,081	83
3	262	50	42	84	2,753	66
4	192	36	23	64	447	19
5	276	51	29	57	3,507	121
6	191	26	21	81	3,154	150
7	326	41	34	83	4,410	130
8	286	39	26	67	3,066	118
Total	1954	324	224	69	21,596	96

Table A.2 Ownership of irrigated land by residence of owner

Place of residence	Amount of land	% of total	Number of households	Mean holding
Wadi Ḍahr	21,596	95.3	324	67
Ṣan'ā'	749	3.3	18	42
Bait Na'am	37	0.2	1	37
Unknown	269	1.2	14	19
Total	22,651	100.0	357	63

1. The percentages in the tables have been rounded arithmetically: thus on occasion row or column per cent totals may add up to 99 or 101 not the 100 per cent shown uniformly as the actual total.
2. Here and in all other tables the measure of land is in water units. See Appendix 1 for the relation between water units and land.

Table A.3 Occupation by birthplace of head of household (per cent)

Occupation	Inside	al-Qariyah	Bait Na'am	Elsewhere	Total	
Landed	97	1	1	1	100	(n=193)
farmer	69	40	25	3	60	
Landless	53	2	6	39	100	(n=53)
labourer	10	20	37	57	16	
Trading	82	–	–	18	100	(n=11)
	3			5	3	
Market	87	4	–	9	100	(n=23)
services	7	20		5	7	
Craft, not	67	–	–	33	100	(n=3)
building	1			3	1	
Mechanic	78	–	–	22	100	(n=9)
& driver	3			5	3	
Building	57	7	22	14	100	(n=14)
	3	20	38	6	4	
Literate	50	–	–	50	100	(n=6)
specialist	1			8	2	
Government	75	–	–	25	100	(n=12)
service & guard	3			8	4	
Total	85	2	2	11	100	
	100	100	100	100	100	
	n=274	n=5	n=8	n=37	n=324	

Appendix 4

Table A.4 Marital histories of women by age of woman

Age of women	Marital history				
	No divorce or death	Widowed	Divorced	Widowed & divorced	Total
Teens	100%	–	–	–	100%
	5				5
20s	72%	5%	23%	–	100%
	16	1	5		22
30s	44%	16%	28%	12%	100%
	11	4	7	3	25
40s	29%	43%	14%	14%	100%
	6	9	3	3	21
50s plus	11%	53%	18%	18%	100%
	3	15	5	5	28
Total	40%	29%	20%	11%	100%
	41	29	20	11	101

Table A.5 Frequency of marriage among women of different age groups

Age group	Number of marriages			
	One	Two	Three or more	Total
Teens	100%	–	–	100%
	5			5
20s	82%	14%	4%	100%
	18	3	1	22
30s	56%	32%	12%	100%
	14	8	3	25
40s	48%	43%	9%	100%
	10	9	2	21
50s	39%	36%	25%	100%
	11	10	7	28
Total	57%	30%	13%	100%
	58	30	13	101

Table A.6 Survival of children born according to age of mother and sex of child

	Women 40 or less (n=40)[1]		Women over 40 (n=51)	
	Female	Male	Female	Male
Surviving	59 52%	82 62%	49 36%	64 38%
Deceased	55 48%	51 38%	87 64%	105 62%
Total births	114 100%	133 100%	136 100%	169 100%
Sex ratio of deliveries reported (boys per 100 girls)[2]	117		124	
Sex ratio of surviving children[2]	139		131	

Notes: 1. Two cases excluded 2. See note to next table concerning sex of children born and rates of survival of children.

Table A.7 Age at death of children according to age of mother

Age at death	Women 40 or less (n=42)		Women over 40 (n=51)	
	Female	Male	Female	Male
Stillbirth				
–30 days	16 (30%)	12 (23%)	10 (11%)	26 (24%)
1–6 months	8 (15%)	10 (19%)	16 (18%)	18 (17%)
6-24 months	28 (52%)	26 (50%)	37 (43%)	40 (38%)
2-4 years	2 (4%)	1 (2%)	12 (14%)	6 (6%)
5-10 years		2 (4%)	6 (7%)	5 (5%)
10-20 years		1 (2%)	5 (6%)	6 (6%)
20+ years			1 (1%)	4 (4%)
Total	54 (100%)	52 (100%)	87 (100%)	105 (100%)

Note: Taking Tables A.6 and A.7 together it appears that older women have reported certain female perinatal deaths as male or have underreported female deaths in early infancy. Although the sex ratio at birth is also high for the deliveries reported by younger women, it is less skewed (117 as opposed to 124). Among the younger women, however, the proportion of female children surviving is markedly lower than that of male children, leading to a highly skewed sex ratio among the surviving children. There may indeed be differential neglect of female children.

Appendix 4

Table A.8 Divorce and the uterine family: distribution of divorce by childbearing history

Childbearing history	Economic status		
	Poor	Rich	All
With children	5 23%	3 18%	8 21%
Without children	17 77%	14 82%	31 79%
Total number	22 100%	17 100%	39 100%

Table A.9 Men's wealth and age difference of spouses: mean difference in age of husband and wife for men over fifty according to landholding per married man of husband's household

Quartile rank	Difference in age of spouses (years)	Total number
First	9.4	n=21
Second	12.8	n=24
Third	12.4	n=34
Fourth	16.3	n=29
All	13.2	n=108

Table A.10 Widow remarriage: widows remarrying or not remarrying according to economic status and childbearing history

Childbearing history	Economic Status		
	Poor	Rich	Total
With children	9/16=56%	5/13=38%	14/29=48%
Without children	8/9=89%	3/6=50%	11/15=73%
Total Number	17/25=68%	8/19=42%	25/44=57%

Table A.11 Polygyny and landholding: proportion of married and widowed women with and without a co-wife according to landholding per married man of husband's household (per cent)

Type of marriage	Quintile rank of husband's household					
	First	Second	Third	Fourth	Fifth	Total
Only wife	93	87	89	85	71	86
Co-wife	7	13	11	15	29	14
Total	100	100	100	100	100	100
	n=118	n=87	n=75	n=82	n=80	n=442

Table A.12 Age and household headship: proportion of men in each age group who are heads of households grouped by wealth of household (per cent)

Age by decade	Wealth category of household			
	Agric 1 & Spec 1	Agric 2 & Spec 2	Agric 3 & Agric 4	All men
Teens	3	6	3	4
Twenties	50	44	17	33
Thirties	79	79	41	60
Forties	88	100	78	85
Fifties	89	100	84	90
Sixties	86	100	88	91
Seventies	100	100	89	93
Eighties +	100	–	92	–
Total	n=146	n=157	n=309	n=613

Table A.13 Residence of widows by wealth of household (per cent)

Residence of widow	Wealth category of household		
	Agric 1 & Spec 1	Agric 2 & Spec 2	Agric 3 & Agric 4
With son	57	56	64
With relative of husband	7	9	22
With daughter	14	13	8
With female relative	–	–	3
With father or brother	–	13	3
Alone	21	9	–
Total	100 n=14	100 n=23	100 n=36

Table A.14 Mean number of married men per household according to age of head and economic grouping

Age of head	Economic grouping			Total
	Agric 1 & Spec 1	Agric 2 & Spec 2	Agric 3 & Agric 4	
Less than 30	0.9	0.9	0.7	0.7 n=51
30–44	1.0	1.1	1.6	1.3 n=89
45–59	0.9	1.1	1.3	1.1 n=99
60 plus	0.8	1.3	2.1	1.5 n=83
Total	0.9 n=107	1.1 n=93	1.6 n=122	1.2 n=322[1]

Note: 1. Two households are excluded from this table

Table A.15 The proportion of women to men in households of agriculturalists according to landholding per married man (per cent)

Proportion of men to women	Landholding per married man of household			
	No land	50 or less	50+/<100	100 plus
Men only	13	3	–	–
More men than women	9	10	10	10
Equal numbers	59	54	60	41
More women than men	11	29	26	49
Women only	8	4	4	–
Total number	100	100	100	100
	n=64	n=70	n=51	n=49

Appendix 4

Table A.16 The number of households structured around women according to economic status of household (per cent)

Type of household	Economic status of household						
	Agric 1	Agric 2	Agric 3	Agric 4	Spec 1	Spec 2	Total
Solitary females	7 n=4	5 n=3	–	–	11 n=5	–	4 n=12
Daughter extension	3 n=2	–	2 n=1	7 n=4	2 n=1	3 n=1	3 n=9
Family from wife's first marriage	3 n=2	2 n=1	–	2 n=1	–	3 n=1	2 n=5
Married or divorced woman and child	3 n=2	–	–	2 n=1	2 n=1	3 n=1	2 n=5
Couple and wife's sister's family	–	–	2 n=1	–	–	–	<1 n=1
Widow and widow's sister's family	–	–	–	2 n=1	–	–	<1 n=1
Widow(s) forming top generation	3 n=2	16 n=10	20 n=12	21 n=13	11 n=5	19 n=6	15 n=48
Households not structured around women	81 n=48	77 n=48	76 n=47	66 n=41	74 n=34	72 n=23	74 n=241
Total	100 n=60	100 n=62	100 n=61	100 n=61	100 n=46	100 n=32	100 n=322[1]

Note: 1. Two households are excluded from this table.

Table A.17 *Mahr* reported by women for marriages during the years 1910–77, mean values per decade[1]

Decade	*Mahr* in first marriage	*Mahr* in second marriage	Total *mahr* and *sharṭ* in first marriage
1910–19	25 RF		53 RF
1920–29	25 RF		85 RF
1930–39	23 RF	25 RF	50 RF
1940–49	20 RF		62 RF
1950–59	25 RF	21 RF	124 RF
1960–64	92 RF	49 RF	224 RF
1965–69	185 RF	55 RF	450 RF
1970–77	1,000 RJ	500 RJ	2,860 RJ

Note: 1. RF = *riyāl faransī*, the silver coinage used in Imamic times. RJ = *riyāl jumhūrī*, the currency introduced after 1962.

Table A.18 Marital payments reported by women of different strata, marriages occurring between 1910 and 1950

Payment	Wealth of woman's family[1]			
	Group 1	Group 2	Group 3	Group 4
Mahr	10 RF	21 RF	27 RF	42 RF
Sharṭ	23 RF	44 RF	66 RF	116 RF
Total	n=6	n=4	n=5	n=5

Note: 1. Here the poor/rich categories used in Tables A.8 and A.10 were further subdivided; the dates were chosen because marriage payments appeared to rise relatively little during the period.

Table A.19 Proportion of men born inside and outside the community according to occupation (per cent)

	Born inside area	Born outside area	Total
Landless agricultural workers	49	51	100 (n=53) 13
Landed farmers	98	2	100 (n=281) 67
Lower specialists	64	36	100 (n=47) 11
Upper specialists	94	6	100 (n=36) 9
Column total	88 (n=366)	12 (n=51)	100 (n=417) 100

Table A.20 Proportion of married and widowed women born inside and outside the community according to occupation of household (per cent)

	Born inside area	Born outside area	Total
Landless agricultural workers	36	64	100 (n=47) 10
Landed farmers	79	21	100 (n=343) 70
Lower specialists	26	74	100 (n=50) 10
Upper specialists	49	51	100 (n=49) 10
Column total	67 (n=326)	33 (n=163)	100 (n=489) 100

Table A.21 Proportion of wives from outside the community according to occupation and landholding of husband's household (per cent)

Land status	Occupation: Trading	Market services	Gov't employ	Trans-port	Building	Literate specs	Total
No land	86	81	60	71	93	100	57
	n=7	n=16	n=5	n=7	n=14	n=3	n=52
Own land	46	86	64	20	–	33	43
	n=11	n=7	n=11	n=5	n=2	n=3	n=39
Total	20	25	18	13	18	6	100
	n=18	n=23	n=16	n=12	n=16	n=6	n=91

Table A.22 Place of wife's home for married women born in the community according to landholding of husband's household, agriculturalists only

Wife's home	Quintile rank of household landholding: First	Second	Third	Fourth	Fifth	Total
In home	7%	17%	12%	3%	6%	8%
	1	6	5	2	6	20
In same ward	57%	46%	28%	32%	27%	33%
	8	16	11	19	26	80
In next ward	7%	20%	25%	32%	29%	26%
	1	7	10	19	27	64
In Wadi	29%	17%	35%	33%	38%	33%
	4	6	14	20	36	80
Total	100%	100%	100%	100%	100%	100%
	14	35	40	60	95	244

Table A.23 Comparative distribution of landholding among agriculturalists calculated through wives and through husbands according to total landholding of natal household[1]

Quintile rank of husband's household	Wives				Husbands		
	% of all land	% of all wives	Mean holding all wives	Mean holding born inside	% of all land	% of all husbands	Mean holding
First	1	19	4 n=60	14 n=19	3	22	2 n=75
Second	9	18	47 n=56	75 n=35	9	19	57 n=62
Third	16	18	85 n=57	121 n=40	16	19	105 n=65
Fourth	24	21	103 n=67	142 n=49	22	21	135 n=70
Fifth	50	24	196 n=74	220 n=66	50	19	316 n=65
Total	100 n=29,256	100 n=314	93 n=314	140 n=209	100 n=40,610	100 n=337	121 n=337

Note: 1. Compare footnote to table A.24. In this table each spouse is credited with the total land of their natal household. This produces a false total amount of land in the first column.

Table A.24 Comparative distribution of landholding among agriculturalists calculated through wives and through husbands according to landholding per married man of natal household[1]

Quintile rank of husband's household	Wives				Husbands		
	% of all land	% of all wives	Mean holding all wives	Mean holding born inside	% of all land	% of all husbands	Mean holding
First	1	19	4 n=57	14 n=16	1	22	1 n=75
Second	12	18	34 n=53	57 n=32	7	19	23 n=62
Third	17	19	47 n=57	67 n=40	14	19	44 n=65
Fourth	25	22	59 n=64	83 n=46	25	21	74 n=70
Fifth	45	22	103 n=66	117 n=58	53	19	167 n=65
Total	100 n=15,345	100 n=297	52 n=297	80 n=192	100 n=20,450	100 n=337	61 n=337

Note: 1. In the calculation, households are first ranked and divided into quintiles according to landownership per married man of husband's household. Each husband is credited with the landholding per married man of his household and each wife with that of her natal household. The relative proportion of the total irrigated land, as thus distributed through husbands and through wives, is computed and compared, as is also the mean value of landholding in each quintile for wives and husbands. The number of missing values is high among the women. For comparison, therefore, all women married in from outside are also included but not credited with any irrigated land. The column "all wives" includes women married in from outside. The mean value of holding is calculated separately for all women and just for those women born inside the community.

Appendix 4

Table A.25 Kin relation of husband in two samples (per cent)

Relationship of husband	Larger survey: marriages in 1975	Sub-sample of women: first marriages only (weighted distribution)
No relation	66	62
Father's brother's son	10	14
Mother's brother's son	3	2
Father's sister's son	3	4
Mother's sister's son	2	4
Through father	13	7
Through mother	3	7
Total	100	100
	n=241	n=101

Note: In the census, relationship between the spouses was unknown to me in 47 per cent of all cases. Because missing values are more likely to occur in cases where there is no relationship between spouses than where there is, this statistic may err on the side of overcounting kin relationship between spouses. The list based on the census also appears to undercount relationship through the mother as compared to relationship through the father when compared to the more carefully controlled smaller survey. Unfortunately the sampling in the smaller survey is not strictly comparable to the larger population; it included a large number of poorer women and women of specialists and so had to be weighted in order to produce comparable statistics on the population as a whole.

In the smaller survey the data on the relation of spouse were obtained by asking the woman (and in many cases I by then knew at least one answer) whether her spouse was related to her. In answering this question women also indicated relationships in the same generation, notably exchange marriages, leviratic marriages (2 per cent of marriages reported) and the sororal double of the levirate, i.e., where a younger sister marries the widower of her older sister (1 per cent of marriages reported).

In the case of the census list, I compiled information for all the marriages where I knew the relationship between spouses or where I knew that there was no relationship between spouses. I indicated only one relationship: there were a handful of cases where I knew that the spouses were related both through mother and father but I gave primacy to the closer relationship and, where relationships were equally close, to the father's side. All women known to be married into their patronymic group, even when I was not entirely certain of other possible relationships, were included in the category "through the father". By contrast any case where I was not entirely certain of relationship was omitted. Thus, if there is a bias in this larger sample it is to overcount patronymic relations as against relationship through the mother or lack of relationship. Furthermore, Ward 4 was excluded because the proportion of missing values was especially high.

Table A.26 Kin marriage by occupation: proportion of women married to a relative grouped according to occupation of husband (per cent) (larger survey: marriages in 1975)

Relationship of husband	Occupation of husband				
	Landed farmers	Landless labourers	Lower spec'ists	Upper spec'ists	Total
No relation	64	86	67	81	67
Some kin relation	36	14	33	19	33
Total	100	100	100	100	100
	n=161	n=14	n=24	n=31	n=230

Note: figures exclude Ward 4.

Table A.27 'Exchange' marriage by occupation: proportion of women married in an 'exchange' marriage grouped according to occupation of husband (per cent)

Type of marriage	Occupation of husband				
	Landless labourers	Landed farmers	Lower spec'ists	Upper spec'ists	Total
'Exchange' marriage	–	21	5	15	17
Simple marriage	100	79	95	85	83
Total	100	100	100	100	100
	n=10	n=148	n=22	n=26	n=206

Appendix 4

Table A.28 Proportion of women married to kin in households of agriculturalists according to landholding per married man of wife's natal family (per cent)

Relationship of husband	Quintile rank of woman's family's landholding					
	First	Second	Third	Fourth	Fifth	Total
No relation	90	53	71	66	49	62 n=73
Kin relation	10	47	29	44	51	38 n=45
Total	100 8 n=10	100 13 n=15	100 18 n=21	100 30 n=35	100 31 n=37	100 100 n=118

Table A.29 Kin marriage and landholding among farmers: women married to a relative in households of agriculturalists grouped according to landholding per married man of husband's household (per cent)

Relationship of husband	Quintile rank of husband's household					
	First	Second	Third	Fourth	Fifth	Total
No relationship	67	71	65	64	56	63
Kin relationship	33	29	35	36	44	37
Total	100 10 n=18	100 14 n=24	100 21 n=37	100 25 n=44	100 30 n=53	100 100 n=176

Table A.30 'Exchange' marriage by landholding among farmers: proportion of women married in an 'exchange' marriage grouped by landholding per married man of the husband's household (per cent)

Type of marriage	Quintile rank of husband's household					
	First	Second	Third	Fourth	Fifth	Total
No exchange	93	77	88	83	69	80
Exchange	7	23	12	17	31	20
Total	100	100	100	100	100	100
	n=14	n=22	n=33	n=41	n=49	n=159

Table A.31 'Crony' marriages in households of agriculturalists: married women with a female relative married in the same household grouped by landholding per married man of the husband's household (per cent)

Type of marriage	Quintile rank of husband's household					
	First	Second	Third	Fourth	Fifth	Total
Crony	4	15	14	8	17	12
No crony	96	85	86	92	83	88
Total	100	100	100	100	100	100
	n=68	n=65	n=71	n=79	n=86	n=369

Table A.32 'Crony' marriages in farming households with two or more married women: proportion of married women with a female relative married in the same household grouped by landholding per married man of the husband's household (per cent)

Type of marriage	Quintile rank of husband's household					
	First	Second	Third	Fourth	Fifth	Total
Crony	16	22	19	12	23	19
No crony	84	78	81	88	77	81
Total	100	100	100	100	100	100
	n=19	n=46	n=52	n=50	n=66	n=233

Table A.33 Type of marriage by relative size of husband's and wife's family land: landholding per married man compared for households of agriculturalists (per cent)[1]

Type of marriage	Comparative size of landholding: Wife's > husband's	About equal	Husband's > wife's	Total
No relation	26	40	34	100
	65	50	68	59
Father's brother's son	13	87	–	100
	7	22		12
Mother's brother's son	–	75	25	100
		5	3	3
Father's sister's son	17	17	66	100
	3	2	11	5
Mother's sister's son	33	–	67	100
	3		5	2
Distant through father	23	54	23	100
	17	21	14	18
Distant through mother	100	–	–	100
	3			1
Total	23	47	30	100
	100	100	100	100
	n=29	n=58	n=37	n=124

Note: 1. Compare the note to Table 7.3 in text concerning the calculation of the comparative size of spouses' landholdings.

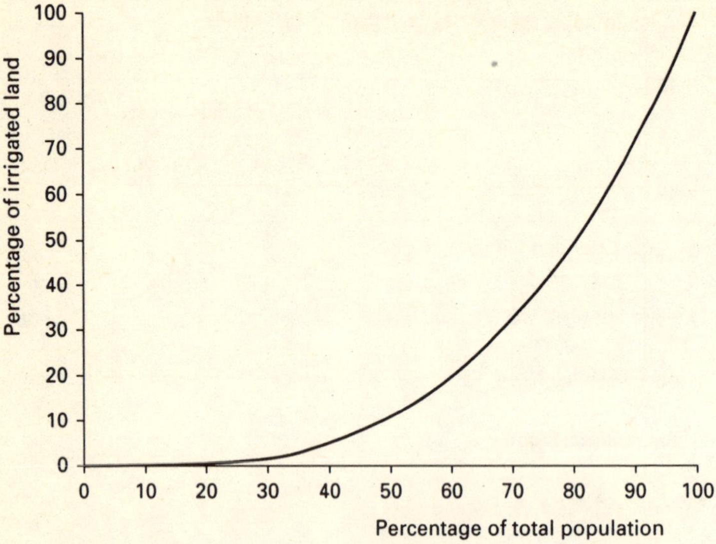

Figure B.1 Graph of irrigated land against total population

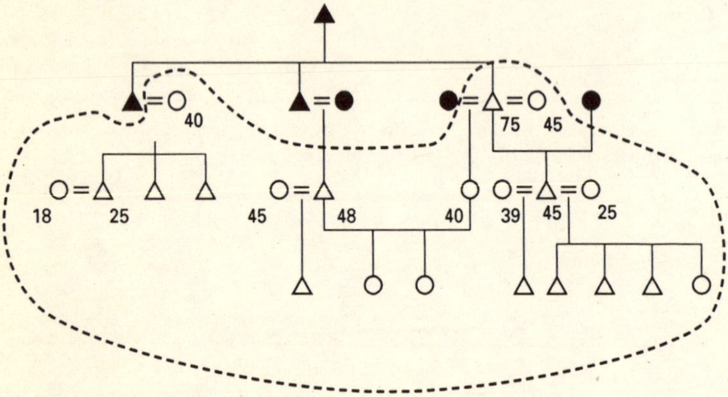

Figure B.2 The household with the largest landholding, *Bait* Murguim (Numbers refer to the age of household members)

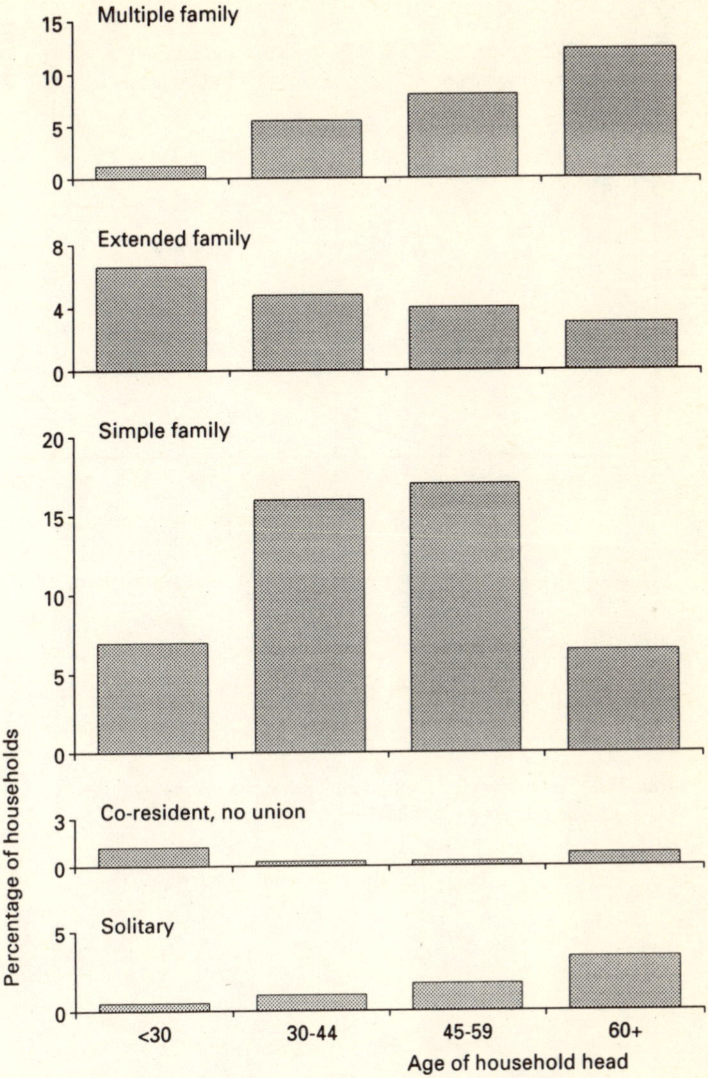

Figure B.3 Typology of households by age of household head

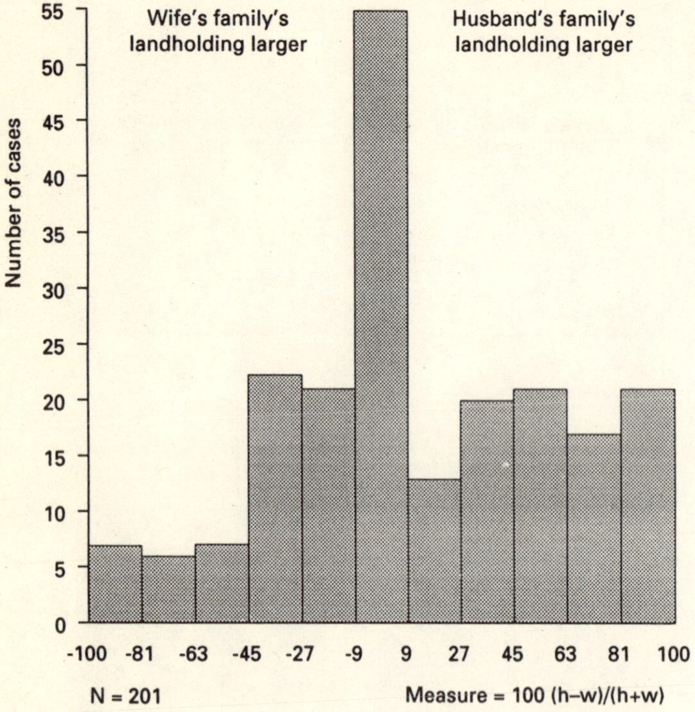

Figure B.4 Comparison of family landholdings of husband and wife (total household landholding; agriculturists only)

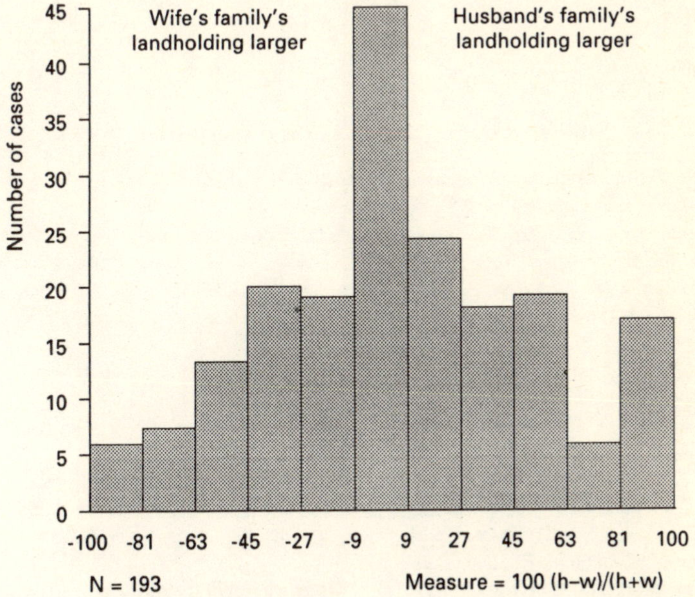

Figure B.5 Comparison of family landholdings of husband and wife (landholding per married man; agriculturists only)

Bibliography

Published books, articles and dissertations

'Abd al-Salām, Muḥammad (1988) *al-Jumhūrīyah bain al-salṭanah wa-'l-qabīlah fī 'l-yaman al-shamālī*, Cairo, Shirkat al-Amal.

Abdel Kader, Suha (1984) "A survey of trends in social science research on women in the Arab region, 1960–1980", in UNESCO, *Social Science Research and Women in the Arab World*, London, Frances Pinter, 139–75.

al-Abdin, al-Tayyib Zein (1975) "Islam and the State (1940–1972, Yemen)", University of Cambridge, Ph.D. dissertation.

— (1979) "The Free Yemeni Movement (1940–48) and its ideas on reform", *Middle Eastern Studies*, 1: 36–48.

Abū Ghānim, Faḍl 'Alī (1985) *al-Bunyah al-qabalīyah fī 'l-yaman bain al-istimrār wa-'l-taghayyur*, Damascus, Maṭba'at al-Kātib al-'Arabī.

Abu Zahra, Nadia (1982) *Sidi Ameur: A Tunisian village*, London, Ithaca Press.

Abu-Lughod, Lila (1990) "Anthropology's orient: the boundaries of theory on the Arab World", in H. Sharabi (ed.), *Theory, Politics and the Arab World: Critical responses*, London, Routledge, 81–131.

Adams, John and Alice Kasakoff (1976) "Factors underlying endogamous group size", in C.A. Smith (1976: 149–73).

Adra, Najwa (1982) "Qabyala: The Tribal Concept in the Central Highlands of the Yemen Arab Republic", Temple University, Ph.D. Dissertation.

— (1985) "The concept of tribe in rural Yemen", in N. Hopkins and S.D. Ibrahim (eds), *Arab Society: Social science perspectives*, Cairo, American University in Cairo, 275–85.

al-Akhras, Muḥammad Ṣafūḥ (1980) *Tarkīb al-'ā'ilah al-'arabīyah wa-waẓā'ifu-hā: dirāsah maidānīyah li-wāqi' al-'ā'ilah fī sūriyah*, Damascus, Wizārat al-Thaqāfah wa-'l-Irshād al-Qaumī.

al-Akwa' al-Ḥiwālī, Ismā'īl 'Alī (1980) *al-Madāris al-islāmīyah fī 'l-yaman*, Damascus, Dār al-Fikr.

al-Akwa' al-Ḥiwālī, Muḥammad 'Alī (1971) *al-Yaman al-khuḍrah, mahd al-ḥaḍārah*, Cairo, Maṭba'at al-Sa'ādah.

Albergoni, Gianni and Geneviève Bédoucha (1991) "Hiérarchie, médiation et tribalisme en Arabie du Sud: la *hijra* yéménite", *L'Homme*, 32/2: 7–36.

al-'Alīmī, Rashshād (n.d.) *al-Qaḍā' al-qabalī fī 'l-mujtama' al-yamanī*, Cairo, Dār al-Wādī.

al-'Amri, Husein (1985) *The Yemen in the 18th & 19th Centuries: a political and intellectual history*, London, Ithaca.

Bibliography

Anderson, Benedict (1983) *Imagined Communities: Reflections on the origin and spread of nationalism*, London, Verso.

al-'Ansī, Aḥmad Qāsim (1938) *al-Tāj al-mudhhab li-aḥkām al-madhhab, sharḥ matn al-azhār*, Cairo, Dār Iḥyā al-Kutub al-'Arabīyah.

Aristotle (1951) *The Politics*, London, Penguin.

Asad, Talal (1986) *The Idea of an Anthropology of Islam, Occasional Papers Series*, Washington, DC, Center for Contemporary Arab Studies, Georgetown University.

Assier-Andrieu, L. (1984) "Le Play et la famille-souche des Pyrénées: politique, juridisme et science sociale", *Annales E.S.C.*, 39: 495–513.

Aswad, Barbara (1971) *Property Control and Social Strategies: Settlers on a Middle Eastern plain*, Ann Arbor, University of Michigan.

Attar, Mohammed Said el (1964) *Le sous-développement économique et sociale du Yémen: perspectives de la révolution yéménite*, Alger, Editions Tiers-Monde.

Augustins, Georges (1982) "Esquisse d'une comparaison des systèmes de perpetuation des groupes domestiques dans les sociétés paysannes européenes", *Archives Européenes de Sociologie*, 23: 39–62.

al-'Azm, Sadik Jalal (1981) "Orientalism and orientalism in reverse", *Khamsin*, 8: 5–26.

al-Azmeh, Aziz (1982) *Ibn Khaldūn: An essay in reinterpretation*, London, Frank Cass.

— (1986) *Arabic Thought and Islamic Societies*, London, Croom Helm.

Barakāt, Ḥalīm (1984) *al-Mujtama' al-'arabī al-mu'āṣir: baḥth istiṭlā'ī ijtimā'ī*, Beirut, Markaz Dirāsāt al-Wiḥdah al-'Arabīyah.

Bédoucha, Geneviève (1987) "Une tribu sédentaire: la tribu des hauts plateaux yéménites", *L'Homme*, 27: 139–49.

— (1994) "Le cercle des proches: la consanguinité et ses détours (Tunisie, Yémen)", in Bonte (1994: 189–219).

Berkner, Lutz and Franklin Mendels (1978) "Inheritance systems, family structure, and demographic patterns in Western Europe, 1700–1900", in Tilly (1978: 209–23).

Berque, Jacques (1944) *Essai sur la méthode juridique maghrébine*, Rabat, n.p.

— (1978) *Structures sociales du Haut-Atlas, suivi de Retour aux Seksawa*, 2nd edn., Paris, Presses Universitaires de France.

Béteille, André (1992) "Caste and family in representations of Indian society", *Anthropology Today*, 8/1: 13–18.

Betzler, Emil (1987) *Sozialer Umbruch und Kulturlanschaftswandel in Südarabien*, Wiesbaden, Ludwig Reichert.

Bloch, Maurice (1977) "The disconnection between power and rank as a process: an outline of the development of kingdoms in central Madagascar" reprinted in Bloch (1989) *Ritual, History and Power: Selected papers in anthropology*, London, Athlone, 46–88.

Bonte, Pierre (1991) "Alliance et rang dans la société maure. Les fonctions du mariage 'arabe'", in Héritier-Augé and Copet-Rougier (eds) (1991, ii: 29–60).

— (ed.) (1994a) *Epouser au plus proche: Inceste, prohibitions et stratégies matrimoniales autour de la Méditerranée*, Paris, Editions de l'EHESS.

— (1994b) "Introduction" in Bonte (1994a: 7–27).

— (1994c) "Manière de dire ou manière de faire: Peut-on parler d'un mariage 'arabe'?" in Bonte (1994a: 371–98).

Bonte, Pierre and Edouard Conte (1991) "La tribu arabe: approches anthropologiques et orientalistes" in P. Bonte, E. Conte, C. Hamès, A.W. Ould Cheikh, *Al-Ansâb: La quête des origines*, Paris, Editions de la Maison des Sciences de l'Homme, 13–48.

Bornstein, Annika (1974) *Food and Society in the Yemen Arab Republic*, Rome, Food and Agriculture Organization, United Nations, MISC/74/4.

Botta, Paul (1880) *Relation d'un voyage dans le Yémen, entrepris en 1837*, Paris, Duprat.

Bourdieu, Pierre (1966) "The sentiment of honour in Kabyle society", in J. Peristiany (ed.) *Honour and Shame*, London, Weidenfeld & Nicholson, 191–241.

— (1970) "La maison kabyle ou le monde renversé" in *Echanges et communications. Mélanges offerts à C. Lévi-Strauss à l'occasion de son 60e anniversaire*, Paris-La Haye, Mouton, 739–58.

— (1972) *Esquisse d'une théorie de la pratique, précédé de trois études d'ethnologie kabyle*, Geneva, Droz.

Bujra, Abdalla (1971) *The Politics of Stratification: a study of political change in a South Arabian town*, Oxford, Oxford University Press.

Burrowes, Robert (1987) *The Yemen Arab Republic: The politics of development 1962–86*, Boulder, Westview.

— (1991) "Prelude to unification: the Yemen Arab Republic, 1962–1990", *International Journal of Middle East Studies*, 23/4: 483–506.

Cain, Maureen (1983) "Gramsci, the state and the place of law", in D. Sugarman (ed.) *Legality, Ideology and the State*, London, Academic Press, 95–117.

Caponera, D.A. (1973) *Water Laws in Moslem Countries*, Irrigation and Drainage Paper 20/1, Rome, Food and Agriculture Organization, United Nations.

Caton, Steven (1987) "Power, persuasion and language: a critique of the segmentary model in the Middle East", *International Journal of Middle Eastern Studies*, 19: 77–102.

— (1990) *"Peaks of Yemen I Summon": Poetry as cultural practice in a North Yemeni tribe*, Berkeley, University of California Press.

Chelhod, Joseph (1965) "Le mariage avec la cousine parallèle dans le système arabe", *L'Homme*, 5: 113–72.

— (1970) "L'organisation sociale au Yemen", *L'Ethnographie*, 64: 61–88.

— (1973) "La parenté et le mariage au Yémen", *L'Ethnographie*, 67: 47–90.

Chelhod, J. et al. (1984 & 1985) *L'Arabie du sud: histoire et civilisation*, Paris, Maisonneuve & Larose, 3 vols.

Claverie, Elisabeth and Pierre Lamaison (1982) *Le mariage impossible: Violence et parenté en Gévaudan, 17e, 18e et 19e siècles*, Paris, Hachette.

Cohen, Abner (1965) *Arab Border-Villages in Israel*, Manchester, Manchester University Press.

Cohen, John, M. Hébert, D. Lewis and J. Swanson (1981) "Development from below: local development associations in the Yemen Arab Republic", *World Development*, 9/11–12: 1039–61.

Cohen, Myron (1976) *House United, House Divided: The Chinese family in Taiwan*, New York, Columbia University Press.

Cole, Juan and Eric Wolf (1974) *The Hidden Frontier: Ecology and ethnicity in an Alpine valley*, New York, Academic Press.

Colonna, Fanny (1987) *Savants paysans: Elements d'histoire sociale sur l'Algérie rurale*, Alger, Office des Publications Universitaires.

Combs-Schilling, M.E. (1989) *Sacred Performances: Islam, sexuality, and sacrifice*, New York, Columbia University Press.

Coulson, Noel (1971) *Succession in the Muslim Family*, Cambridge, Cambridge University Press.

Cresswell, Robert (1970) "Parenté et propriété dans la montagne libanaise", *Etudes rurales*, 40: 7–79.

Cuisenier, Jean (1975) *Economie et parenté, leurs affinités de structure dans le domaine turc et le domaine arabe*, Paris, Mouton.

Davis, John (1977) *People of the Mediterranean: An essay in comparative social anthropology*, London, Routledge and Kegan Paul.

Donzelot, Jacques (1977) *La police des familles*, Paris, Minuit.

Dorsky, Susan (1986) *Women of 'Amran: A Middle Eastern ethnographic study*, Salt Lake City, University of Utah Press.

Dostal, Walter (1974) "Sozio-ökonomische Aspekte der Stammesdemokratie in Nordost-Yemen", *Sociologus* N.S. 24/1: 1–15.

Douglas, J. Leigh (1987) *The Free Yemeni Movement, 1935–1962*, Beirut, American University of Beirut.

Dresch, Paul (1984) "The position of shaykhs among the northern tribes of the Yemen", *Man*, NS 19: 31–49.

— (1986) "The significance of the course events take in segmentary systems", *American Ethnologist*, 13: 309–24.

— (1988) "Segmentation: Its roots in Arabia and its flowering elsewhere", *Cultural Anthropology*, 3/1: 50–67.

— (1989) *Tribes, Government, and History in Yemen*, Oxford, Clarendon Press.

— (1990a) "Guaranty of the market in Ḥūth", *Arabian Studies*, 8: 63–91.

— (1990b) "Imams and tribes: the writing and acting of history in Upper Yemen", in Khoury and Kostiner (eds) (1990: 252–87).

— (1994) "Tribalism and democracy in Yemen", *Chroniques Yéménites*, Centre Français d'Etudes Yéménites, Ṣan'ā': 65–79.

Duben, Alan and Cem Behar (1991) *Istanbul Households, 1880–1940*, Cambridge, Cambridge University Press.

Durkheim, Emile (1933) *The Division of Labor in Society*, New York, Macmillan (first French edition 1893).

Eickelman, Dale (1981) *The Middle East: An anthropological approach*, Englewood Cliffs, Prentice Hall.

Erder, Türköz (ed.) (1985) *Family in Turkish Society*, Ankara, Turkish Social Science Association.

Evans-Pritchard, E.E. (1940) *The Nuer: A description of the modes of livelihood and political institutions of a Nilotic people*, London, Oxford University Press.

— (1949) *The Sanusi of Cyrenaica*, Oxford, Clarendon Press.

Ferchiou, Sophie (ed.) (1992) *Hasab wa Nasab: Parenté, alliance et patrimoine en Tunisie*, Paris, Editions du C.N.R.S.

Fortes, Meyer (1953) "The structure of unilineal descent groups", *American Anthropologist*, 55: 17–41.

Fortes, Meyer and E.E. Evans-Pritchard (eds) (1940) *African Political Systems*, London, Oxford University Press.

Foucault, Michel (1970) *The Order of Things: An archaeology of the human sciences*, London, Tavistock (first French edition 1966).

— (1976) *Histoire de la sexualité 1: La volonté de savoir*, Paris, Gallimard.

— (1979) "On Governmentality", *Ideology and Consciousness*, 6: 5–46.

Fox, Richard (1971) *Kin, Clan, Raja and Rule: State-hinterland relations in pre-industrial India*, Berkeley, University of California Press.

Gauffrey, Christian (1990) *Ni père, ni mère: Critique de la parenté, le cas makhuwa*, Paris, Le Seuil.

Gautier, Emile-Félix (1931) *Moeurs et coutumes des Musulmans*, Paris, Payot.

Geertz, Hildred (1979) "The meaning of family ties" in C. Geertz, H. Geertz and L. Rosen, *Meaning and Order in Moroccan Society*, Cambridge, Cambridge University Press, 315–91.

Gellner, Ernest (1969) *Saints of the Atlas*, London, Weidenfeld & Nicholson.

— (1981) *Muslim Society*, Cambridge, Cambridge University Press.

— (1990) "Tribalism and the state in the Middle East", in Khoury and Kostiner (1990: 109–26).

Gerber, Haim (1980) "Social and economic position of women in an Ottoman city, Bursa", *International Journal of Middle Eastern Studies*, 12: 231–44.

Gerholm, Tomas (1977) *Market, Mosque and Mafraj: social inequality in a Yemeni town*, Stockholm, Department of Social Anthropology, University of Stockholm.

— (1985) "Aspects of inheritance and marriage payment in North Yemen", in Ann E. Mayer (ed.), *Property, Social Structure, and Law in the Modern Middle East*, Albany, State University of New York Press, 129–51.

Gingrich, André (1989) "How the chiefs' daughters marry: tribes, marriage patterns and hierarchies in Northwest Yemen", in A. Gingrich, S. Haas et al. (eds) (1989: 75–86).

— (1993) "Tribes and rulers in Northern Yemen" in A. Gingrich, S. Haas, G. Paleczek, T. Fillitz (eds) *Studies in Oriental Culture and History*, Frankfurt, Peter Lang, 253–80.

Gingrich, André and Johann Heiss (1986) *Beiträge zur Ethnographie der Provinz Ṣa'da* (Nordjemen), Vienna, Austrian Academy of Science.

Gingrich, André, Siegfried Haas, Sylvia Haas, Gabriele Paleczek (eds) (1989), *Kinship, Social Change and Evolution, Vienna Contributions to Ethnology and Anthropology*, 5, Vienna, F. Berger.

Ghālib, Muḥammad An'am (1962) *Niẓām al-ḥukm wa-'l-takhalluf al-iqtiṣādī fī 'l-yaman*, Cairo, Maṭba'at Dār al-Hanā.

Glaser, Eduard (1885) "Die kastengliederung im Jemem", *Das Ausland*, 68/11: 201–5.

Goitein, S.D. (1955) "Portrait of a Yemenite Weaving Village", *Jewish Social Studies*, 17/1: 1–16.

— (1978) *A Mediterranean Society. Volume III: The Family*, Berkeley, University of California Press.

Goody, J.R. (ed.) (1958) *The Developmental Cycle in Domestic Groups*, Cambridge, Cambridge University Press.

— (1972) "The evolution of the family", in P. Laslett (1972: 103–24).

— (1977a) *The Domestication of the Savage Mind*, Cambridge, Cambridge University Press.

— (1977b) *Production and Reproduction: A comparative study of the domestic domain*, Cambridge, Cambridge University Press.

— (1983) *The Development of the Family and Marriage in Europe*, Cambridge, Cambridge University Press.

— (1989) "Kinship, comparison and long-term development: a methodological and substantive comment on the woman's property complex among the Arabs", in A. Gingrich, S. Haas, et al. (1989: 249–54).

Granqvist, H. (1931 and 1935) *Marriage Conditions in a Palestinian Village*, Commentationes Humanarum Litterarum 3/8 and 6/8, Helsingfors, Societas Scientarum Fennica.

Grosrichard, A. (1979) *Structure du serail: la fiction du despotisme asiatique dans l'occident classique*, Paris, Le Seuil.

Guichard, Pierre (1977) *Structures sociales "orientales" et "occidentales" dans l'Espagne musulmane*, Paris, Mouton.

Haddad, Yvonne (1982) *Contemporary Islam and the Challenge of History*, Albany, State University of New York Press.

al-Hamdānī, al-Ḥasan ibn Aḥmad (1931) *al-Iklīl VIII* (ed. A.M. al-Karmalī), Baghdad, n.p.

— (1948) *al-Iklīl min akhbār al-yaman wa-insān ḥimyar*, X, (ed. Muḥibb al-Dīn al-Khaṭīb), Cairo, al-Maṭba'ah al-Salafīyah.

— (1968) *Geographie der Arabischen Halbinsel: Ṣifat jazīrat al-'arab*, reprint of 1891 edition of D.H. Muller, Amsterdam, Oriental Press.

Hammoudi, Abdellah (1974) "Segmentarité, stratification sociale, pouvoir politique et saintèté: réflexions sur les thèses de Gellner", *Hespéris-Tamuda*, 15: 147–79.

— (1988) *Les masques de la victime*, Paris, Le Seuil.

Hatab, Zuhair (1976) *Taṭawwur bunā al-usrah al-'arabīyah wa-'l-judhūr al-ta'rīkhīyah wa-'l-ijtimā'īyah li-qaḍāyā-hā al-mu'āṣirah*, Beirut, Ma'had al-Inmā' al-'Arabīy.

Héritier, Françoise (1981) *L'exercise de la parenté*, Paris, E.H.E.S.S.-Gallimard-Le Seuil.

Héritier-Augé, Françoise and Elizabeth Copet-Rougier (eds) (1990 and 1991) *Les complexités de l'alliance*, Paris, Editions des archives contemporaines, 2 vols.

al-Hibri, Aziza (ed.) (1982) *Women and Islam*, Oxford, Pergamon.

al-Ḥibshī, 'Abdullāh Muḥammad (ed.) (n.d.) *Ḥawlīyāt yamānīyah min sinat 1224h ilā sinat 1316h*, Ṣan'ā', Ministry of Culture.

Holy, Ladislav (1989) *Kinship, Honour and Solidarity: Cousin marriage in the Middle East*, Manchester, Manchester University Press.

Hughes, D.O. (1978) "From brideprice to dowry in Mediterranean Europe", *Journal of Family History*, 3: 262–96.

Ibn al-Murtaḍā, al-Mahdī li-dīn allāh Aḥmad b. Yaḥyā (1947–49) *al-Baḥr al-zakhkhār al-jāmi' li-madhāhib 'ulamā' al-amṣār*, Cairo, Maṭba'at Anṣār al-Sunnah al-Muḥammadīyah, 5 vols.

— (1972) *Kitāb al-Azhār fī fiqh al-a'immat al-aṭhār*, Beirut, Dār Maktabat al-Ḥayāt.

Jackson, Jean (1976) "Vaupés marriage: a network system in the Northwest Amazon", in C.A. Smith (1976: 65–93).

al-Jāwī, 'Umar (1975) *Ḥiṣār Ṣan'ā'*, Aden, Mu'assasat Ṣaut al-'Ummāl.

Keddie, Nikki and Beth Baron (eds) (1991) *Women in Middle Eastern History: Shifting boundaries in sex and gender*, New Haven, Yale University Press.

Kelley, Donald R. (1984) *History, Law and the Human Sciences: Medieval and Renaissance perspectives*, London, Variorum Reprints.

Kennedy, John (1987) *The Flower of Paradise: The institutionalized use of the drug qat in North Yemen*, Dordrecht, Reidel.

Khoury, Philip and Joseph Kostiner (eds) (1990) *Tribes and State Formation in the Middle East*, Berkeley, University of California Press.

Khury, Fuad (1976) "A profile of family associations in two suburbs of Beirut" in Peristiany (1976: 81–100).

Klorman-Eraqi, Bat-Zion (1981) "Messianism in the 19th Century Yemeni Jewish Community of Yemen", University of California at Los Angeles, Ph.D. dissertation.

Lackner, Helen (1978) *A House Built on Sand: A political economy of Saudi Arabia*, London, Ithaca.

— (1985) *P.D.R. Yemen: Outpost of socialist development in Arabia*, London, Ithaca.

Lamaison, Pierre (1991) "Les structures complexes ont-elles une unité?", in Héritier-Augé and Copet-Rougier (1991:ii: 227–69).

Lambardi, Nello (1947) "Divisioni amministrativi del Yemen", *Oriente Moderno*, 27: 142–63.

Lambert, Jean (1991) "Saba et le barrage de Mareb: récit fondateur et temps imaginé", *Peuples Méditerranéens*, 56/57: 141–76.

Lancaster, William and Fidelity Lancaster (1992) "Tribal formations in the Arabian Peninsula", *Arabian Archaeology and Epigraphy*, 3: 145–72.

Landberg, Carlo (Comte de) (1920, 1923, 1942) *Glossaire Datînois*, Leiden, Brill, 3 vols.

Lane, Edward W. (1893) *An Arabic-English Lexicon*, Part I, London, Williams and Norgate, 8 volumes.

Laslett, Peter with Richard Wall (eds) (1972) *Household and Family in Past Time*, Cambridge, Cambridge University Press.

Lecerf, Jean (1956) "Note sur la famille dans le monde arabe et islamique", *Arabica*, 3: 31–60.

Lévi-Strauss, Claude (1949) *Les structures élémentaires de la parenté*, Paris, Mouton.

Lewcock, R., P. Costa, R.B. Serjeant and R. Wilson (1983) "The urban development of Ṣan'ā'" in Serjeant and Lewcock (1983: 122–43).

Lucas, P. and J.-C. Vatin (1982) *L'Algérie des anthropologues*, Paris, Maspero.

Mahé, Alain (1993) "Laïcisme et sacralité dans les *Qānuns* Kabyles", *Annales islamologiques*, 27: 137–56.

Maher, Vanessa (1974) *Women and Property in Morocco: Their changing relation to the process of social stratification in the Middle Atlas*, Cambridge, Cambridge University Press.

al-Maqramī, ʻAbd al-Mālik (1987) *al-Qāt bain al-siyāsah wa-ʻilm al-ijtimāʻ*, Beirut, Dār Azāl li-'l-Ṭibāʻah.

— (1991) *al-Ta'rīkh al-ijtimāʻī li-'l-thaurah al-yamanīyah*, Beirut, Dār al-Fikr al-Muʻāṣir.

Meillassoux, Claude (1990) "Les faux-nés de la parenté ou comment la nature imite la culture", *L'Ethnographie*, 86/1: 39–53.

Meissner, Jeffrey (1987) "Tribes at the Core: Legitimacy, Structure and Power in Zaydi Yemen", Columbia University, Ph.D. dissertation.

Mermier, Franck (1985) "Patronyme et hiérarchie sociale à Sanaa: le langage pris dans les mots", *Peuples Méditerranéens*, 33: 33–41.

— (1989) "De l'usage d'un concept: la citadinité à Sanaa", *Peuples Méditerranéens*, 46: 31–48.

Mernissi, Fatima (1982a) *al-Sulūk al-jinsī fī mujtamaʻ islāmī ra'smālī tabaʻī*, Beirut, Dār al-Ḥadāthah.

— (1982b) "Virginity and patriarchy" in al-Hibri (1982: 183–91).

Messick, Brinkley (1978) "Transactions in Ibb: Economy and Society in a Yemeni Highland Town", Princeton University, Ph.D. dissertation.

— (1990) "Literacy and the law: documents and document specialists in Yemen", in D.H. Dwyer (ed.), *Law and Islam in the Middle East*, New York, Bergin and Garvey, 61–76.

— (1993) *The Calligraphic State: Textual domination and history in a Muslim society*, Berkeley, University of California Press.

ibn Miftāḥ, Fakhr ad-Dīn ʻAlī b. Muḥammad (1938) *al-Muntazaʻ al-mukhtār min al-ghaith al-midrār*, Cairo, 2nd edn Maṭbaʻah al-Ḥijāzī, 4 vols. (1st edn Maṭbaʻah al-Maʻāhid, 1921).

Montagne, Robert (1930) *Les Berbères et le Makhzen dans le Sud du Maroc. Essai sur la transformation politique des berbères sédentaires (groupe chleuh)*, Paris, Alcan.

Moore, Sally F. (1978) *Law as Process: An anthropological approach*, London, Routledge.

al-Muʻallimī, Aḥmad ʻAbd al-Raḥmān (1981), "al-Sharīʻah al-mutawakkilīyah 'aw al-qaḍā' fī 'l-yaman", *al-Iklīl*, 5: 65–120.

Mundy, Martha (1979) "Women's inheritance of land in highland Yemen", *Arabian Studies*, 5: 161–87.

— (1983) "Ṣanʻā' dress: 1920–75", in R.B. Serjeant and R. Lewcock (1983: 529–40).

— (1985) "Agricultural development in the Yemeni Tihama: the past ten years", in B.R. Pridham (ed.), *Economy, Society and Culture in Contemporary Yemen*, London, Croom Helm, 22–40.

— (1988) "The family, inheritance and Islam: a reexamination of the sociology of *farā'iḍ* law", in A. al-Azmeh (ed.), *Islamic Law: Social and historical contexts*, London, Routledge, 1–123.

— (1989) "Irrigation and society in a Yemeni valley: on the life and death of a bountiful source", *Peuples Méditerranéens*, 46/1: 97–128.

Munson, Henry (1993) "Rethinking Gellner's segmentary analysis of Morocco's Ait ʻAtta", *Man*, 28/2: 267–80.

Nasir, J.J. (1955) "The Doctrine of Kafā'ah, A Critical Edition of *al-Mar'ah al-*

mubayyinah li-'l-nāẓir mā huwa 'l-ḥaqq fī mas'alat al-kafā'ah", University of London, Ph.D. dissertation.

Netting, R. McC., R. Wilk and E.J. Arnould (eds) (1984) *Households: Comparative and historical studies of the domestic group*, Berkeley, University of California Press.

Niebuhr, Carsten (1792) *Travels through Arabia and Other Countries in the East* (trans. R. Heron), Edinburgh, G. Mudie, 2 vols (facsimile reprint, Beirut, Librarie du Liban, n.d.).

Obermeyer, Gerald J. (1981) "*Taghūt, man'* and *sharī'a*: the realms of law in tribal Arabia", in Widad Qadi (ed.), *Studia Arabica et Islamica*, Beirut, American University of Beirut, 365–71.

Oexle, Otto (1992) "Les groupes sociaux du Moyen Age et les débuts de la sociologie contemporaine", *Annales E.S.C.*, 47/3: 751–65.

Pasternak, Burton (1972) *Kinship in Two Chinese Villages*, Stanford, Stanford University Press.

Patai, R. (1969) "The family" in *Golden River to Golden Road: Society, culture and change in the Middle East*, Philadelphia, University of Pennsylvania, 84–114.

— (1973) *The Arab Mind*, New York, Scribner.

Peristiany, J.G. (ed.) (1976) *Mediterranean Family Structures*, Cambridge, Cambridge University Press.

Peters, Emrys (1963) "Aspects of rank and status among Muslims in a Lebanese village" reprinted in L.E. Sweet (1970) *Peoples and Cultures of the Middle East*, Garden City, The Natural History Press, ii: 76–123.

— (1976) "Aspects of affinity in a Lebanese Maronite village" in Peristiany, (1976: 27–79).

— (1980a) "Aspects of Bedouin bridewealth in Cyrenaica", in Comaroff, J.L. (ed.) *The Meaning of Marriage Payments*, London, Academic Press, 125–60.

— (1980b) "The status of women in four Middle Eastern communities", in Beck, L. and N. Keddie (eds) *Women in the Muslim World*, Cambridge, Harvard University Press, 311–51.

Piamenta, Moshe (1990, 1991) *Dictionary of Post-Classical Yemeni Arabic*, Leiden, Brill, 2 vols.

al-Qaṣīr, Ahmad (1986) *Sharkh fī bunyat al-wahm: al-hijrah wa-'l-taḥawwul fī 'l-yaman*, Cairo, Dār Thābit.

Rathjens, Carl (1951) "Taghut gegen Scheri'a Gewohnheitsrecht und islamisches Recht den Gabilen des jemenitischen Hochlandes", *Jahrbuch des Stadtischen Museum für Völkerkunde*, Leipzig, 172–87.

Rosenfeld, Henry (1957) "An analysis of marriage and marriage statistics in a Moslem Christian Arab village", *International Archives of Ethnography*, Amsterdam, 48: 32–62.

— (1976) "Social and economic factors in explanation of the increased rate of patrilineal endogamy in the Arab village in Israel", in Peristiany (1976: 115–36).

Rossi, Ettore (1948) "Il diritto consuetudinario delle tribu arabe del Yemen", *Rivista degli Studi Orientali*, 23: 1–36.

— (1953) "Note sull'irrigazione, l'agricoltura e le stagione nel Yemen", *Oriente Moderno*, 33/8, 9: 349–61.

Rousseau, Jean-Jacques (1755) "Economie politique" in D. Diderot and J. d'Alembert (eds), *Encyclopédie, ou Dictionnaire raisonné des sciences, des arts et métiers, par une société de gens de lettres*, Paris, Briasson, David (et al), 5: 337–49.

Saadawi, Nawal El (1982) "Woman and Islam", in al-Hibri (1982: 193–206).

Sabean, David (1990) *Property, Production and Family in Neckarhausen, 1700–1870*, Cambridge, Cambridge University Press.

Sālim, Sayyid M. (1971) *Takwīn al-yaman al-hadīth wa-'l-imām yaḥyā*, Cairo, Maktabah Sa'īd Rāfit.

al-Sayāghī, Ḥusain A. (ed.) (1978) *Ṣafaḥāt majhūlah min ta'rīkh al-yaman*, Ṣan'ā', Markaz al-Dirāsāt al-Yamanīyah.

Schacht, Joseph (1964) *An Introduction to Islamic Law*, Oxford, Oxford University Press.

Schopen, Armin (1978) *Das Qat: Geschichte und Gebrauch des Genussmittels Catha Edulis Forsk. in der Arabischen Republik Jemen*, Wiesbaden, Franz Steiner Verlag.

Seddon, David (1976) "Aspects of kinship and family structure among the Ulad Stut of Zaio rural commune, Nador province, Morocco" in Peristiany (1976: 173–94).

Segalen, Martine (1991) *Fifteen Generations of Bretons: Kinship and society in Lower Brittany, 1720–1980*, Cambridge, Cambridge University Press.

Serjeant, Robert B. (1962) "Ḥaram and ḥawṭah: the sacred enclaves in Arabia", in 'Abd al-Raḥmān al-Badawī, *Mélanges Taha Husein*, Cairo, Dār al-Ma'ārif, 41–58.

— (1976) *South Arabian Hunt*, London, Luzac.

— (1977) "South Arabia" in C.A.O. van Nieuwenhuijze (ed.) *Commoners, Climbers and Notables: A sampler of studies on social ranking in the Middle East*, Leiden, Brill, 226–47.

— (1979) "The Yemeni poet al-Zubayrī and his polemic against the Zaydi Imams", *Arabian Studies*, 5: 87–130.

— (1982) "The Interplay between tribal affinities and religious (Zaydī) authority in the Yemen" reprinted in Serjeant (1991) *Customary and Shari'ah Law in Arabian Society*, Aldershot, Variorum.

— (1983) "The post-medieval and modern history of Ṣan'ā' and the Yemen, ca. 953–1382/1515–1962", in Serjeant and Lewcock (1983: 68–107).

Serjeant, R.B. and R. Lewcock (eds) (1983) *Ṣan'ā': An Arabian Islamic city*, London, Scorpion.

Shalan, Thaira (1993) "L'Interférence entre les concepts de classe et de catégorie sociale dans la société yéménite", Université Paris X Nanterre, Ph.D. dissertation.

al-Shamāḥī, 'Abdullāh b. 'Abd al-Wahhāb al-Mujāḥid (1939) *Ṣirāṭ al-ārifīn ilā idrāk al-ikhtiyārāt amīr al-mu'minīn*, Ṣan'ā', Maṭba'at al-Ma'ārif al-Jalīlah.

— (1972) *al-Yaman: al-insān wa-'l-ḥaḍārah*, Cairo, Dār al-Ḥadīthah.

Sharābī, Hishām (1977) *Muqaddimāt li-dirāsat al-mujtama' al-'arabī*, Beirut, al-Ahlīyah.

— (1992) *al-Niẓām al-'abawī wa-ishkālīyat takhalluf al-mujtama' al-'arabīy*, Beirut, Markaz Dirāsāt al-Wiḥdah al-'Arabīyah.

Sharārah, Waḍḍāḥ (1981) *al-Ahl wa-'l-ghanīmah, muqawwimāt al-siyāsah fī 'l-mamlakah al-'arabīyah al-sa'ūdīyah*, Beirut, Dār al-Ṭalī'ah.

al-Sharjabī, Qā'id (1986), *al-Sharā'iḥ al-ijtimā'īyah al-taqlīdīyah fī 'l-mujtama' al-yamanī*, Beirut, Dār al-Ḥadāthah.

Sharma, Ursula (1980) *Women, Work and Property in North-West India*, London, Tavistock.

al-Shaukānī, Muḥammad 'Alī (1348 AH/1929) *Al-badr al-ṭāli' bi-maḥāsin min ba'd al-qarn al-sābi'*, 2 vols, Cairo, Maṭba'at al-Sa'ādah.

Skinner, G. William (1964) "Marketing and social structure in China", *Journal of Asian Studies*, 24: 3–43, 195–228, 363–99.

Smith, Carol A. (ed.) (1976) *Regional Systems*, London, Academic Press, 2 vols.

Smith, Jonathan Z. (1987) *To Take Place: Toward theory in ritual*, Chicago, Chicago University Press.

Smith, Richard M. (ed.) (1984) *Land, Kinship and Life-cycle*, Cambridge, Cambridge University Press.

Stevenson, Thomas (1985) *Social Change in a Yemeni Highlands Town*, Salt Lake City, University of Utah Press.

al-Suwaidī, Abī 'l-Fauz Muḥammad Amīn al-Baghdādī (n.d.) *Sabā'ik al-dhahab fī ma'rifat qabā'il al-'arab*, Beirut, Dār Iḥyā al-'Ulūm.

Swagman, Charles (1988a) "Tribe and politics: an example from Highland Yemen", *Journal of Anthropological Research*, 44: 251–61.

— (1988b) *Development and Change in Highland Yemen*, Salt Lake City, University of Utah Press.

Swanson, Jon (1979) *Emigration and Economic Development: The case of the Yemen Arab Republic*, Boulder, Westview.

Tapper, Nancy (1991) *Bartered Brides: Politics, gender and marriage in an Afghan tribal society*, Cambridge, Cambridge University Press.

Tapper, Richard and Nancy Tapper (1992–93) "Marriage, honour and responsibility: Islamic and local models in the Mediterranean and the Middle East", *Cambridge Anthropology*, 16/2: 3–21.

Ṭarābīshī, Jūrj (1977) *Sharq wa-gharb, rujūlah wa-unūthah*, Beirut, Dār al-Ṭalī'ah.

al-Taufīq, Aḥmad (1983) *al-Mujtama' al-maghribī fī 'l-qarn al-tāsi' 'ashar (Aynūltān 1850–1912)*, Casablanca, Maṭba'at al-Najāḥ al-Jadīdah.

Thomson, W.M. (1886) *The Land and the Book or, Biblical Illustrations Drawn from the Manner and Customs, the Scenes and Scenery of the Holy Land*, London, T. Nelson.

Tillion, Germaine (1966) *Le Harem et les cousins*, Paris, Le Seuil.

Tilly, Charles (ed.) (1978) *Historical Studies of Changing Fertility*, Princeton, Princeton University Press.

Tuchscherer, Michel (ed.) (1994) *Le Yémen, passé et présent de l'unité. Revue du Monde Musulman et de la Méditerranéen*, 67.

Tucker, Judith (1985) *Women in Nineteenth Century Egypt*, Cambridge, Cambridge University Press.

Tutwiler, Richard (1987) "Tribe, Tribute and Trade: Social Class Formation in Highland Yemen", State University of New York at Binghamton, Ph.D. dissertation.

'Ubayd Allāh, 'Alī Muḥammad (1972) *Sīrat al-hādī ilā 'l-ḥaqq yaḥyā ibn al-ḥusain*, ed. S. Zakkār, Beirut, Dār al-Fikr.

Uberoi, Patricia (1993) "Introduction" in P. Uberoi (ed.) *Family, Kinship and Marriage in India*, Delhi, Oxford University Press, 1–44.

'Umar, Sulṭān Aḥmad (1970) *Naẓrah fī taṭawwur al-mujtama' al-yamanī*, Beirut, Dār al-Ṭalī'ah.

Valensi, Lucette (1977) *Fellahs tunisiens: L'Economie rurale et la vie des campagnes au 18ème et 19ème siecles*, Paris, Mouton.

Varanda, Fernando (1981) *Art of Building in Yemen*, London and Cambridge, AARP and MIT.

Varisco, Daniel (1982) "The Adaptive Dynamics of Water Allocation in al-Ahjur, Yemen Arab Republic", University of Pennsylvania, Ph.D. dissertation.

— (1983) "*Sayl* and *ghail*: the ecology of water allocation in Yemen", *Human Ecology*, 11: 365–83.

Verdon, Michel (1991) *Contre la culture: Fondements d'une anthropologie sociale opérationnelle*, Paris, Editions des Archives Contemporaines.

Vom Bruck, Gabriele (1991) "Descent and Religious Knowledge: 'Houses of Learning' in Modern San'a, Yemen Arab Republic", London School of Economics, Ph.D. dissertation.

al-Waisī, Ḥusain ibn 'Alī (1962) *al-Yaman al-kubrā: kitāb jughrāfī jiyūlūjī ta'rīkhī*, Cairo, Maṭba'at al-Nahḍah al-'Arabīyah.

Wakin, Jeanette (1972) *The Function of Documents in Islamic Law: The chapters on sales from Ṭaḥāwī's Kitāb al-shurūṭ al-kabīr*, Albany, State University of New York Press.

al-Wāsi'ī al-Yamānī, 'Abd al-Wāsi' (1927) *Ta'rīkh al-yaman*, Cairo, al-Maṭba'ah al-Salafīyah.

Watson, Ruth (1985) *Inequality among Brothers: Class and kinship in South China*, Cambridge, Cambridge University Press.

Weber, Max (1978) *Economy and Society: An outline of interpretive sociology*, Berkeley, University of California Press, 2 vols.

Weir, Shelagh (1985) *Qat in Yemen: Consumption and social change*, London, British Museum.

— (1986) "Tribe, hijrah and madinah in North-West Yemen", in K. Brown, M. Jolé, P. Sluglett and S. Zubaida (eds) *Middle Eastern Cities in Comparative Perspective*, London, Ithaca, 225–39.

— (1991) "Trade and tribal structures in North West Yemen", *Cahiers du GREMAMO: Arabie du Sud*, 10: 87–101.

Wilson, R.T.O. (1989) *Gazetteer of Historical North-West Yemen*, Hildesheim, George Olms.

Wolf, Arthur and Chieh-shan Huang (1980) *Marriage and Adoption in China, 1845–1945*, Stanford, Stanford University Press.

World Bank (1979) *Yemen Arab Republic: Development of a traditional economy*, Washington, DC, World Bank.

Wrigley, E.A. (1978) "Fertility strategy for the group and the individual", in Tilly (1978: 135–52).

Yanagisako, S.J. (1979) "Family and household: the analysis of domestic groups", *Annual Review of Anthropology*, 8: 161–205.

Yemen Arab Republic (1971) United Nations Development Programme, *Information Paper No. 9*, Ṣan'ā'.

Yemen Arab Republic (1978) *Final Report on the Airphoto Interpretation Project of the Swiss Technical Co-operation Service, Berne, carried out for the Central Planning Organisation*, Ṣan'ā' and Zurich, Swiss Technical Co-operation.

al-Zabārah, Muḥammad b. Muḥammad (1348 AH/1929) *Nail al-waṭar min tarājim rijāl al-yaman fī 'l-qarn al-thālith 'ashar*, Cairo, al-Matba'ah al-Salafīyah, 2 vols.

— (1360/1941 and 1357/1958) *Nashr al-'arf li-nubalā' al-yaman ba'd al-alf ilā 1357*, Cairo, Maṭba'at al-Sa'ādah, 2 vols.

— (1376/1957) "Nail al-ḥasaniyīn" in *Anbā' 'an daulat bilqīs wa saba'*, Cairo, al-Maṭba'ah al-Salafīyah, 86–212.

Ziyādah, Khālid (1991) *Kātib al-Sulṭān*, London, Riyāḍ al-Rayyis.

Manuscripts and unpublished works

Anonymous (n.d.) British Museum Arabic Ms., Supplement 411, Glaser Collection 349, folios 190–95: fragment of a dissertation on the service due by wives to their husbands according to the decisions of al-Hādī.

Anonymous or uncertain authorship (n.d.) Three manuscripts on tribal law. The first two were collected by E. Rossi, see Rossi (1948); the last by R.B. Serjeant. In the papers bequeathed by R.B. Serjeant to the library of the University of Edinburgh.

Kitāb talqīḥ al-ḥukkām

Kitāb al-tabyīn fī 'l-man'

Kitāb al-man'ah

Colonna, Fanny (1990) "Les sciences sociales au Maghreb et le paradigme durkheimien", paper presented to the Conference on the Social Sciences in and about the Arab World, Institut du Monde Arabe and Groupe de Sociologie Politique et Morale EHESS-CNRS, Paris, December 1990.

al-'Ulufī, Ibrāhīm b. Khālid (n.d.) *al-Ajwibah al-mufīdah 'alā 'l-su'ālāt al-ḥamīdah*, British Museum Or. 3923, Arabic Ms., Supplement 431, Glaser Collection 217.

Varisco, Daniel (n.d.) translation of "A legal discussion of irrigation and water rights by Yemeni jurist, Ḥusain ibn Aḥmad al-Siyāghī, dated 1386 AH/1966", unpublished manuscript.

Index

Note: Only conceptually important Arabic terms and only authors discussed in the text (not those cited in the notes) appear in this index.

Egypt, Egyptian role in Yemen, 15
Eickelman, D., 169

farā'iḍ see law of inheritance
fiqh (see also law, *sharī'ah*), 50–52, 58, 62–64, 170–171, 212n.41, 215n.1, 216n.20,n.24, 219n.13, 213n.54, 240, 253n.19
Free Officers, 48, 88

Gellner, E., 4, 8, 52, 54, 215n.13,n.14
geography, of area of Wadi Ḍahr, 19, 63–64; historical geography, 24, 209n.4, 218n.1; of Yemen, 10–11, 205n.2
al-Ghashmī, President Aḥmad, 215n.11
Goitein, S.D., 14
government (see also Imamate, law and political conditions), character of central government (see also Imamic and Republican), 6, 161, 202; government employment (see also army), 86–88, 115, 158; of house, 4–5, 53, 56, 58, 79, 165, 195; Imamic (see also Imamate and Ḥamīd al-Dīn) 13–14, 210n.18; local government, 6, 29–30, 32, 36, 38–39, 53–54, 56–58, 161, 199–201, 211n.29; relation of central government to local government, 30–31, 33–35, 39, 51, 83, 161–162, 165, 201–203; Republican, 8, 14, 30, 48, 51, 58, 83, 88, 172, 202–204, 207n.51, 215n.10, 243

hajar/tahjiir, 215n.8, 248, 249n.4, 253, 254, 257n.26, 259n.29, 261n.37, 265n.44
al-Ḥajrī, 'Abdullāh, 16
ḥākim (see law, role of *ḥākim*)
al-ḥarīw/al-ḥarīwah, 79
Hamdān, 17, 22, 26, 115, 122, 175, 177, 201, 209n.86, 210n.13, 216n.24
al-Hamdānī, al-Ḥasan, 19, 27, 210n.5,n.7,n.13, 212n.40, 217n.27
al-Ḥamdī, President Ibrāhīm, 16, 215n.11
Ḥāmīd al-Dīn Imams, 26, 43; Imam Aḥmad, 9, 26; Imam Yaḥyā, 9, 12–14, 26, 28, 40, 63, 74, 208n.73, 216n.19,n.24
the harem, 4
Ḥāshid (see also Ḥāshid and Bakīl), 8, 15, 17, 37–38, 202, 207n.51
Ḥāshid and Bakīl, 1, 8, 9, 23, 37, 40, 206n.39, 209n.78,n.86
ḥijāb, 139, 145, 228n.23; *muḥajjabah*, 127, 227n.23;
hijrah, 4, 29, 39, 115, 172, 210n.20, 217n.31
historiography and sociology, of Arab society, 90–92, 124–125, 168–171, 205n.16, 206n.42, 213n.45, 221n.4, 222n.17,n.20, 224n.45,n.46, 227n.18, 229n.35; of European peasantry or society, 167–168, 200–201; of Yemeni society 5–10, 199–202, 206n.40,n.42, 210n.7, 213n.47
house/s, 2–3, 93–96, 163–164, 181–82, 185–187, 187–196, 222n.23,n.24, 223n.27, 226n.60, 237n.56, 238n.59
household, contracts within, 69; developmental cycle of domestic group, 100–101, 109–110, 145, 165–166; division of labour within, 77–79, 11–112, 115–118, 143–145, 226n.63; government of, 4–5, 53, 56, 58, 195, 203, 218n.49; labour in agriculture 67, 69, 73, 76–79, 191; land and property 72, 134, 145, 149, 152–153, 165–166, 190–191, 194, 232n.68, 235n.44; size and composition of, 76, 96–100, 110–112, 115–119, 140, 152–3, 200, 223n.30,n.31, 226n.61, 245
al-Ḥudaydah, 84, 111

Ibn Khaldun, 60–61, 215n.14, 218n.3
Imamate (see also Ḥamīd al-Dīn and political conditions), 3, 7, 9, 12–14, 25, 28, 43, 45, 160, 210n.11, 216n.19,n.24; overthrowal of, 14, 175; and status rank, 40, 175, 212n.41, 213n.44; of Sharaf al-Dīn Imams, 25–26, 210n.11
irrigation, in Yemen, 10–11; in Wadi Ḍahr, 19, 23–26, 31–32, 36, 42–43,

public spaces, 3, 55; shops and traders, 82–84; specialists, 96, 112, 176–177
marriage, as alliance 141, 171, 182, 230n.43, (and economic relations) 44, 48, 81, 83, 107–08, 122, 125, 135–138, 154–55, 159, 171, 173, 174, 177–181, 183–184, 195–8, 234n.38,n.39,n.42, 236n.47, 238n.57, (and political relations) 36, 45, 122, 125, 135–138, 173–174, 177, 194–95; ceremony, 126–130, 133, 146, 228n.25,n.26,n.27, 229n.28,n.30; and childbearing, 102–03, 141; "close", 89, 180–185, 195–196, 237n.52,n.53,n.55; comparative study of, 89, 167–170; cousin, 168, 179–180, 227n.17, 233n.13–15, 236n.48, 239n.2; and divorce, 103–4; exchange, 183–85, 195; first, 101–102, 224n.40; payments, 131–136, 183, 229n.32,n.35; plural, 106–109, 190; second and third, 104–106
Marxism, and kinship 168; Arab Marxism 91; Yemeni Marxism 71
mazāyinah see *muzayyin*
methodology, 5–6, 89–90, 123–124, 166, 172, 201, 207n.40, 223n.24,n.32,n.36, 224n.38,n.39, 235n.44, 239–246
Montagne, R., 14
mourning, 138–139, 146–147, 150, 231n.49
mukhuwwah, 32, 211n.27,n.28
muzayyin, *muzayyinah/mazāyinah*, 13, 45, 46, 82, 85, 126–127, 130, 131, 137–139, 146, 173, 175, 177, 184, 214n.50, 215n.59, 217n.37, 228n.20,n.22,n.27, 263

nasab, 236n.50
nuqqāṣ, 13 (see also *mazaayinah*)

orality, 4, 58, 64, 210n.10, 219n.12; oral tradition, 4, 12, 210n.5,n.7
Ottoman rule, 12, 26, 75, 208n.60, 219n.10

patronymic group (see house and kinship)
peasantry, 7, 8, 9, 14, 123–124, 167, 206n.25; peasant production, 6, 14
People's Democratic Republic of Yemen, 7, 172
Peristiany, J., 169
political conditions, during the Imamate 13–15, 208n.65,n.69; local administration, 17, 51, 58, 63, 215n.10; local community, (common fund) 32, 54, 57, 64–65, 211n.29,n.30, 217n.40, 219n.9, (control of market) 31, (corporate protection by) 30, (nature of) 36, 54, 212n.37,n.38, (principles of membership) 29, 36, 211n.29, (rights of residence in) 29, 31, 57, (rights over land) 31; national political culture (see also the army), 2–3, 7–8, 10, 55, 207n.51,n.52, 208n.53; unification of the two Yemens, 10, 207n.51, 209n.85; Yemeni civil war, 15, 83
property (see also under land and *māl*), 59, 62, 70, 199; community property, 31, 62, 199, 211n.25, 219n.13; in land, 31, 62–63; and litigation (see also law of inheritance), 53, 151; state property, 63, 21n.12, 219n.13; in trees and plantings, 65, 66, 68; in water, 62, 65–66, 199–200, 219n.8, 226n.68, 242–243, 246n.1,n.5

qabīlah/qabā'il, 7, 172, 201, 216n.24; *qabīlī*, 40, 45, 61, 213n.44
qāḍī/quḍāh, 39–40, 44, 45–9, 61, 86, 172–173, 213n.44, 226n.59
qarābah, 169, 181, 197, 236n.50
Qariyat al-Qābil, 20–22, 36–37, 42–43, 67, 74, 153, 161, 173, 175, 210n.11, 219n.9
qāt, 17, 63, 65–66, 69, 70, 74–8, 80–82, 84, 111, 116, 120, 164, 209n.87, 220n32–35, 221n.39–42, 226n.1, 243–244, 248, 249n.1, 250
qishr, 83, 140

al-Rauḍah, 86
ritual (see marriage ceremony and mourning), bloodletting 127, 139,

200; liminality, 127, 138, 139, 200; structure, 126

Ṣa'dah, 13
Ṣāliḥ, President 'Alī 'Abdullāh, 7, 206n.35
Sallāl, President 'Abdullāh, 83
Ṣān'ā', city, 3, 9, 12, 15, 30–31, 38, 41, 46, 48, 80–82, 87, 102, 108, 111, 114, 115, 131, 142, 160, 177, 203, 205n.9, 213n.44, 214n.52, 216n.19, 220n.38; plateau, 1, 12, 16, 27
Saudi Arabia, 10, 175; Saudi role in Yemen, 10, 15–17
sayyid/sādah, 26, 39–40, 43, 45–49, 61, 172–175, 206n.30, 213n.43,n.44, 213n.47, 223n.28
schools, under the Ottomans 12
segmentation, and segmentary analysis, 4–5, 9, 25, 52, 54–56, 58, 95, 197, 201, 205n.12, 215n.13,n.14; segmentary society, 5, 7, 8, 10, 52, 54
servants, 3, 211n.22,n.29, 214n.50,n.51
sha'b, 7, 206n.34
shabāb, 212n.30
shaikh(s) (see also law, role of shaikhs in), 8, 12–17, 25, 28–38, 45, 51–58, 62, 64–65, 86, 95–96, 117, 150, 151, 161, 164, 165, 181, 201–204, 219n.17, 223n.26
shāfi'ī, 14, 207n.44,n.51
sharī'ah (see under law)
shaqīyah, 68–70, 214n.54, 226n.1
Skinner, G.W., 175
slaves, 3
Smith, Jonathan Z., 127
sociology (see historiography)
status, categories and hierarchy, 1, 6–7, 13, 39–42, 55, 59, 172, 212n.41, 234n.33; groups, 1, 30–31, 217n.34; and kinship, 42; and marital alliance, 172–175; in Wadi Ḍahr, 4, 45–49, 172–175

Ṭaibah, 22, 24, 207n.44
Ta'izz, 108, 216n.19, 226n.1
Tapper, R. and N., 170
taxation (see under land)
Ṭayyibī Fāṭimīs, 24, 26, 44, 207n.44, 210n.11
Tihāmah, 4, 7, 8, 10, 12, 17, 85, 205n.6, 207n.44,n.51, 220n.25
Tillion, G., 169
trade (see under markets)
tribe, 1, 4–7, 14, 17, 90, 201–202, 251n.9; tribal custom/law (see also under law and custom on specific topics), 13, 49, 51, 200–201; tribal history, 27; tribal society or organization (see also under political conditions and segmentation), 4, 8, 9, 52–55, 61, 91–92, 202–204, 205n.13, 206n.36,n.38, 212n.37,n.38

ulema (see under literacy)

veiling (see dress and ritual)
virginity, 127, 130, 132, 133, 139, 227n.22, 228n.31

waqf, 26, 44, 62–63, 88, 148, 149, 155, 159, 160, 214n.54, 219n.11, 221n.4, 227n.18, 231n.52, 232n.61,n.62, 232n.70
Weber, M., 1, 89, 199–201, 204
weddings (see marriage ceremony)
women, and inheritance, 34, 142, 144, 148, 153–160; labourers, 79, 110–112; in law, 53, 56, 57, 216n.18; and lending, 84; and literacy, 87; as mothers, 102–103, 105–106, 141, 144–145, 151, 230n.39,n.42,n.43,n.44,n.45; nature of, 90–91; and property, 79, 101, 119, 120–123, 133–134, 135–138, 142–144, 151–152, 192; and *qāt*, 78; and ritual, 126–130, 138–141, 232n.64; social life of, 116, 129, 140–142, 144, 146–147, 151; and work, 77–80, 110–112, 116–117, 133, 138, 141, 143–144, 174
writing (see literacy)

Yemen Arab Republic, 7, 205n.2

al-Zabārah, Muḥammad, 40
Zaidism, 13